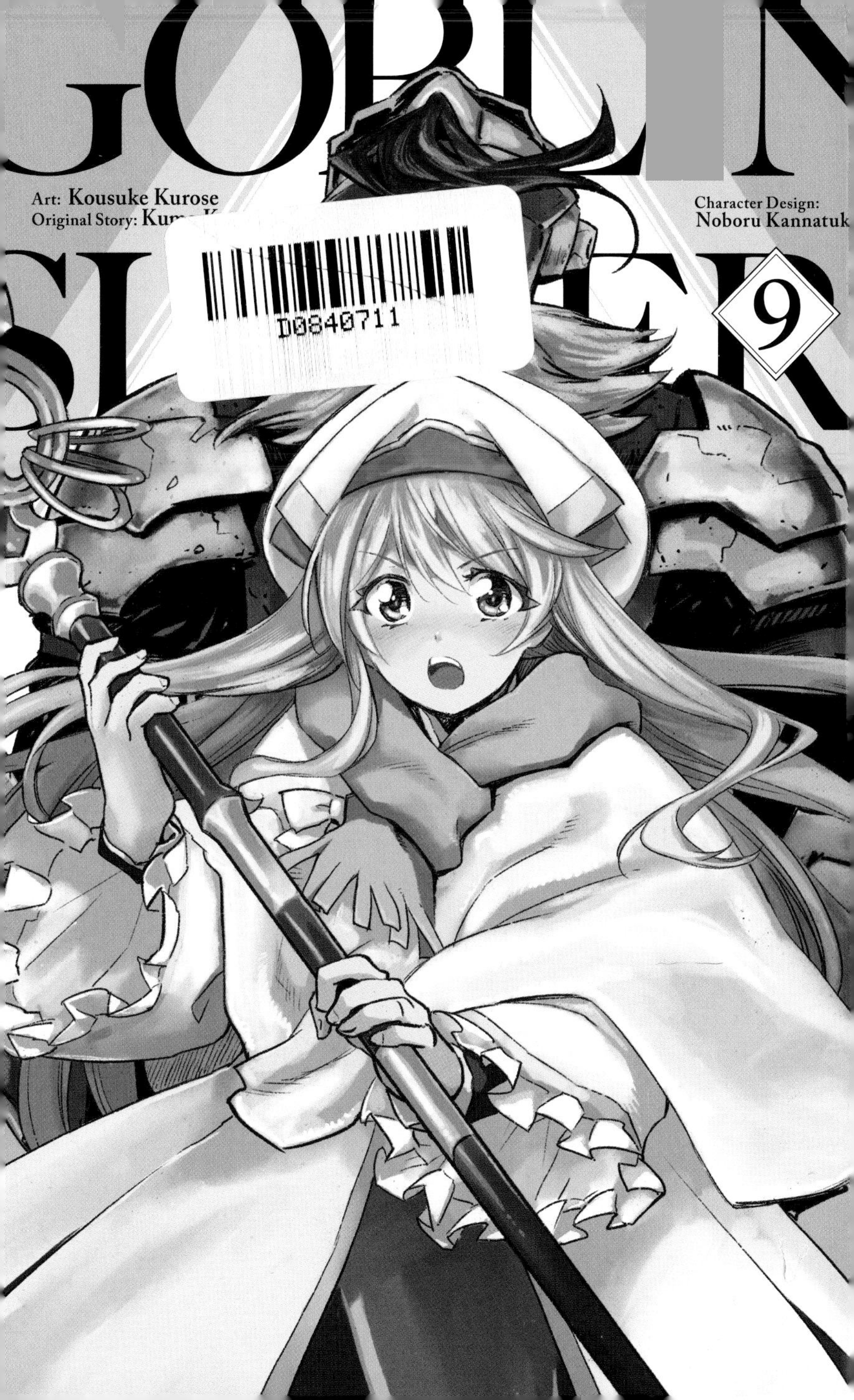
Art: Kousuke Kurose
Original Story: Kum
Character Design:
Noboru Kannatuk
9

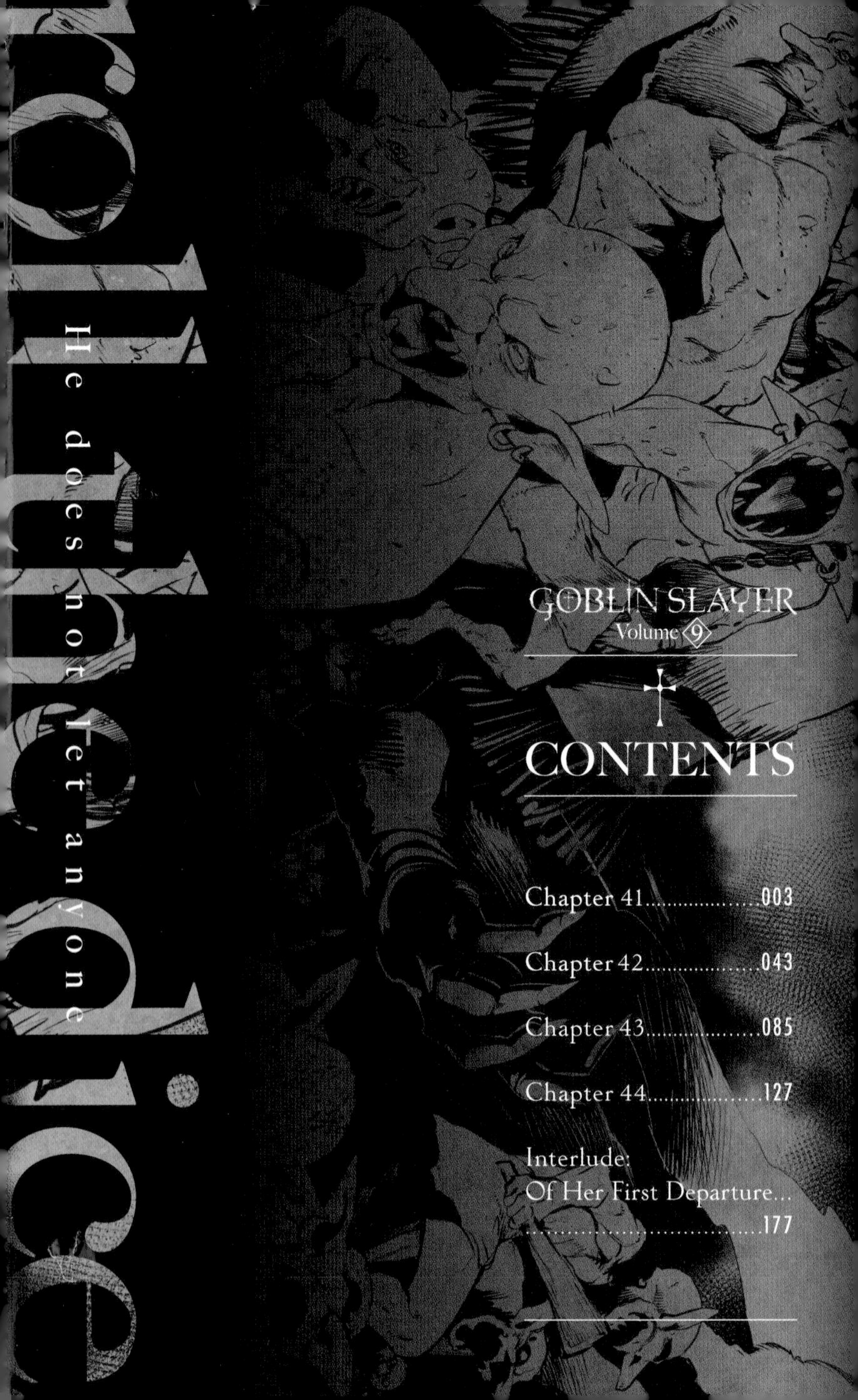
He does not let anyone

GOBLIN SLAYER
Volume 9

CONTENTS

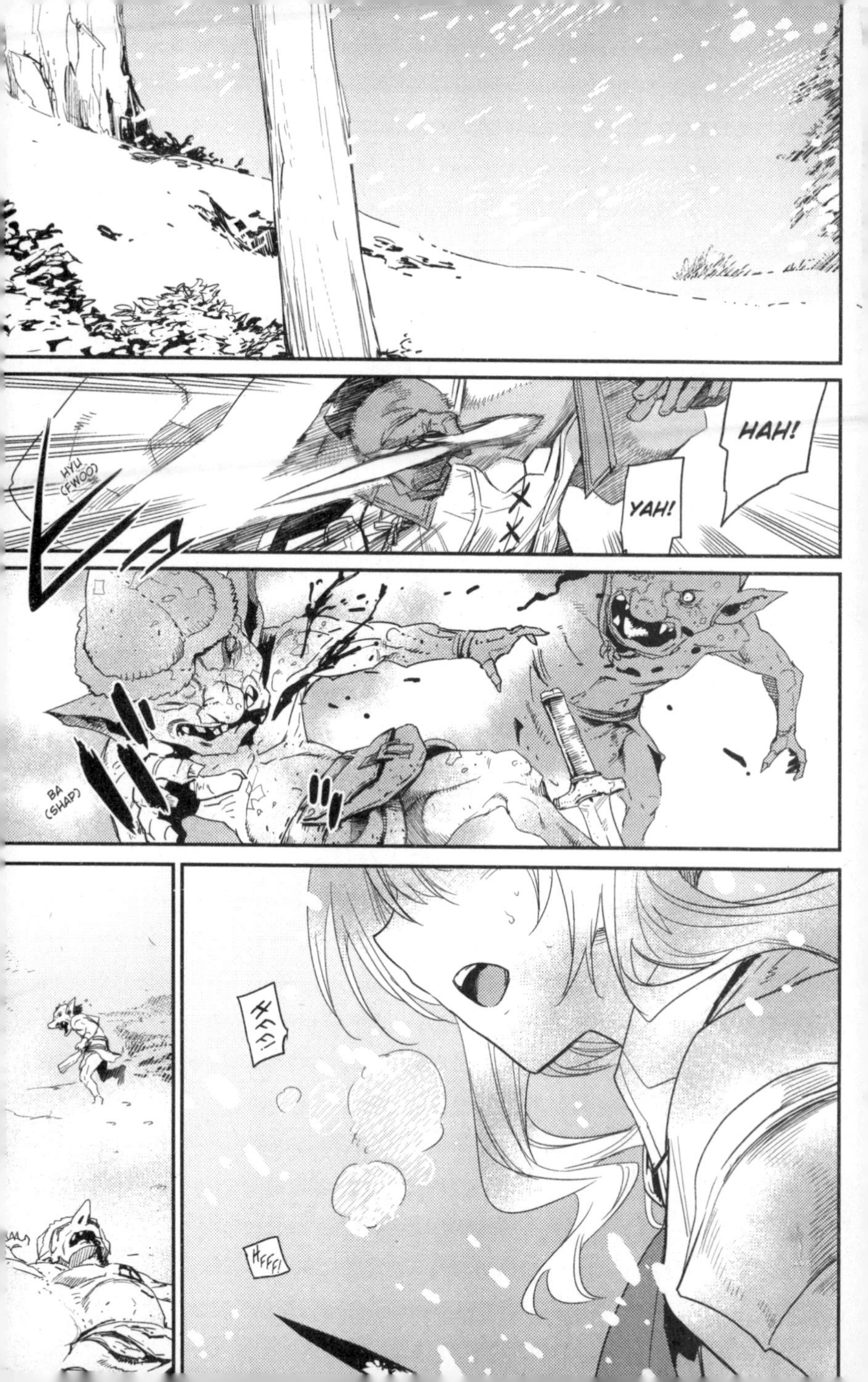
HAH!
YAH!
HYU (FWOO)
BA (SHAP)
HFF!
HFFF!

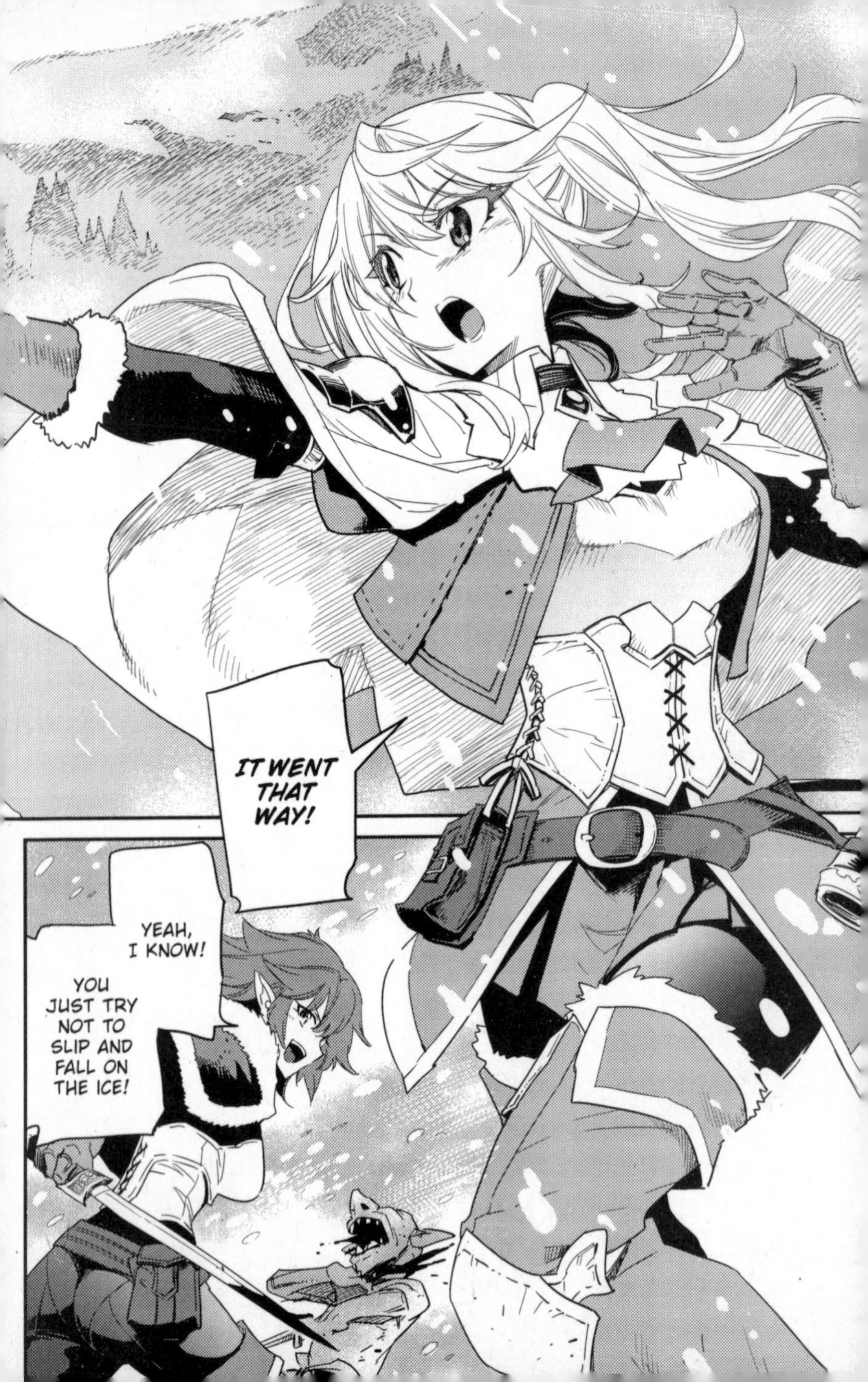
IT WENT THAT WAY!
YEAH, I KNOW!
YOU JUST TRY NOT TO SLIP AND FALL ON THE ICE!

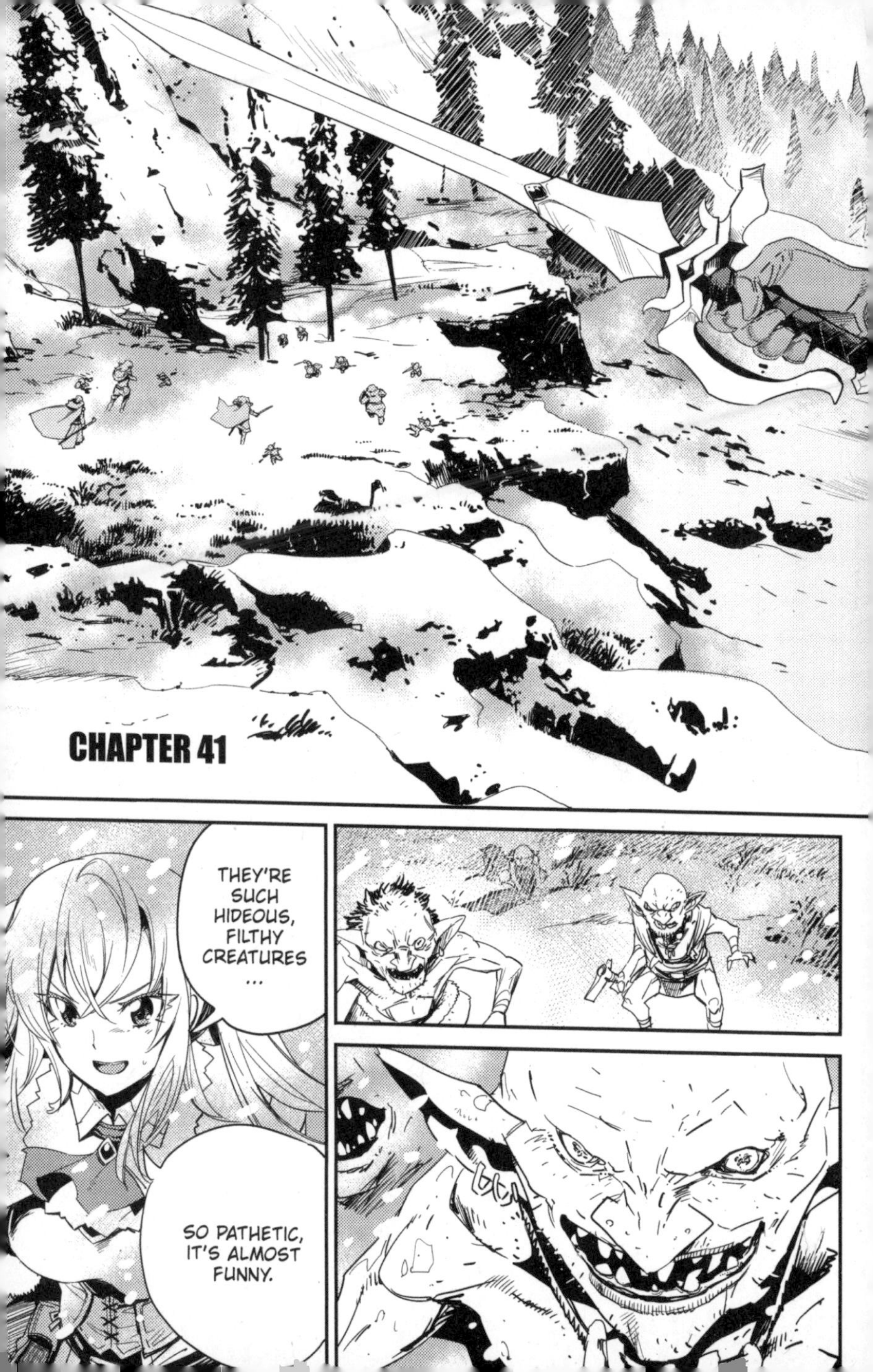
CHAPTER 41
THEY'RE SUCH HIDEOUS, FILTHY CREATURES ...
SO PATHETIC, IT'S ALMOST FUNNY.

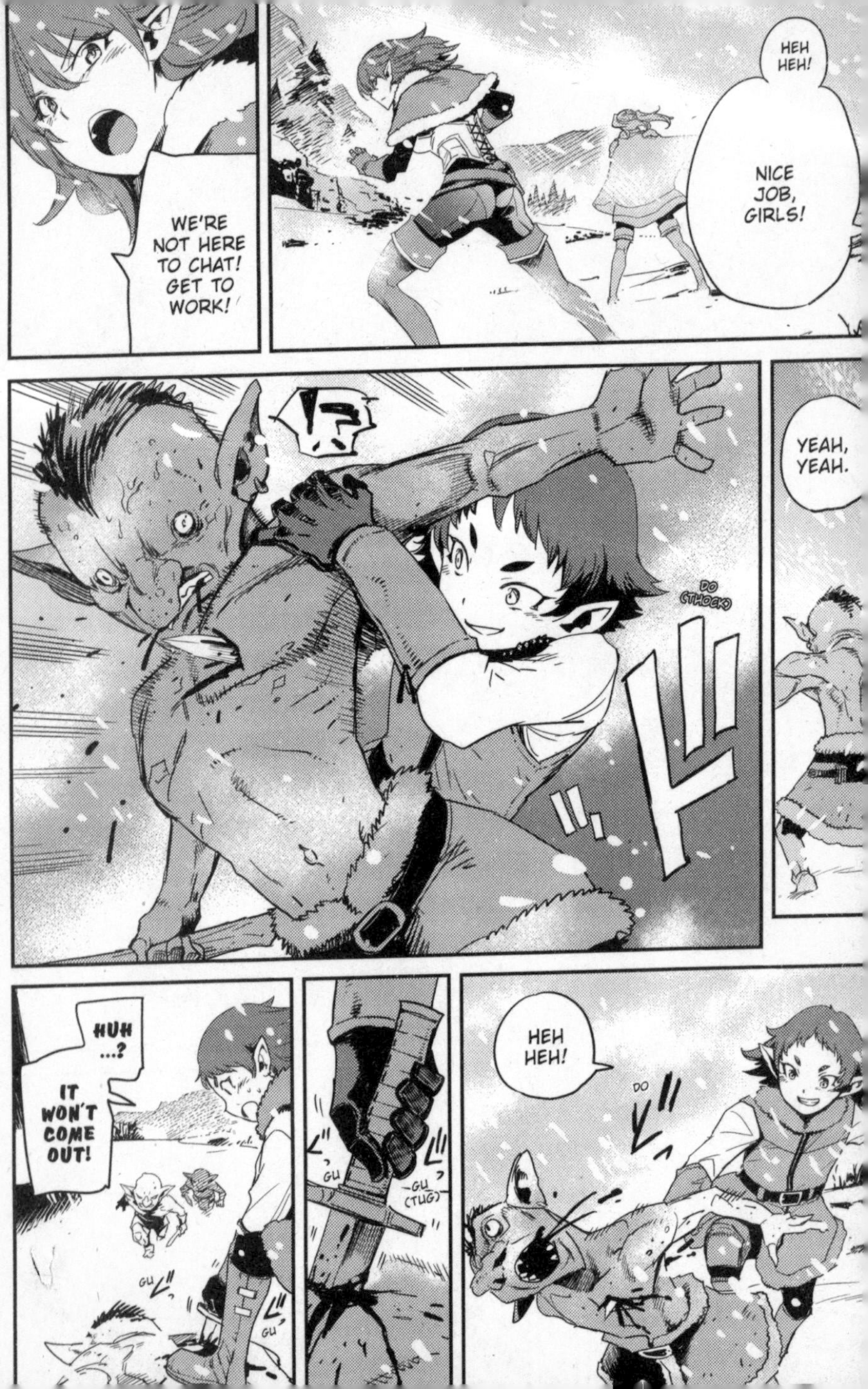
HEH HEH!
NICE JOB, GIRLS!
WE'RE NOT HERE TO CHAT! GET TO WORK!
YEAH, YEAH.
!?
DO (THOCK)
HEH HEH!
DO
GU
GU (TUG)
HUH ...?
IT WON'T COME OUT!
GU
GU

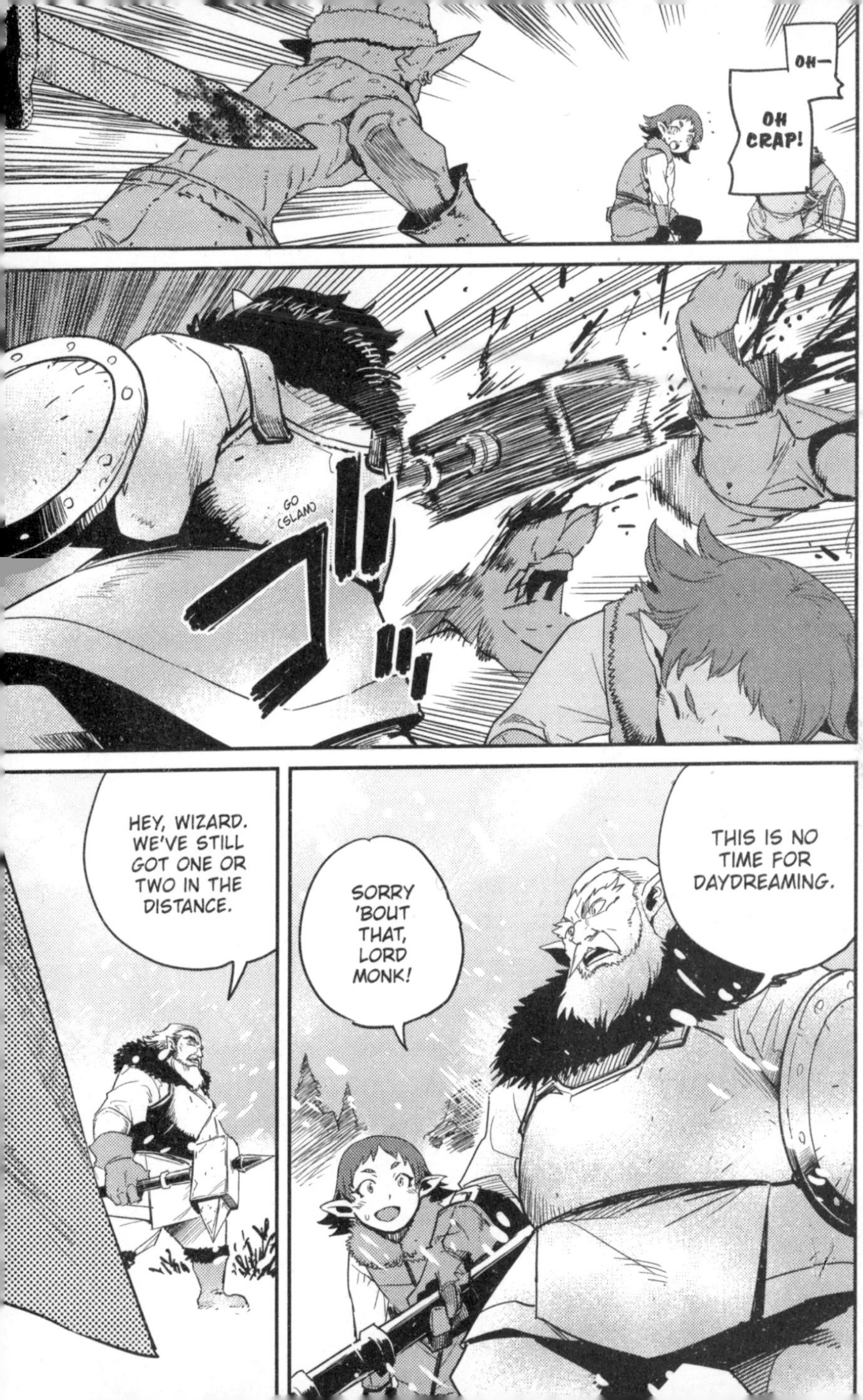
OH—
OH CRAP!
GO (SLAM)
THIS IS NO TIME FOR DAYDREAMING.
SORRY 'BOUT THAT, LORD MONK!
HEY, WIZARD. WE'VE STILL GOT ONE OR TWO IN THE DISTANCE.

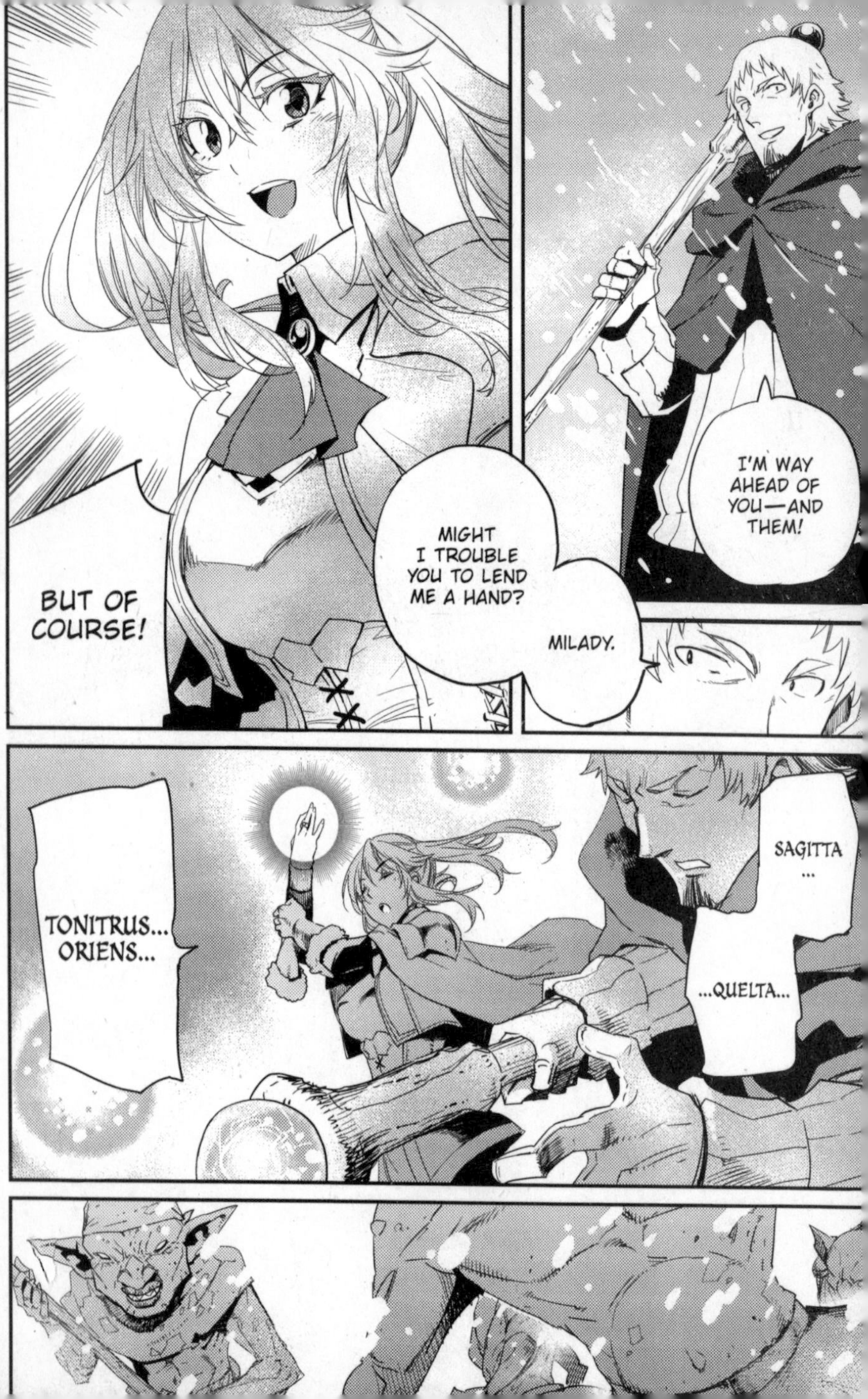
I'M WAY AHEAD OF YOU—AND THEM!
MIGHT I TROUBLE YOU TO LEND ME A HAND?
MILADY.
BUT OF COURSE!
SAGITTA ...
...QUELTA...
TONITRUS... ORIENS...

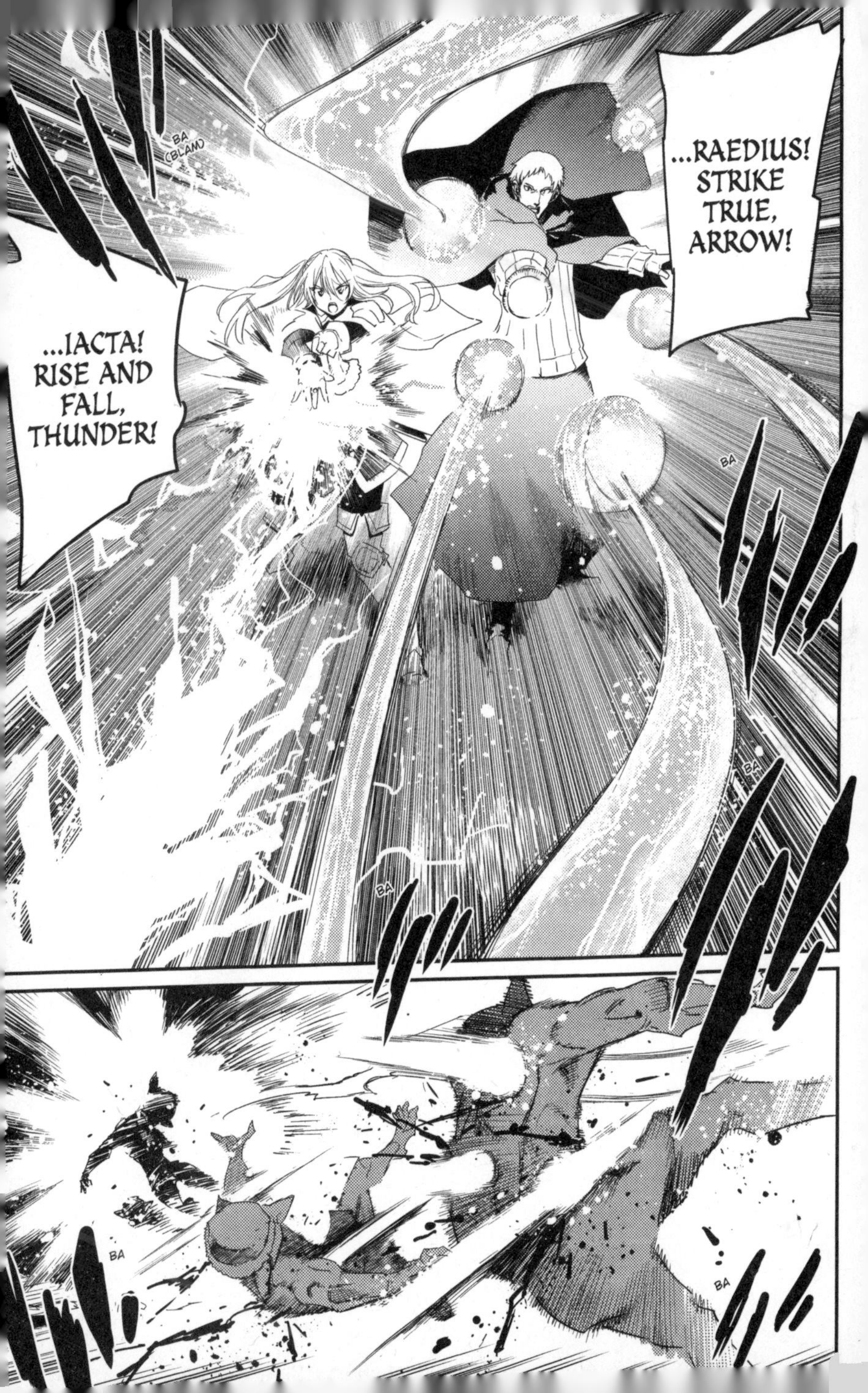
...RAEDIUS! STRIKE TRUE, ARROW!
BA (BLAM)
...IACTA! RISE AND FALL, THUNDER!
BA
BA
BA
BA
BA

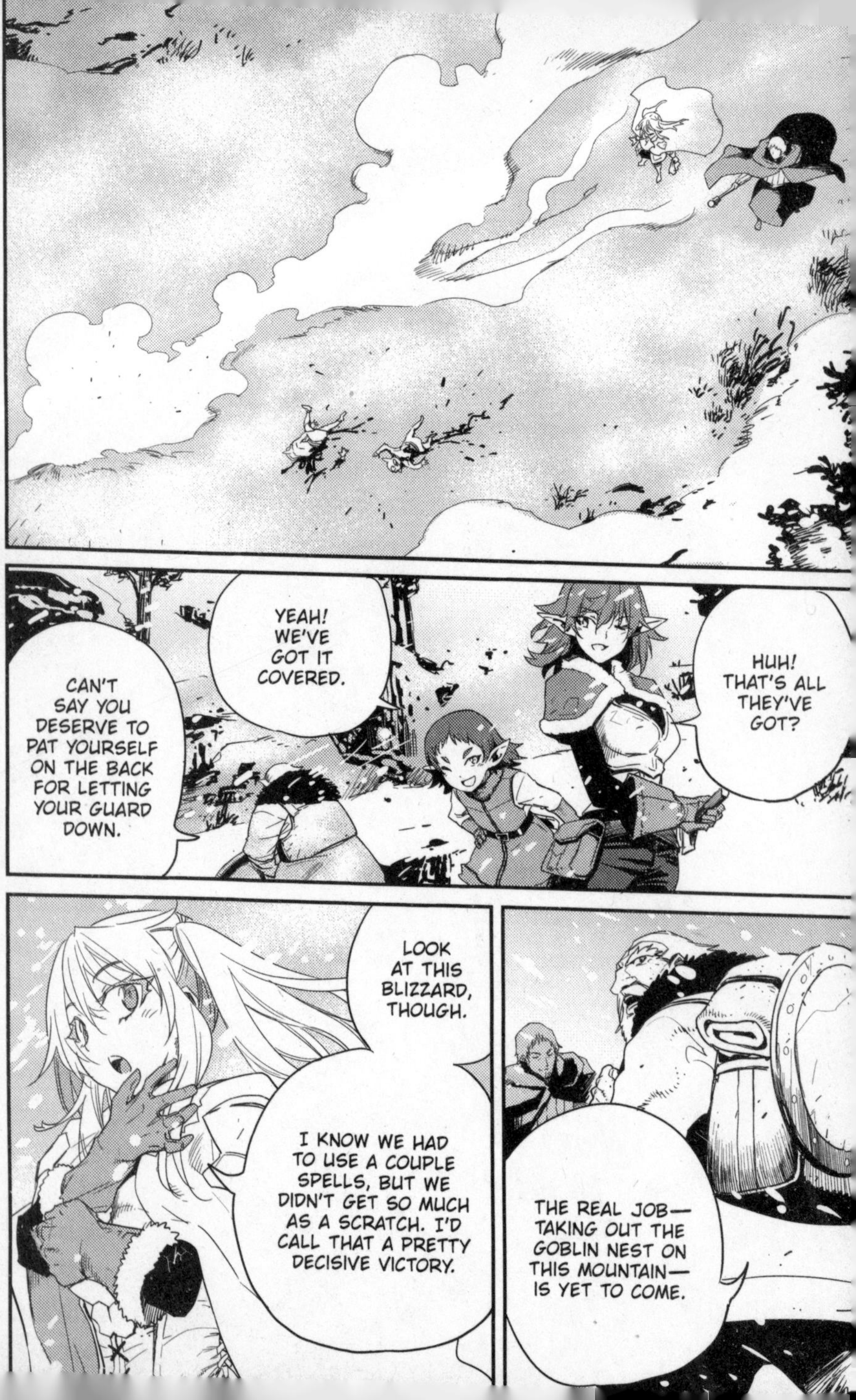
HUH! THAT'S ALL THEY'VE GOT?
YEAH! WE'VE GOT IT COVERED.
CAN'T SAY YOU DESERVE TO PAT YOURSELF ON THE BACK FOR LETTING YOUR GUARD DOWN.
THE REAL JOB—TAKING OUT THE GOBLIN NEST ON THIS MOUNTAIN—IS YET TO COME.
LOOK AT THIS BLIZZARD, THOUGH.
I KNOW WE HAD TO USE A COUPLE SPELLS, BUT WE DIDN'T GET SO MUCH AS A SCRATCH. I'D CALL THAT A PRETTY DECISIVE VICTORY.

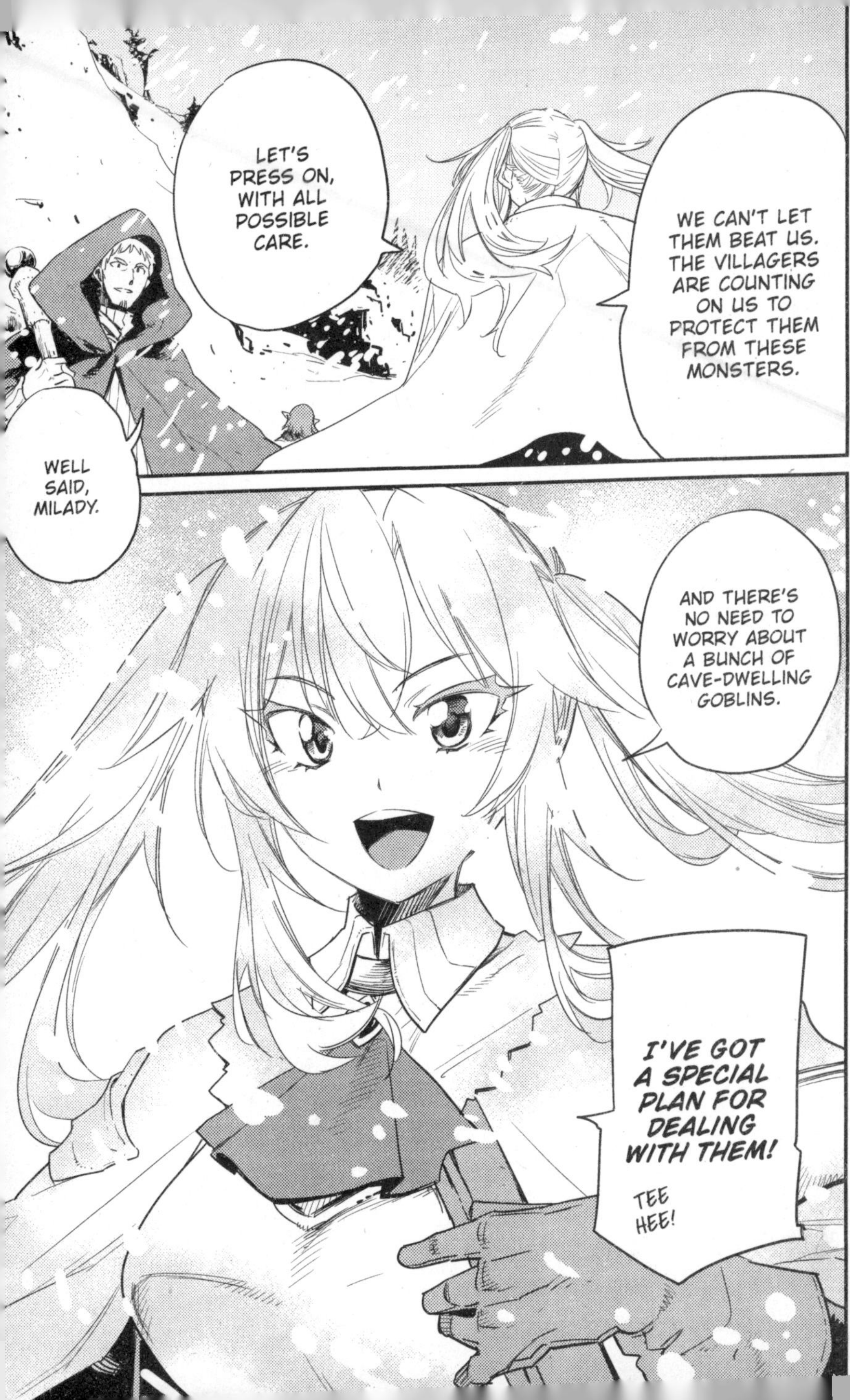
WE CAN'T LET THEM BEAT US. THE VILLAGERS ARE COUNTING ON US TO PROTECT THEM FROM THESE MONSTERS.
LET'S PRESS ON, WITH ALL POSSIBLE CARE.
WELL SAID, MILADY.
AND THERE'S NO NEED TO WORRY ABOUT A BUNCH OF CAVE-DWELLING GOBLINS.
I'VE GOT A SPECIAL PLAN FOR DEALING WITH THEM!
TEE HEE!

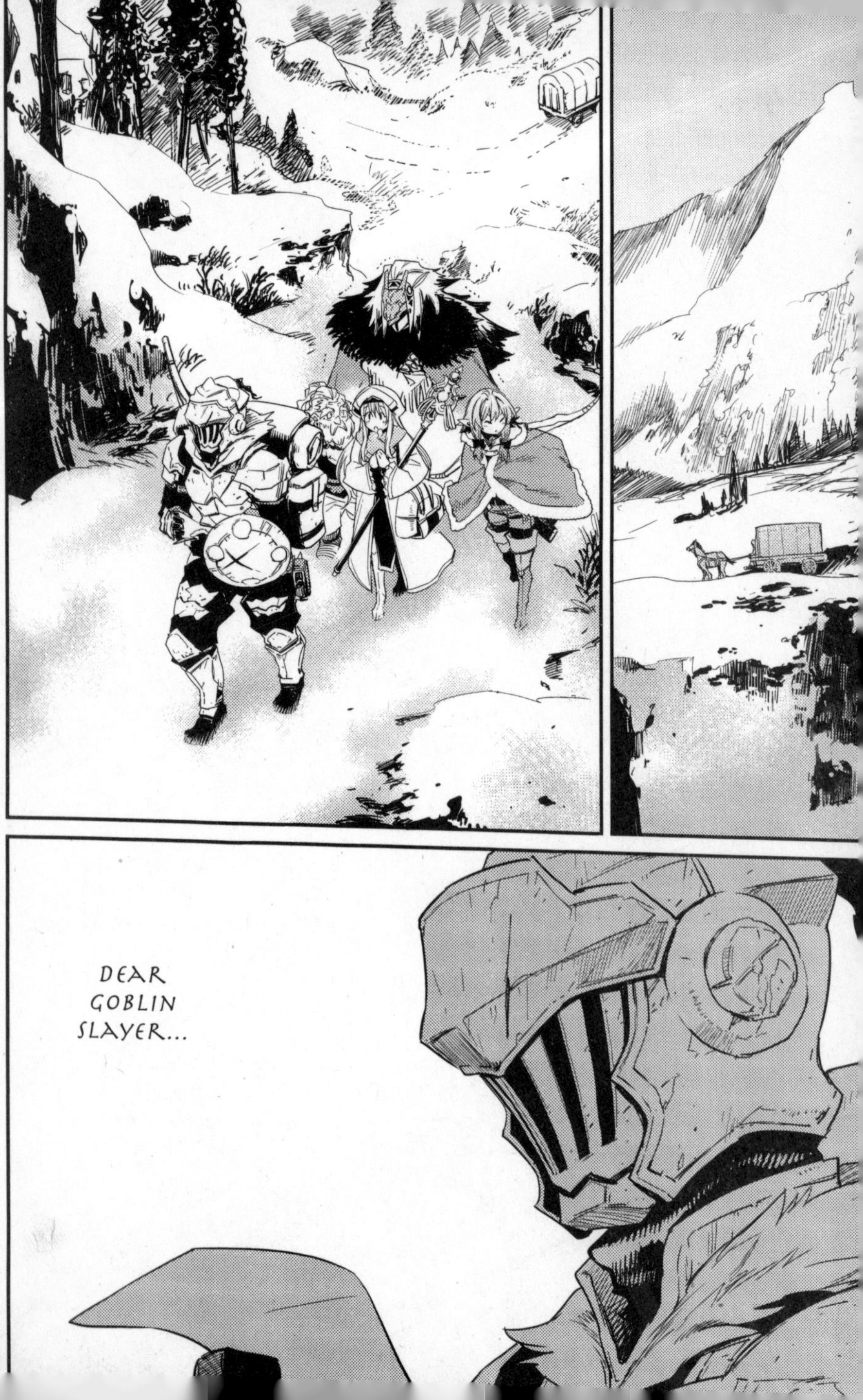
DEAR GOBLIN SLAYER...

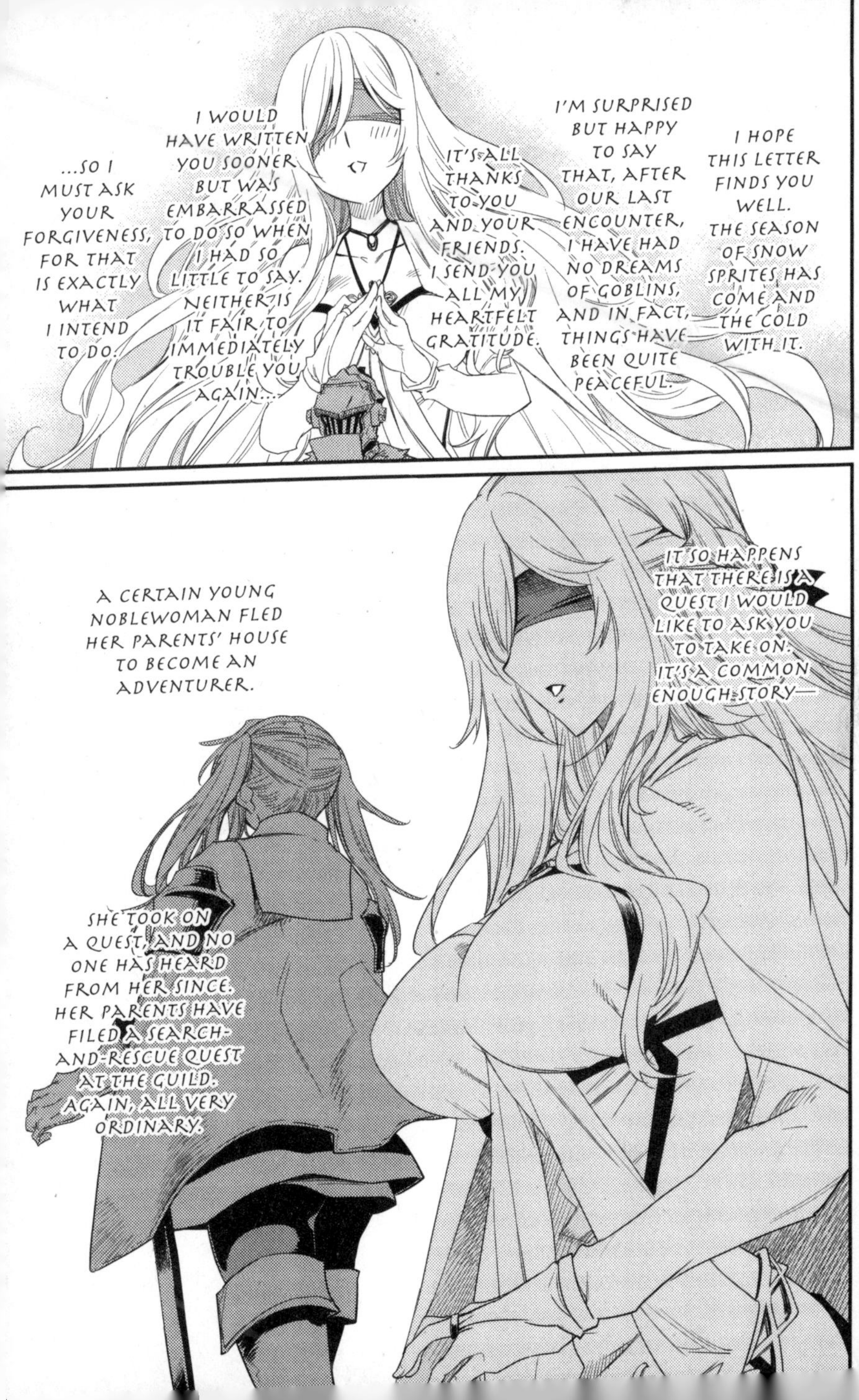
I HOPE THIS LETTER FINDS YOU WELL. THE SEASON OF SNOW SPRITES HAS COME AND THE COLD WITH IT.
I'M SURPRISED BUT HAPPY TO SAY THAT, AFTER OUR LAST ENCOUNTER, I HAVE HAD NO DREAMS OF GOBLINS, AND IN FACT, THINGS HAVE BEEN QUITE PEACEFUL.
IT'S ALL THANKS TO YOU AND YOUR FRIENDS. I SEND YOU ALL MY HEARTFELT GRATITUDE.
I WOULD HAVE WRITTEN YOU SOONER BUT WAS EMBARRASSED TO DO SO WHEN I HAD SO LITTLE TO SAY. NEITHER IS IT FAIR TO IMMEDIATELY TROUBLE YOU AGAIN...
...SO I MUST ASK YOUR FORGIVENESS, FOR THAT IS EXACTLY WHAT I INTEND TO DO.
IT SO HAPPENS THAT THERE IS A QUEST I WOULD LIKE TO ASK YOU TO TAKE ON. IT'S A COMMON ENOUGH STORY—
A CERTAIN YOUNG NOBLEWOMAN FLED HER PARENTS' HOUSE TO BECOME AN ADVENTURER.
SHE TOOK ON A QUEST, AND NO ONE HAS HEARD FROM HER SINCE. HER PARENTS HAVE FILED A SEARCH-AND-RESCUE QUEST AT THE GUILD. AGAIN, ALL VERY ORDINARY.

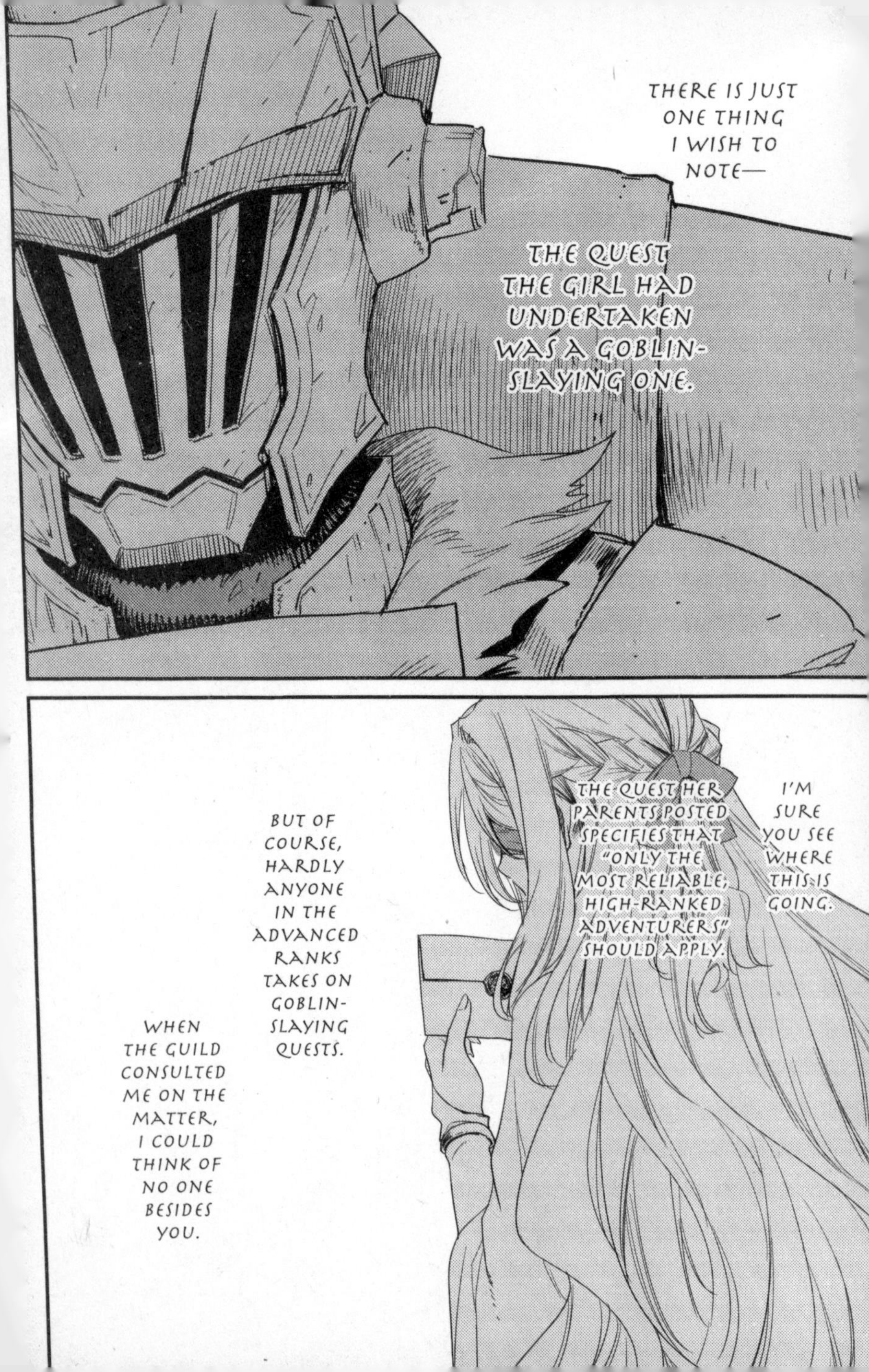
THERE IS JUST ONE THING I WISH TO NOTE—
THE QUEST THE GIRL HAD UNDERTAKEN WAS A GOBLIN-SLAYING ONE.
I'M SURE YOU SEE WHERE THIS IS GOING.
THE QUEST HER PARENTS POSTED SPECIFIES THAT "ONLY THE MOST RELIABLE, HIGH-RANKED ADVENTURERS" SHOULD APPLY.
BUT OF COURSE, HARDLY ANYONE IN THE ADVANCED RANKS TAKES ON GOBLIN-SLAYING QUESTS.
WHEN THE GUILD CONSULTED ME ON THE MATTER, I COULD THINK OF NO ONE BESIDES YOU.

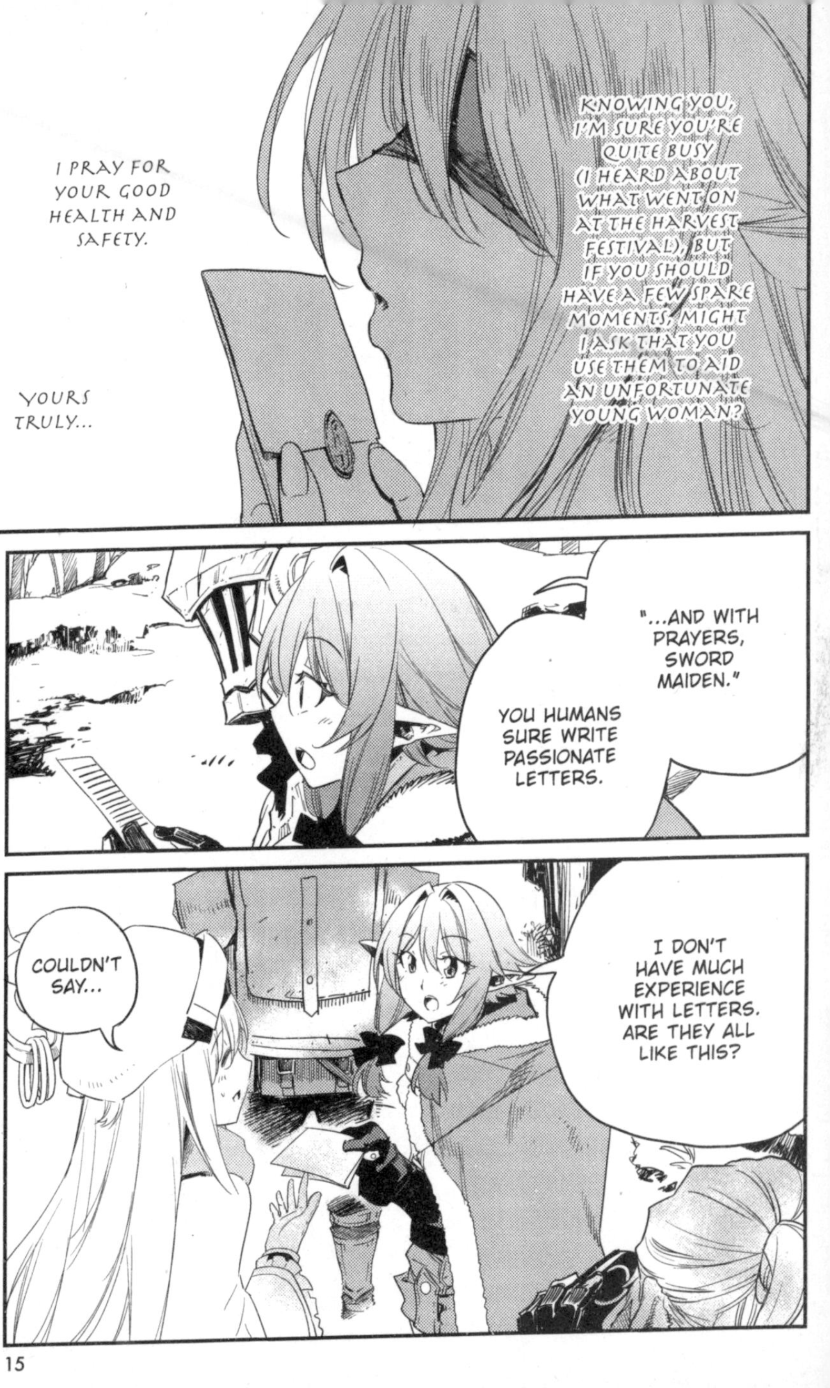
KNOWING YOU, I'M SURE YOU'RE QUITE BUSY (I HEARD ABOUT WHAT WENT ON AT THE HARVEST FESTIVAL), BUT IF YOU SHOULD HAVE A FEW SPARE MOMENTS, MIGHT I ASK THAT YOU USE THEM TO AID AN UNFORTUNATE YOUNG WOMAN?
I PRAY FOR YOUR GOOD HEALTH AND SAFETY.
YOURS TRULY...
"...AND WITH PRAYERS, SWORD MAIDEN."
YOU HUMANS SURE WRITE PASSIONATE LETTERS.
I DON'T HAVE MUCH EXPERIENCE WITH LETTERS. ARE THEY ALL LIKE THIS?
COULDN'T SAY...

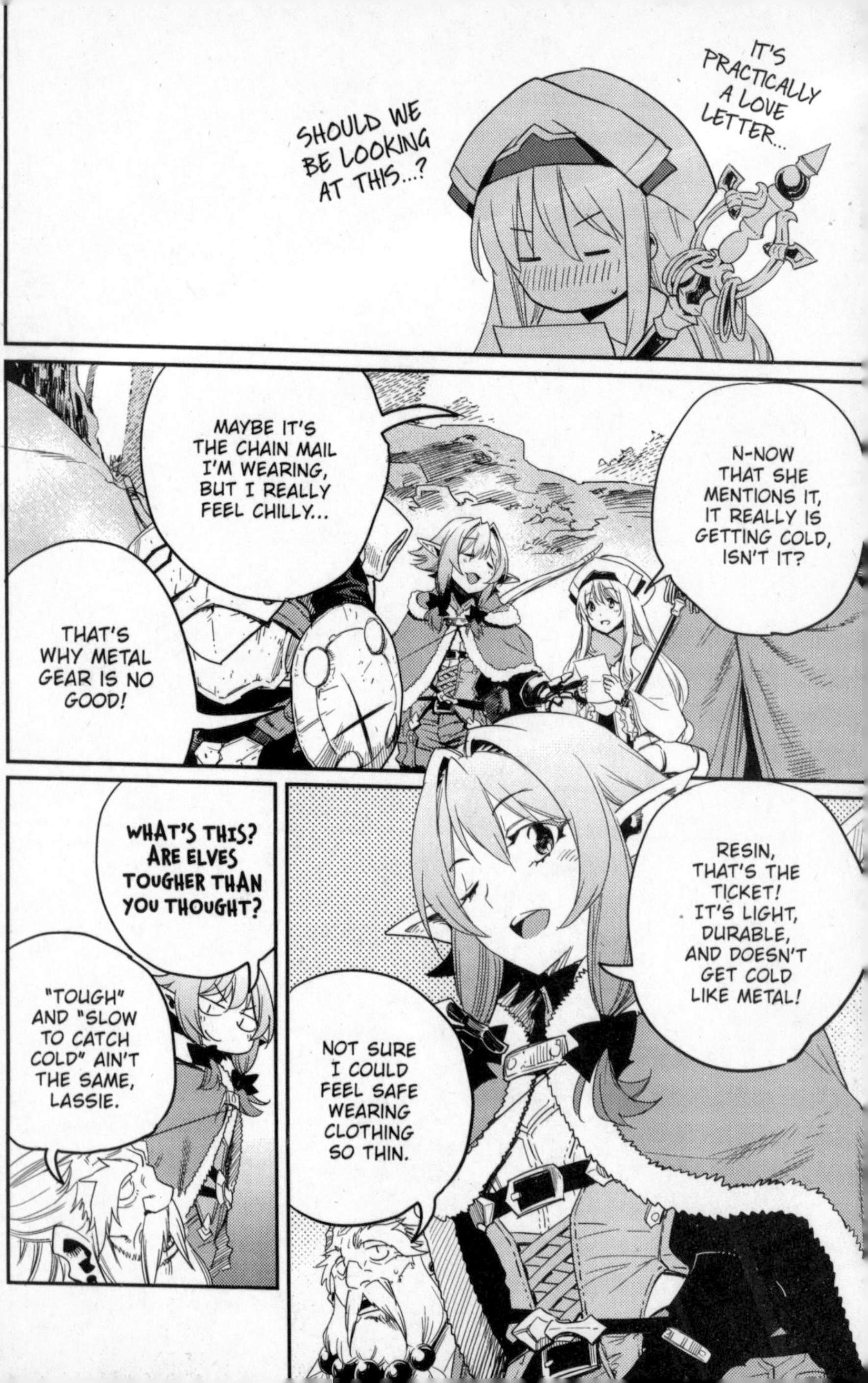
IT'S PRACTICALLY A LOVE LETTER...
SHOULD WE BE LOOKING AT THIS...?
N-NOW THAT SHE MENTIONS IT, IT REALLY IS GETTING COLD, ISN'T IT?
MAYBE IT'S THE CHAIN MAIL I'M WEARING, BUT I REALLY FEEL CHILLY...
THAT'S WHY METAL GEAR IS NO GOOD!
RESIN, THAT'S THE TICKET! IT'S LIGHT, DURABLE, AND DOESN'T GET COLD LIKE METAL!
NOT SURE I COULD FEEL SAFE WEARING CLOTHING SO THIN.
WHAT'S THIS? ARE ELVES TOUGHER THAN YOU THOUGHT?
"TOUGH" AND "SLOW TO CATCH COLD" AIN'T THE SAME, LASSIE.

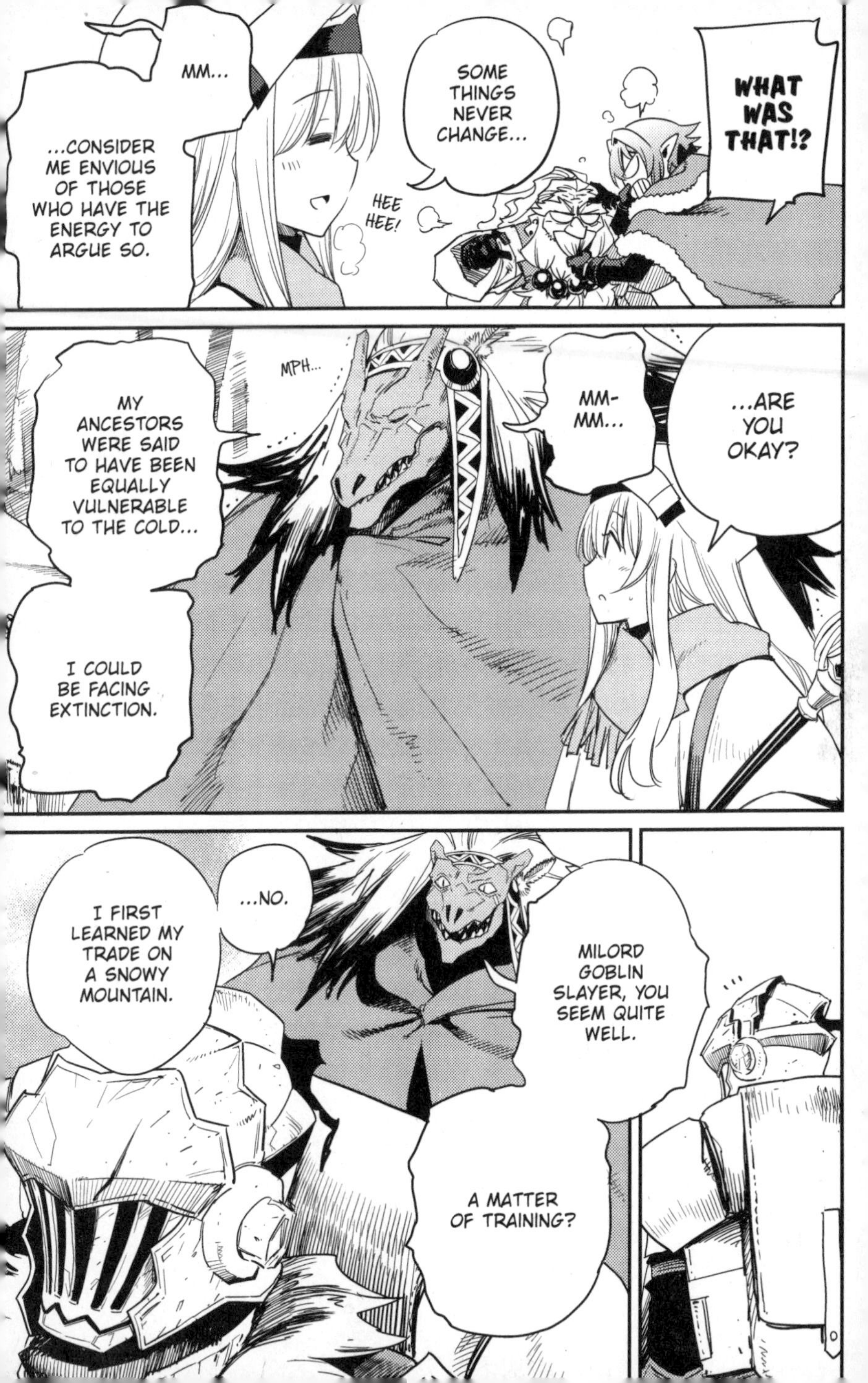
WHAT WAS THAT!?
SOME THINGS NEVER CHANGE...
HEE HEE!
MM...
...CONSIDER ME ENVIOUS OF THOSE WHO HAVE THE ENERGY TO ARGUE SO.
...ARE YOU OKAY?
MM-MM...
MPH...
MY ANCESTORS WERE SAID TO HAVE BEEN EQUALLY VULNERABLE TO THE COLD...
I COULD BE FACING EXTINCTION.
...
MILORD GOBLIN SLAYER, YOU SEEM QUITE WELL.
A MATTER OF TRAINING?
...NO.
I FIRST LEARNED MY TRADE ON A SNOWY MOUNTAIN.

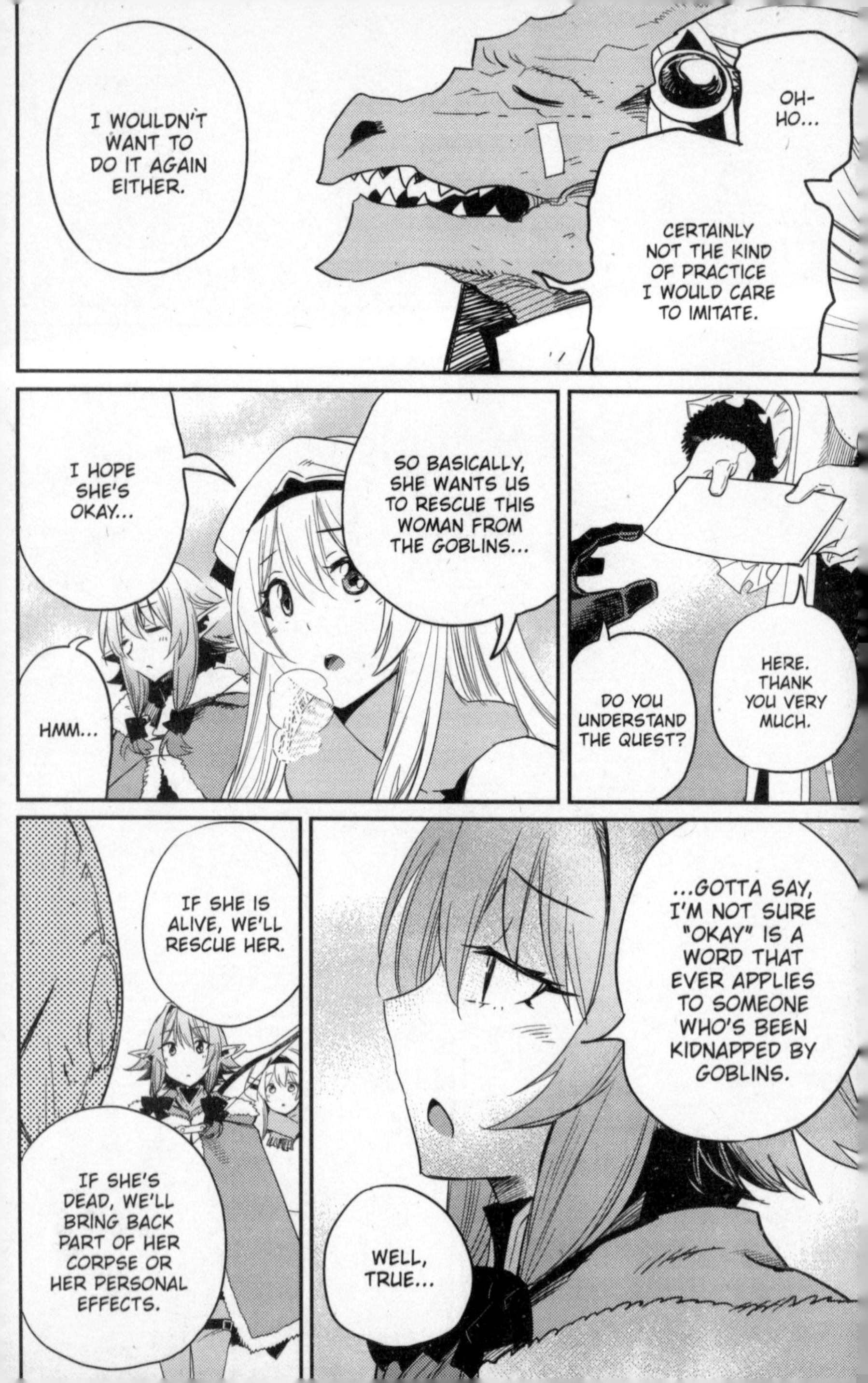
OH-HO...
CERTAINLY NOT THE KIND OF PRACTICE I WOULD CARE TO IMITATE.
I WOULDN'T WANT TO DO IT AGAIN EITHER.
HERE. THANK YOU VERY MUCH.
DO YOU UNDERSTAND THE QUEST?
SO BASICALLY, SHE WANTS US TO RESCUE THIS WOMAN FROM THE GOBLINS...
I HOPE SHE'S OKAY...
HMM...
...GOTTA SAY, I'M NOT SURE "OKAY" IS A WORD THAT EVER APPLIES TO SOMEONE WHO'S BEEN KIDNAPPED BY GOBLINS.
WELL, TRUE...
IF SHE IS ALIVE, WE'LL RESCUE HER.
IF SHE'S DEAD, WE'LL BRING BACK PART OF HER CORPSE OR HER PERSONAL EFFECTS.

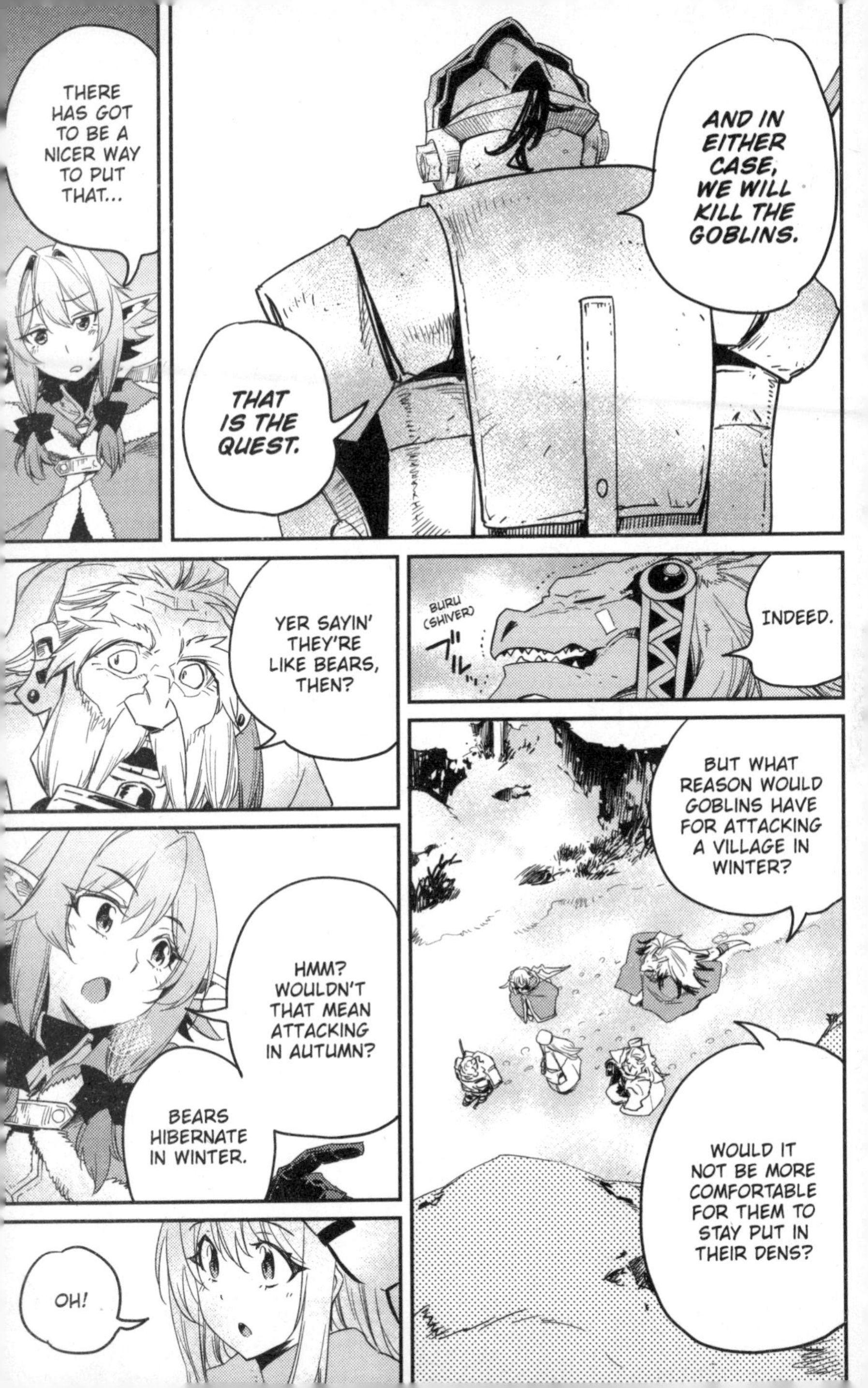
AND IN EITHER CASE, WE WILL KILL THE GOBLINS.
THAT IS THE QUEST.
THERE HAS GOT TO BE A NICER WAY TO PUT THAT...
INDEED.
BURU (SHIVER)
ブル
YER SAYIN' THEY'RE LIKE BEARS, THEN?
BUT WHAT REASON WOULD GOBLINS HAVE FOR ATTACKING A VILLAGE IN WINTER?
WOULD IT NOT BE MORE COMFORTABLE FOR THEM TO STAY PUT IN THEIR DENS?
HMM? WOULDN'T THAT MEAN ATTACKING IN AUTUMN?
BEARS HIBERNATE IN WINTER.
OH!

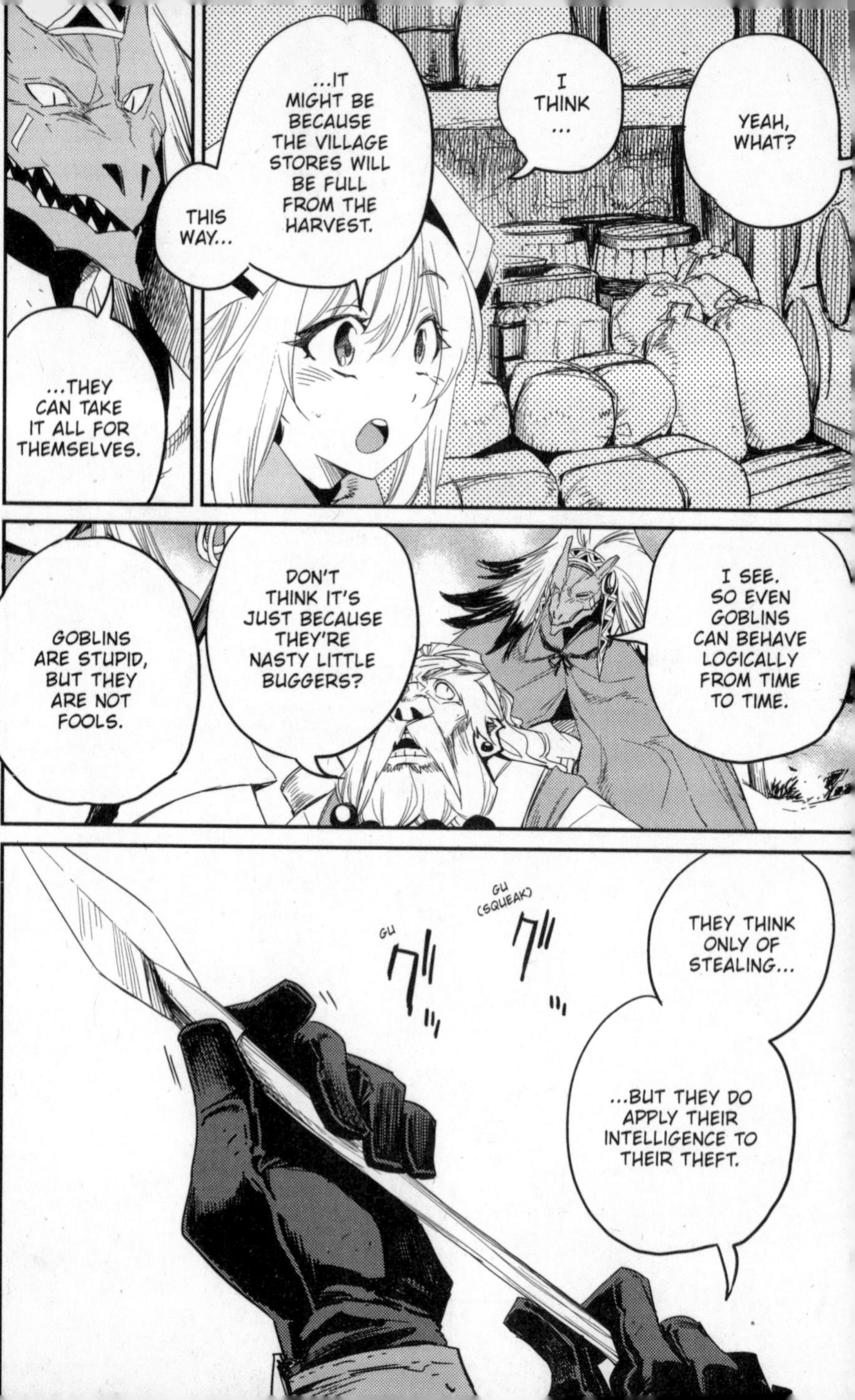
YEAH, WHAT?
I THINK ...
...IT MIGHT BE BECAUSE THE VILLAGE STORES WILL BE FULL FROM THE HARVEST.
THIS WAY...
...THEY CAN TAKE IT ALL FOR THEMSELVES.
I SEE. SO EVEN GOBLINS CAN BEHAVE LOGICALLY FROM TIME TO TIME.
DON'T THINK IT'S JUST BECAUSE THEY'RE NASTY LITTLE BUGGERS?
GOBLINS ARE STUPID, BUT THEY ARE NOT FOOLS.
THEY THINK ONLY OF STEALING...
...BUT THEY DO APPLY THEIR INTELLIGENCE TO THEIR THEFT.
GU (SQUEAK)
グ
GU
グ

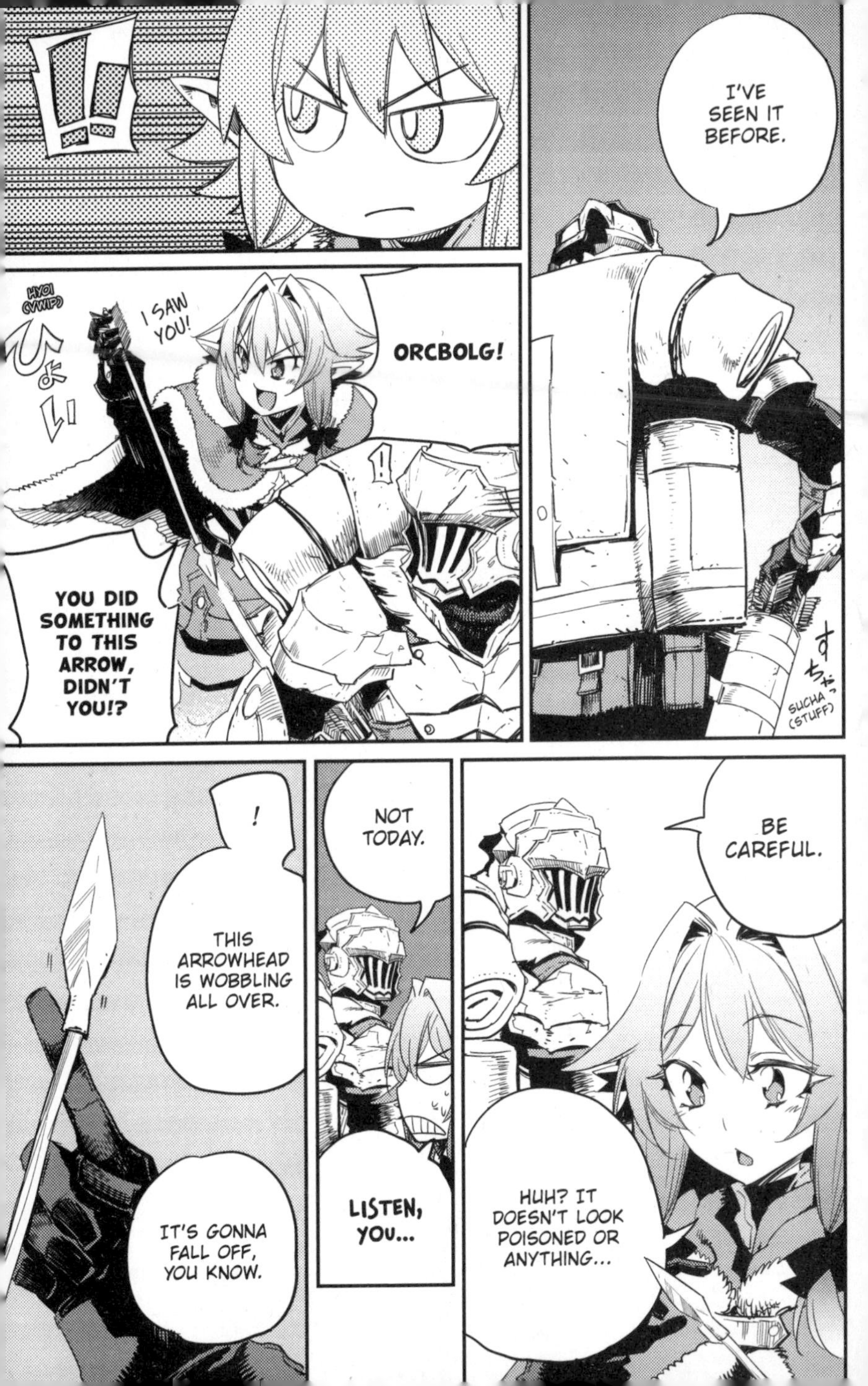
I'VE SEEN IT BEFORE.
すちゃっ
SUCHA (STUFF)
!!
HYOI (YWIP)
ひょい
I SAW YOU!
ORCBOLG!
!
YOU DID SOMETHING TO THIS ARROW, DIDN'T YOU!?
BE CAREFUL.
HUH? IT DOESN'T LOOK POISONED OR ANYTHING...
NOT TODAY.
LISTEN, YOU...
!
THIS ARROWHEAD IS WOBBLING ALL OVER.
IT'S GONNA FALL OFF, YOU KNOW.

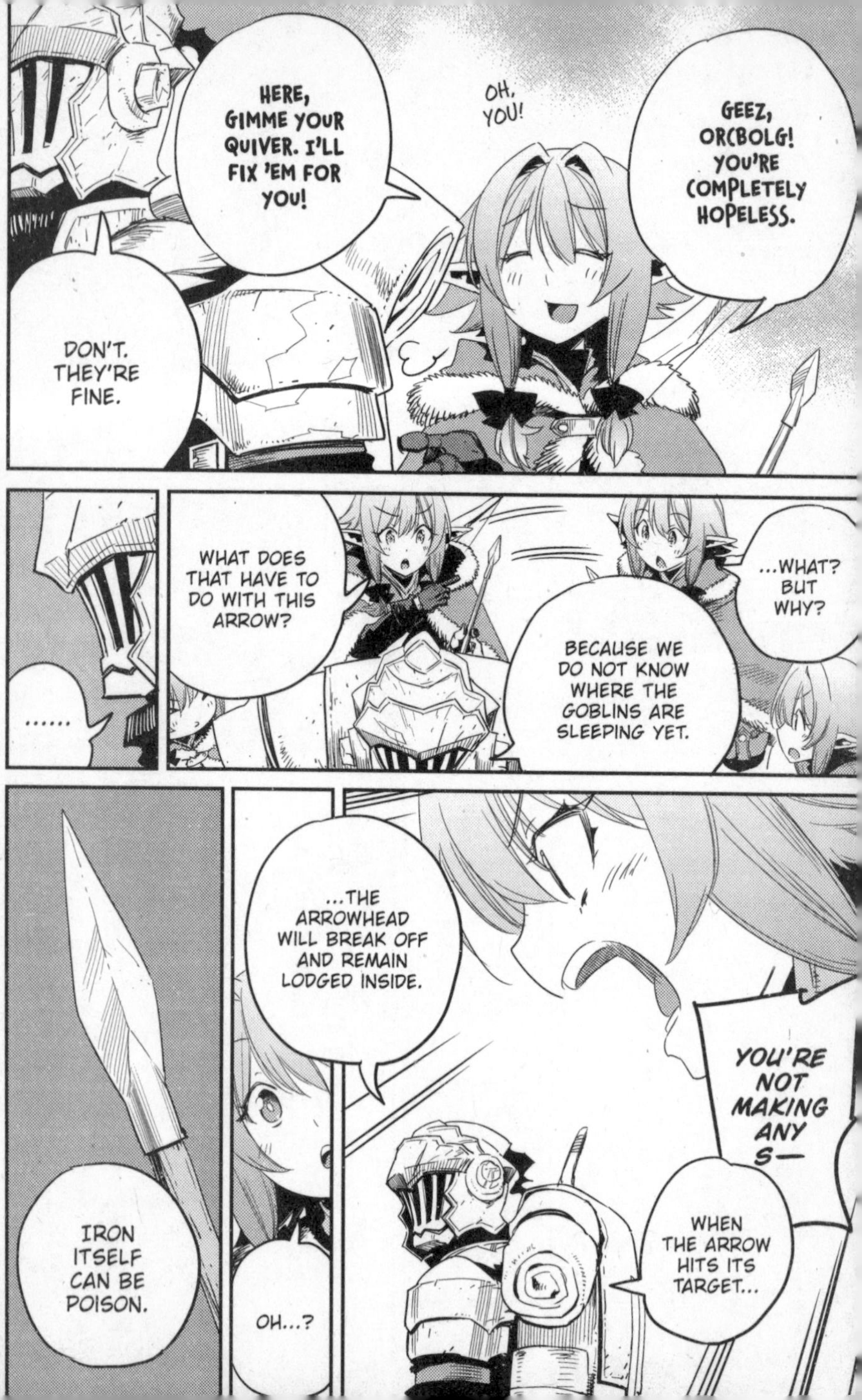
GEEZ, ORCBOLG! YOU'RE COMPLETELY HOPELESS.
OH, YOU!
HERE, GIMME YOUR QUIVER. I'LL FIX 'EM FOR YOU!
DON'T. THEY'RE FINE.
...WHAT? BUT WHY?
BECAUSE WE DO NOT KNOW WHERE THE GOBLINS ARE SLEEPING YET.
WHAT DOES THAT HAVE TO DO WITH THIS ARROW?
......
YOU'RE NOT MAKING ANY S—
WHEN THE ARROW HITS ITS TARGET...
...THE ARROWHEAD WILL BREAK OFF AND REMAIN LODGED INSIDE.
OH...?
IRON ITSELF CAN BE POISON.

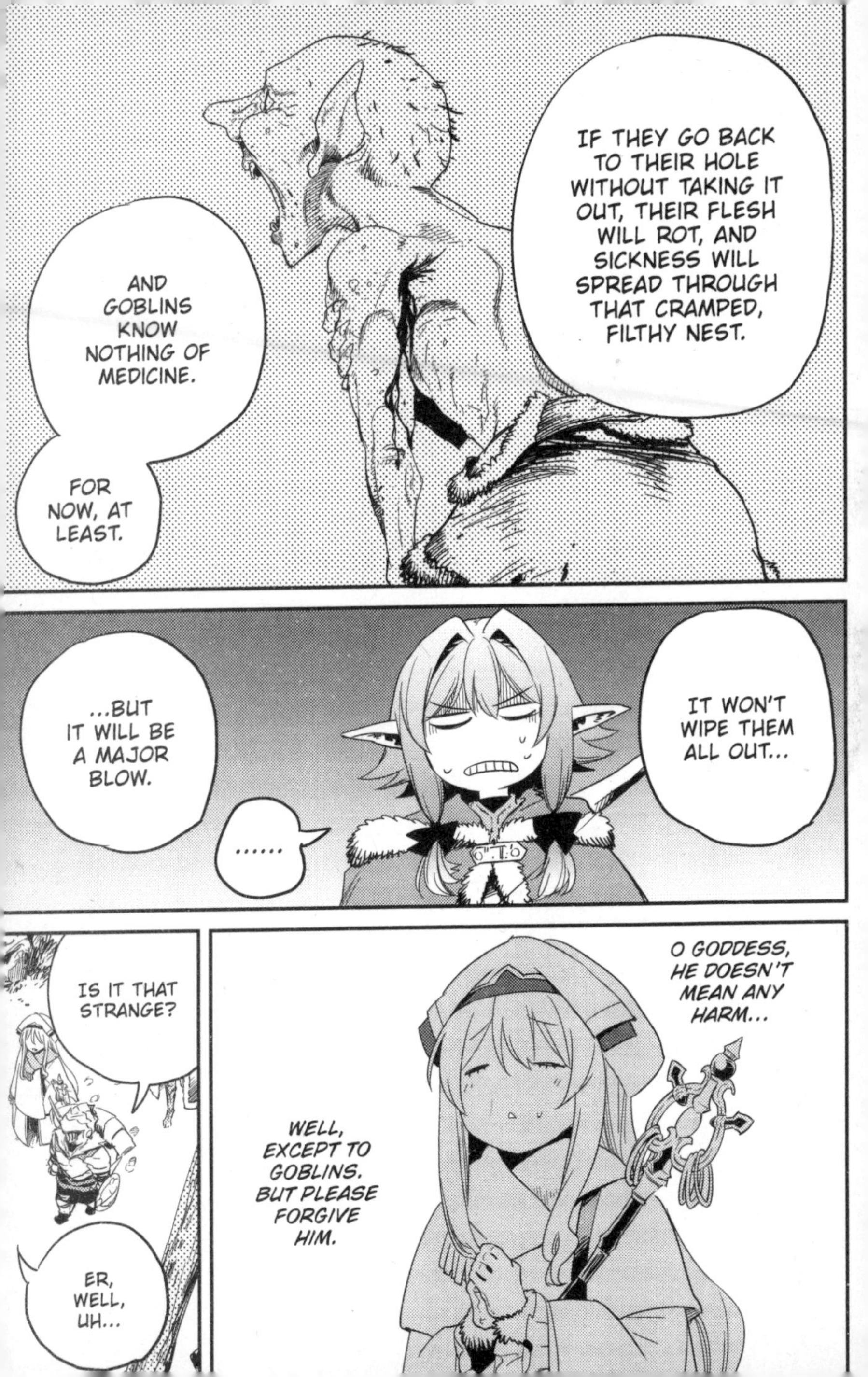
IF THEY GO BACK TO THEIR HOLE WITHOUT TAKING IT OUT, THEIR FLESH WILL ROT, AND SICKNESS WILL SPREAD THROUGH THAT CRAMPED, FILTHY NEST.
AND GOBLINS KNOW NOTHING OF MEDICINE.
FOR NOW, AT LEAST.
IT WON'T WIPE THEM ALL OUT...
...BUT IT WILL BE A MAJOR BLOW.
......
O GODDESS, HE DOESN'T MEAN ANY HARM...
WELL, EXCEPT TO GOBLINS. BUT PLEASE FORGIVE HIM.
IS IT THAT STRANGE?
ER, WELL, UH...

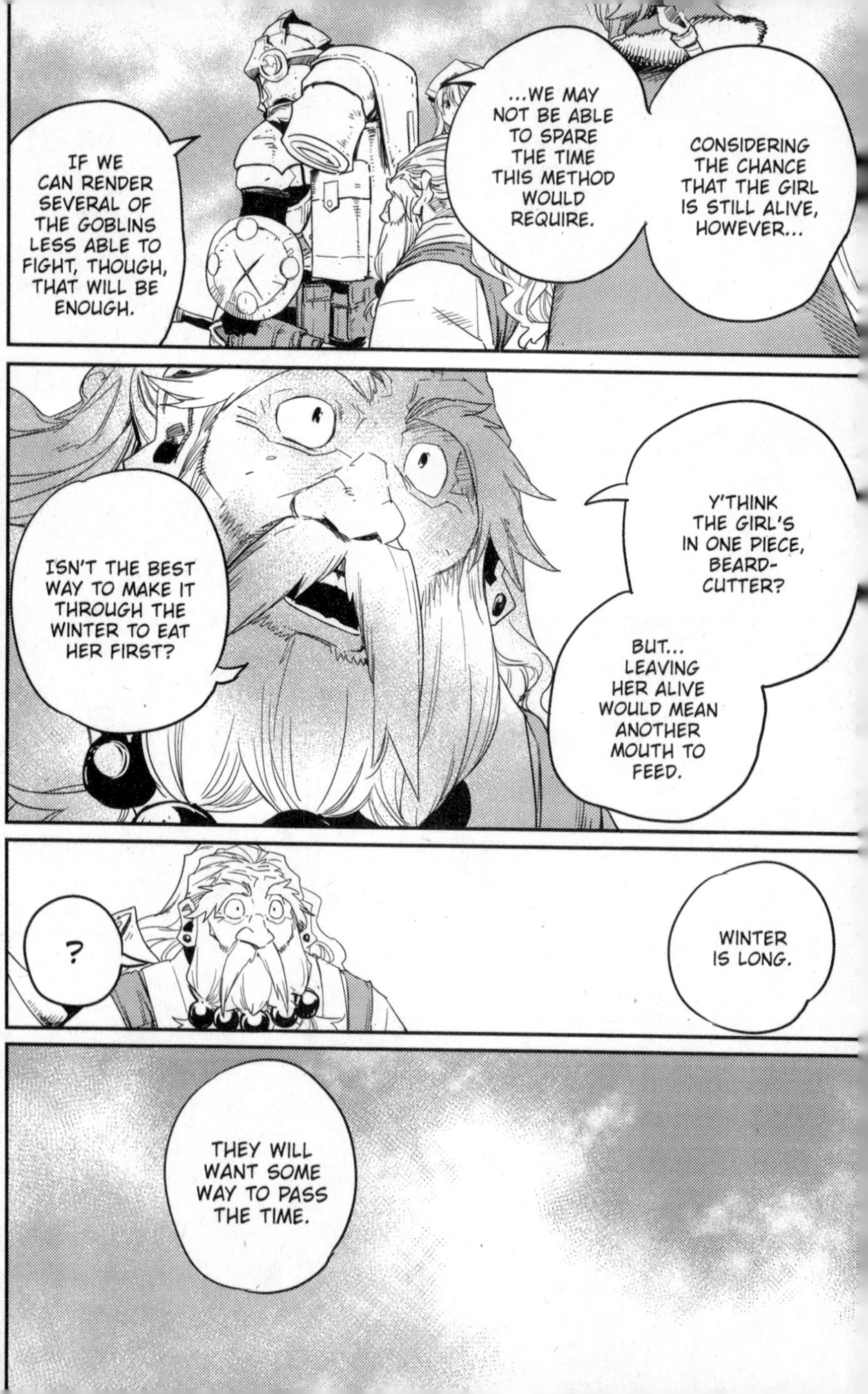
CONSIDERING THE CHANCE THAT THE GIRL IS STILL ALIVE, HOWEVER...
...WE MAY NOT BE ABLE TO SPARE THE TIME THIS METHOD WOULD REQUIRE.
IF WE CAN RENDER SEVERAL OF THE GOBLINS LESS ABLE TO FIGHT, THOUGH, THAT WILL BE ENOUGH.
Y'THINK THE GIRL'S IN ONE PIECE, BEARD-CUTTER?
BUT... LEAVING HER ALIVE WOULD MEAN ANOTHER MOUTH TO FEED.
ISN'T THE BEST WAY TO MAKE IT THROUGH THE WINTER TO EAT HER FIRST?
WINTER IS LONG.
?
THEY WILL WANT SOME WAY TO PASS THE TIME.

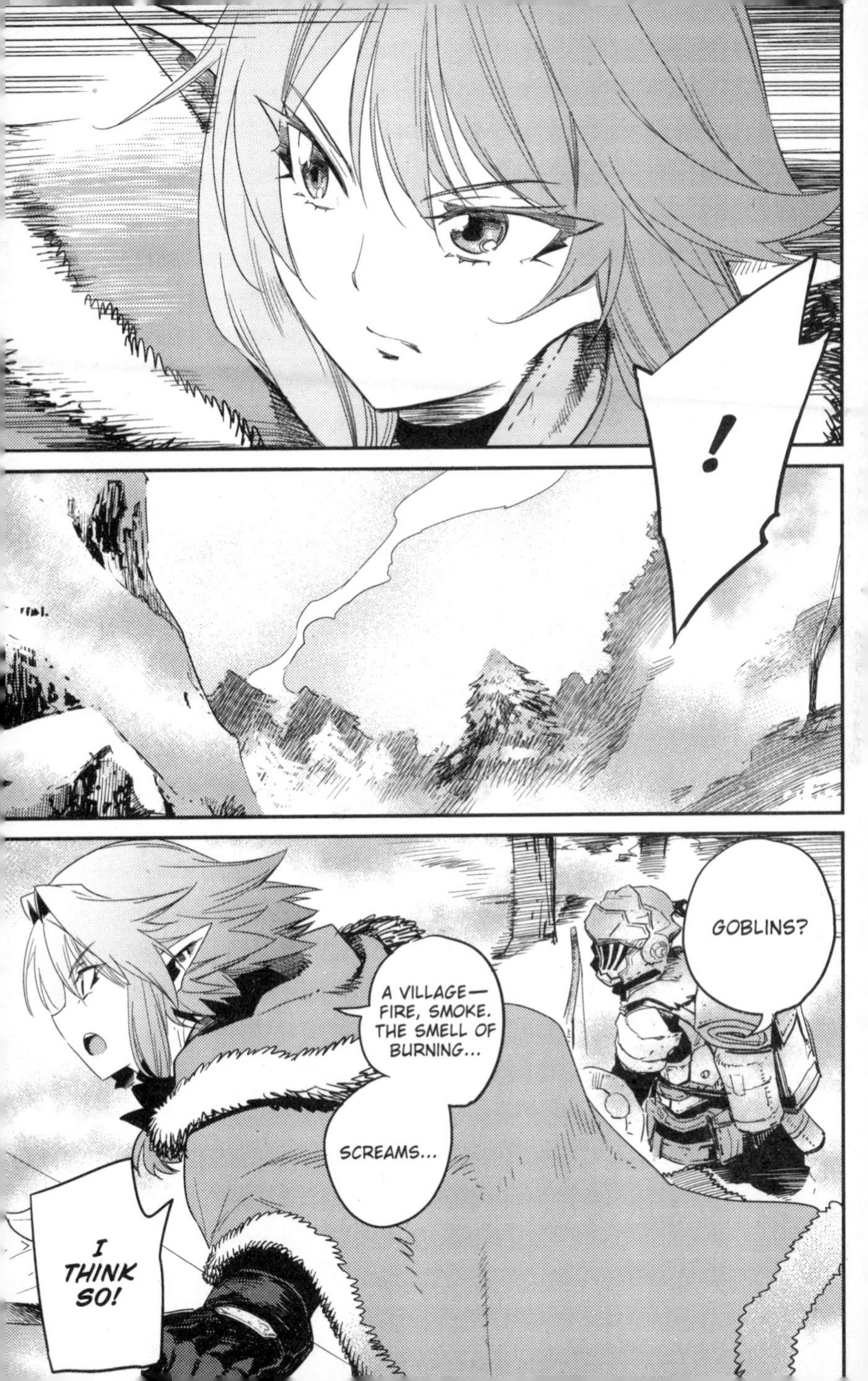
!
GOBLINS?
A VILLAGE—FIRE, SMOKE. THE SMELL OF BURNING...
SCREAMS...
I THINK SO!

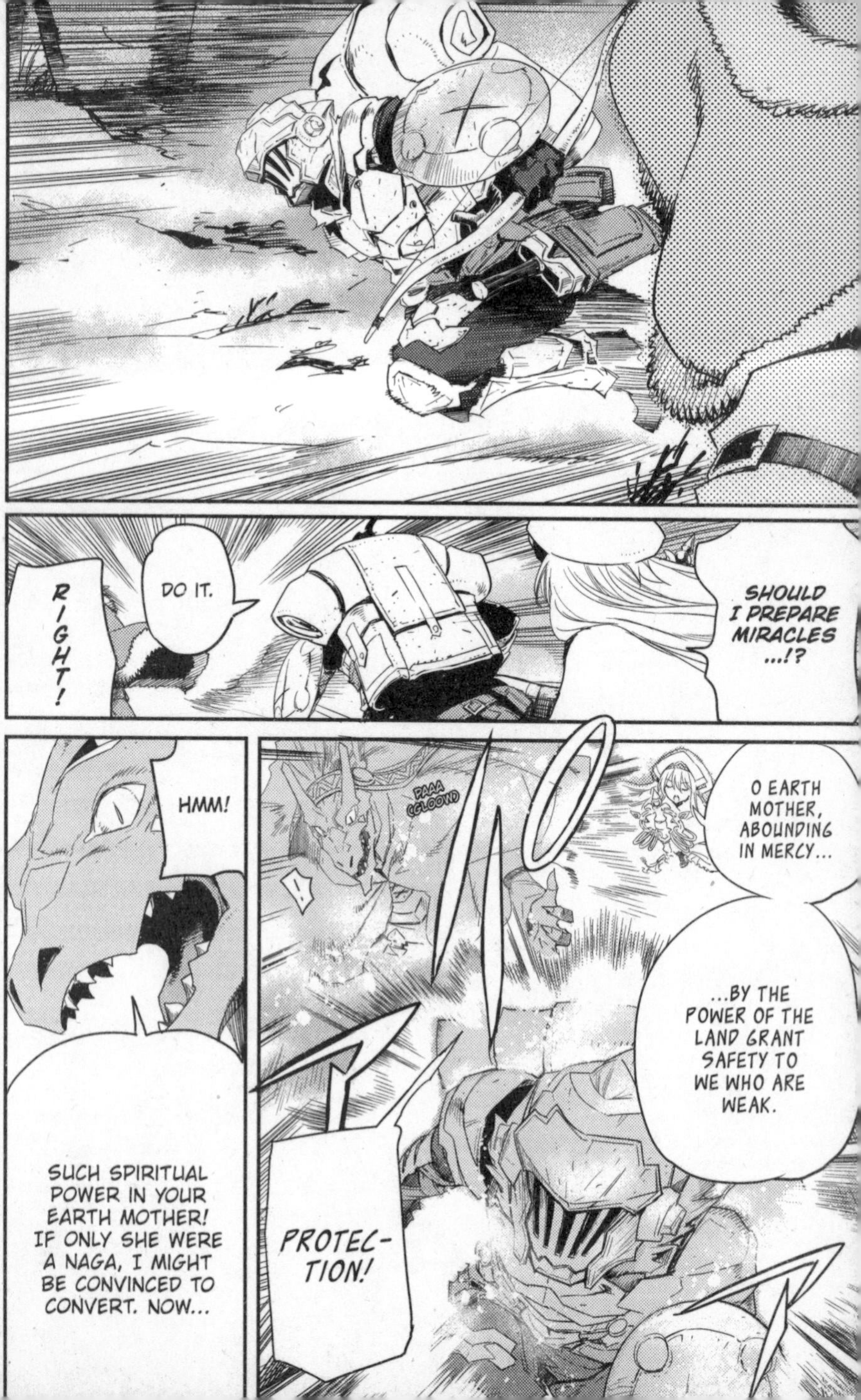
SHOULD I PREPARE MIRACLES ...!?
DO IT.
RIGHT!
O EARTH MOTHER, ABOUNDING IN MERCY...
...BY THE POWER OF THE LAND GRANT SAFETY TO WE WHO ARE WEAK.
PAAA (GLOOW)
!
PROTECTION!
HMM!
SUCH SPIRITUAL POWER IN YOUR EARTH MOTHER! IF ONLY SHE WERE A NAGA, I MIGHT BE CONVINCED TO CONVERT. NOW...

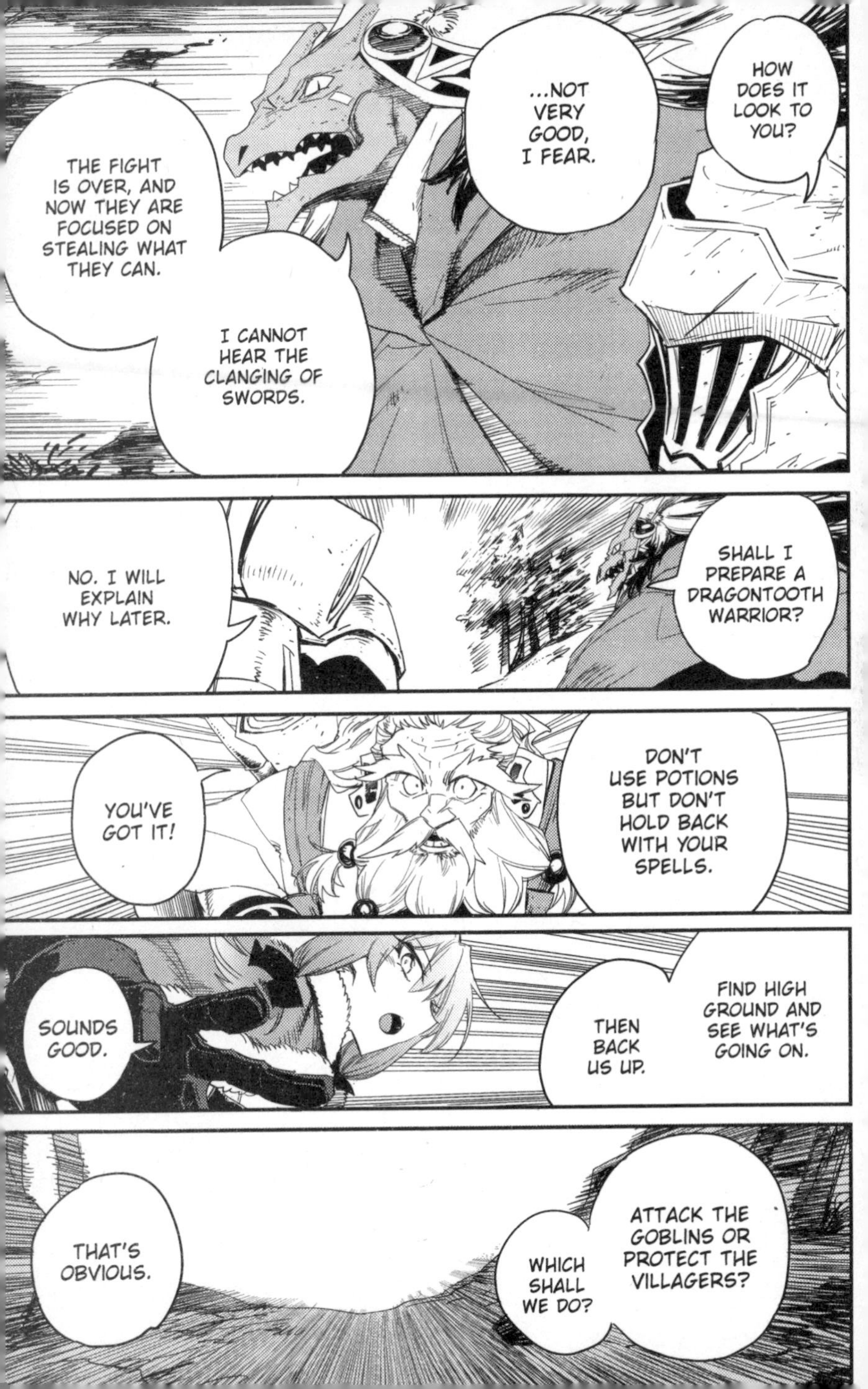
HOW DOES IT LOOK TO YOU?
...NOT VERY GOOD, I FEAR.
THE FIGHT IS OVER, AND NOW THEY ARE FOCUSED ON STEALING WHAT THEY CAN.
I CANNOT HEAR THE CLANGING OF SWORDS.
SHALL I PREPARE A DRAGONTOOTH WARRIOR?
NO. I WILL EXPLAIN WHY LATER.
DON'T USE POTIONS BUT DON'T HOLD BACK WITH YOUR SPELLS.
YOU'VE GOT IT!
FIND HIGH GROUND AND SEE WHAT'S GOING ON.
THEN BACK US UP.
SOUNDS GOOD.
ATTACK THE GOBLINS OR PROTECT THE VILLAGERS?
WHICH SHALL WE DO?
THAT'S OBVIOUS.

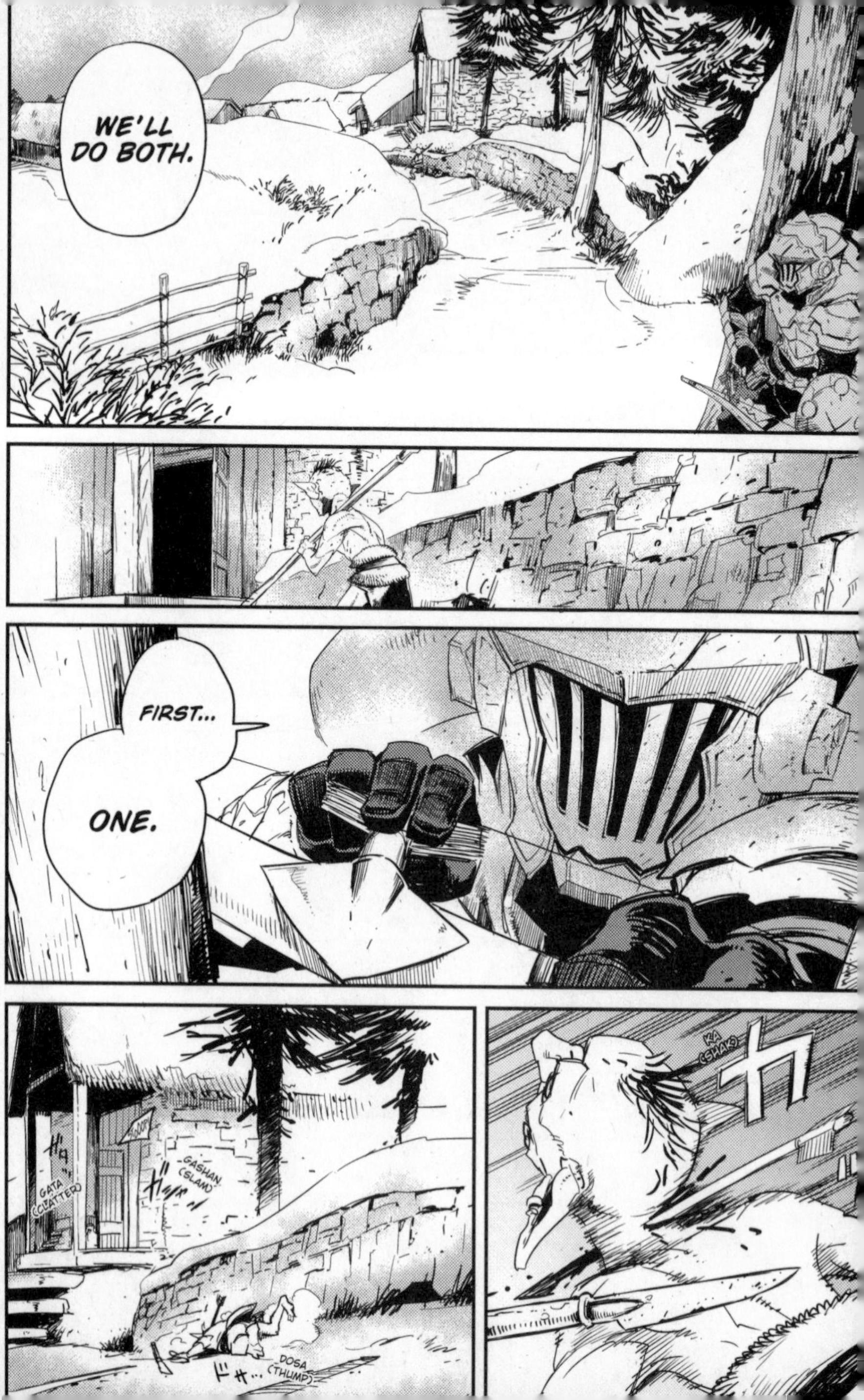
WE'LL DO BOTH.
FIRST...
ONE.
KA (SHAK)
カ
STOOOP!
GATA (CLATTER)
ガタ
GASHAN (SLAM)
ガシャン
DOSA (THUMP)
ドサ…

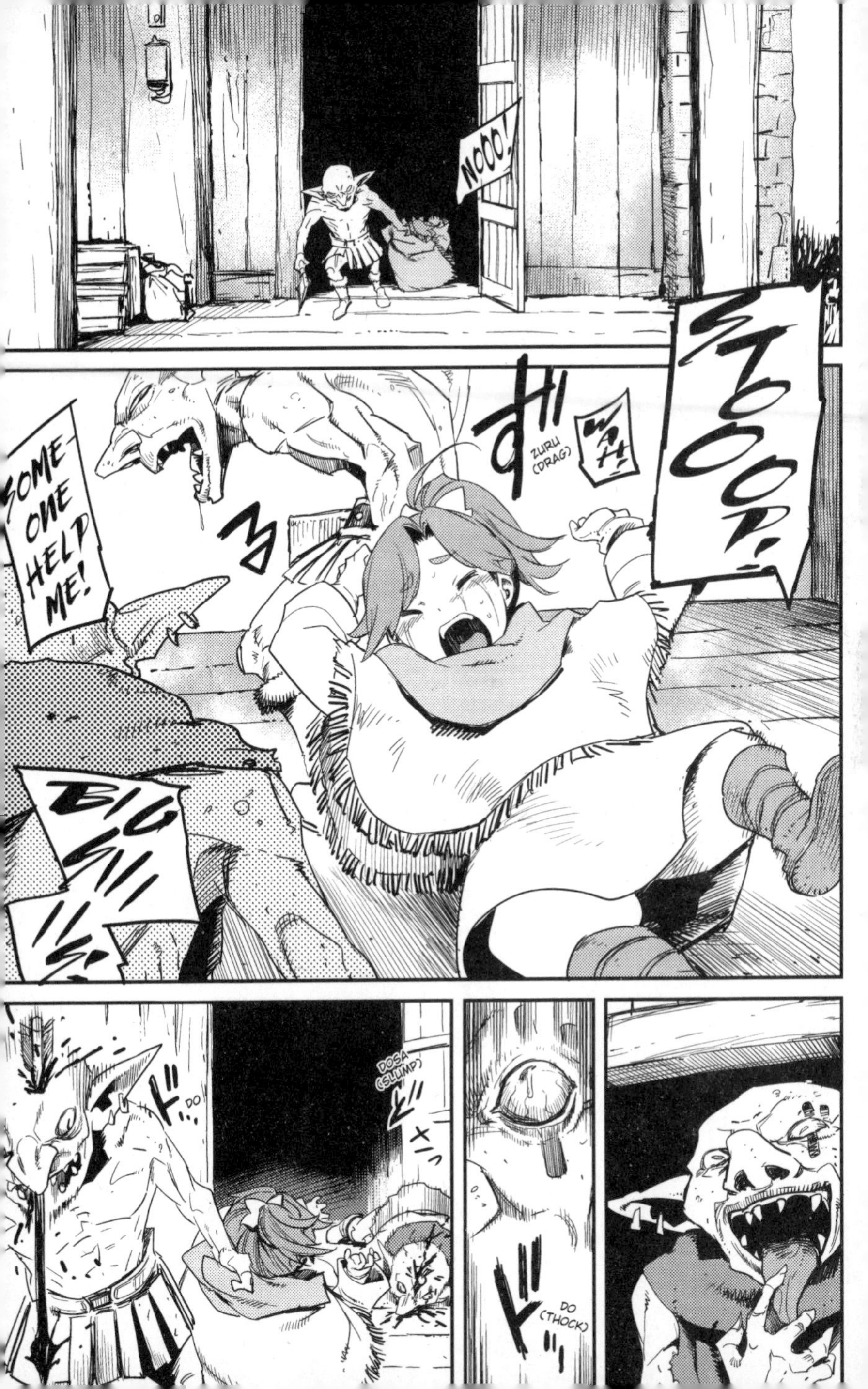
NOOO!
STOOOP!
WAH!
ZURU (DRAG)
SOME-ONE HELP ME!
BIG SIS!!
DO (THOCK)
DOSA (SLUMP)
DO

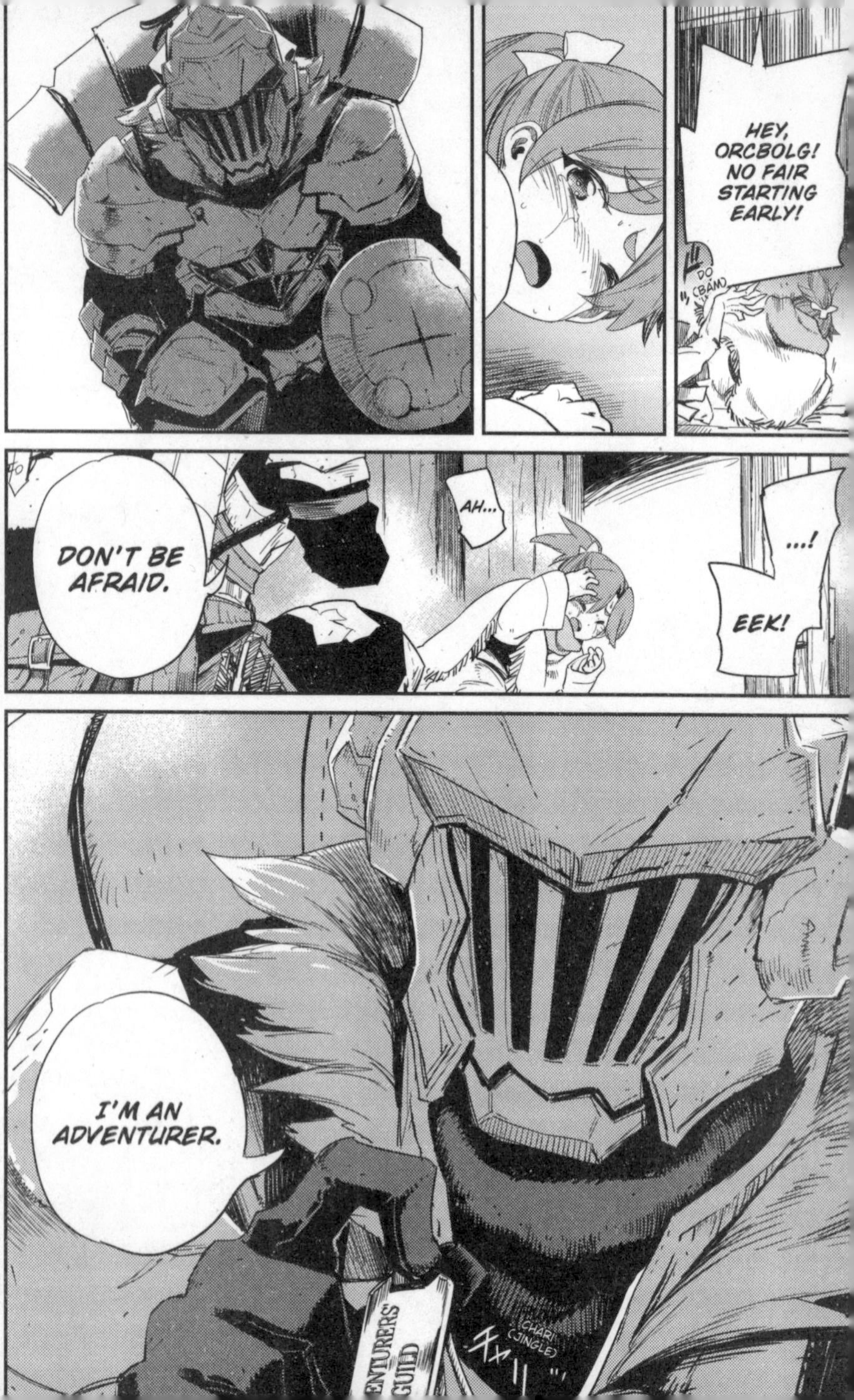
HEY, ORCBOLG! NO FAIR STARTING EARLY!
DO (BAM)
...!
EEK!
AH...
DON'T BE AFRAID.
I'M AN ADVENTURER.
CHARI (JINGLE)
ENTURERS' GUILD

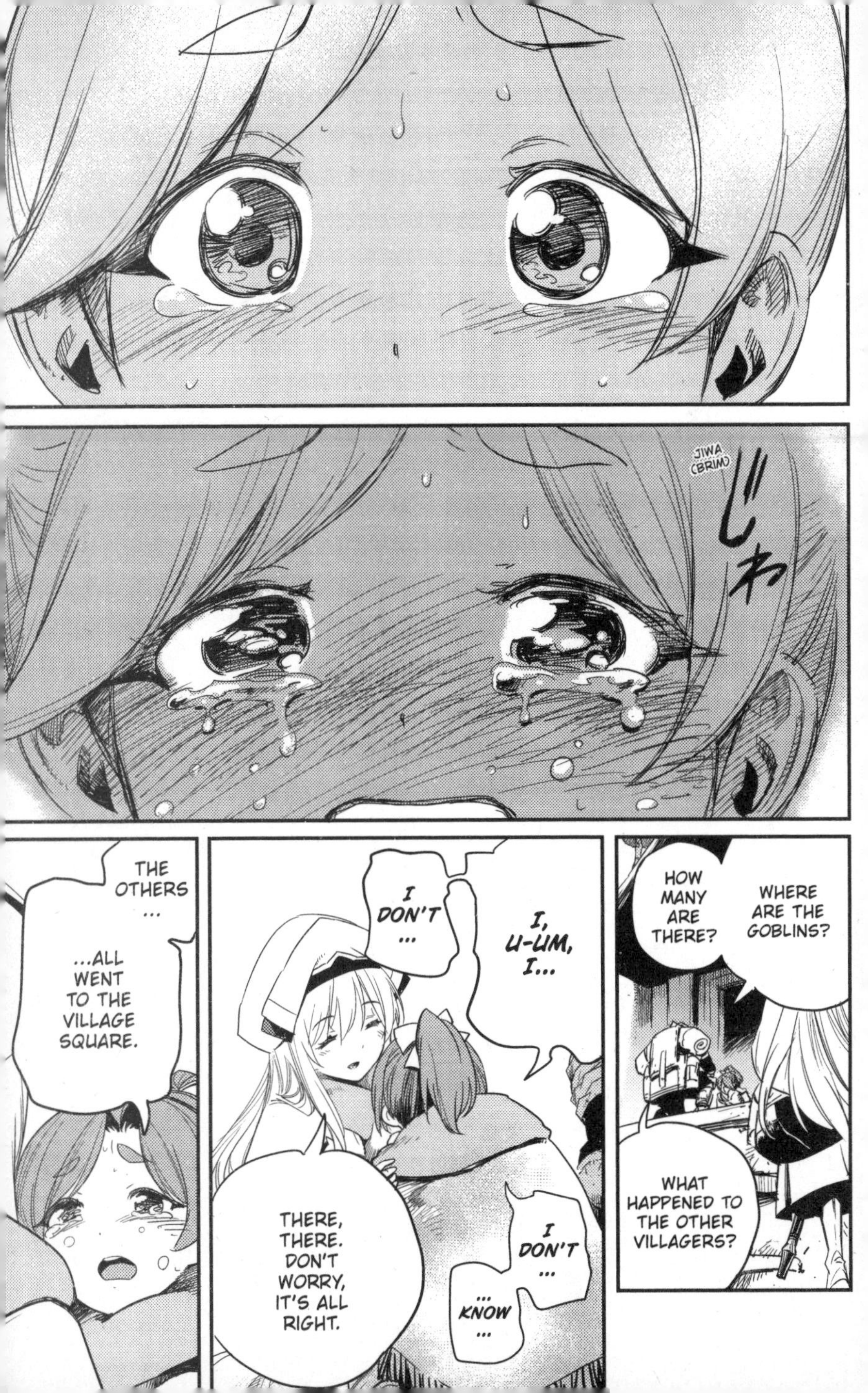
JIWA (BRIM)
じわ
WHERE ARE THE GOBLINS?
HOW MANY ARE THERE?
WHAT HAPPENED TO THE OTHER VILLAGERS?
I, U-UM, I...
I DON'T ...
I DON'T ...
... KNOW ...
THERE, THERE. DON'T WORRY, IT'S ALL RIGHT.
THE OTHERS ...
...ALL WENT TO THE VILLAGE SQUARE.

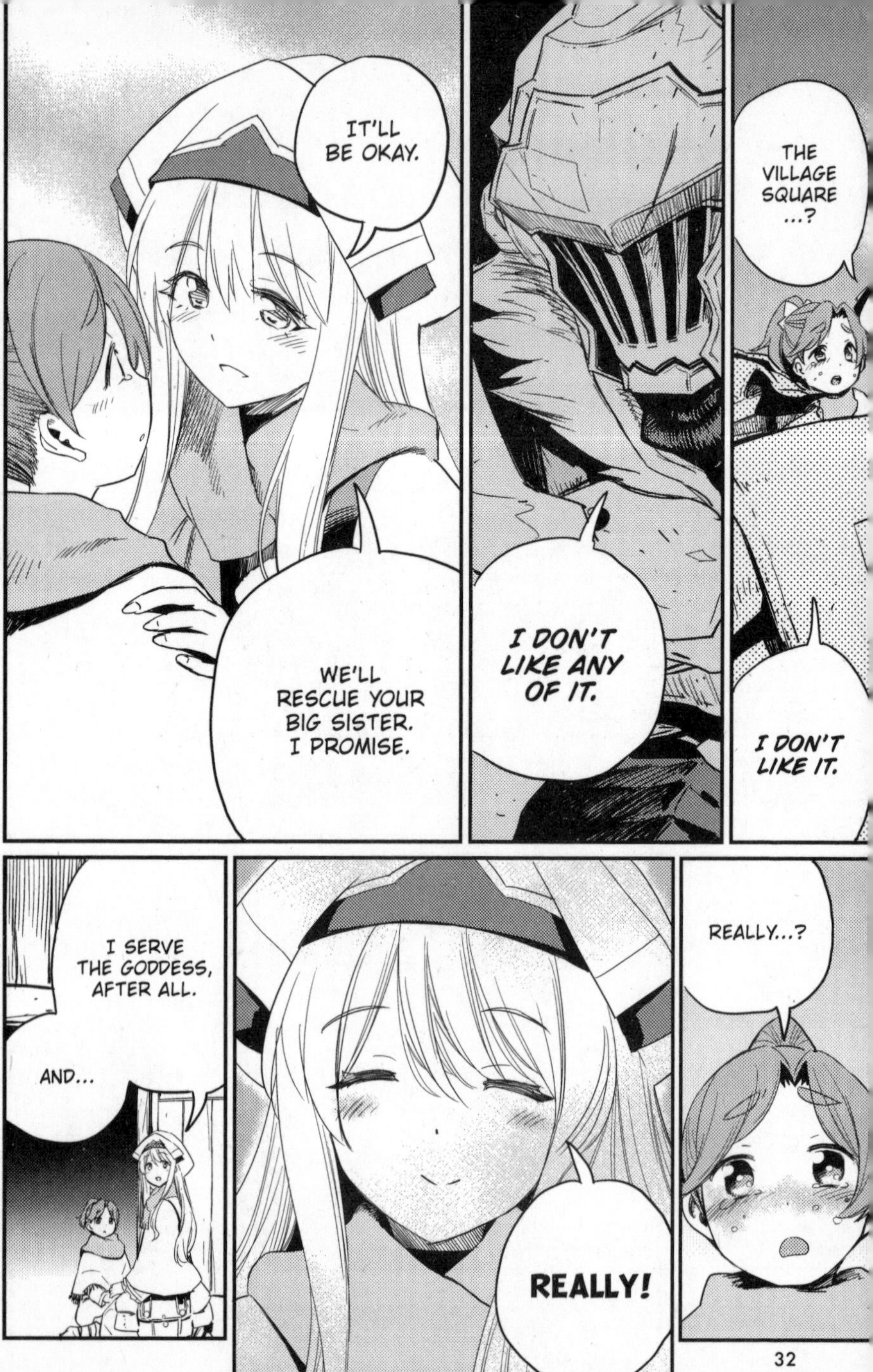
THE VILLAGE SQUARE ...?
I DON'T LIKE IT.
I DON'T LIKE ANY OF IT.
IT'LL BE OKAY.
WE'LL RESCUE YOUR BIG SISTER. I PROMISE.
REALLY...?
REALLY!
I SERVE THE GODDESS, AFTER ALL.
AND...

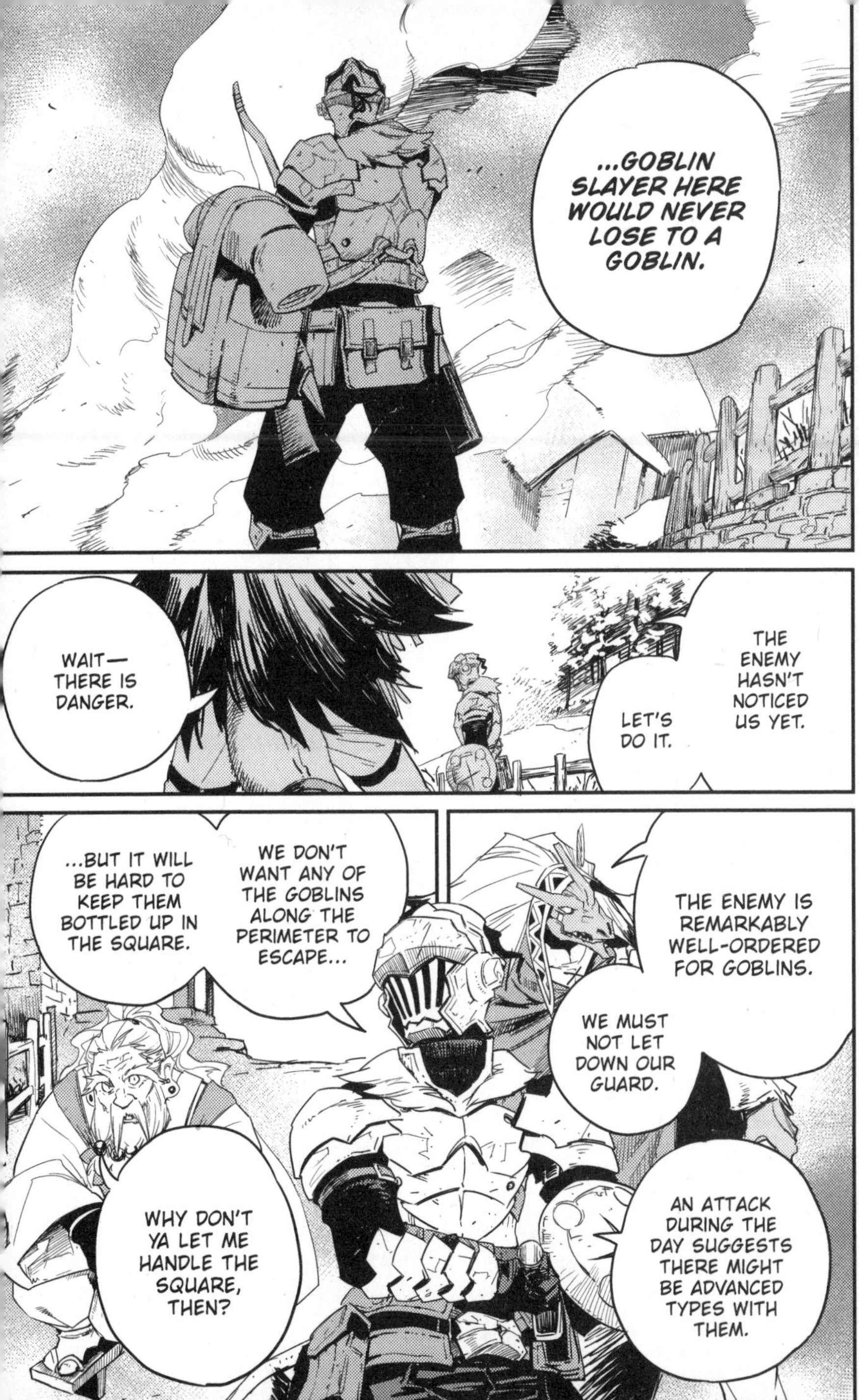
...GOBLIN SLAYER HERE WOULD NEVER LOSE TO A GOBLIN.
THE ENEMY HASN'T NOTICED US YET.
LET'S DO IT.
WAIT— THERE IS DANGER.
THE ENEMY IS REMARKABLY WELL-ORDERED FOR GOBLINS.
WE MUST NOT LET DOWN OUR GUARD.
AN ATTACK DURING THE DAY SUGGESTS THERE MIGHT BE ADVANCED TYPES WITH THEM.
WE DON'T WANT ANY OF THE GOBLINS ALONG THE PERIMETER TO ESCAPE...
...BUT IT WILL BE HARD TO KEEP THEM BOTTLED UP IN THE SQUARE.
WHY DON'T YA LET ME HANDLE THE SQUARE, THEN?

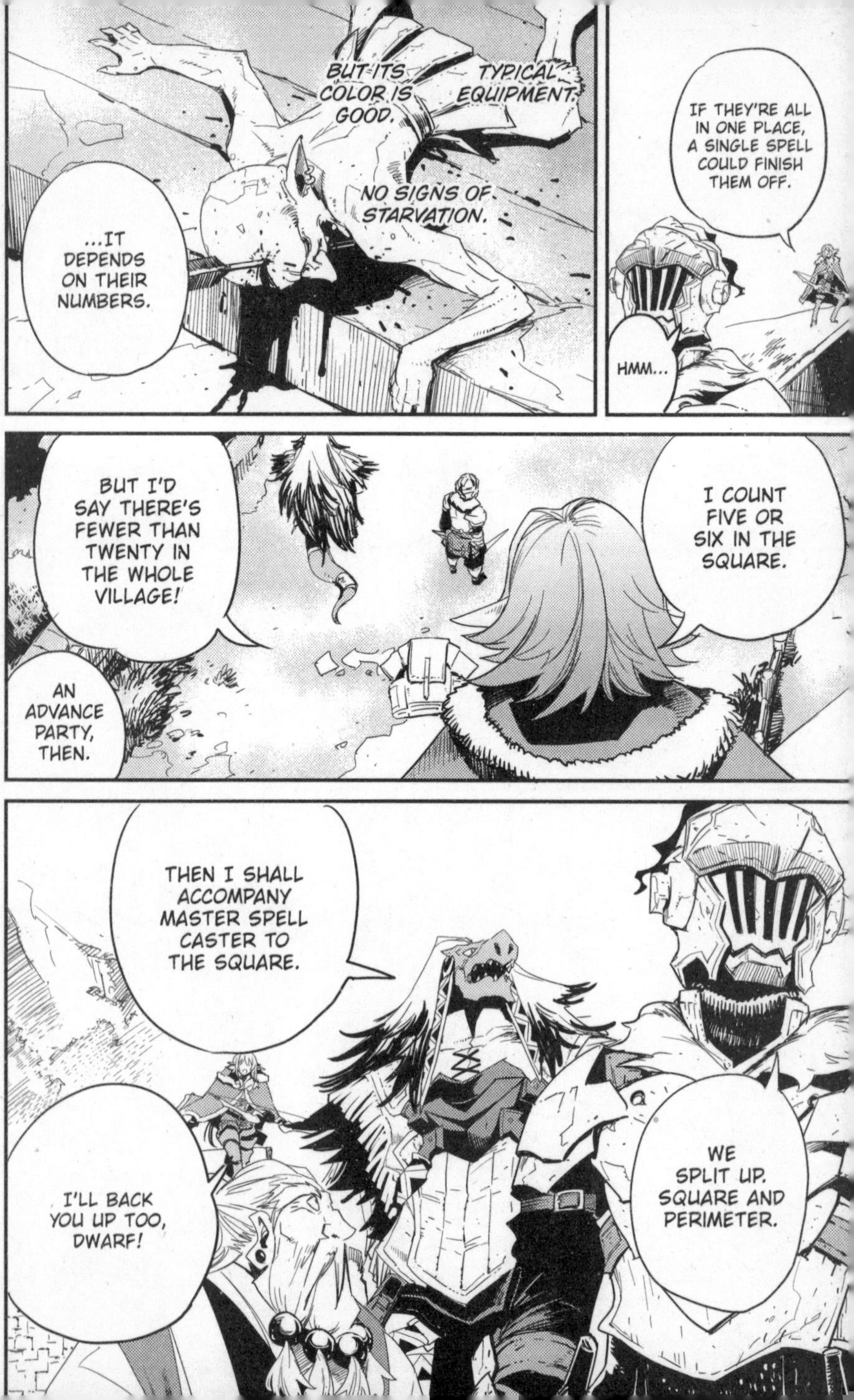
IF THEY'RE ALL IN ONE PLACE, A SINGLE SPELL COULD FINISH THEM OFF.
HMM...
TYPICAL EQUIPMENT.
BUT ITS COLOR IS GOOD.
NO SIGNS OF STARVATION.
...IT DEPENDS ON THEIR NUMBERS.
I COUNT FIVE OR SIX IN THE SQUARE.
BUT I'D SAY THERE'S FEWER THAN TWENTY IN THE WHOLE VILLAGE!
AN ADVANCE PARTY, THEN.
WE SPLIT UP. SQUARE AND PERIMETER.
THEN I SHALL ACCOMPANY MASTER SPELL CASTER TO THE SQUARE.
I'LL BACK YOU UP TOO, DWARF!

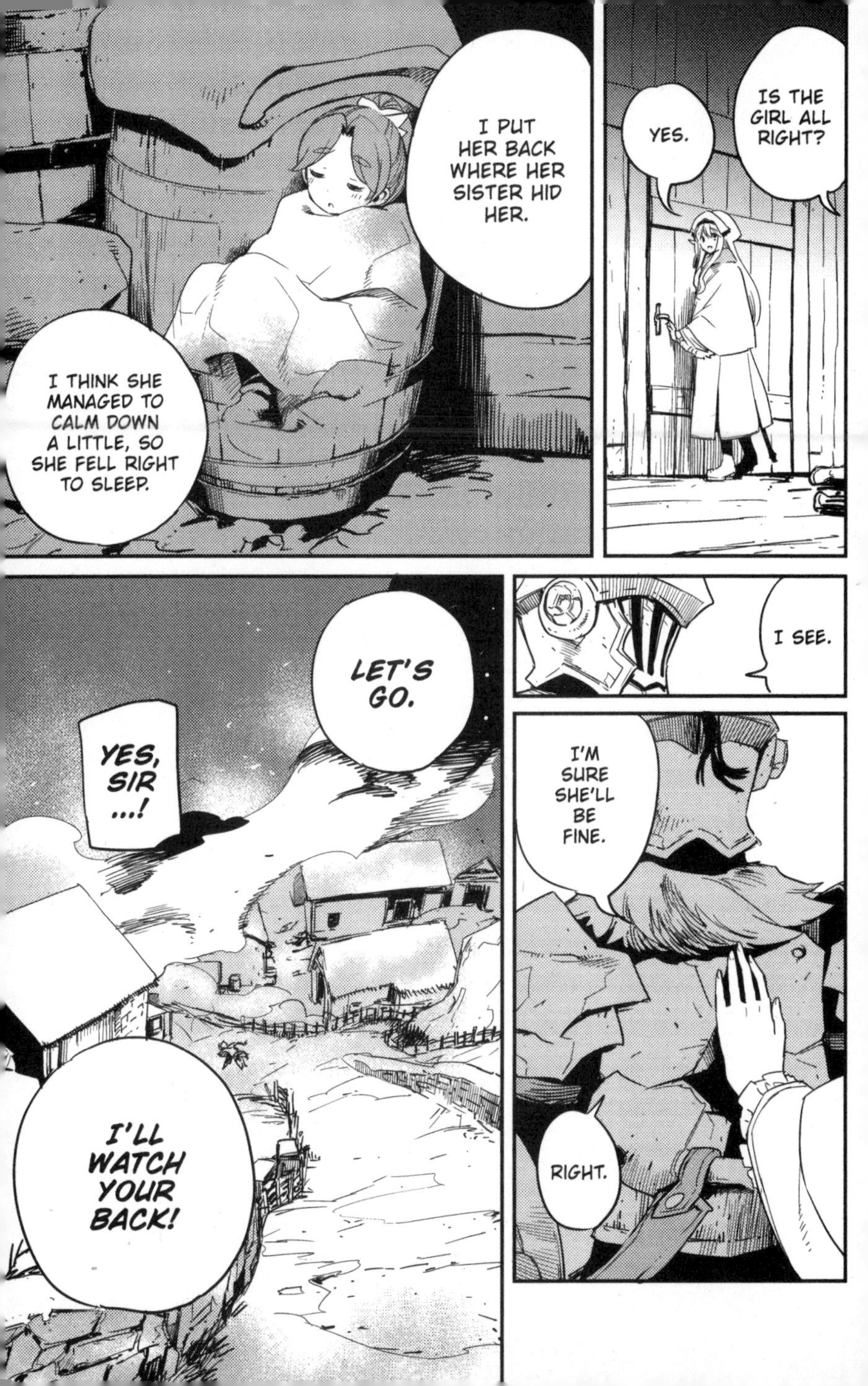
IS THE GIRL ALL RIGHT?
YES.
I PUT HER BACK WHERE HER SISTER HID HER.
I THINK SHE MANAGED TO CALM DOWN A LITTLE, SO SHE FELL RIGHT TO SLEEP.
I SEE.
I'M SURE SHE'LL BE FINE.
RIGHT.
LET'S GO.
YES, SIR ...!
I'LL WATCH YOUR BACK!

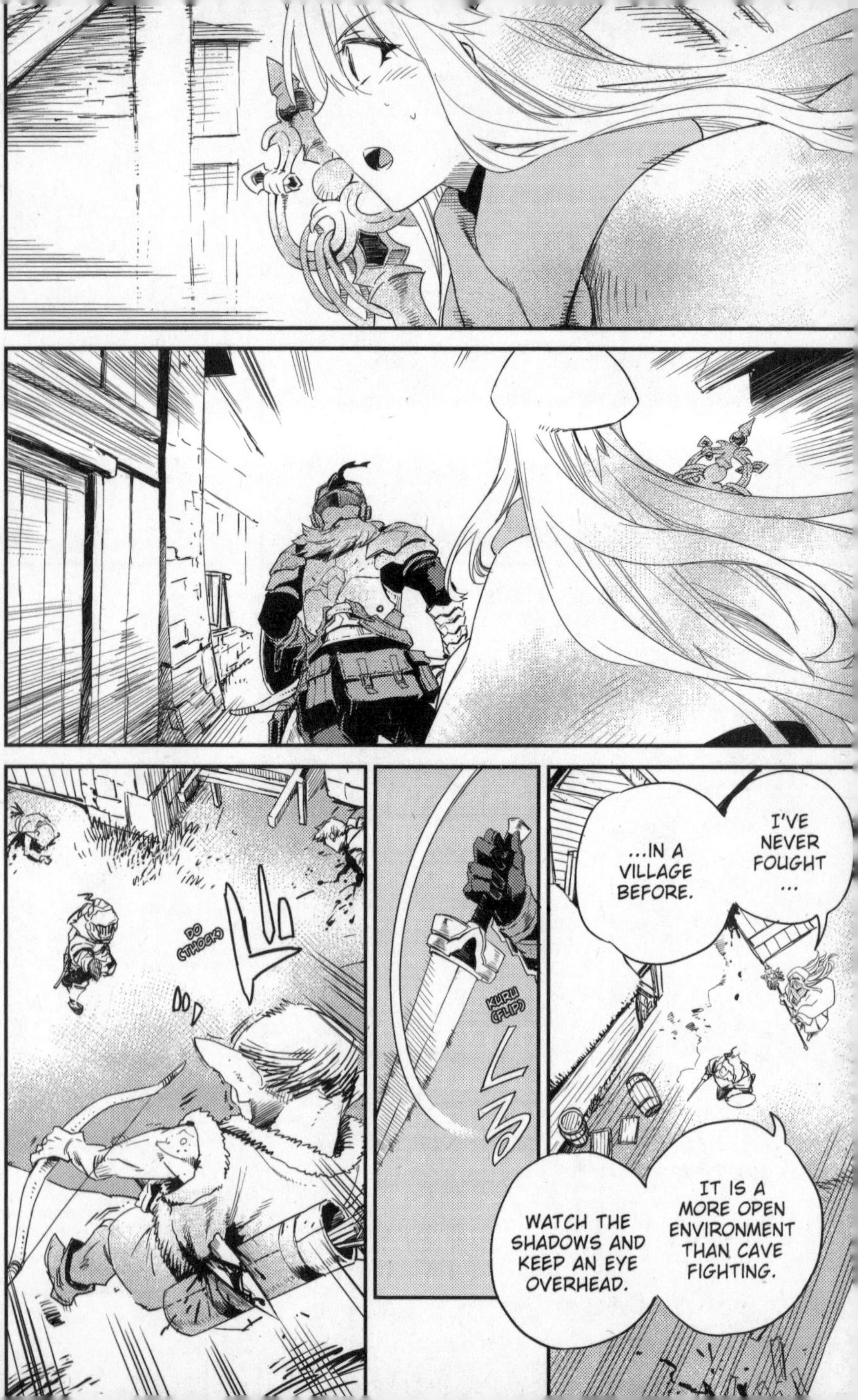
I'VE NEVER FOUGHT ...
...IN A VILLAGE BEFORE.
IT IS A MORE OPEN ENVIRONMENT THAN CAVE FIGHTING.
WATCH THE SHADOWS AND KEEP AN EYE OVERHEAD.
KURU (FLIP)
DO (THOCK)

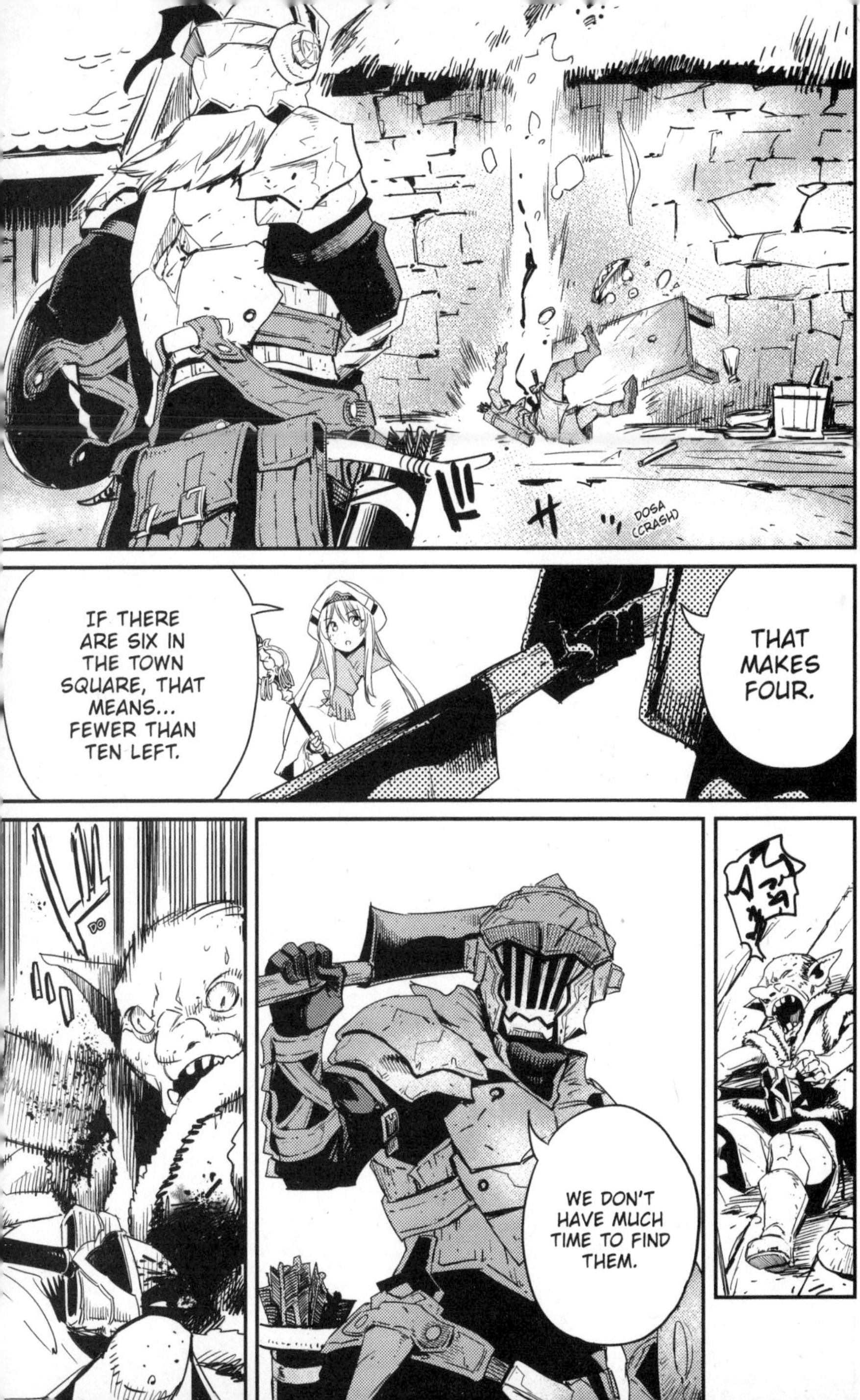
DOSA (CRASH)
THAT MAKES FOUR.
IF THERE ARE SIX IN THE TOWN SQUARE, THAT MEANS... FEWER THAN TEN LEFT.
WE DON'T HAVE MUCH TIME TO FIND THEM.
DO

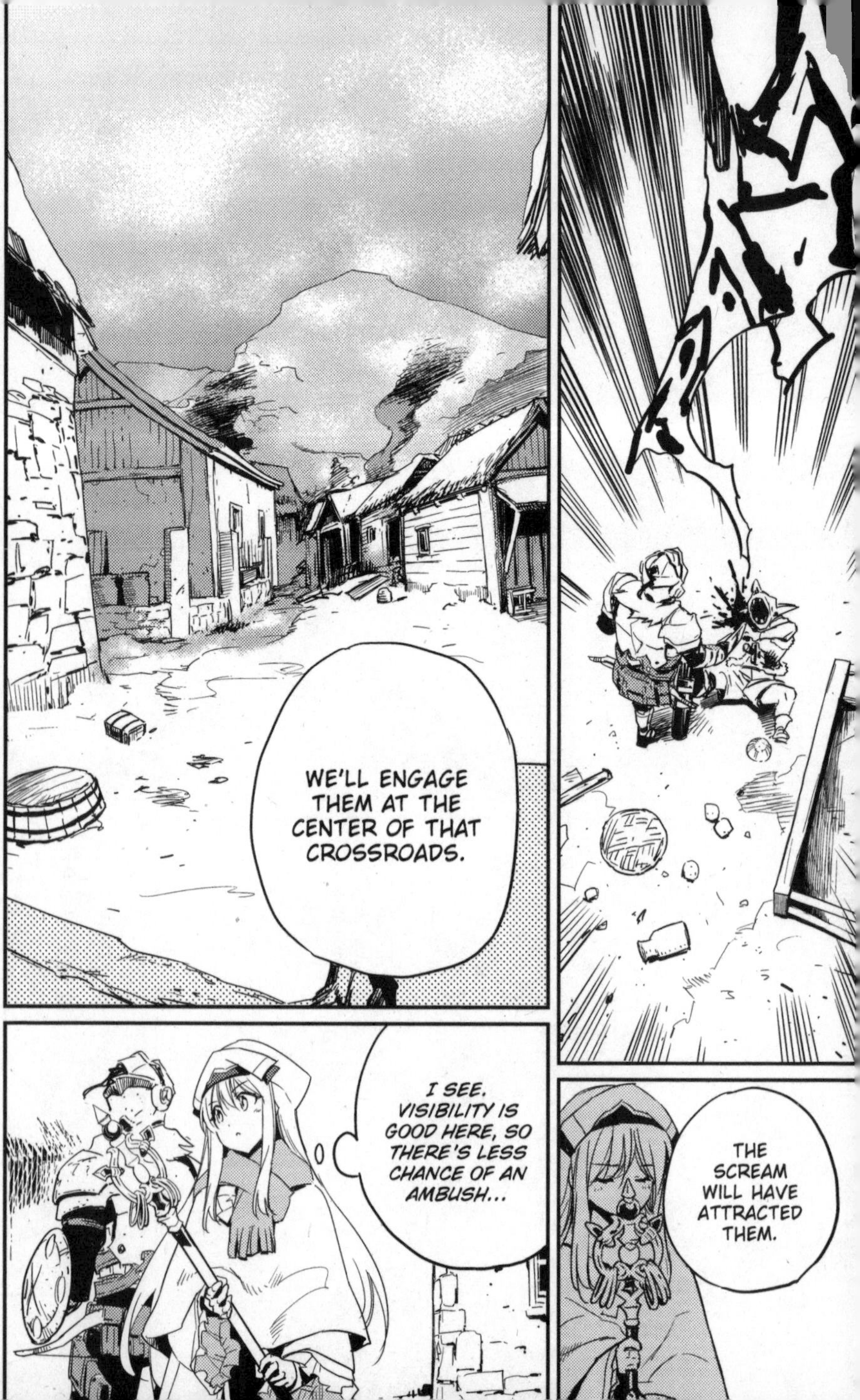
THE SCREAM WILL HAVE ATTRACTED THEM.
WE'LL ENGAGE THEM AT THE CENTER OF THAT CROSSROADS.
I SEE. VISIBILITY IS GOOD HERE, SO THERE'S LESS CHANCE OF AN AMBUSH...

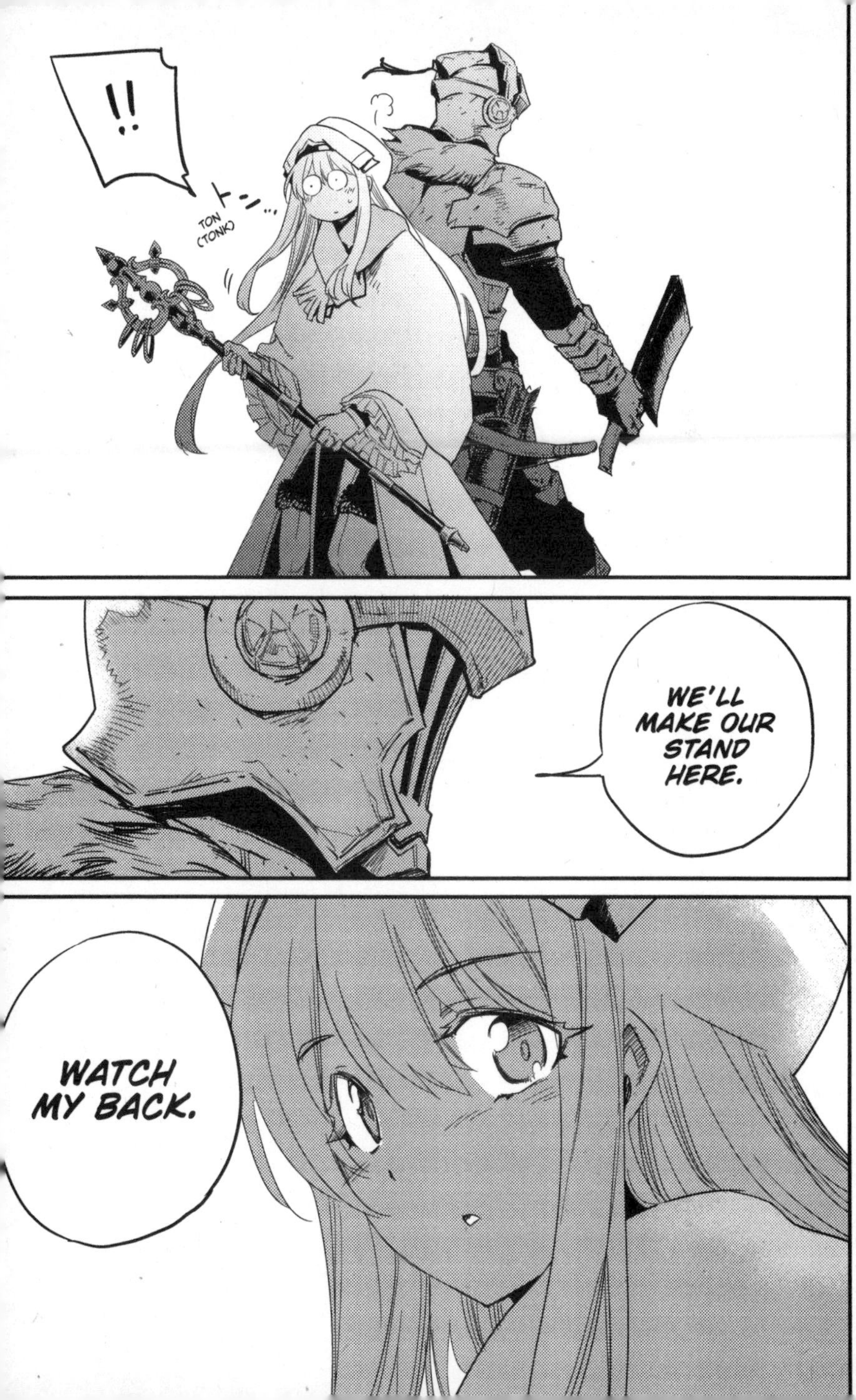
!!
TON (TONK)
WE'LL MAKE OUR STAND HERE.
WATCH MY BACK.

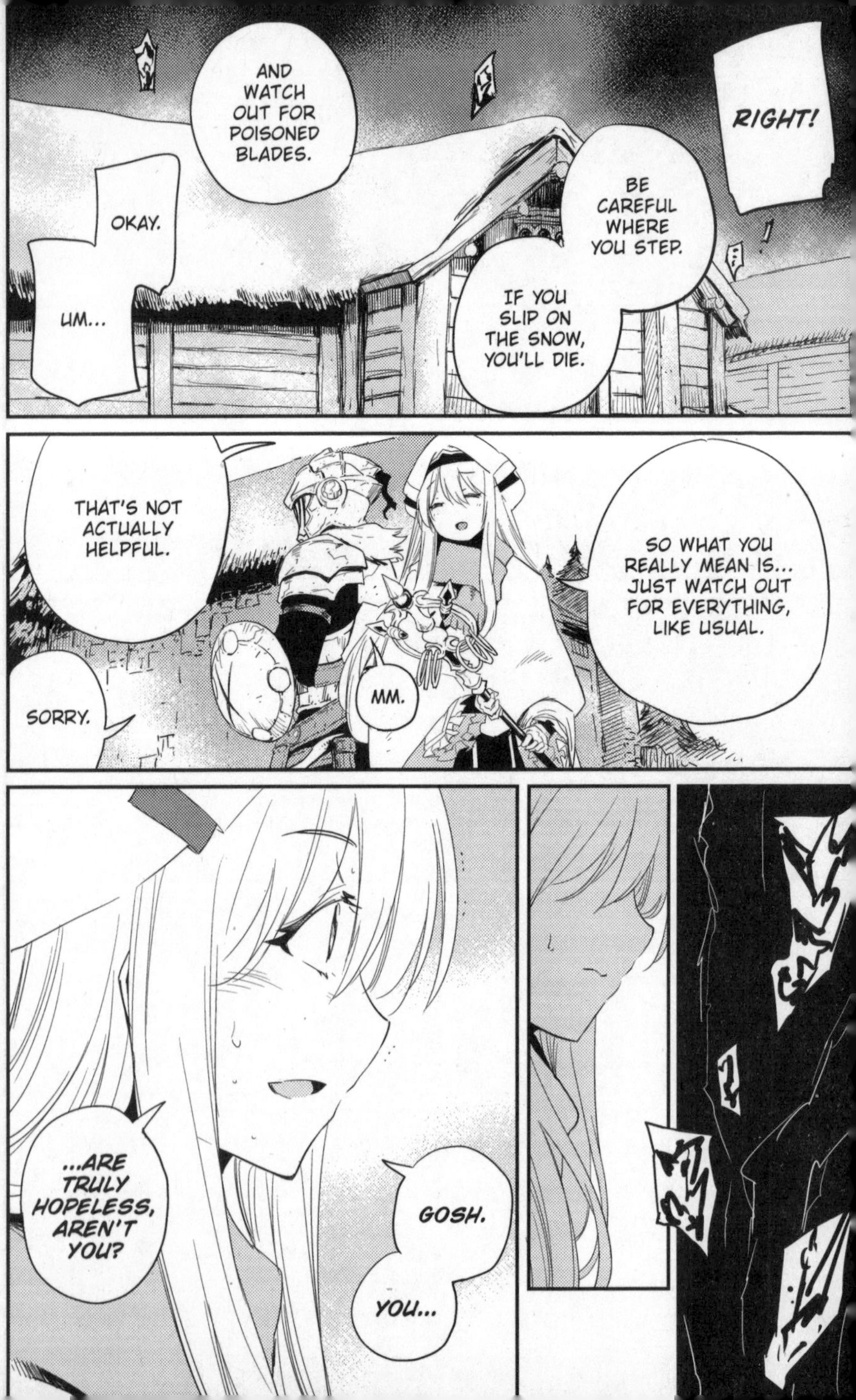
RIGHT!
BE CAREFUL WHERE YOU STEP.
IF YOU SLIP ON THE SNOW, YOU'LL DIE.
AND WATCH OUT FOR POISONED BLADES.
OKAY.
UM...
SO WHAT YOU REALLY MEAN IS... JUST WATCH OUT FOR EVERYTHING, LIKE USUAL.
MM.
THAT'S NOT ACTUALLY HELPFUL.
SORRY.
GOSH.
YOU...
...ARE TRULY HOPELESS, AREN'T YOU?

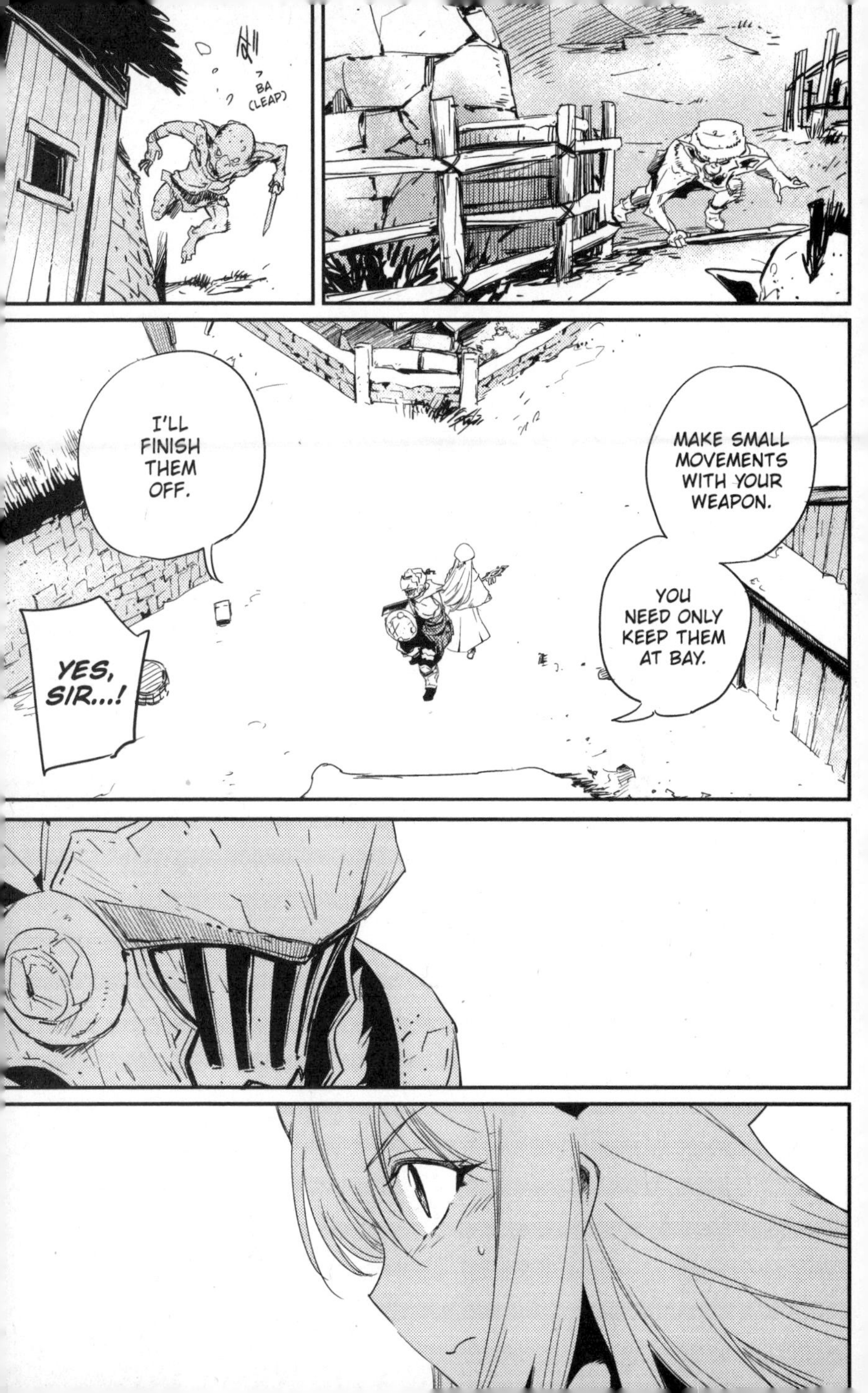
BA (LEAP)
MAKE SMALL MOVEMENTS WITH YOUR WEAPON.
YOU NEED ONLY KEEP THEM AT BAY.
I'LL FINISH THEM OFF.
YES, SIR...!

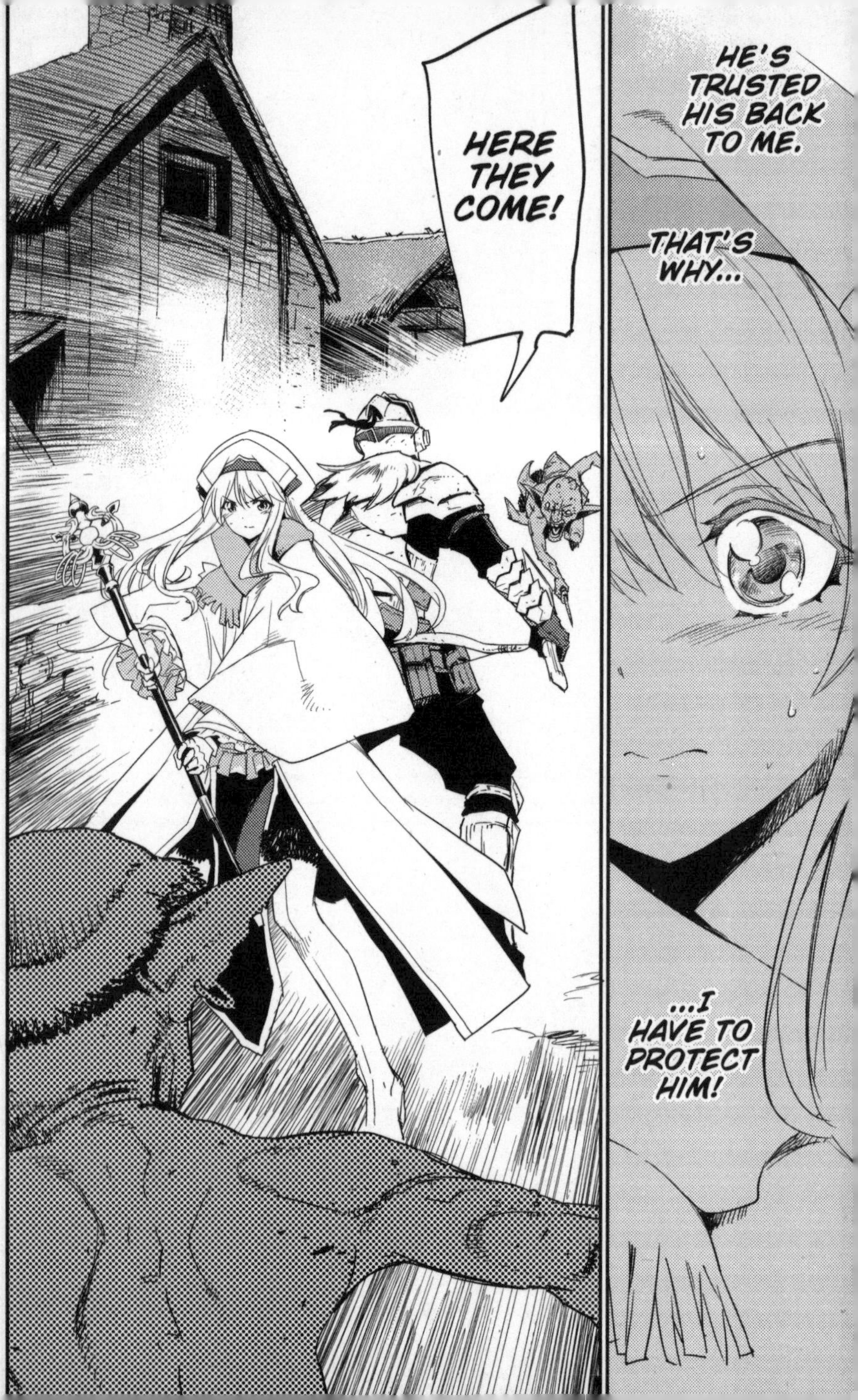
HE'S TRUSTED HIS BACK TO ME.
THAT'S WHY...
...I HAVE TO PROTECT HIM!
HERE THEY COME!

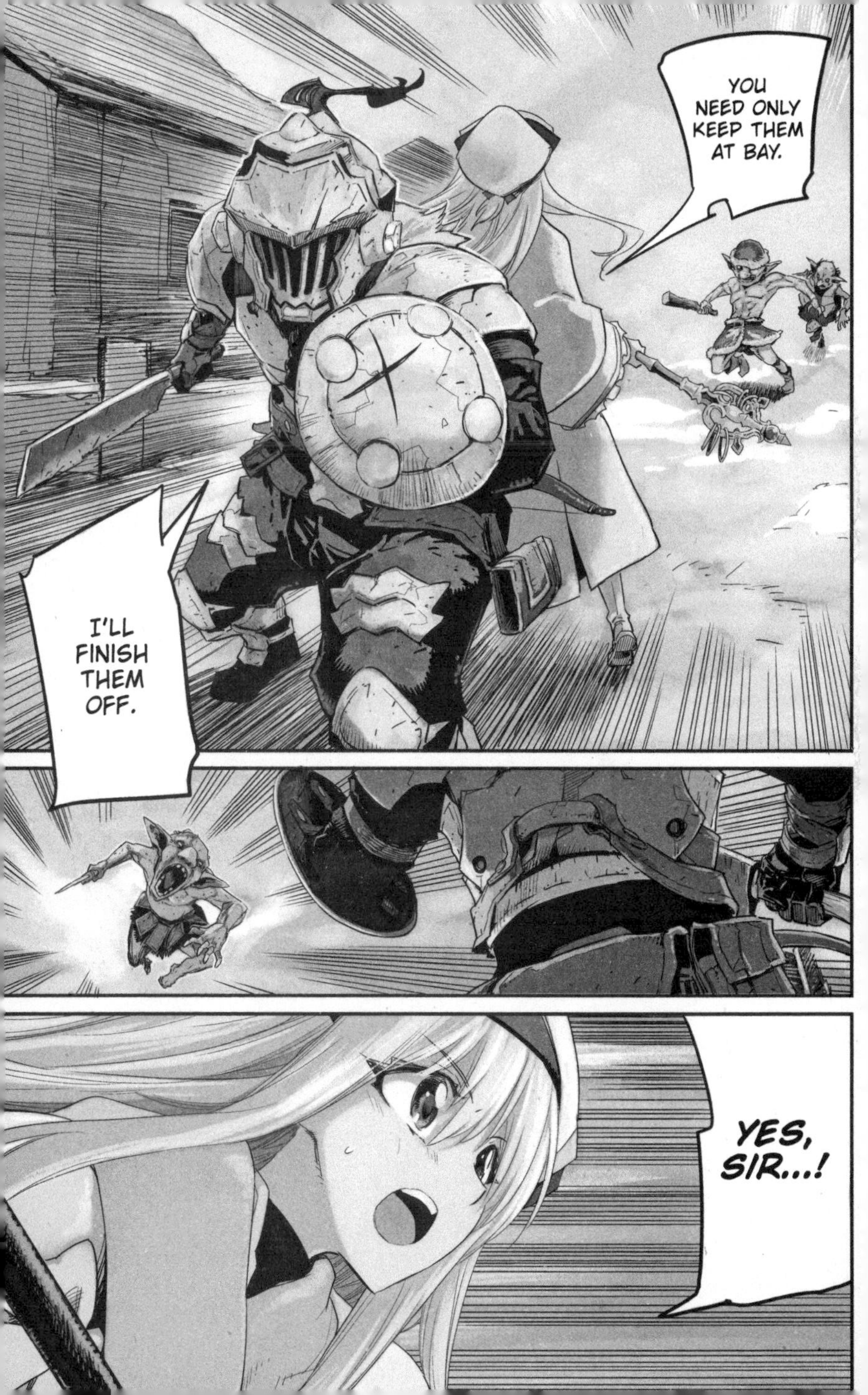
YOU NEED ONLY KEEP THEM AT BAY.
I'LL FINISH THEM OFF.
YES, SIR...!

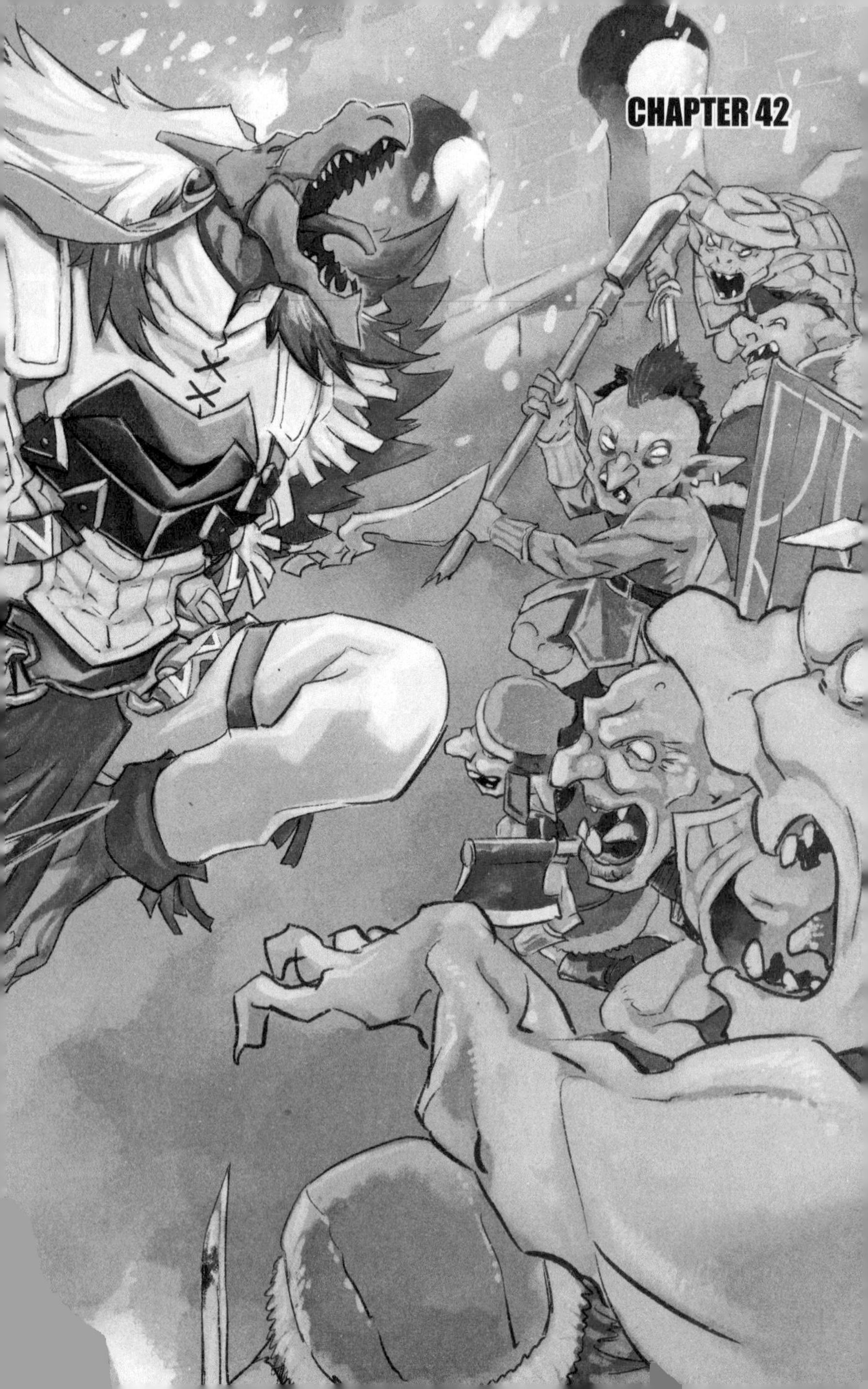
CHAPTER 42

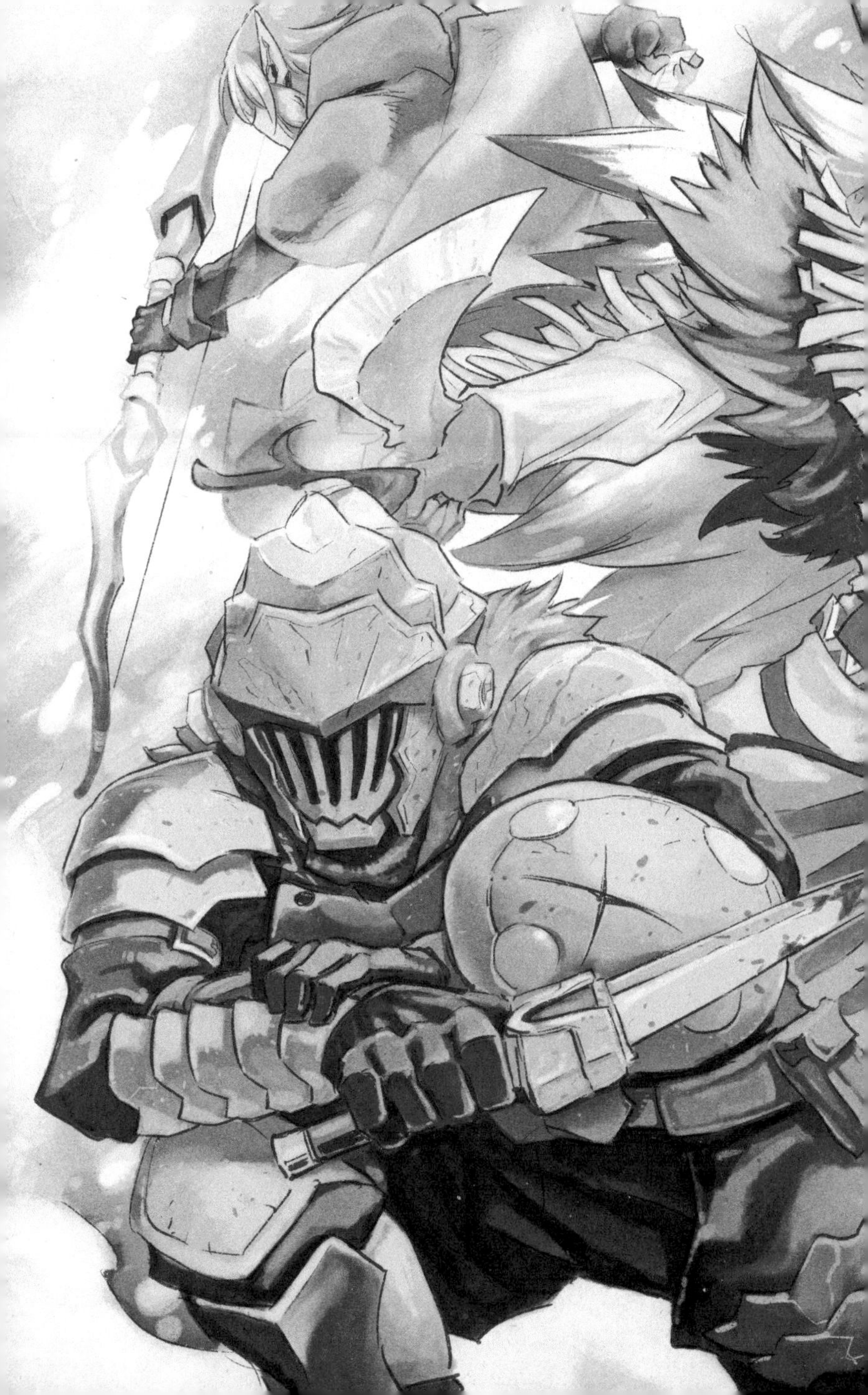

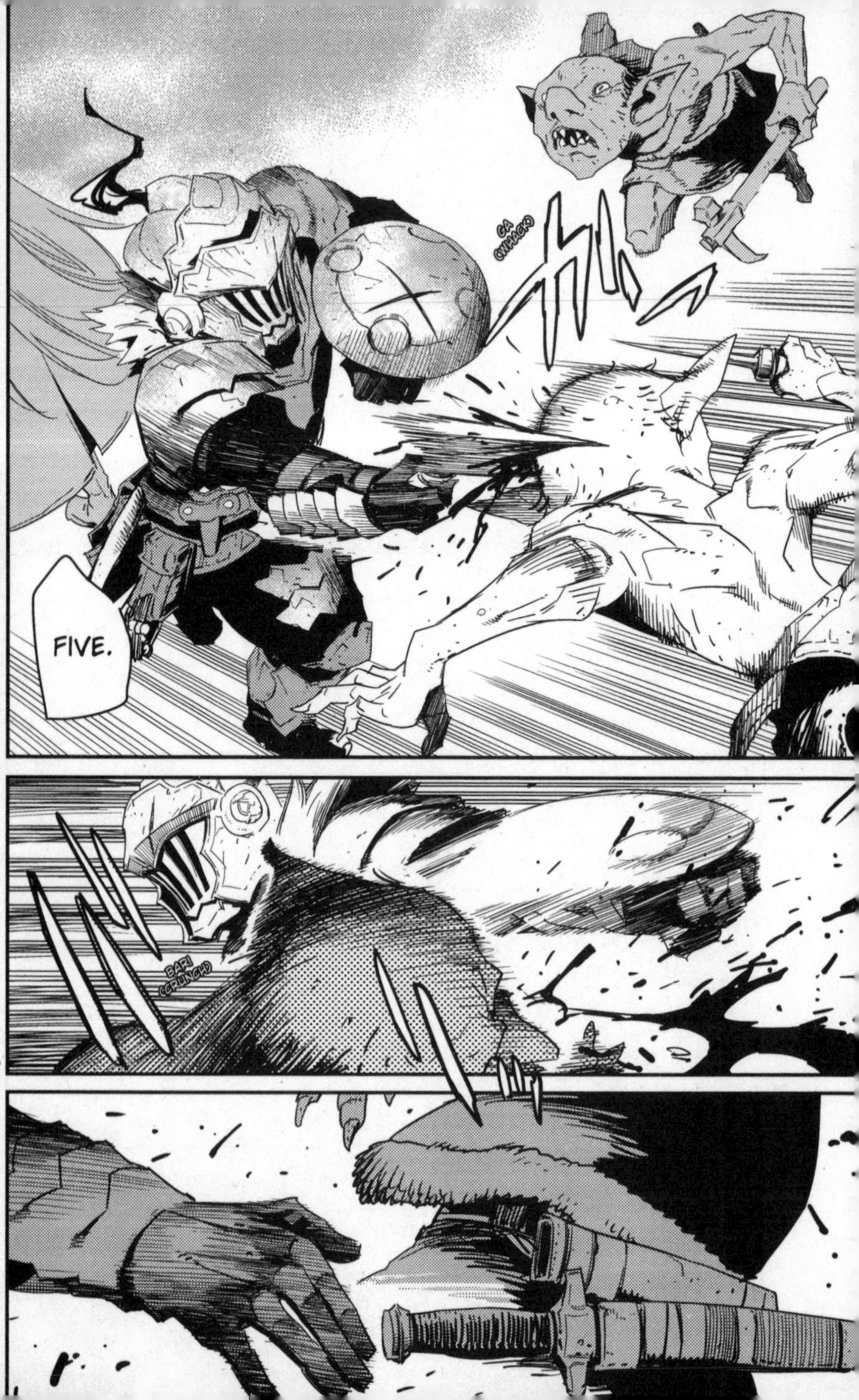
GA (WHACK)
FIVE.
BARI (CRUNCH)

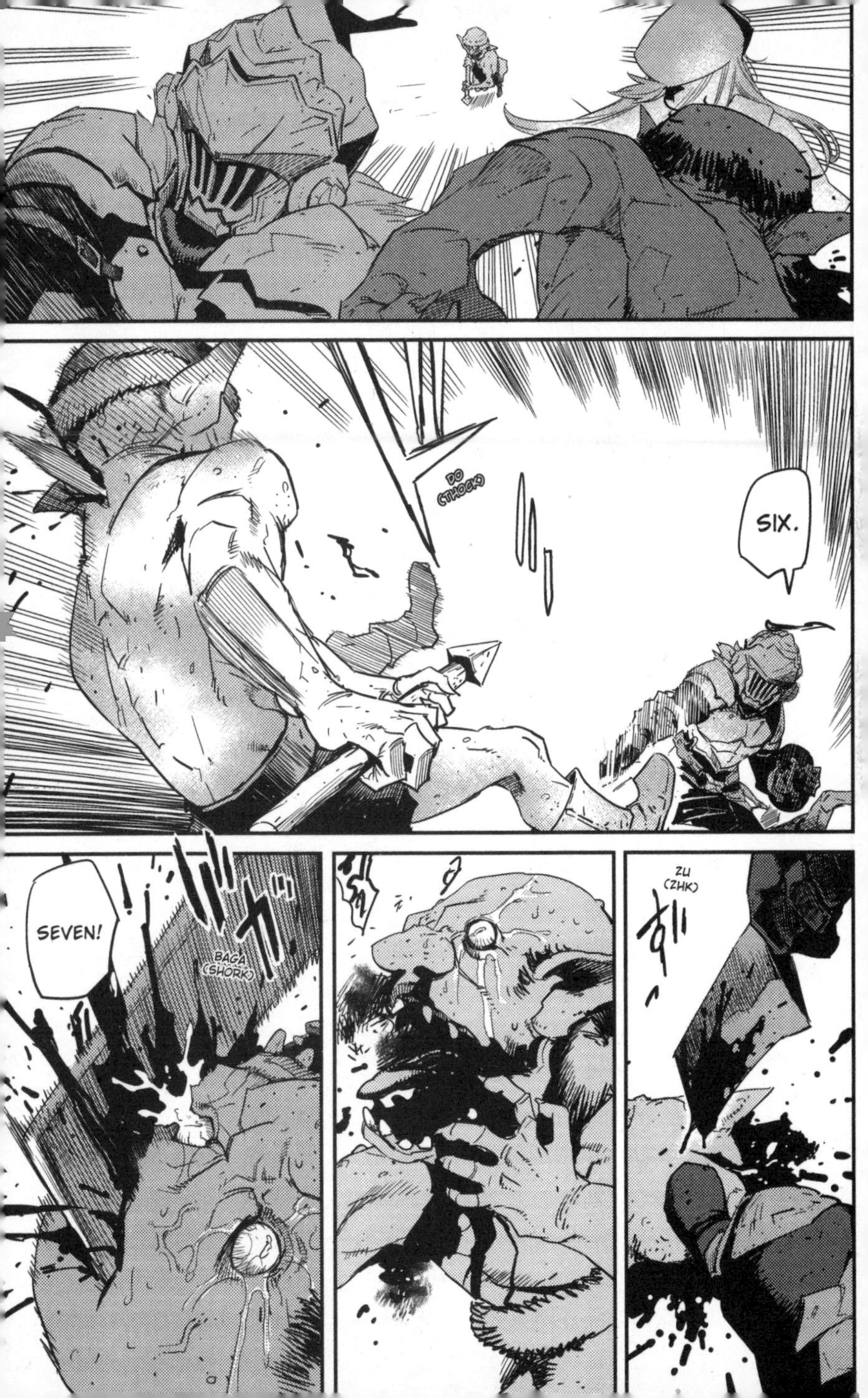
SIX.
DO (THOCK)
ZU (ZHK)
SEVEN!
BAGA (SHORK)

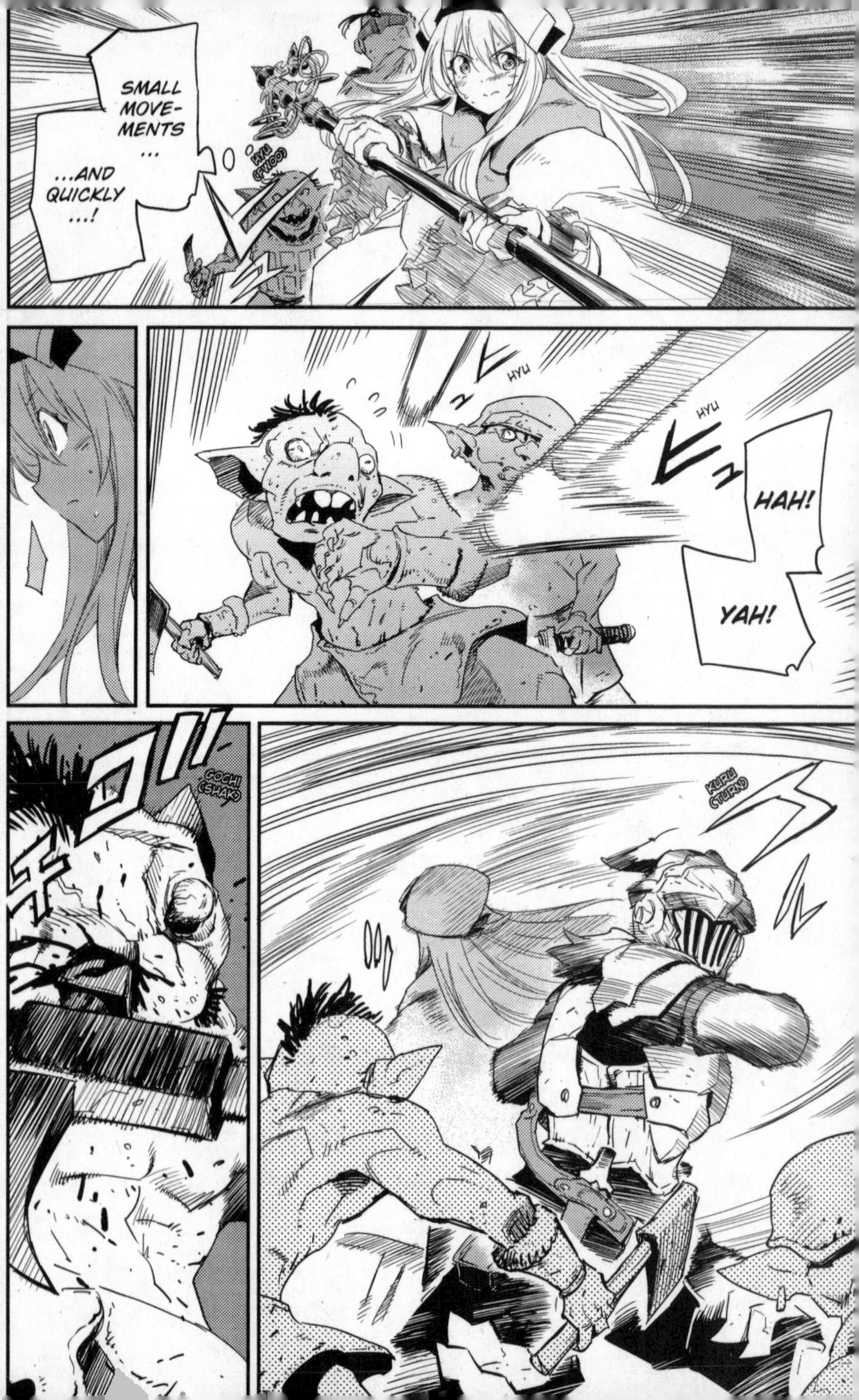
SMALL MOVEMENTS ...
...AND QUICKLY ...!
HYU (FWOO)
HYU
HYU
HAH!
YAH!
KURU (TURN)
GOCHI (SHAK)

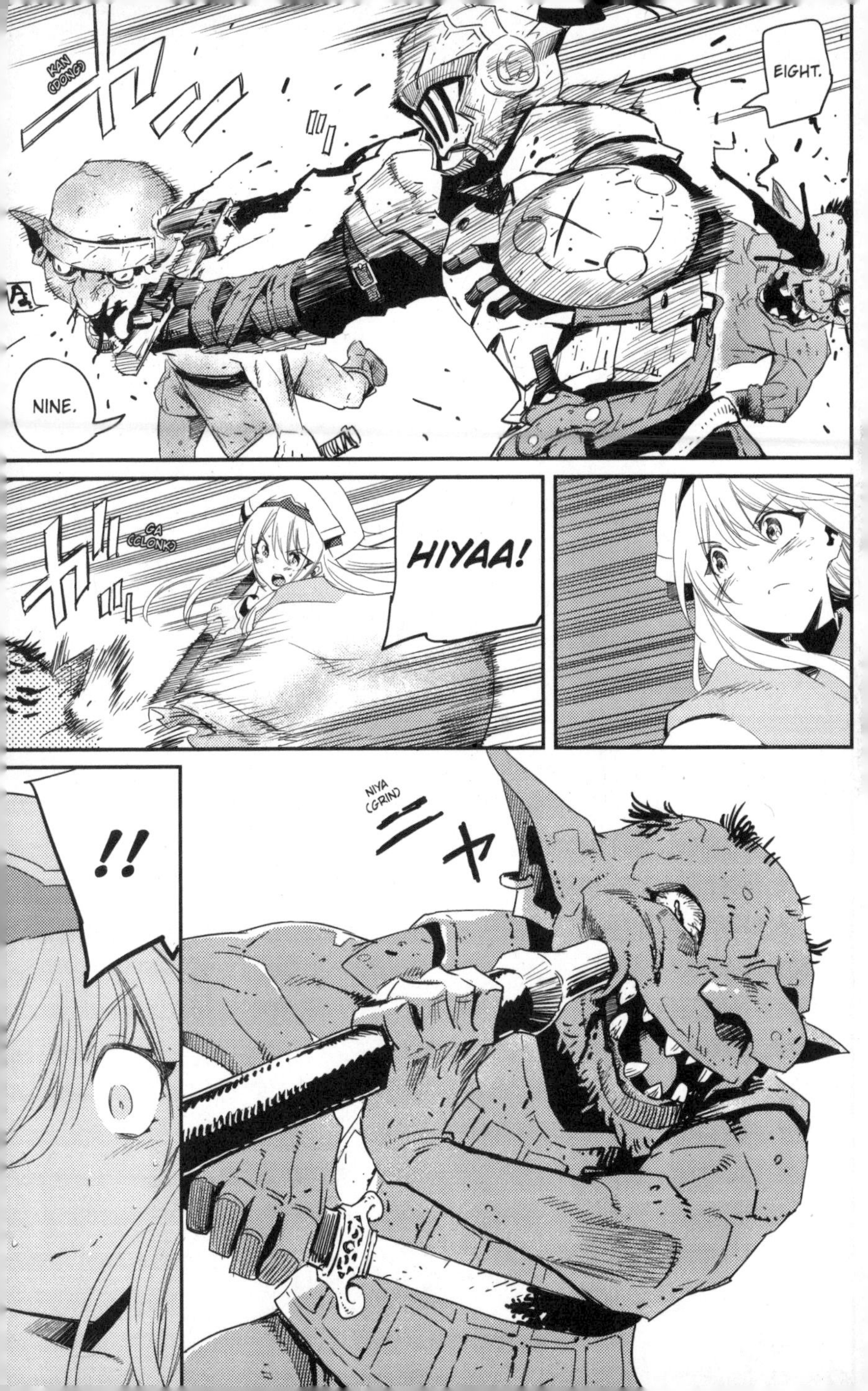

EIGHT.
KAN (DONG)
NINE.
HIYAA!
GA (CLONK)
NIYA (GRIND)
!!

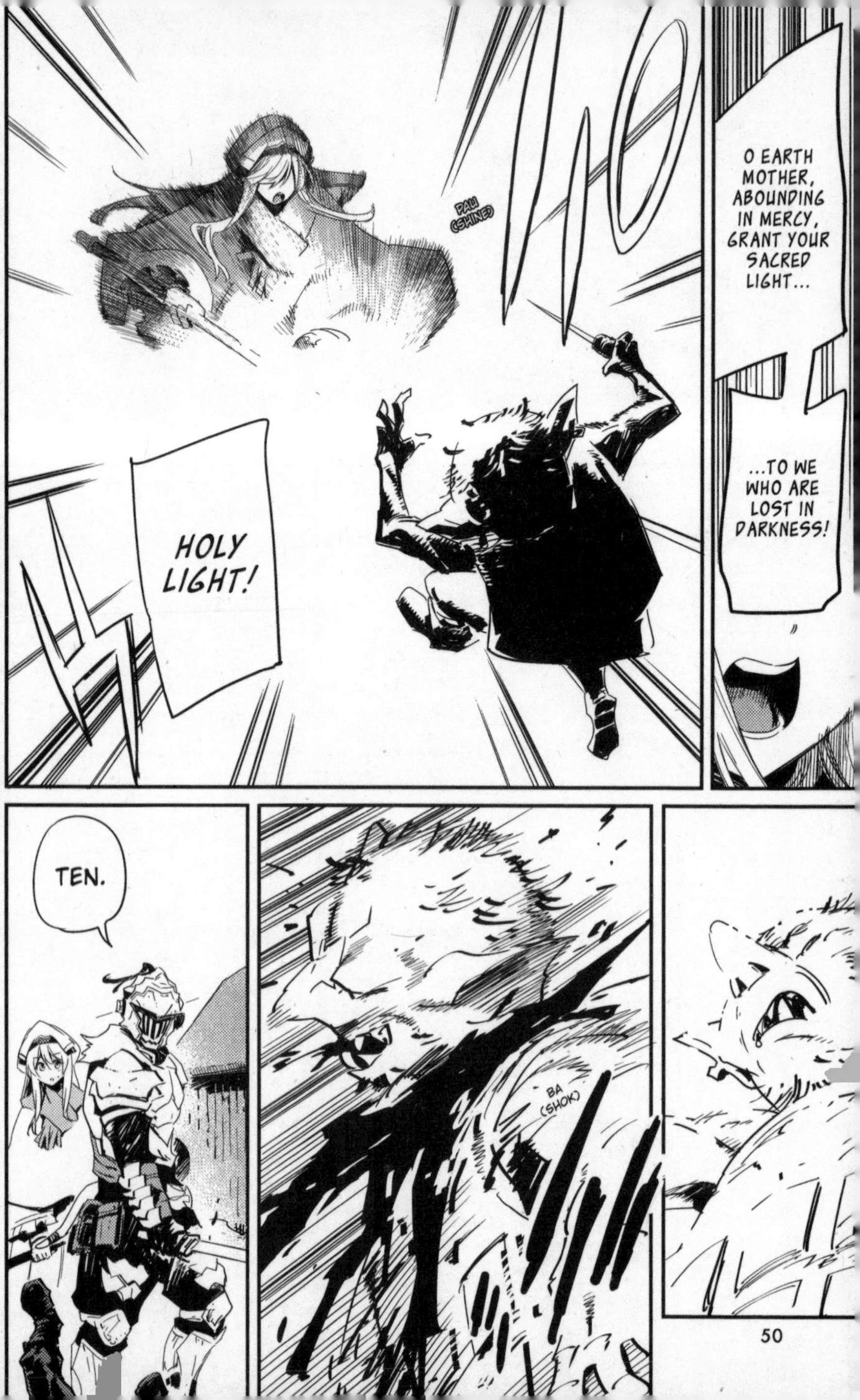
O EARTH MOTHER, ABOUNDING IN MERCY, GRANT YOUR SACRED LIGHT...
...TO WE WHO ARE LOST IN DARKNESS!
PALI (SHINED)
HOLY LIGHT!
BA (SHOK)
TEN.

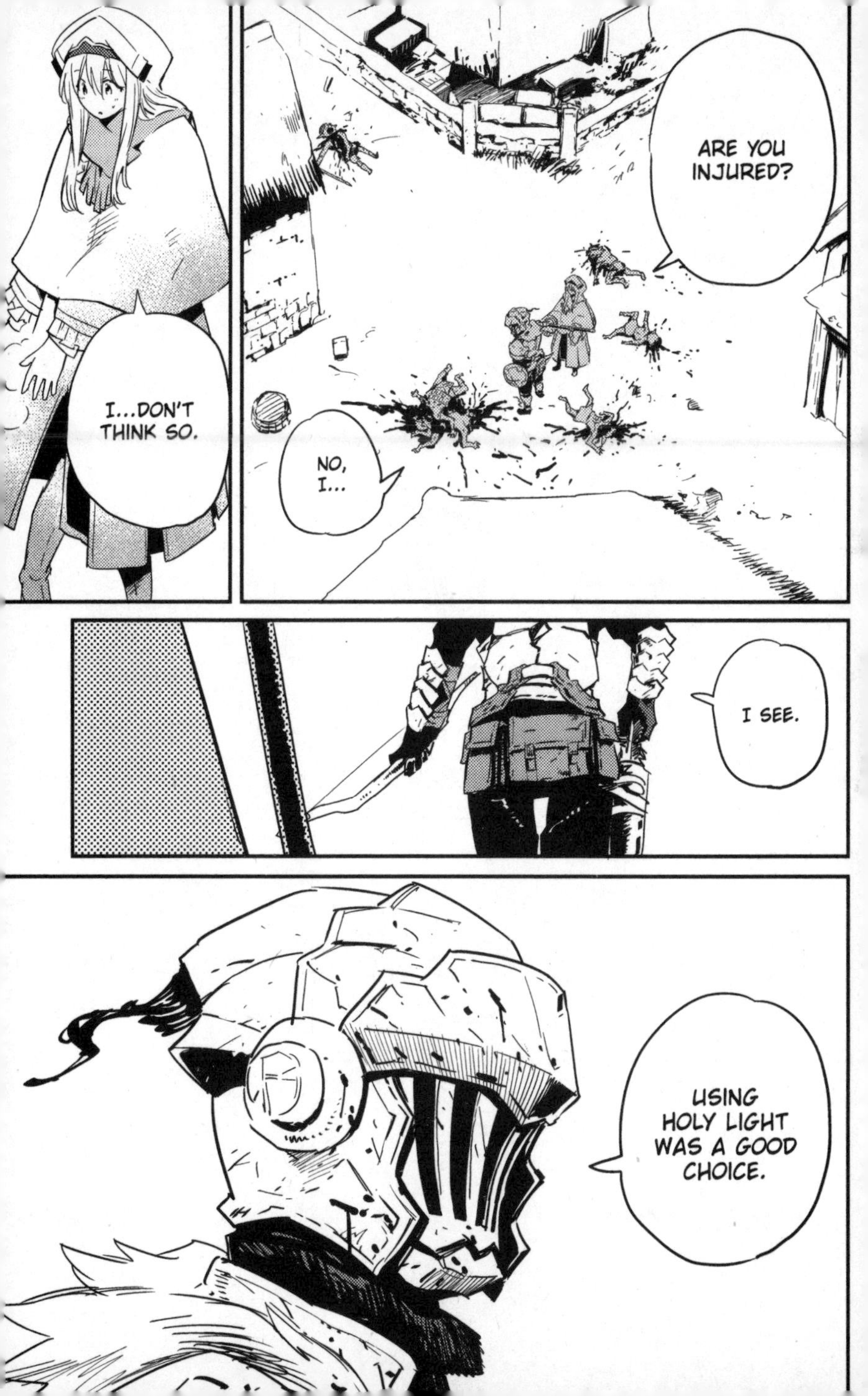
ARE YOU INJURED?
NO, I...
I...DON'T THINK SO.
I SEE.
USING HOLY LIGHT WAS A GOOD CHOICE.

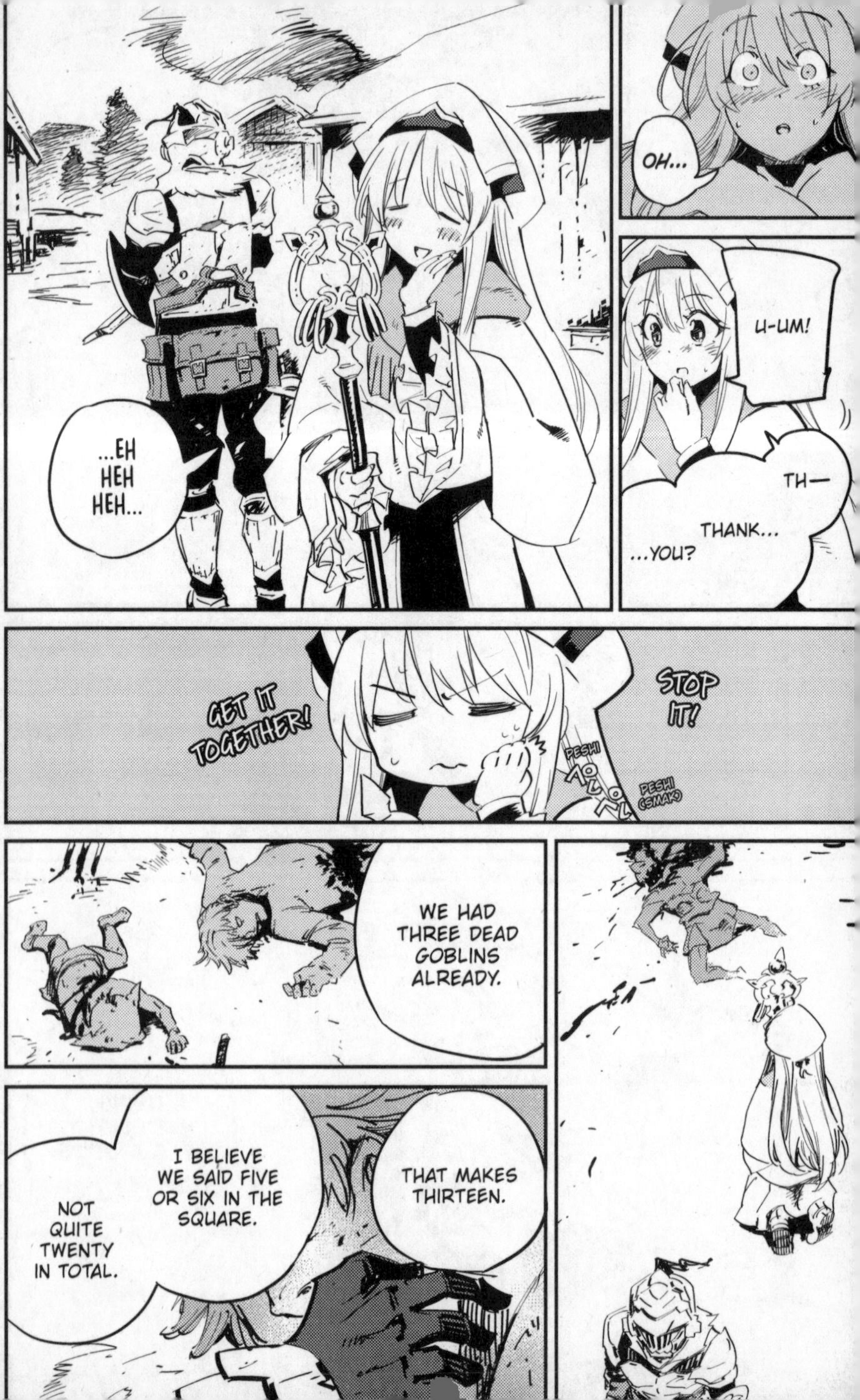
OH...
U-UM!
TH— THANK... ...YOU?
...EH HEH HEH...
STOP IT!
PESHI
PESHI (SMAK)
GET IT TOGETHER!
WE HAD THREE DEAD GOBLINS ALREADY.
THAT MAKES THIRTEEN.
I BELIEVE WE SAID FIVE OR SIX IN THE SQUARE.
NOT QUITE TWENTY IN TOTAL.

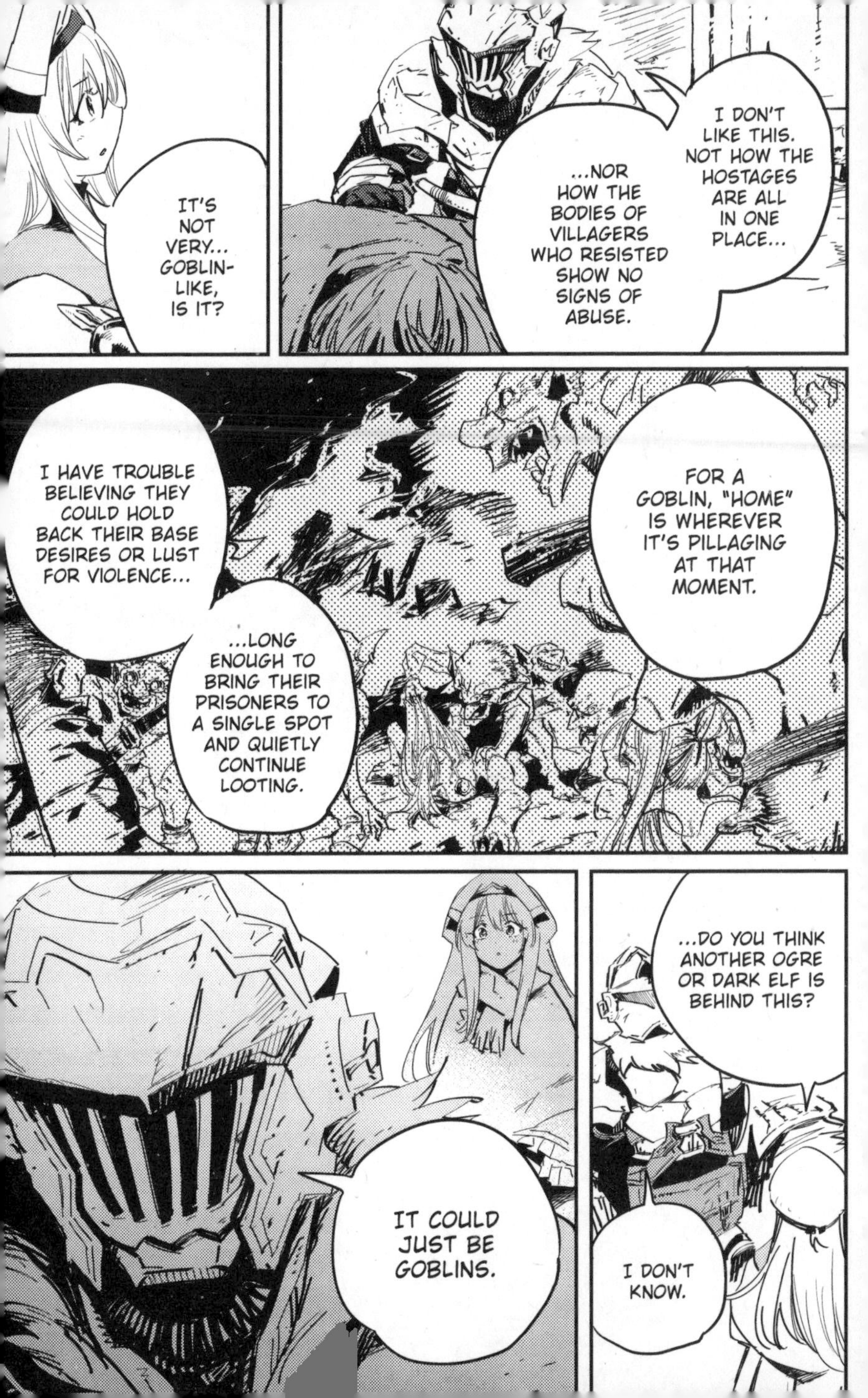
I DON'T LIKE THIS. NOT HOW THE HOSTAGES ARE ALL IN ONE PLACE...
...NOR HOW THE BODIES OF VILLAGERS WHO RESISTED SHOW NO SIGNS OF ABUSE.
IT'S NOT VERY... GOBLIN-LIKE, IS IT?
FOR A GOBLIN, "HOME" IS WHEREVER IT'S PILLAGING AT THAT MOMENT.
I HAVE TROUBLE BELIEVING THEY COULD HOLD BACK THEIR BASE DESIRES OR LUST FOR VIOLENCE...
...LONG ENOUGH TO BRING THEIR PRISONERS TO A SINGLE SPOT AND QUIETLY CONTINUE LOOTING.
...DO YOU THINK ANOTHER OGRE OR DARK ELF IS BEHIND THIS?
I DON'T KNOW.
IT COULD JUST BE GOBLINS.

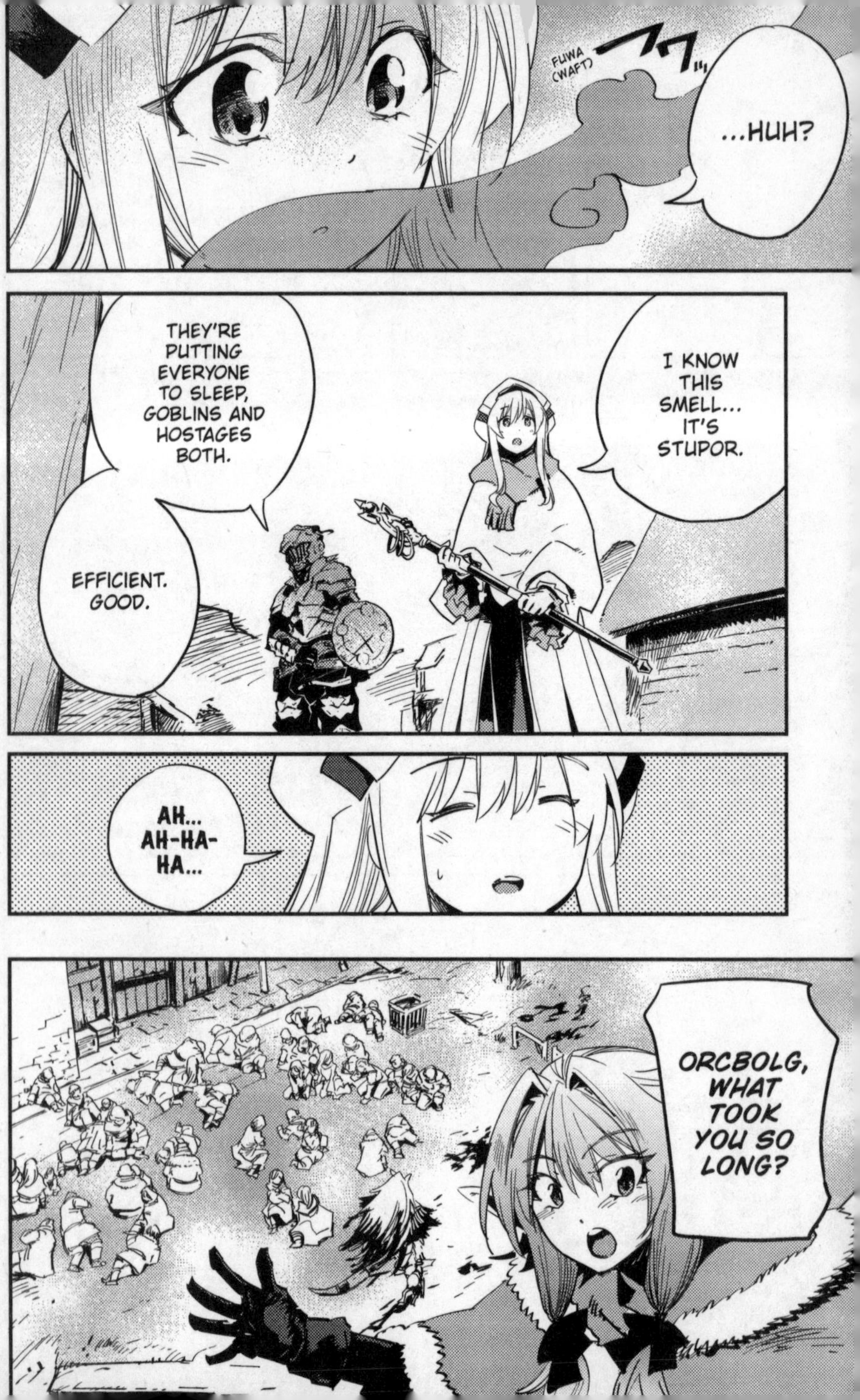
FUWA (WAFT)
...HUH?
I KNOW THIS SMELL... IT'S STUPOR.
THEY'RE PUTTING EVERYONE TO SLEEP, GOBLINS AND HOSTAGES BOTH.
EFFICIENT. GOOD.
AH... AH-HA-HA...
ORCBOLG, WHAT TOOK YOU SO LONG?

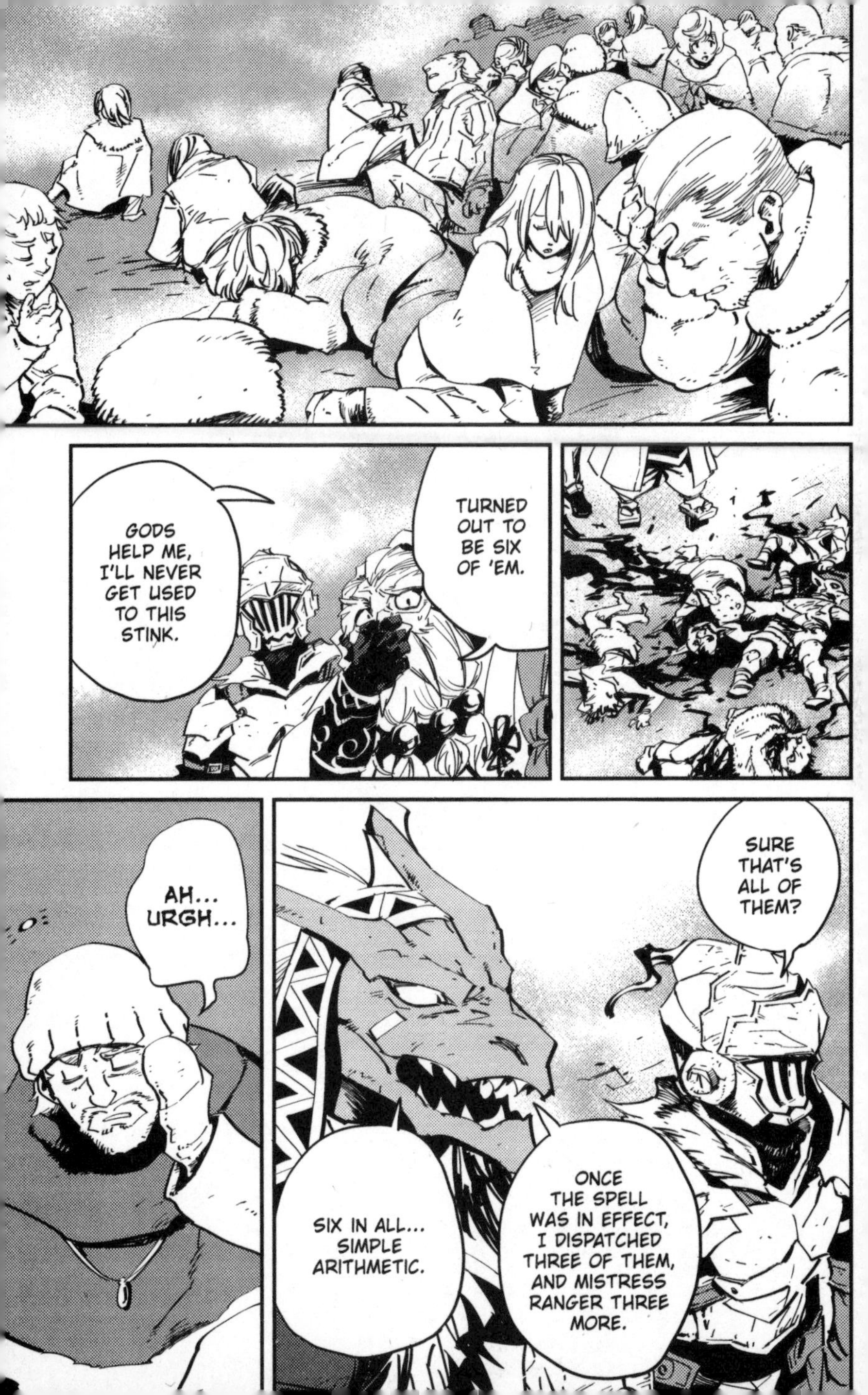
TURNED OUT TO BE SIX OF 'EM.
GODS HELP ME, I'LL NEVER GET USED TO THIS STINK.
SURE THAT'S ALL OF THEM?
ONCE THE SPELL WAS IN EFFECT, I DISPATCHED THREE OF THEM, AND MISTRESS RANGER THREE MORE.
SIX IN ALL... SIMPLE ARITHMETIC.
AH... URGH...

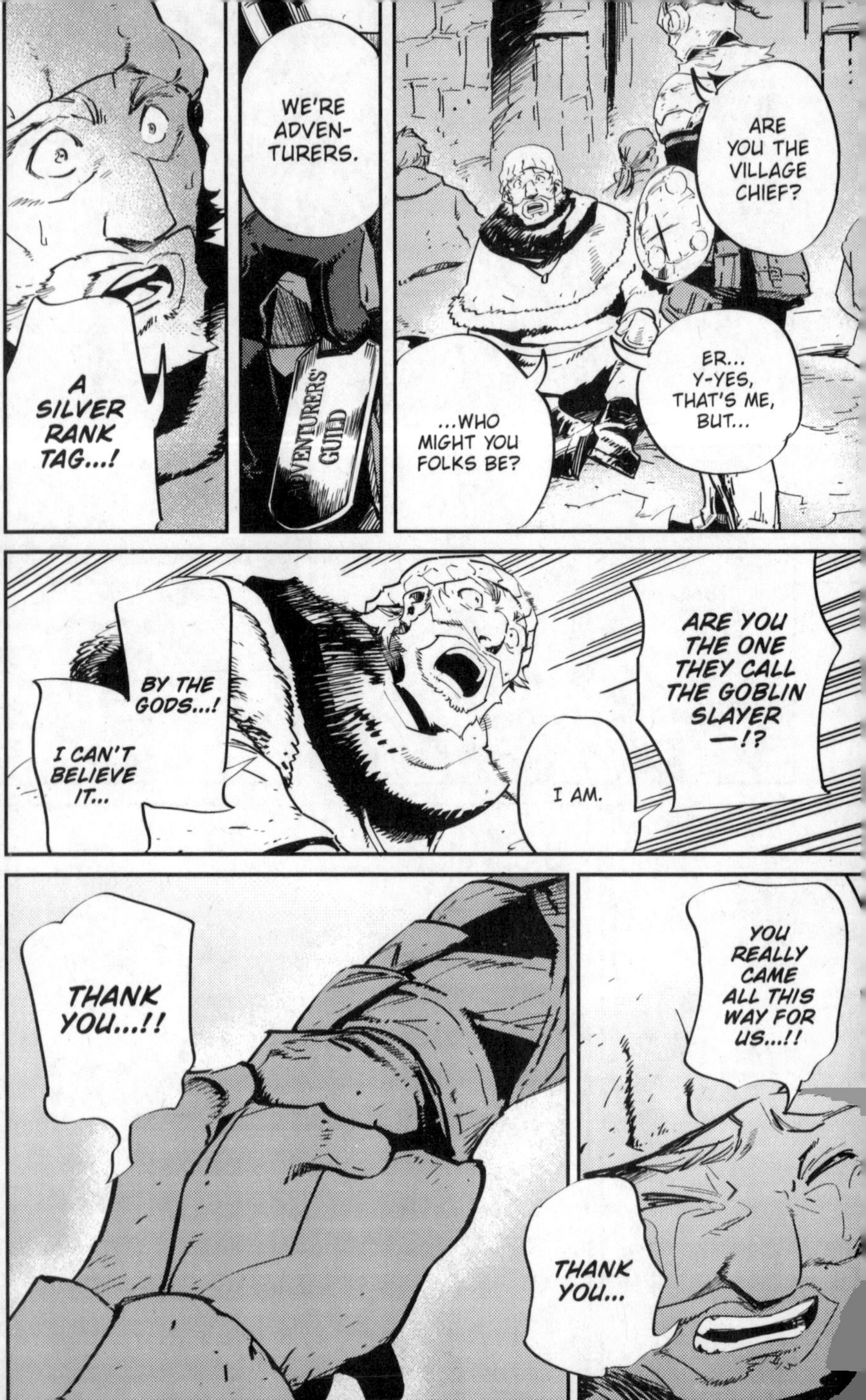
ARE YOU THE VILLAGE CHIEF?
ER... Y-YES, THAT'S ME, BUT...
...WHO MIGHT YOU FOLKS BE?
WE'RE ADVEN-TURERS.
ADVENTURERS' GUILD
A SILVER RANK TAG...!
ARE YOU THE ONE THEY CALL THE GOBLIN SLAYER—!?
I AM.
BY THE GODS...!
I CAN'T BELIEVE IT...
YOU REALLY CAME ALL THIS WAY FOR US...!!
THANK YOU...
THANK YOU...!!

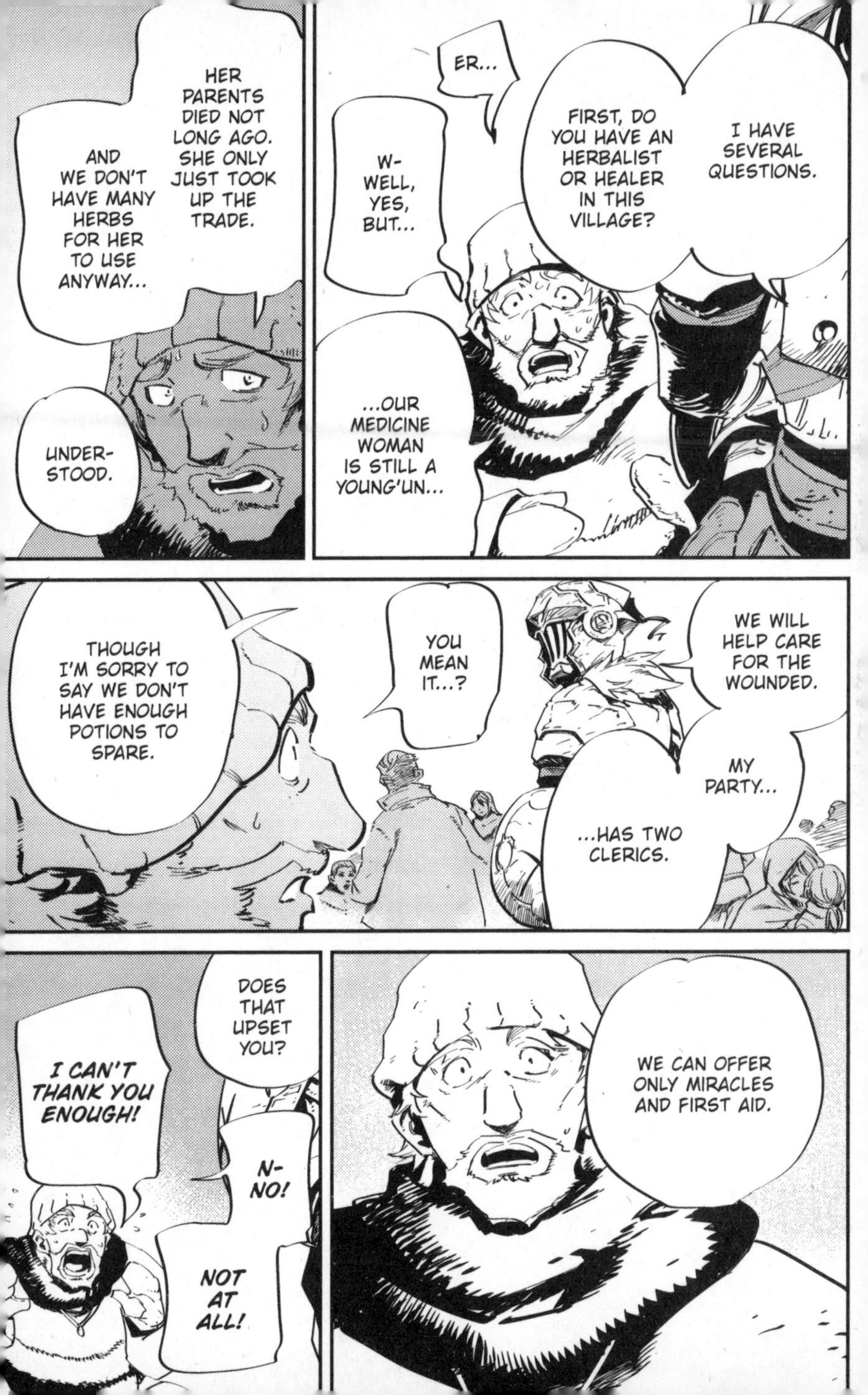
I HAVE SEVERAL QUESTIONS.
FIRST, DO YOU HAVE AN HERBALIST OR HEALER IN THIS VILLAGE?
ER...
W-WELL, YES, BUT...
...OUR MEDICINE WOMAN IS STILL A YOUNG'UN...
HER PARENTS DIED NOT LONG AGO. SHE ONLY JUST TOOK UP THE TRADE.
AND WE DON'T HAVE MANY HERBS FOR HER TO USE ANYWAY...
UNDER-STOOD.
WE WILL HELP CARE FOR THE WOUNDED.
MY PARTY...
...HAS TWO CLERICS.
YOU MEAN IT...?
THOUGH I'M SORRY TO SAY WE DON'T HAVE ENOUGH POTIONS TO SPARE.
WE CAN OFFER ONLY MIRACLES AND FIRST AID.
DOES THAT UPSET YOU?
N-NO!
NOT AT ALL!
I CAN'T THANK YOU ENOUGH!

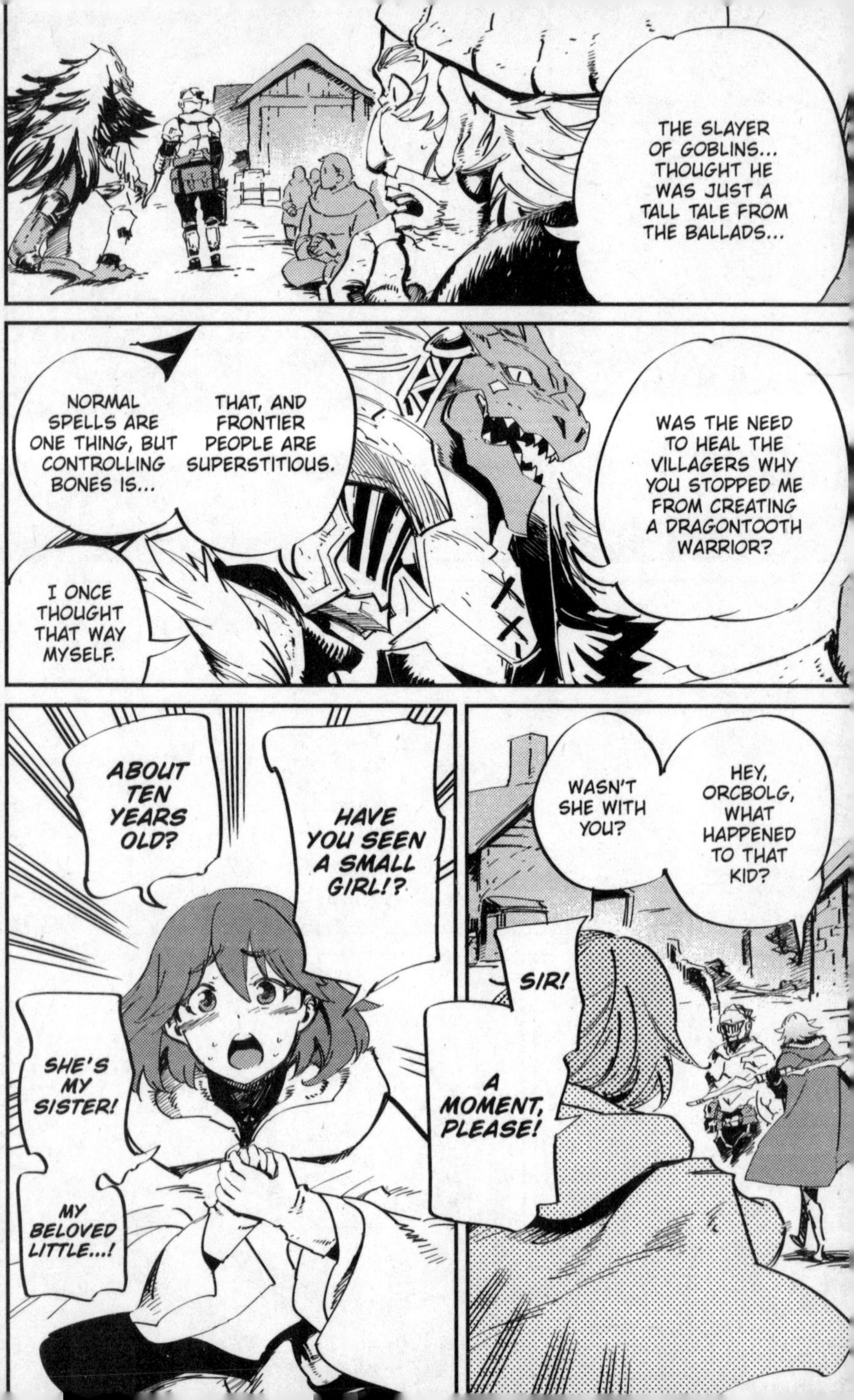
THE SLAYER OF GOBLINS... THOUGHT HE WAS JUST A TALL TALE FROM THE BALLADS...
WAS THE NEED TO HEAL THE VILLAGERS WHY YOU STOPPED ME FROM CREATING A DRAGONTOOTH WARRIOR?
THAT, AND FRONTIER PEOPLE ARE SUPERSTITIOUS.
NORMAL SPELLS ARE ONE THING, BUT CONTROLLING BONES IS...
I ONCE THOUGHT THAT WAY MYSELF.
HEY, ORCBOLG, WHAT HAPPENED TO THAT KID?
WASN'T SHE WITH YOU?
SIR!
A MOMENT, PLEASE!
HAVE YOU SEEN A SMALL GIRL!?
ABOUT TEN YEARS OLD?
SHE'S MY SISTER!
MY BELOVED LITTLE...!

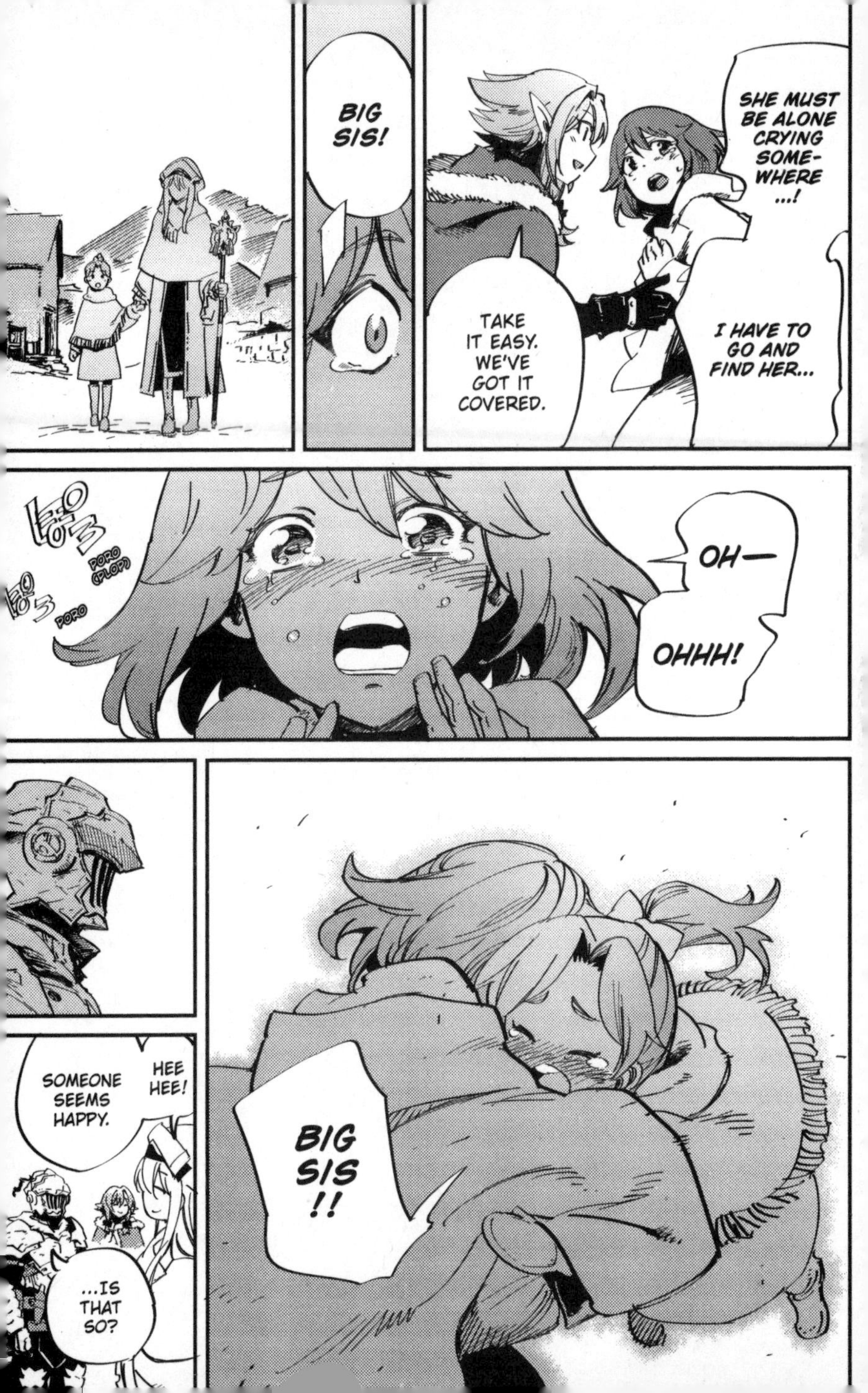
SHE MUST BE ALONE CRYING SOME-WHERE ...!
I HAVE TO GO AND FIND HER...
TAKE IT EASY. WE'VE GOT IT COVERED.
BIG SIS!
OH—
OHHH!
PORO (PLOP)
PORO
BIG SIS!!
HEE HEE!
SOMEONE SEEMS HAPPY.
...IS THAT SO?

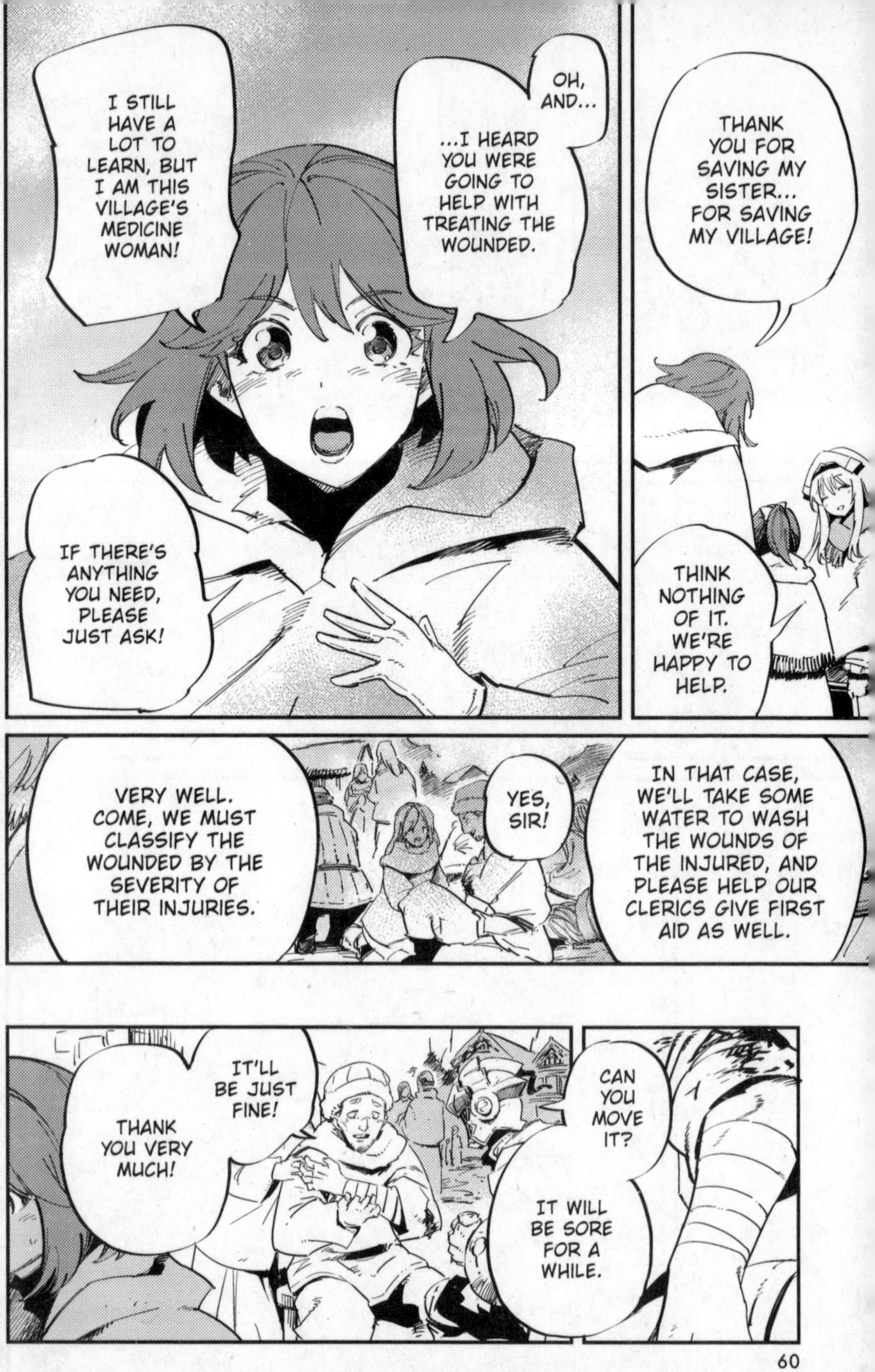
THANK YOU FOR SAVING MY SISTER... FOR SAVING MY VILLAGE!
THINK NOTHING OF IT. WE'RE HAPPY TO HELP.
OH, AND...
...I HEARD YOU WERE GOING TO HELP WITH TREATING THE WOUNDED.
I STILL HAVE A LOT TO LEARN, BUT I AM THIS VILLAGE'S MEDICINE WOMAN!
IF THERE'S ANYTHING YOU NEED, PLEASE JUST ASK!
IN THAT CASE, WE'LL TAKE SOME WATER TO WASH THE WOUNDS OF THE INJURED, AND PLEASE HELP OUR CLERICS GIVE FIRST AID AS WELL.
YES, SIR!
VERY WELL. COME, WE MUST CLASSIFY THE WOUNDED BY THE SEVERITY OF THEIR INJURIES.
CAN YOU MOVE IT?
IT WILL BE SORE FOR A WHILE.
IT'LL BE JUST FINE!
THANK YOU VERY MUCH!

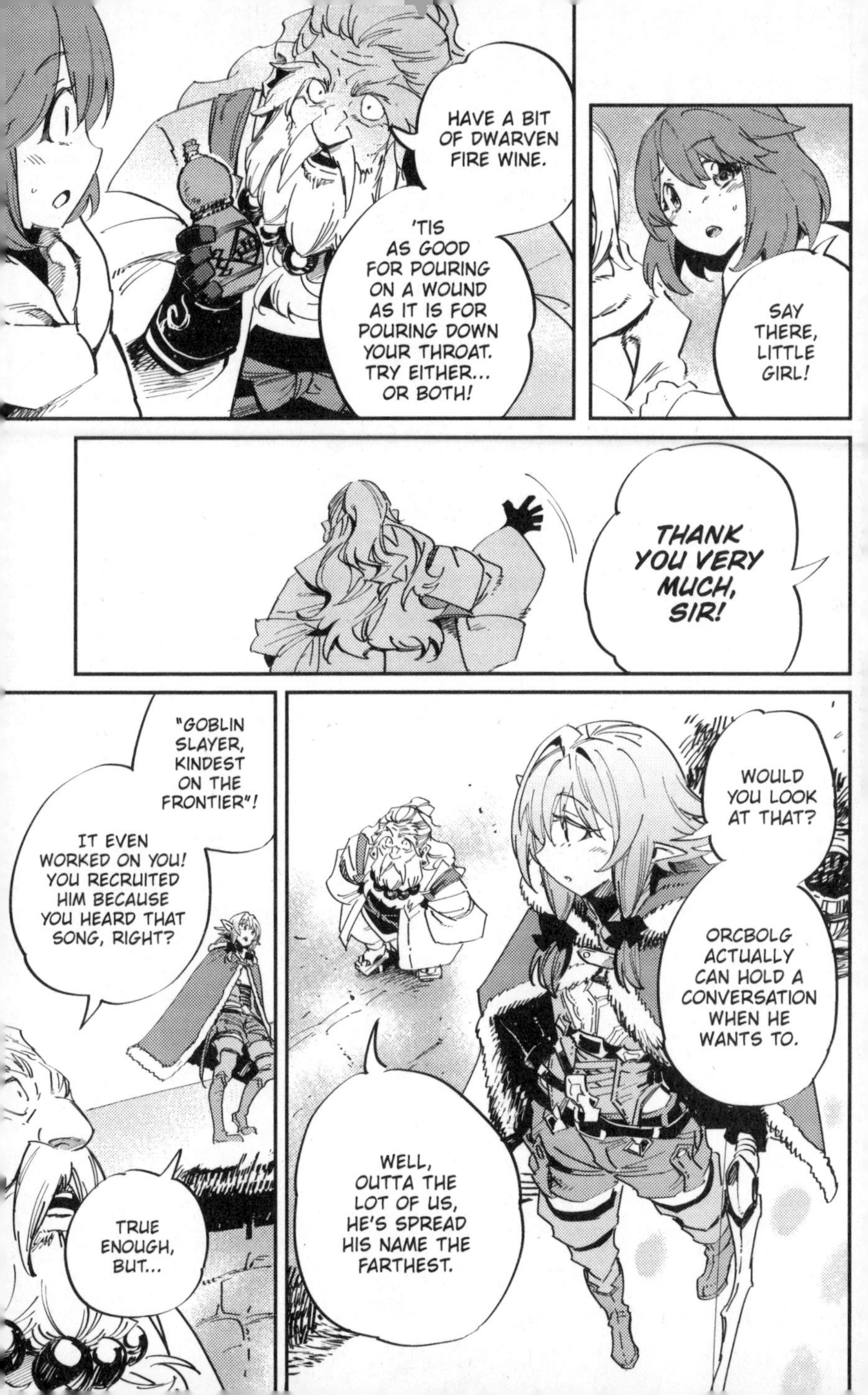
SAY THERE, LITTLE GIRL!
HAVE A BIT OF DWARVEN FIRE WINE.
'TIS AS GOOD FOR POURING ON A WOUND AS IT IS FOR POURING DOWN YOUR THROAT. TRY EITHER... OR BOTH!
THANK YOU VERY MUCH, SIR!
WOULD YOU LOOK AT THAT?
ORCBOLG ACTUALLY CAN HOLD A CONVERSATION WHEN HE WANTS TO.
WELL, OUTTA THE LOT OF US, HE'S SPREAD HIS NAME THE FARTHEST.
"GOBLIN SLAYER, KINDEST ON THE FRONTIER"!
IT EVEN WORKED ON YOU! YOU RECRUITED HIM BECAUSE YOU HEARD THAT SONG, RIGHT?
TRUE ENOUGH, BUT...

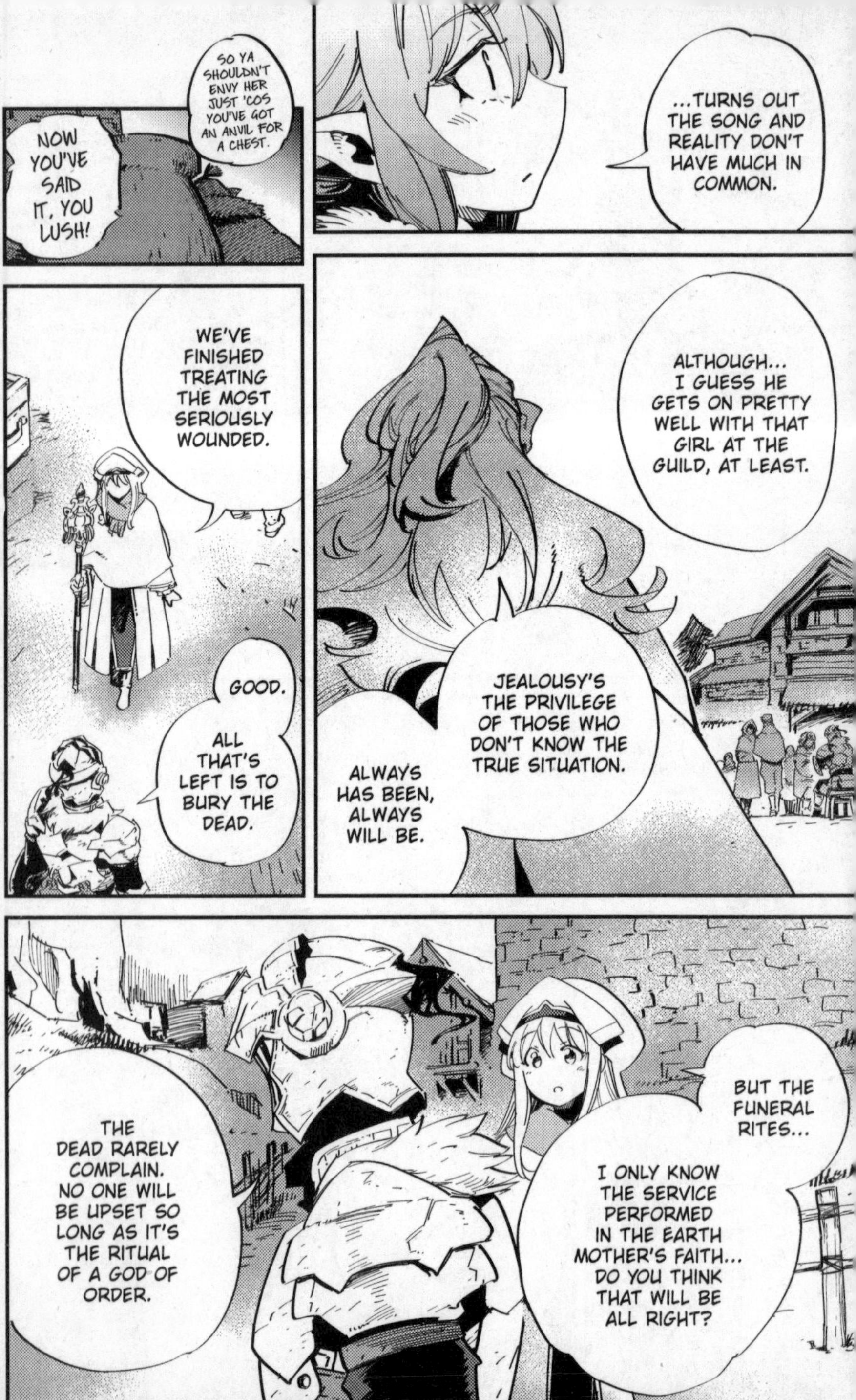
...TURNS OUT THE SONG AND REALITY DON'T HAVE MUCH IN COMMON.
SO YA SHOULDN'T ENVY HER JUST 'COS YOU'VE GOT AN ANVIL FOR A CHEST.
NOW YOU'VE SAID IT, YOU LUSH!
ALTHOUGH... I GUESS HE GETS ON PRETTY WELL WITH THAT GIRL AT THE GUILD, AT LEAST.
JEALOUSY'S THE PRIVILEGE OF THOSE WHO DON'T KNOW THE TRUE SITUATION.
ALWAYS HAS BEEN, ALWAYS WILL BE.
WE'VE FINISHED TREATING THE MOST SERIOUSLY WOUNDED.
GOOD.
ALL THAT'S LEFT IS TO BURY THE DEAD.
BUT THE FUNERAL RITES...
I ONLY KNOW THE SERVICE PERFORMED IN THE EARTH MOTHER'S FAITH... DO YOU THINK THAT WILL BE ALL RIGHT?
THE DEAD RARELY COMPLAIN. NO ONE WILL BE UPSET SO LONG AS IT'S THE RITUAL OF A GOD OF ORDER.

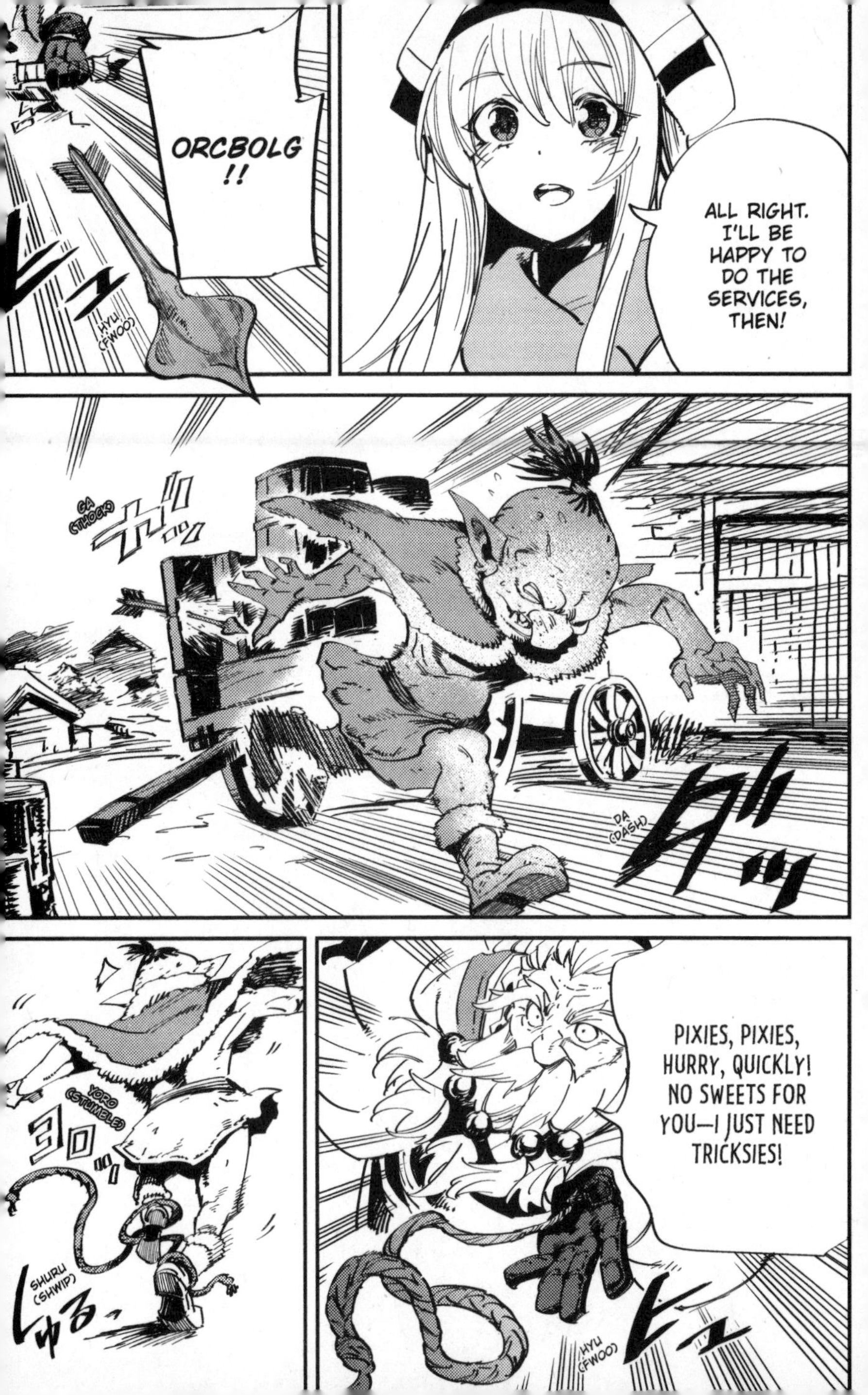
ALL RIGHT. I'LL BE HAPPY TO DO THE SERVICES, THEN!
ORCBOLG!!
HYU (FWOO)
GA (THOCK)
DA (DASH)
PIXIES, PIXIES, HURRY, QUICKLY! NO SWEETS FOR YOU—I JUST NEED TRICKSIES!
HYU (FWOO)
YORO (STUMBLE)
SHURU (SHWIP)

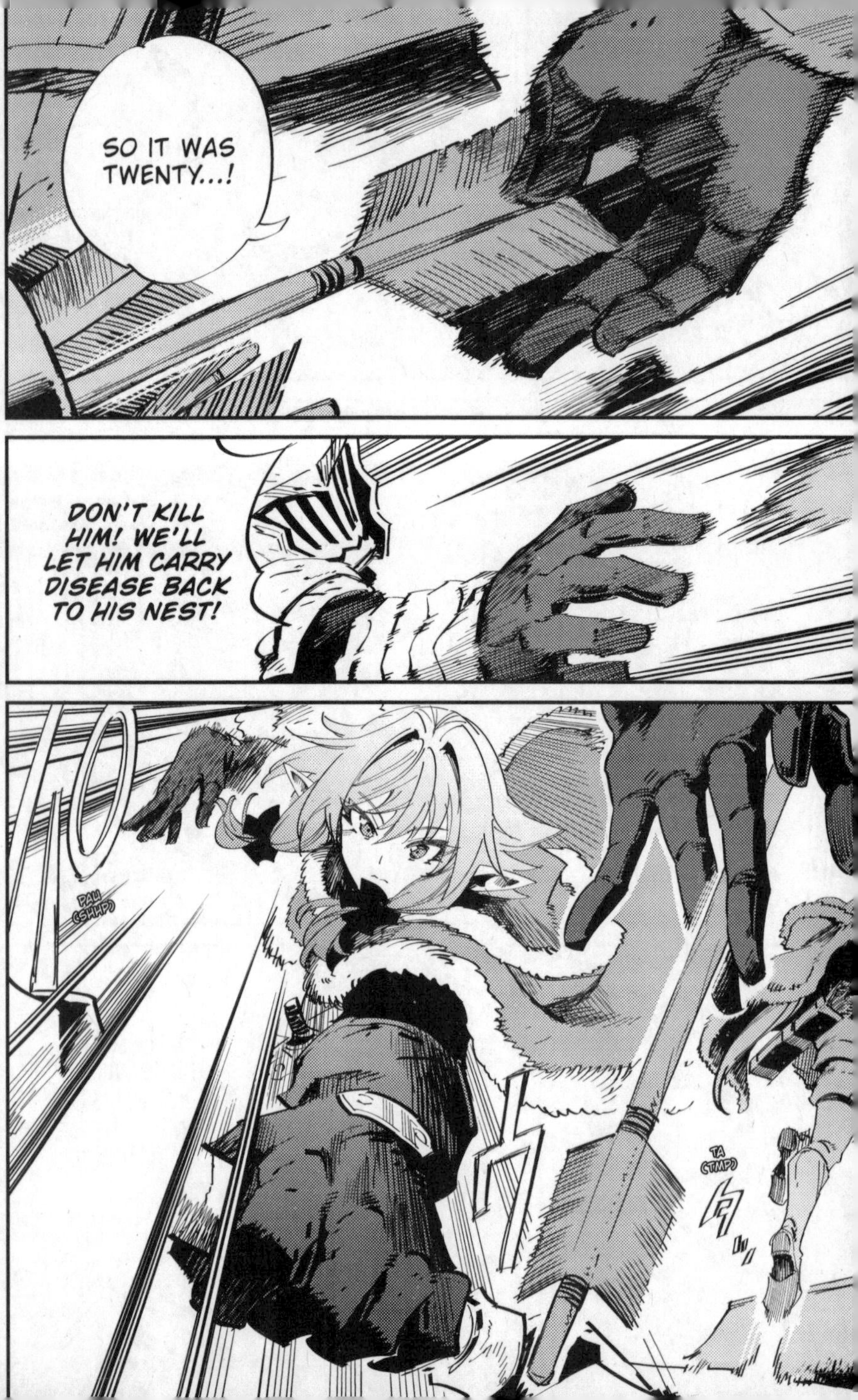
SO IT WAS TWENTY...!
DON'T KILL HIM! WE'LL LET HIM CARRY DISEASE BACK TO HIS NEST!
TA (TMP)
PAU (SHHP)

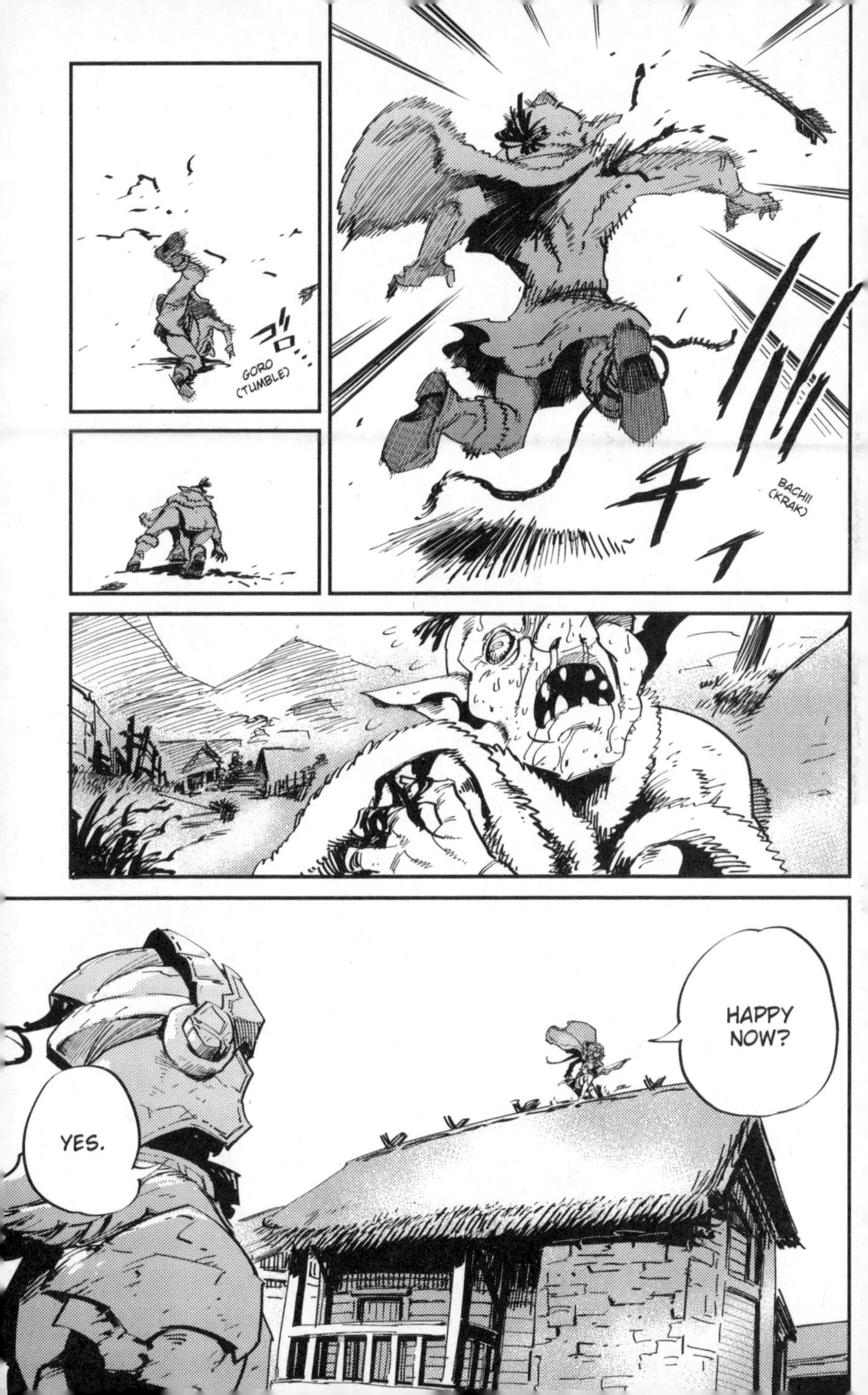
BACHII
(KRAK)
ゴロ…
GORO
(TUMBLE)
HAPPY NOW?
YES.

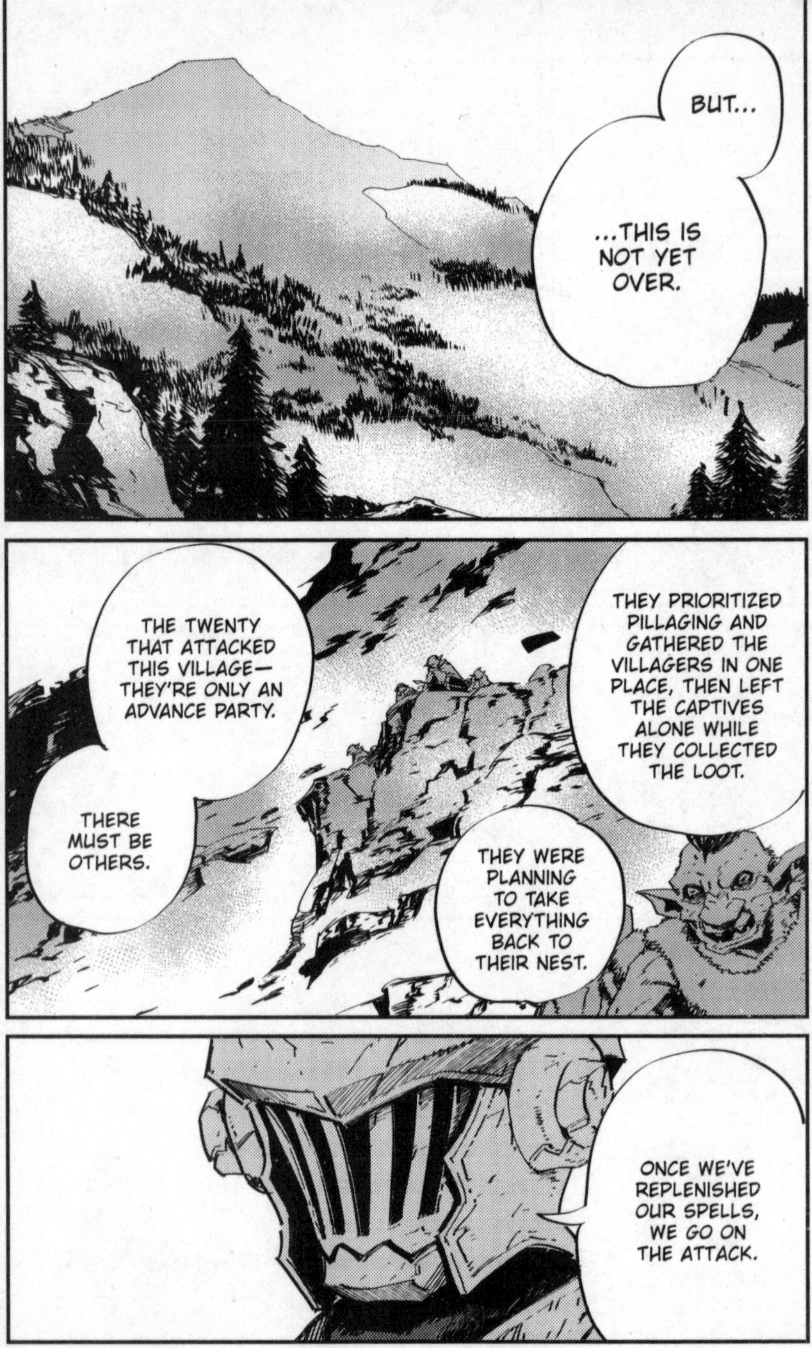
BUT...
...THIS IS NOT YET OVER.
THEY PRIORITIZED PILLAGING AND GATHERED THE VILLAGERS IN ONE PLACE, THEN LEFT THE CAPTIVES ALONE WHILE THEY COLLECTED THE LOOT.
THEY WERE PLANNING TO TAKE EVERYTHING BACK TO THEIR NEST.
THE TWENTY THAT ATTACKED THIS VILLAGE—THEY'RE ONLY AN ADVANCE PARTY.
THERE MUST BE OTHERS.
ONCE WE'VE REPLENISHED OUR SPELLS, WE GO ON THE ATTACK.

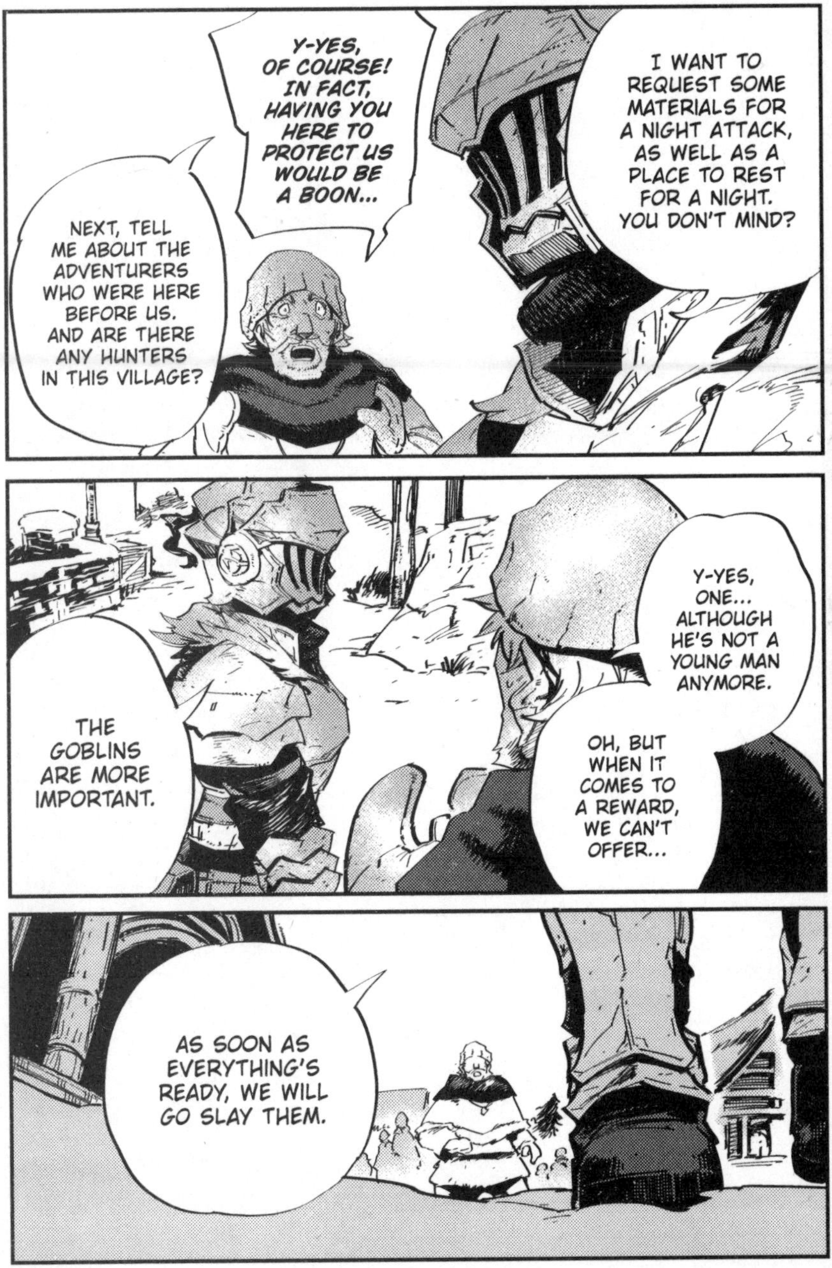
I WANT TO REQUEST SOME MATERIALS FOR A NIGHT ATTACK, AS WELL AS A PLACE TO REST FOR A NIGHT. YOU DON'T MIND?
Y-YES, OF COURSE! IN FACT, HAVING YOU HERE TO PROTECT US WOULD BE A BOON...
NEXT, TELL ME ABOUT THE ADVENTURERS WHO WERE HERE BEFORE US. AND ARE THERE ANY HUNTERS IN THIS VILLAGE?
Y-YES, ONE... ALTHOUGH HE'S NOT A YOUNG MAN ANYMORE.
OH, BUT WHEN IT COMES TO A REWARD, WE CAN'T OFFER...
THE GOBLINS ARE MORE IMPORTANT.
AS SOON AS EVERYTHING'S READY, WE WILL GO SLAY THEM.

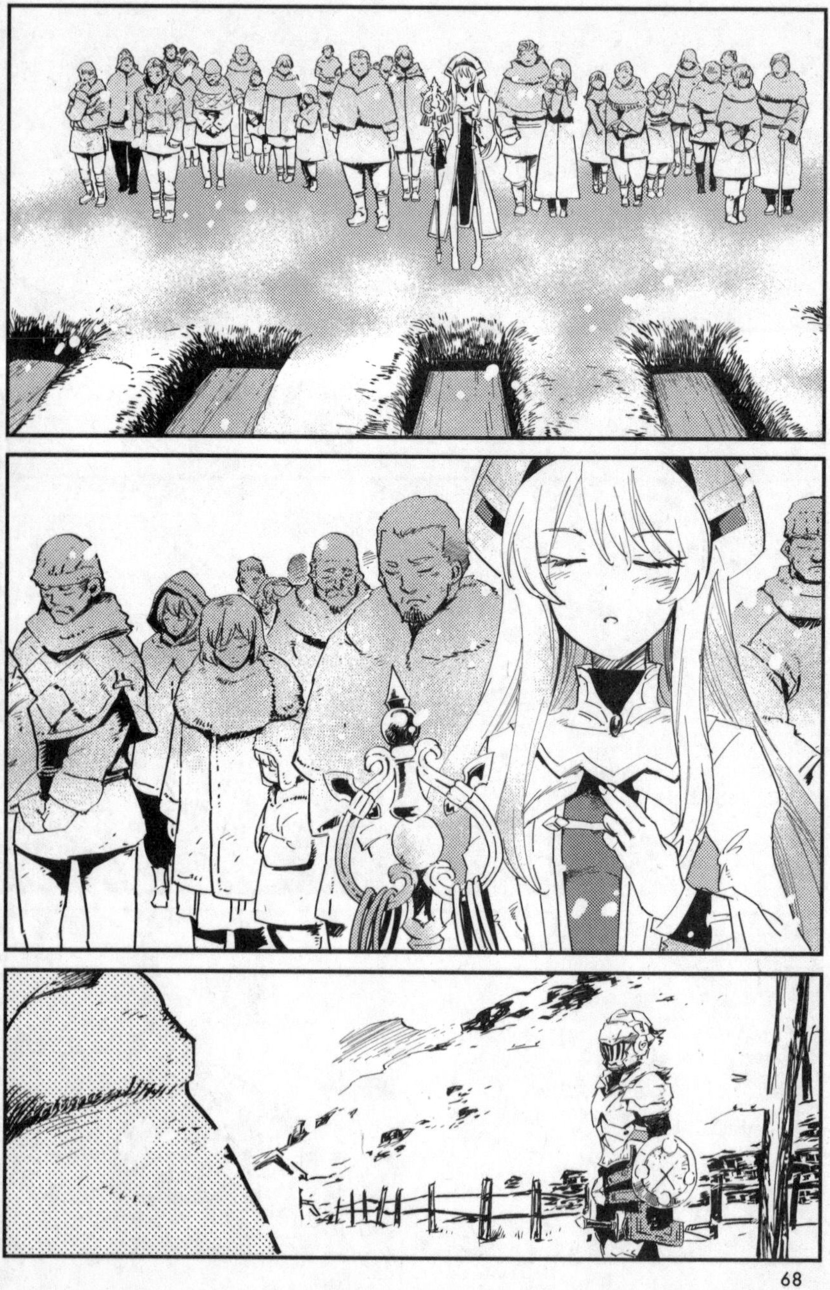

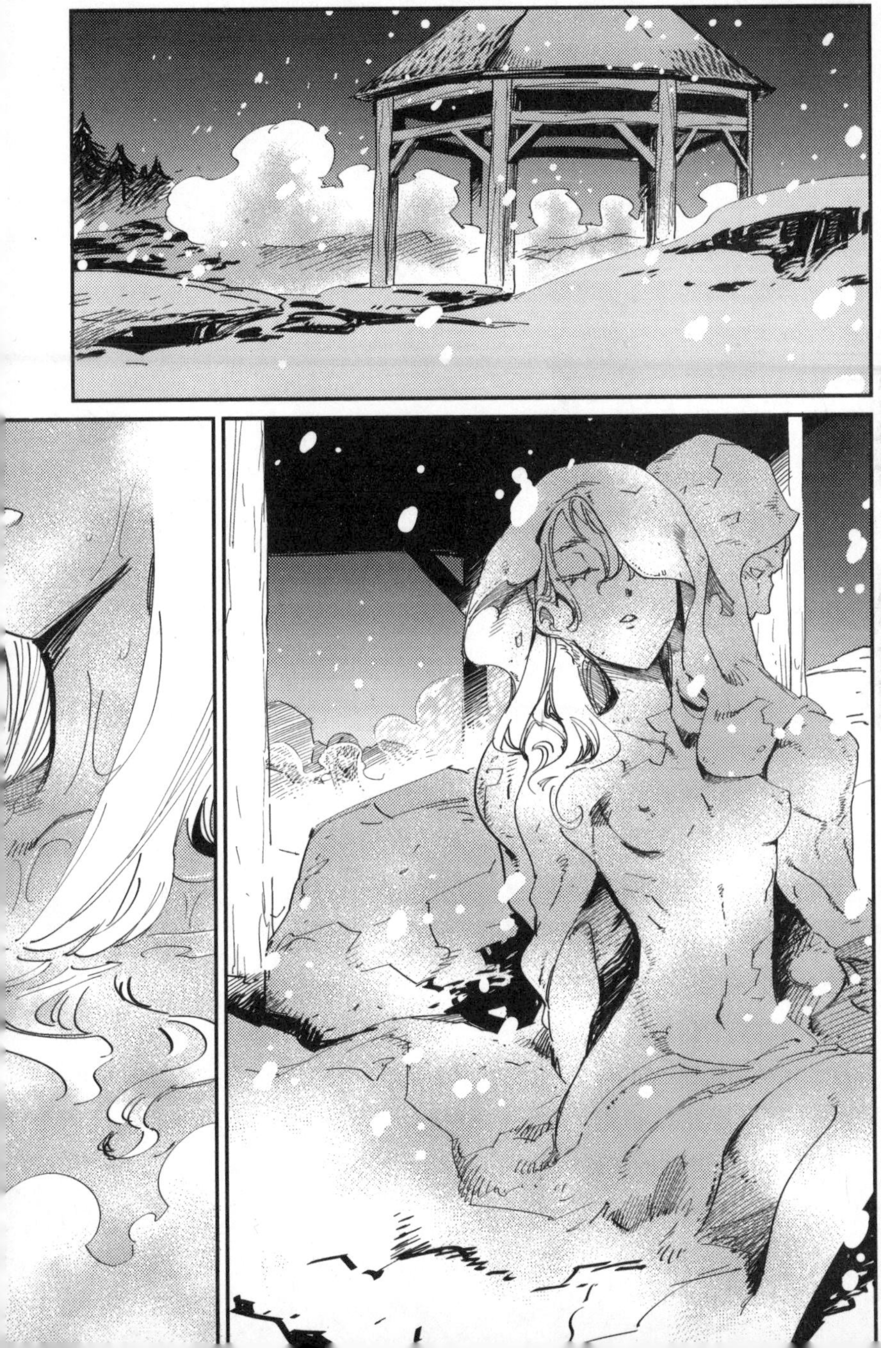

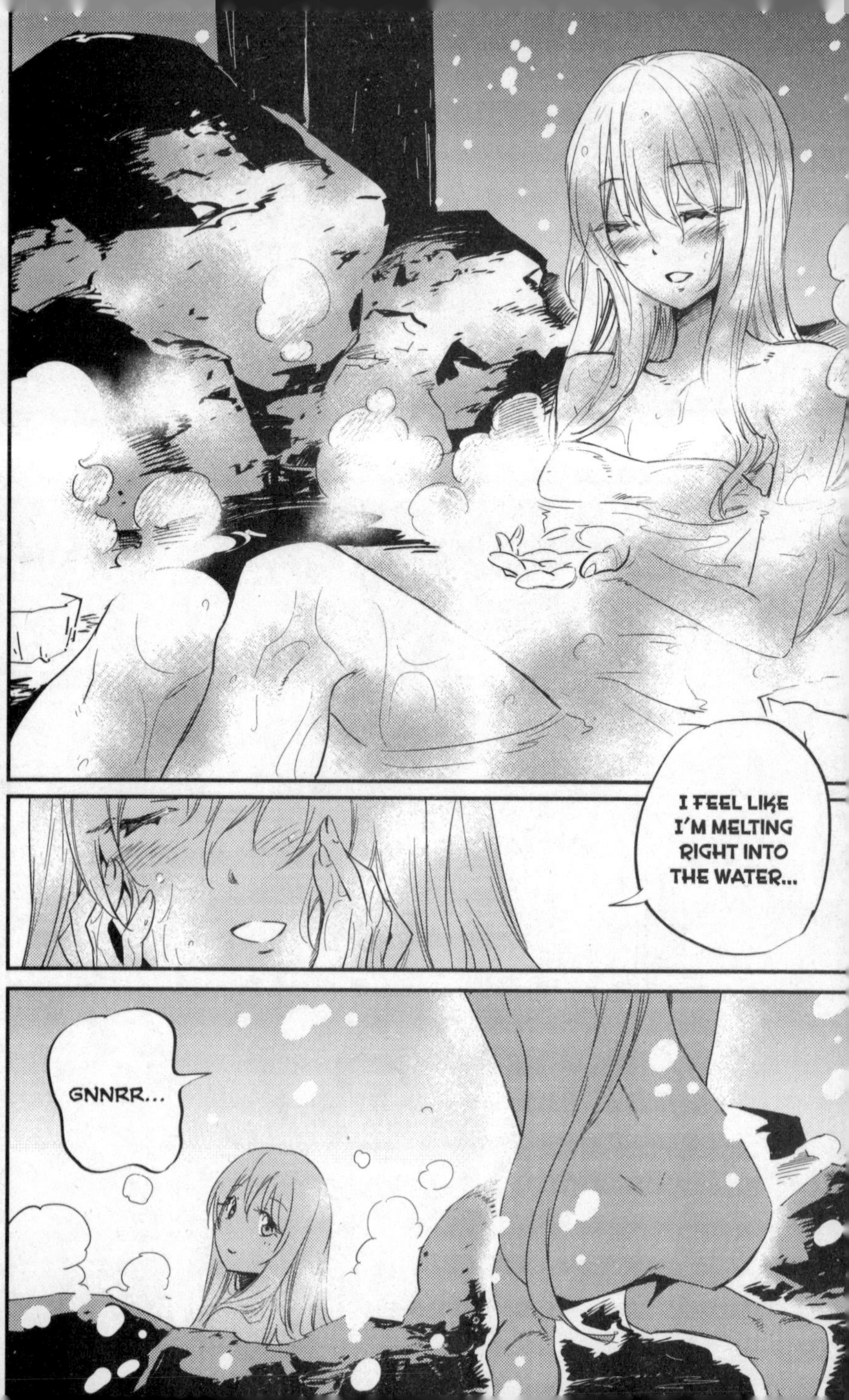
I FEEL LIKE I'M MELTING RIGHT INTO THE WATER...
GNNRR...

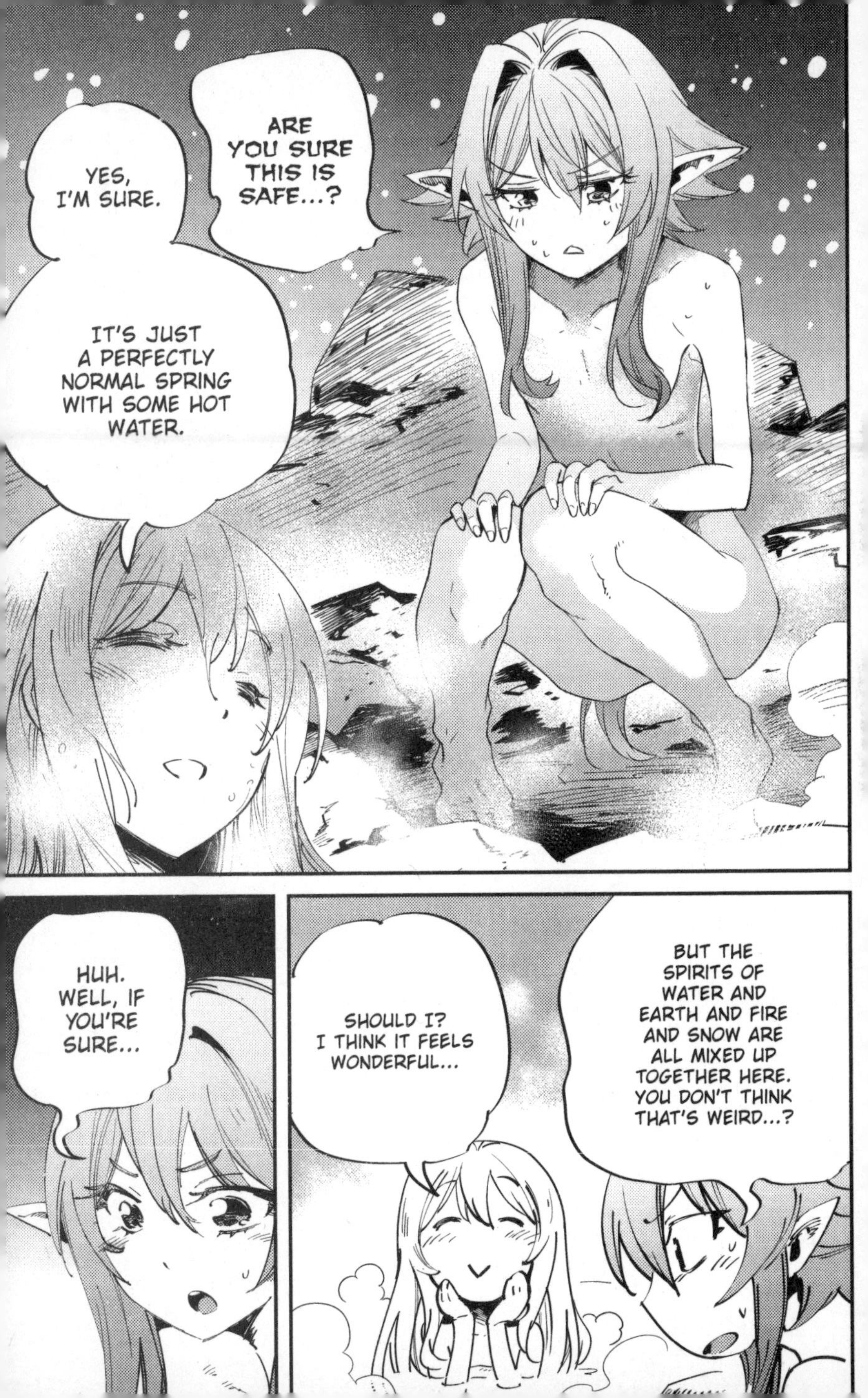
ARE YOU SURE THIS IS SAFE...?
YES, I'M SURE.
IT'S JUST A PERFECTLY NORMAL SPRING WITH SOME HOT WATER.
BUT THE SPIRITS OF WATER AND EARTH AND FIRE AND SNOW ARE ALL MIXED UP TOGETHER HERE. YOU DON'T THINK THAT'S WEIRD...?
SHOULD I? I THINK IT FEELS WONDERFUL...
HUH. WELL, IF YOU'RE SURE...

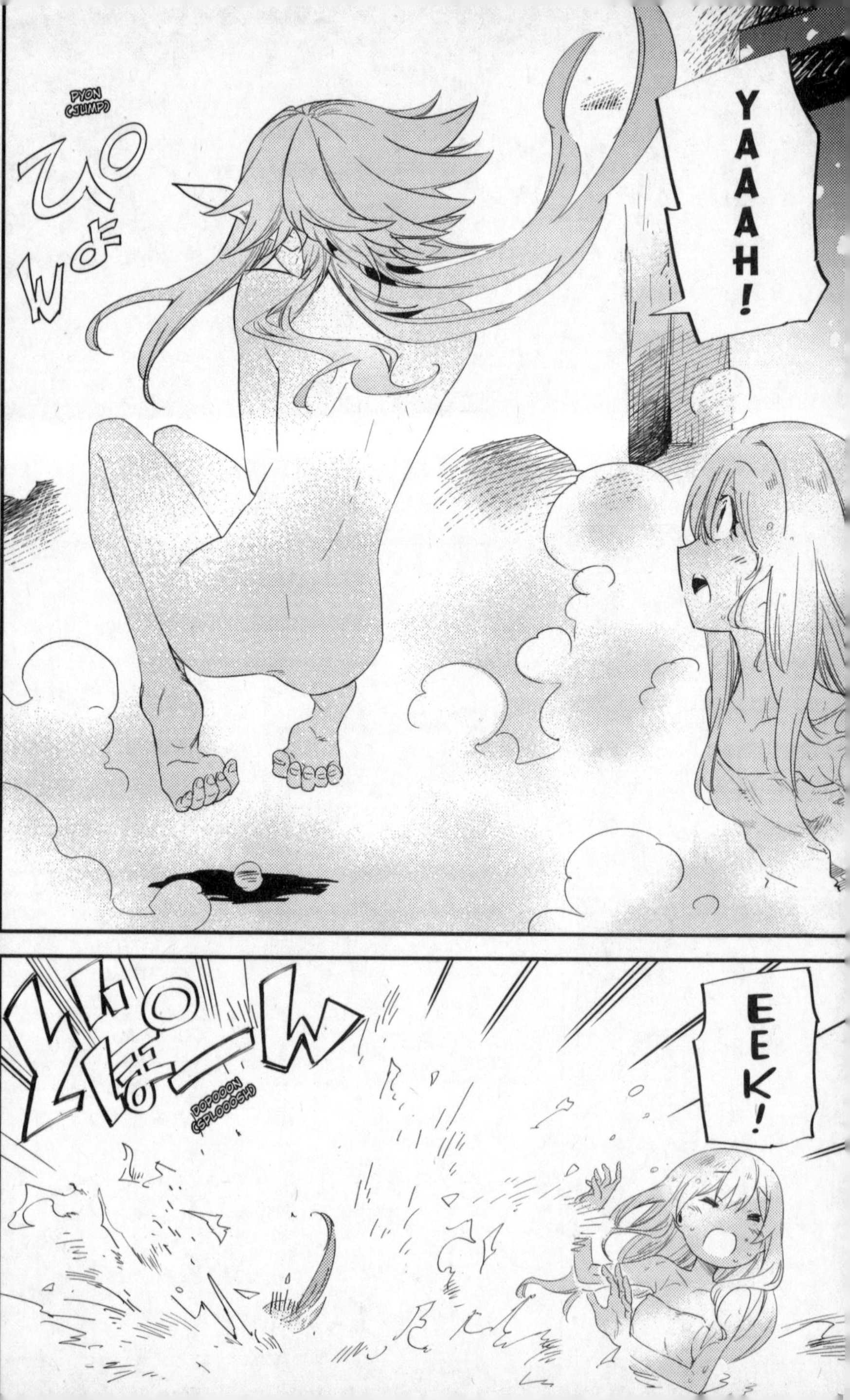
YAAAH!
ぴょん
PYON (JUMP)
EEK!
どぽーん
DOPOOON (SPLOOOSH)

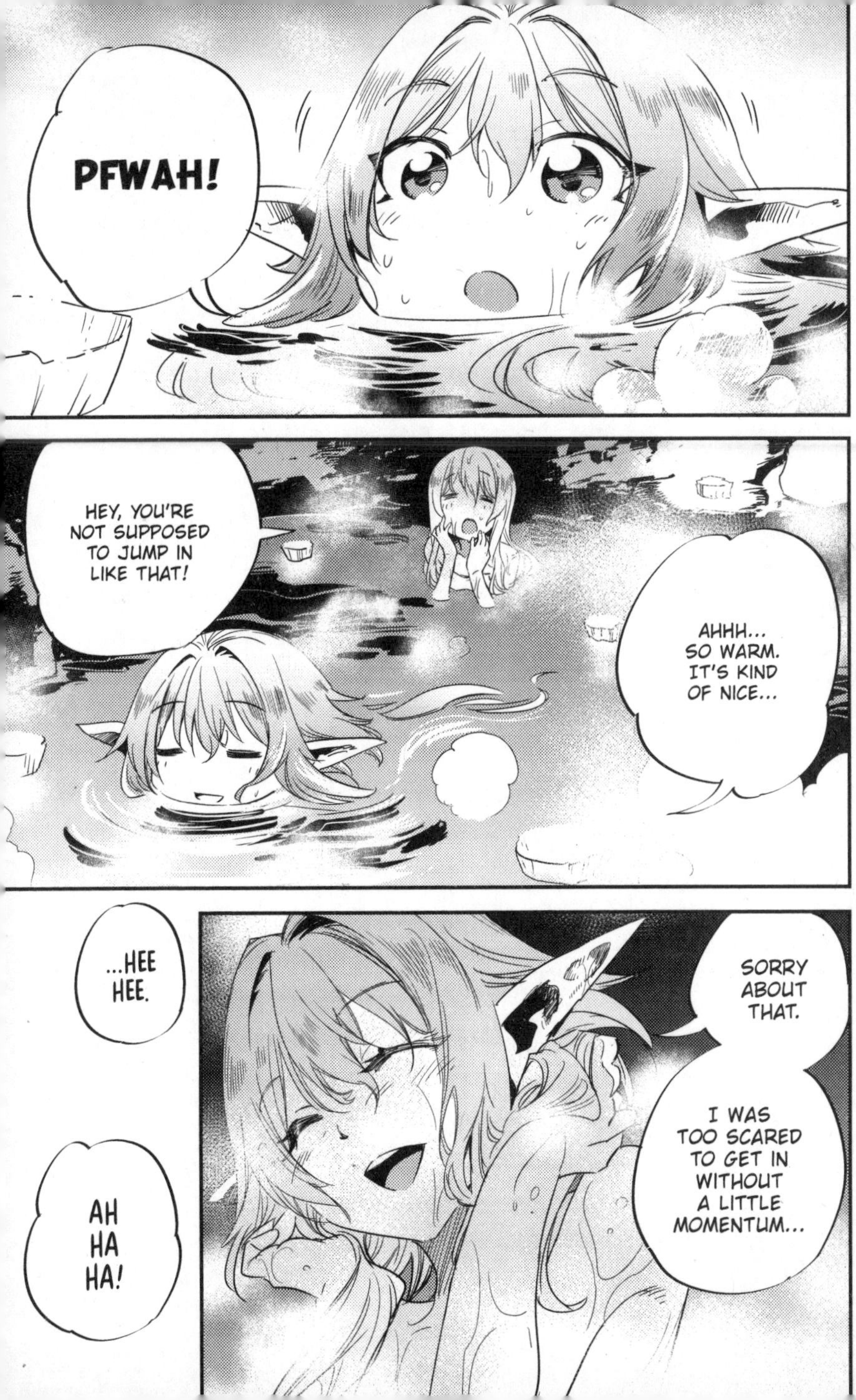
PFWAH!
AHHH... SO WARM. IT'S KIND OF NICE...
HEY, YOU'RE NOT SUPPOSED TO JUMP IN LIKE THAT!
SORRY ABOUT THAT.
I WAS TOO SCARED TO GET IN WITHOUT A LITTLE MOMENTUM...
...HEE HEE.
AH HA HA!

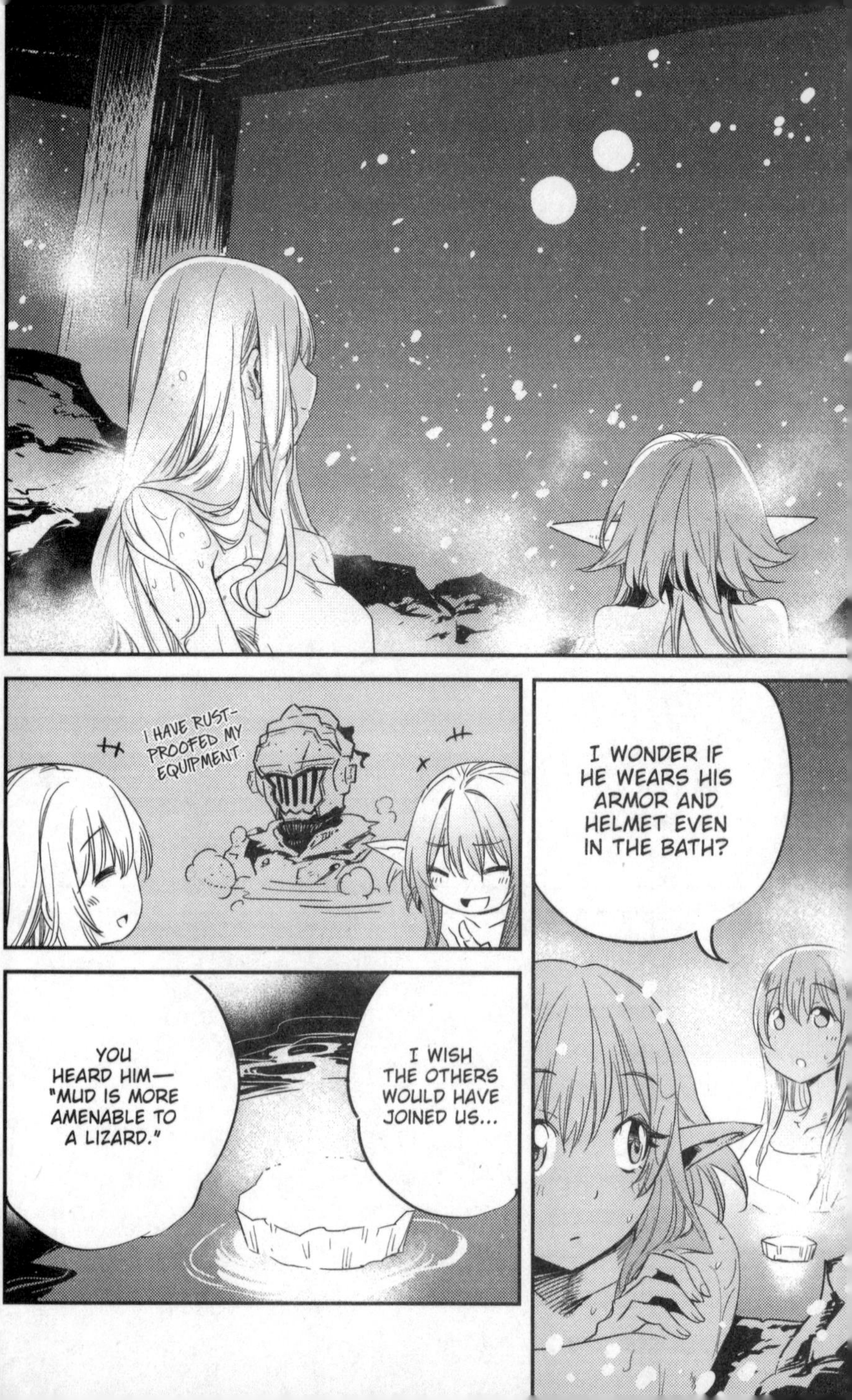
I WONDER IF HE WEARS HIS ARMOR AND HELMET EVEN IN THE BATH?
I HAVE RUST-PROOFED MY EQUIPMENT.
I WISH THE OTHERS WOULD HAVE JOINED US...
YOU HEARD HIM—"MUD IS MORE AMENABLE TO A LIZARD."

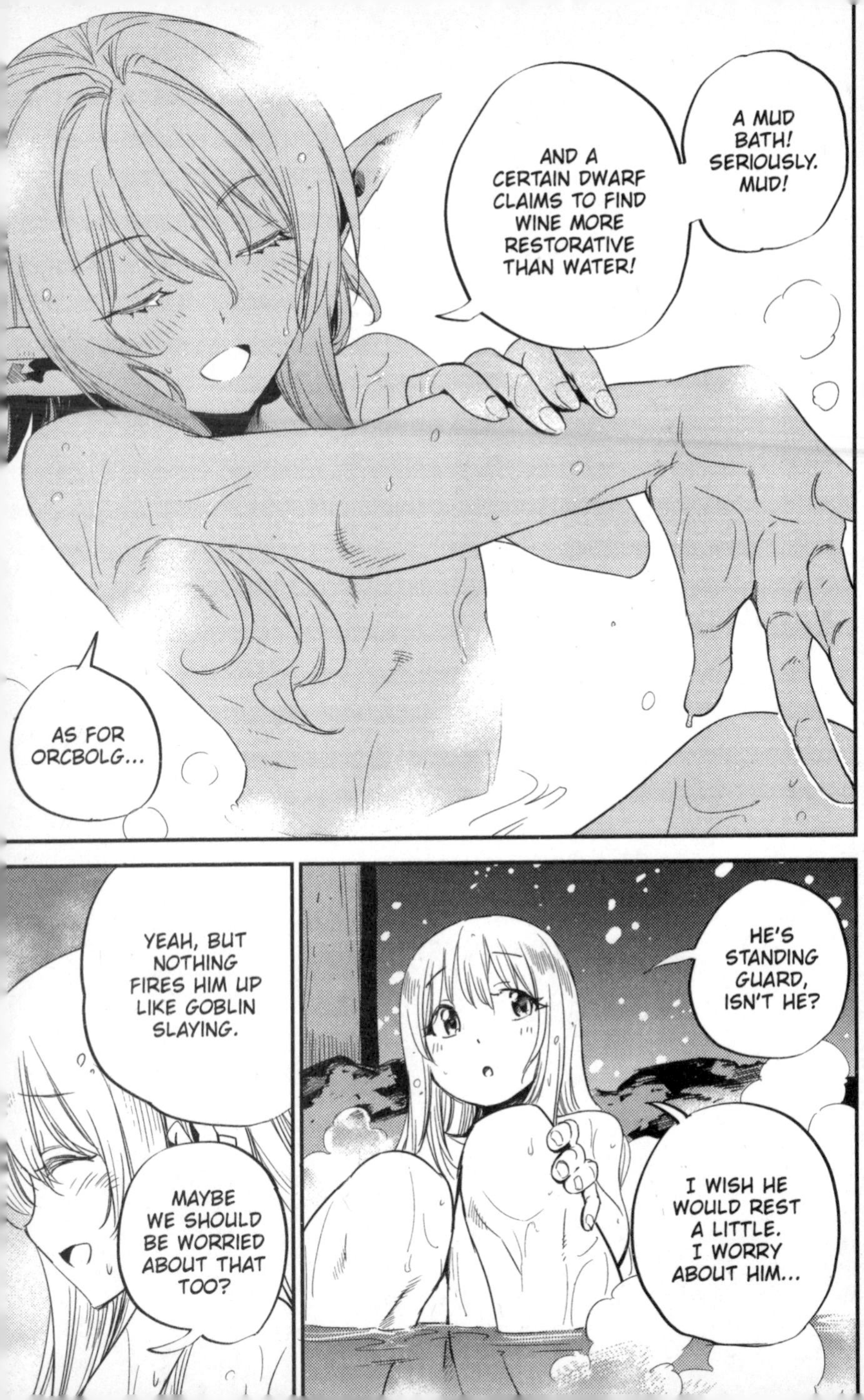
A MUD BATH! SERIOUSLY. MUD!
AND A CERTAIN DWARF CLAIMS TO FIND WINE MORE RESTORATIVE THAN WATER!
AS FOR ORCBOLG...
HE'S STANDING GUARD, ISN'T HE?
I WISH HE WOULD REST A LITTLE. I WORRY ABOUT HIM...
YEAH, BUT NOTHING FIRES HIM UP LIKE GOBLIN SLAYING.
MAYBE WE SHOULD BE WORRIED ABOUT THAT TOO?

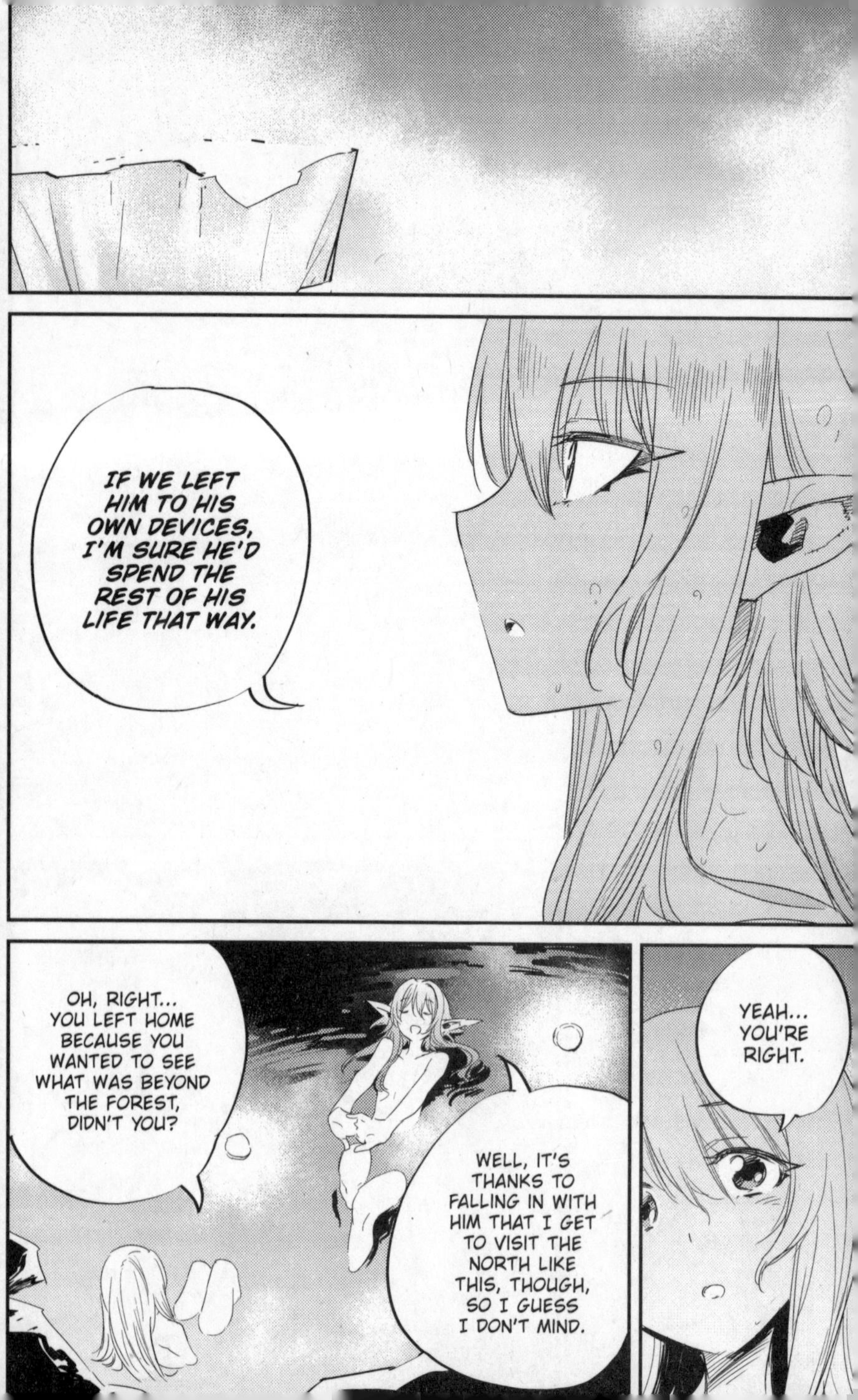
IF WE LEFT HIM TO HIS OWN DEVICES, I'M SURE HE'D SPEND THE REST OF HIS LIFE THAT WAY.
YEAH... YOU'RE RIGHT.
OH, RIGHT... YOU LEFT HOME BECAUSE YOU WANTED TO SEE WHAT WAS BEYOND THE FOREST, DIDN'T YOU?
WELL, IT'S THANKS TO FALLING IN WITH HIM THAT I GET TO VISIT THE NORTH LIKE THIS, THOUGH, SO I GUESS I DON'T MIND.

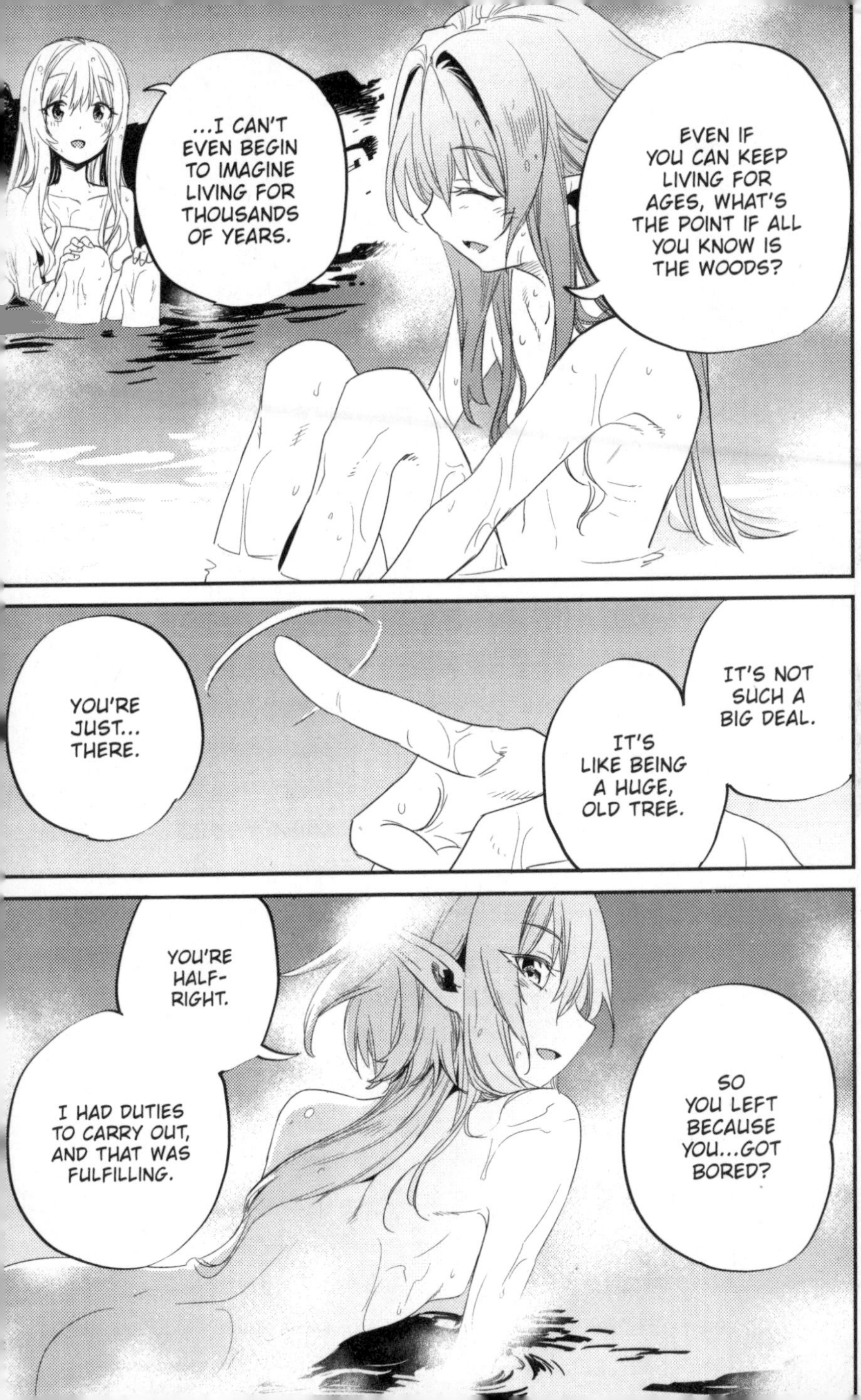
EVEN IF YOU CAN KEEP LIVING FOR AGES, WHAT'S THE POINT IF ALL YOU KNOW IS THE WOODS?
...I CAN'T EVEN BEGIN TO IMAGINE LIVING FOR THOUSANDS OF YEARS.
IT'S NOT SUCH A BIG DEAL.
IT'S LIKE BEING A HUGE, OLD TREE.
YOU'RE JUST... THERE.
SO YOU LEFT BECAUSE YOU...GOT BORED?
YOU'RE HALF-RIGHT.
I HAD DUTIES TO CARRY OUT, AND THAT WAS FULFILLING.

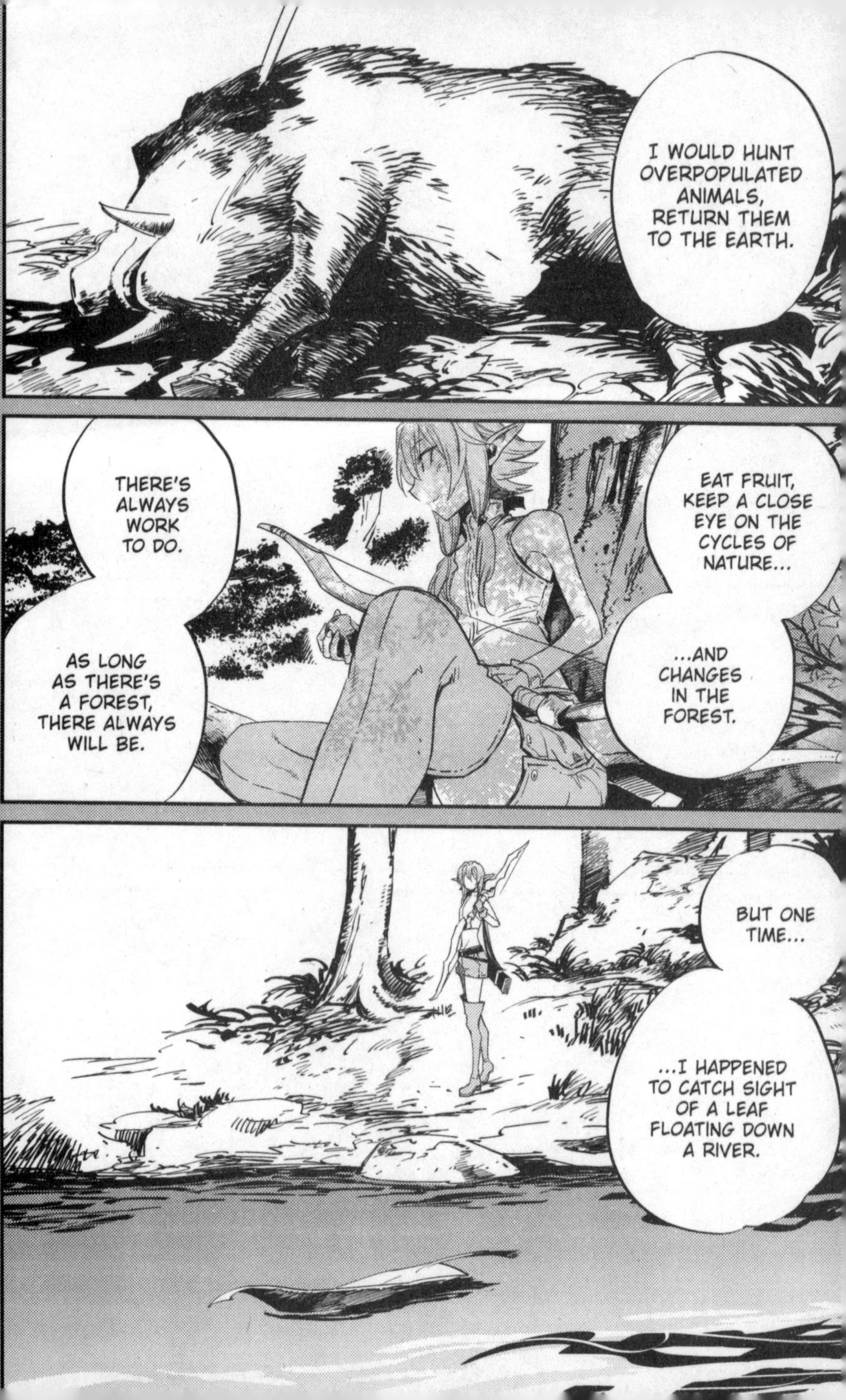
I WOULD HUNT OVERPOPULATED ANIMALS, RETURN THEM TO THE EARTH.
EAT FRUIT, KEEP A CLOSE EYE ON THE CYCLES OF NATURE...
...AND CHANGES IN THE FOREST.
THERE'S ALWAYS WORK TO DO.
AS LONG AS THERE'S A FOREST, THERE ALWAYS WILL BE.
BUT ONE TIME...
...I HAPPENED TO CATCH SIGHT OF A LEAF FLOATING DOWN A RIVER.

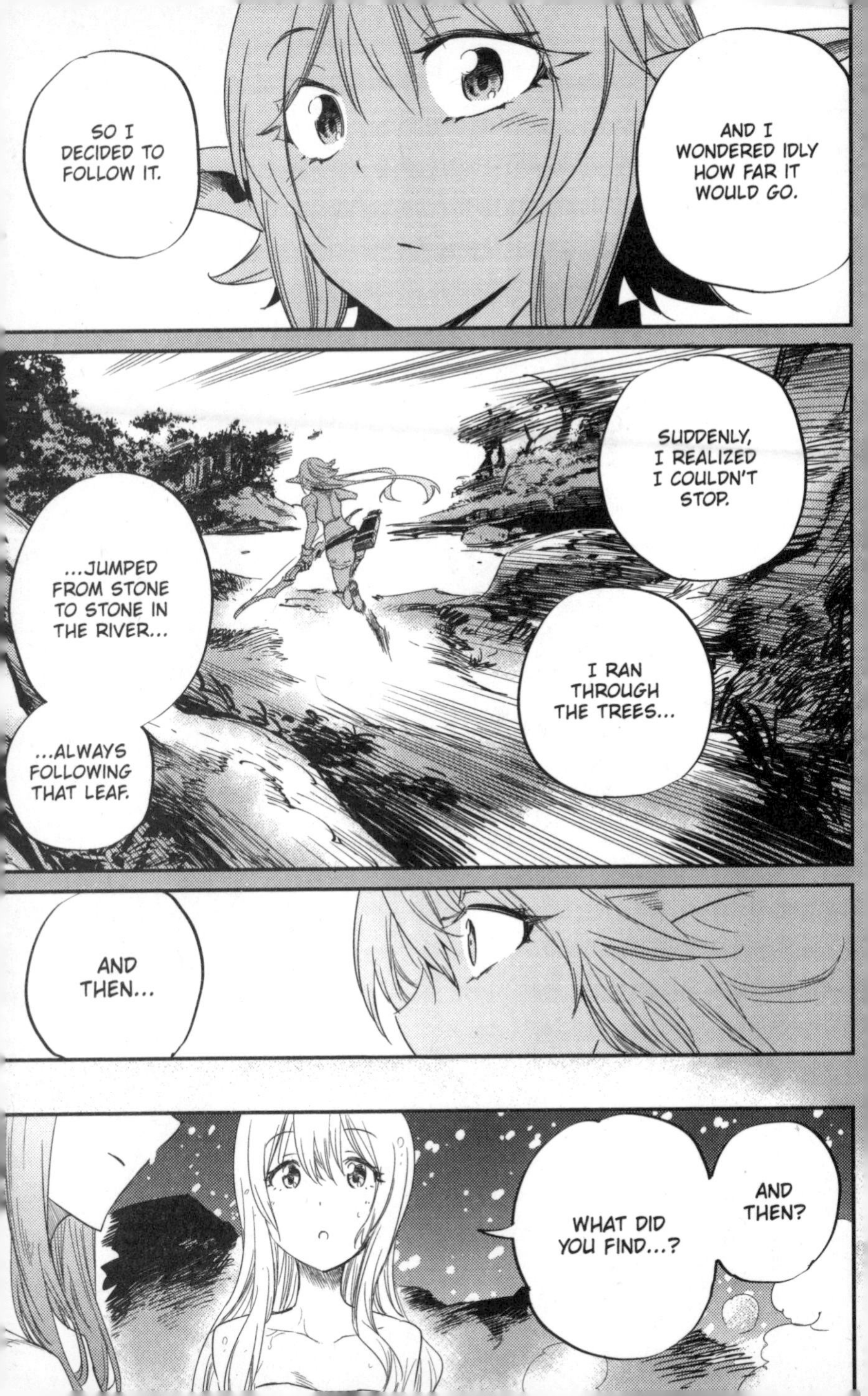
AND I WONDERED IDLY HOW FAR IT WOULD GO.
SO I DECIDED TO FOLLOW IT.
SUDDENLY, I REALIZED I COULDN'T STOP.
I RAN THROUGH THE TREES...
...JUMPED FROM STONE TO STONE IN THE RIVER...
...ALWAYS FOLLOWING THAT LEAF.
AND THEN...
AND THEN?
WHAT DID YOU FIND...?

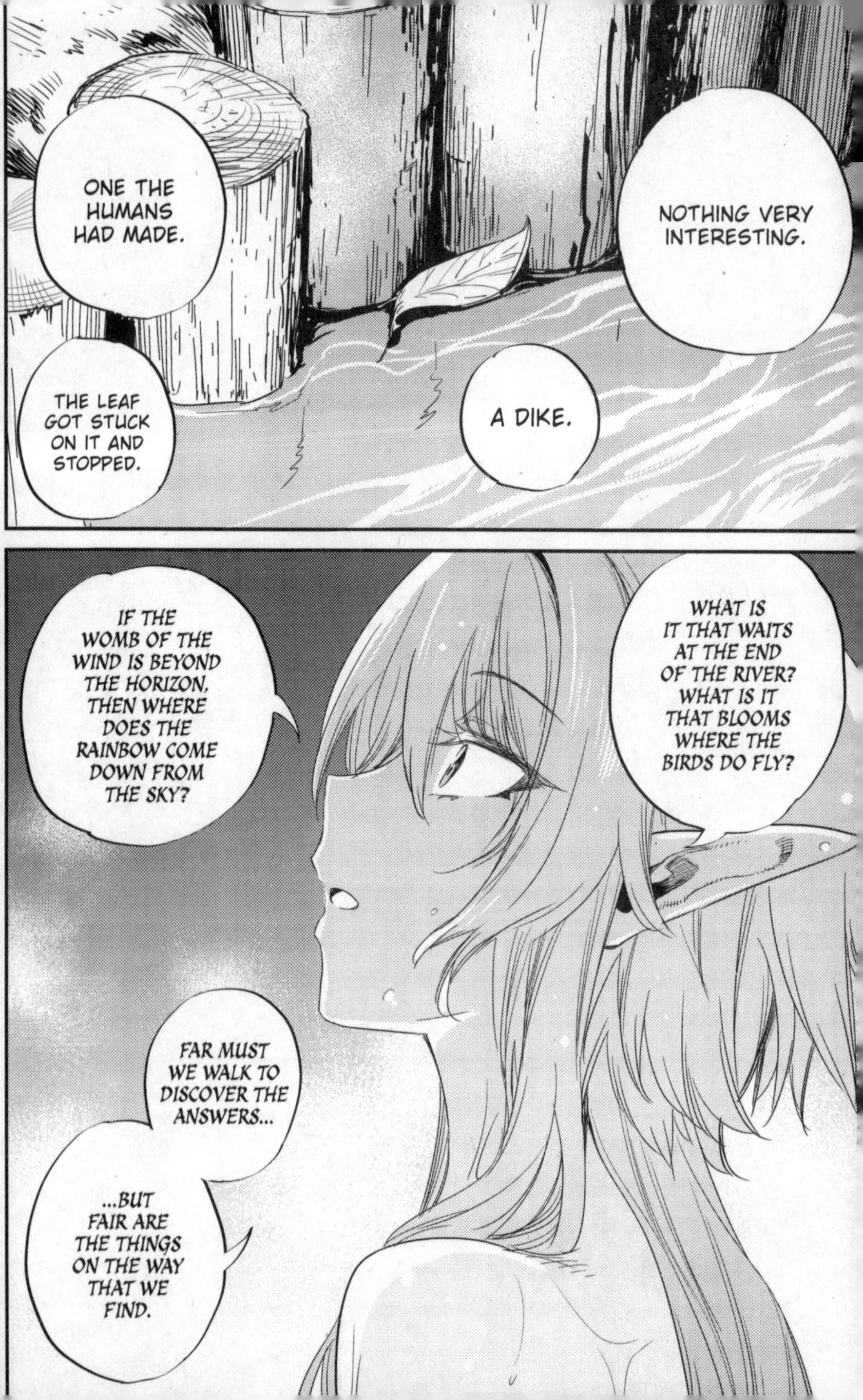
NOTHING VERY INTERESTING.
A DIKE.
ONE THE HUMANS HAD MADE.
THE LEAF GOT STUCK ON IT AND STOPPED.
WHAT IS IT THAT WAITS AT THE END OF THE RIVER? WHAT IS IT THAT BLOOMS WHERE THE BIRDS DO FLY?
IF THE WOMB OF THE WIND IS BEYOND THE HORIZON, THEN WHERE DOES THE RAINBOW COME DOWN FROM THE SKY?
FAR MUST WE WALK TO DISCOVER THE ANSWERS...
...BUT FAIR ARE THE THINGS ON THE WAY THAT WE FIND.

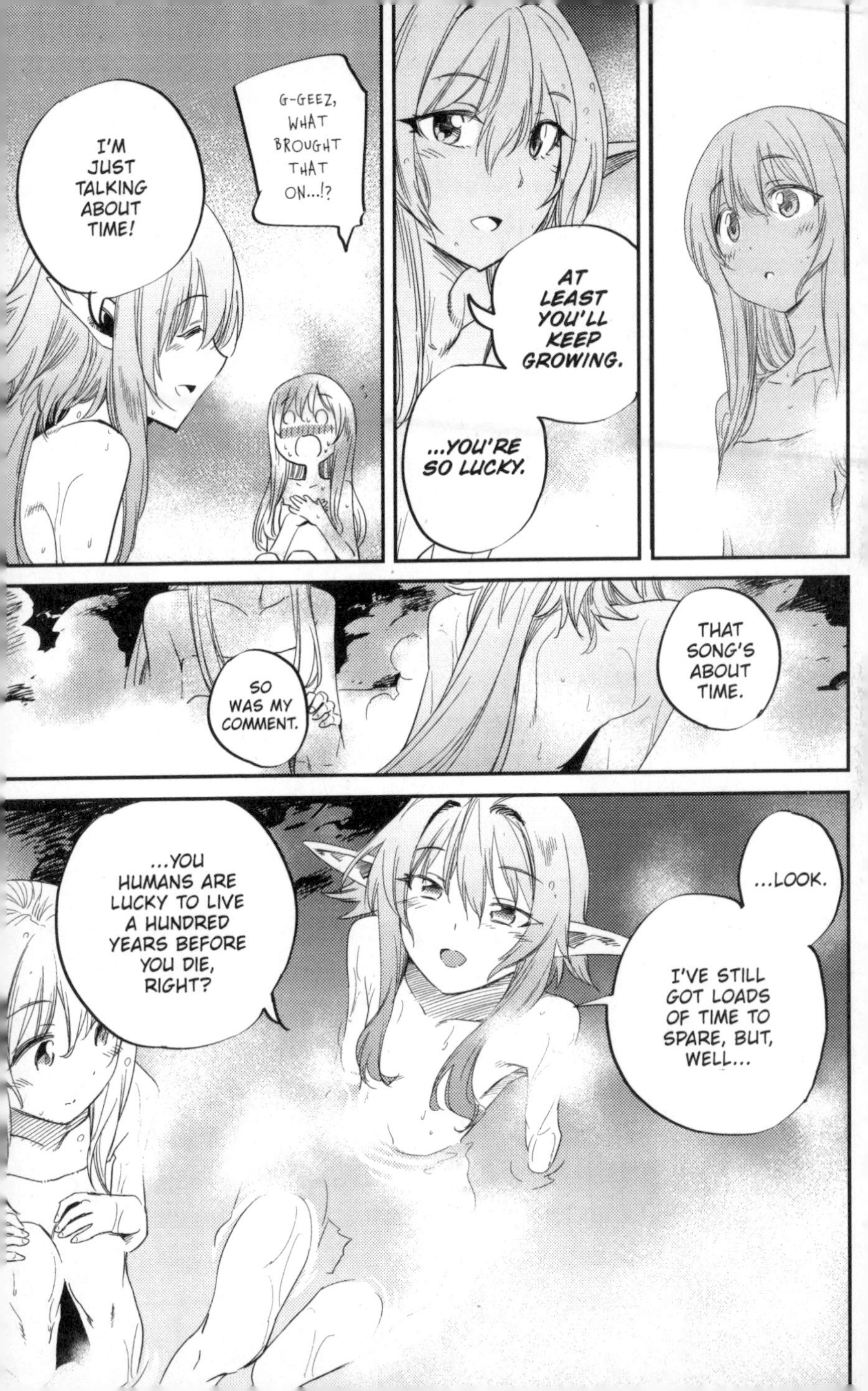
AT LEAST YOU'LL KEEP GROWING.
...YOU'RE SO LUCKY.
G-GEEZ, WHAT BROUGHT THAT ON...!?
I'M JUST TALKING ABOUT TIME!
THAT SONG'S ABOUT TIME.
SO WAS MY COMMENT.
...LOOK.
I'VE STILL GOT LOADS OF TIME TO SPARE, BUT, WELL...
...YOU HUMANS ARE LUCKY TO LIVE A HUNDRED YEARS BEFORE YOU DIE, RIGHT?

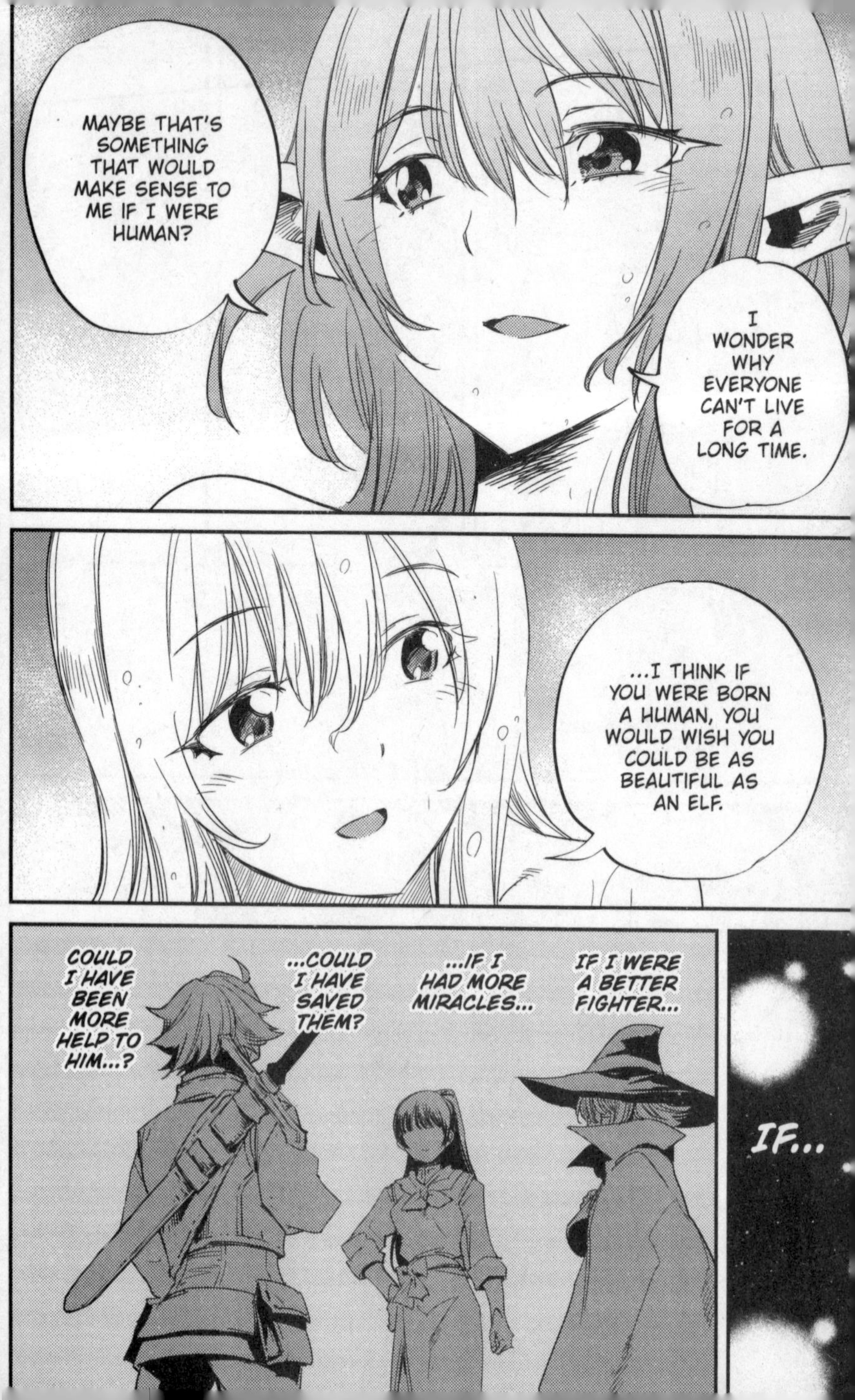
I WONDER WHY EVERYONE CAN'T LIVE FOR A LONG TIME.
MAYBE THAT'S SOMETHING THAT WOULD MAKE SENSE TO ME IF I WERE HUMAN?
...I THINK IF YOU WERE BORN A HUMAN, YOU WOULD WISH YOU COULD BE AS BEAUTIFUL AS AN ELF.
IF...
IF I WERE A BETTER FIGHTER...
...IF I HAD MORE MIRACLES...
...COULD I HAVE SAVED THEM?
COULD I HAVE BEEN MORE HELP TO HIM...?

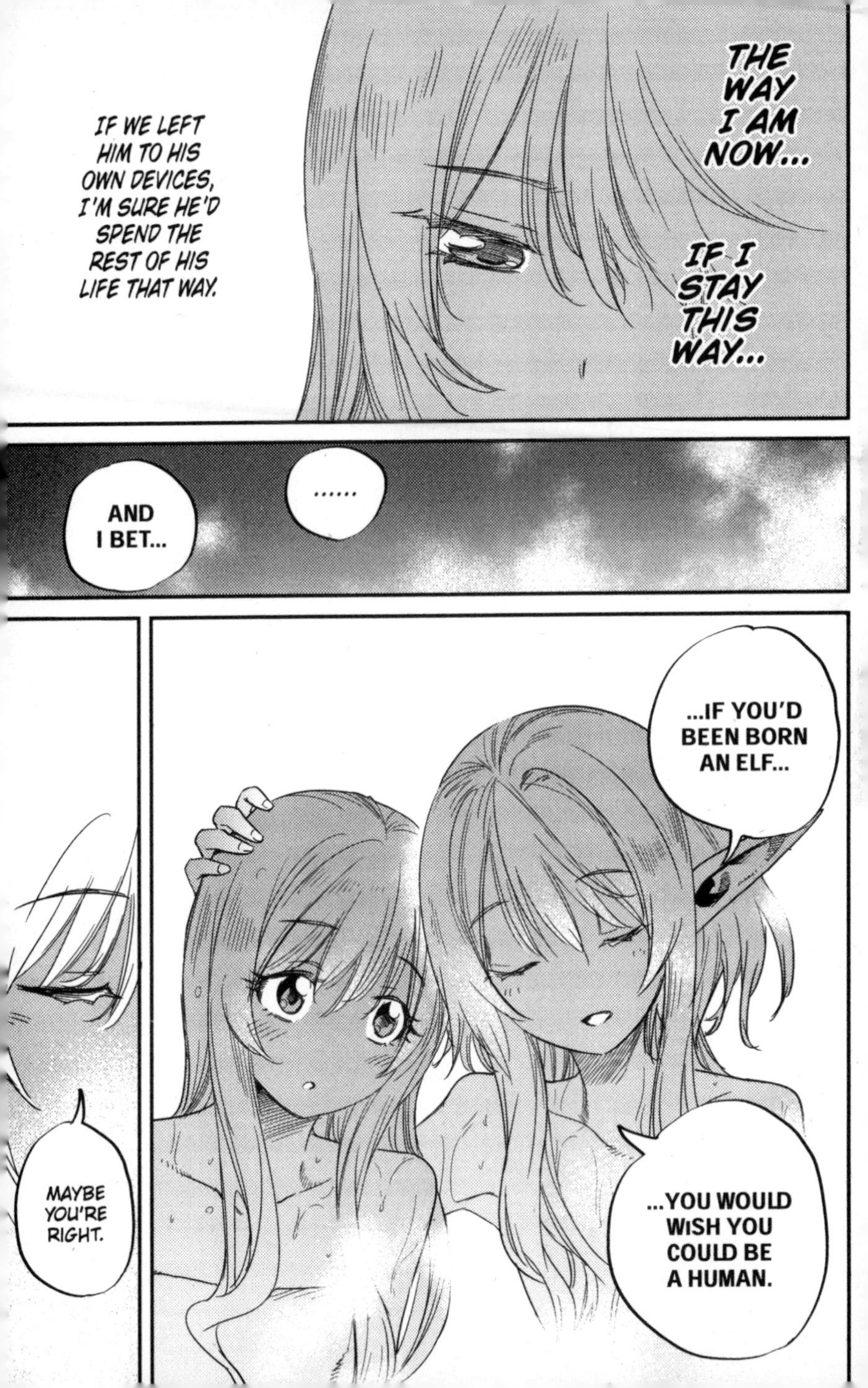
THE WAY I AM NOW...
IF I STAY THIS WAY...
IF WE LEFT HIM TO HIS OWN DEVICES, I'M SURE HE'D SPEND THE REST OF HIS LIFE THAT WAY.
......
AND I BET...
...IF YOU'D BEEN BORN AN ELF...
...YOU WOULD WISH YOU COULD BE A HUMAN.
MAYBE YOU'RE RIGHT.

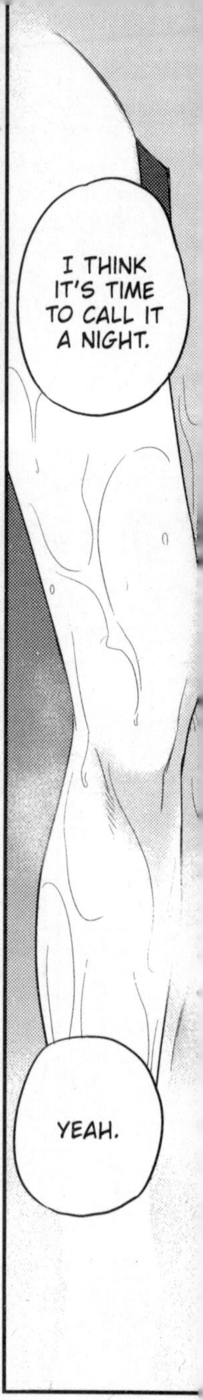
I THINK IT'S TIME TO CALL IT A NIGHT.
YEAH.
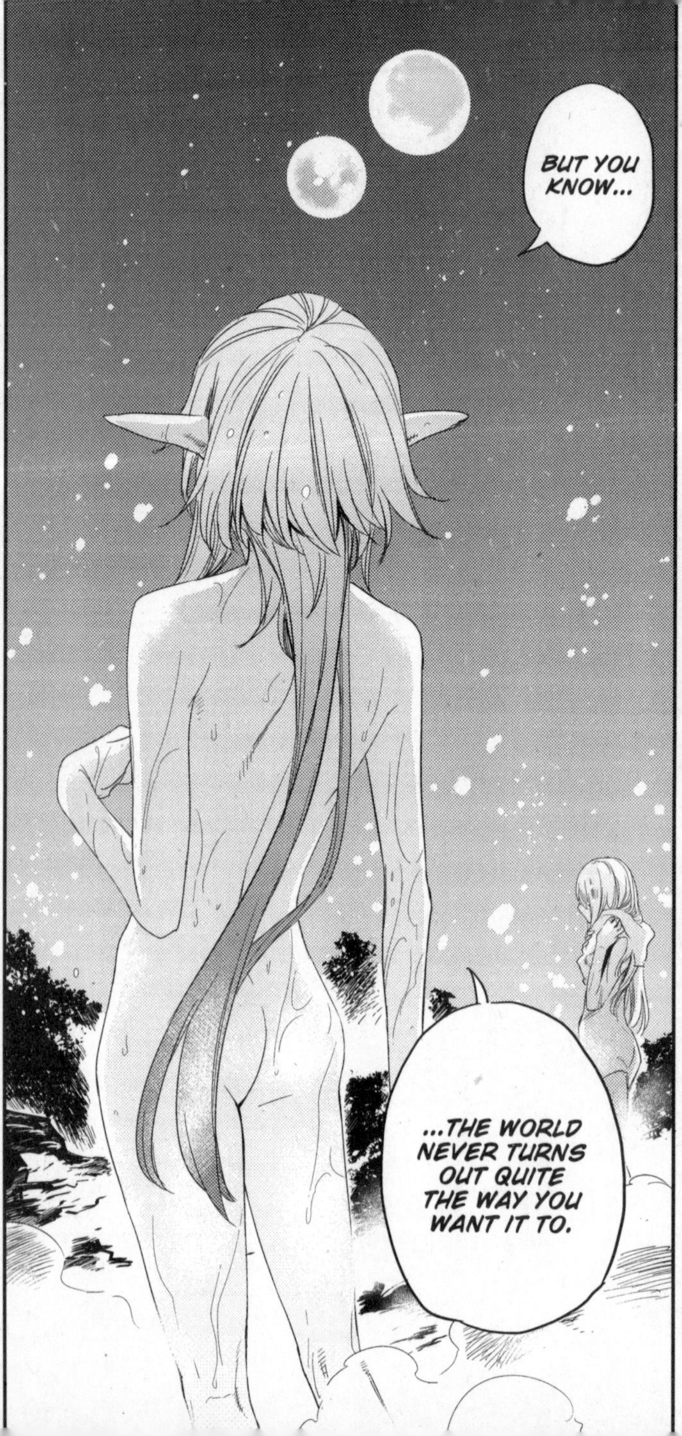
BUT YOU KNOW...
...THE WORLD NEVER TURNS OUT QUITE THE WAY YOU WANT IT TO.

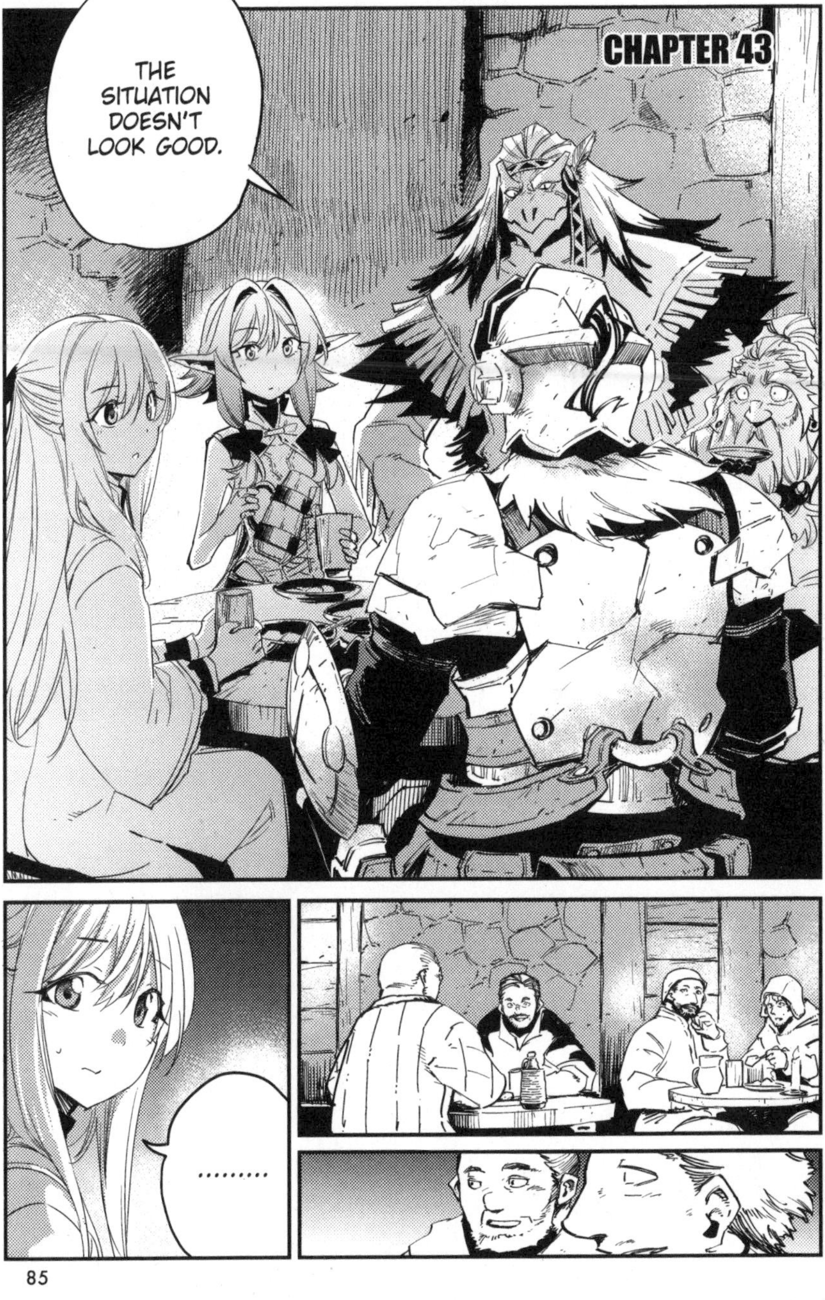
CHAPTER 43
THE SITUATION DOESN'T LOOK GOOD.
....

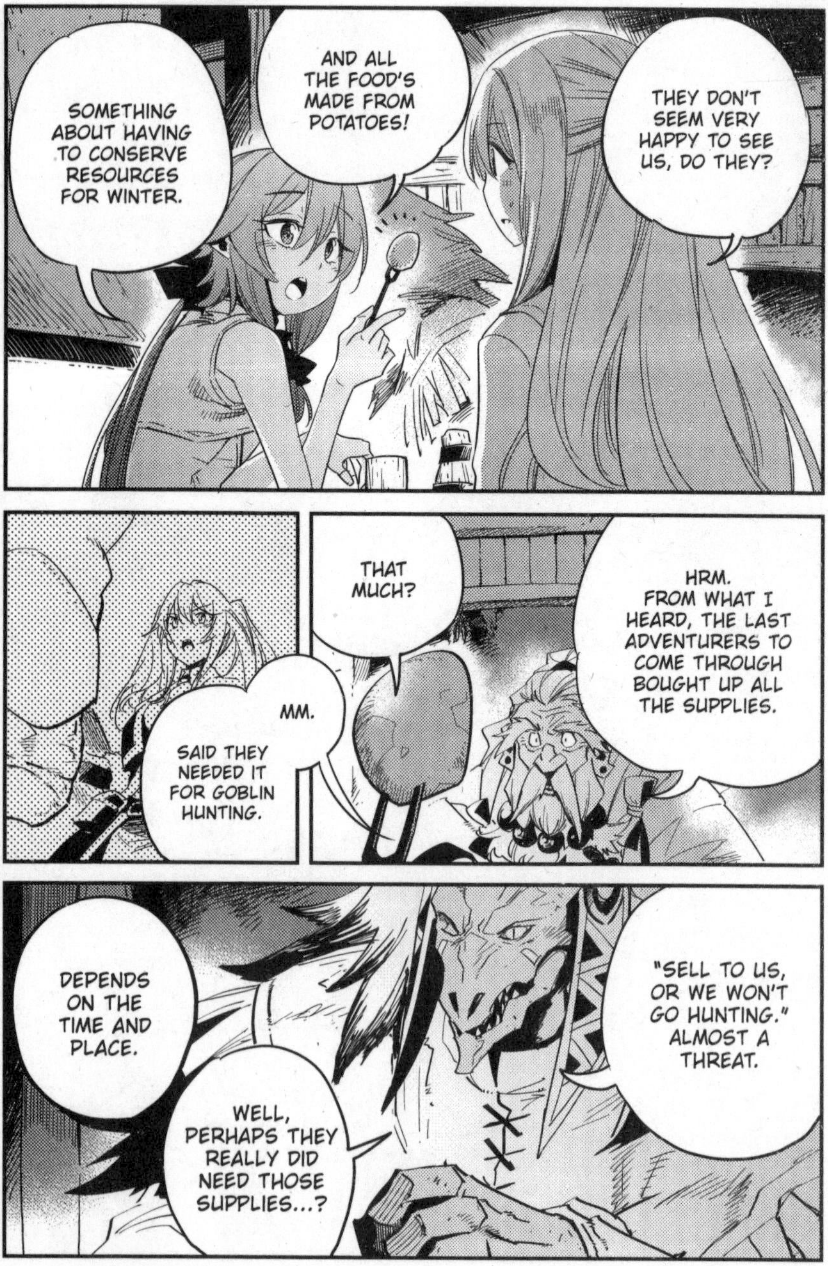
THEY DON'T SEEM VERY HAPPY TO SEE US, DO THEY?
AND ALL THE FOOD'S MADE FROM POTATOES!
SOMETHING ABOUT HAVING TO CONSERVE RESOURCES FOR WINTER.
HRM. FROM WHAT I HEARD, THE LAST ADVENTURERS TO COME THROUGH BOUGHT UP ALL THE SUPPLIES.
THAT MUCH?
MM.
SAID THEY NEEDED IT FOR GOBLIN HUNTING.
"SELL TO US, OR WE WON'T GO HUNTING." ALMOST A THREAT.
WELL, PERHAPS THEY REALLY DID NEED THOSE SUPPLIES...?
DEPENDS ON THE TIME AND PLACE.

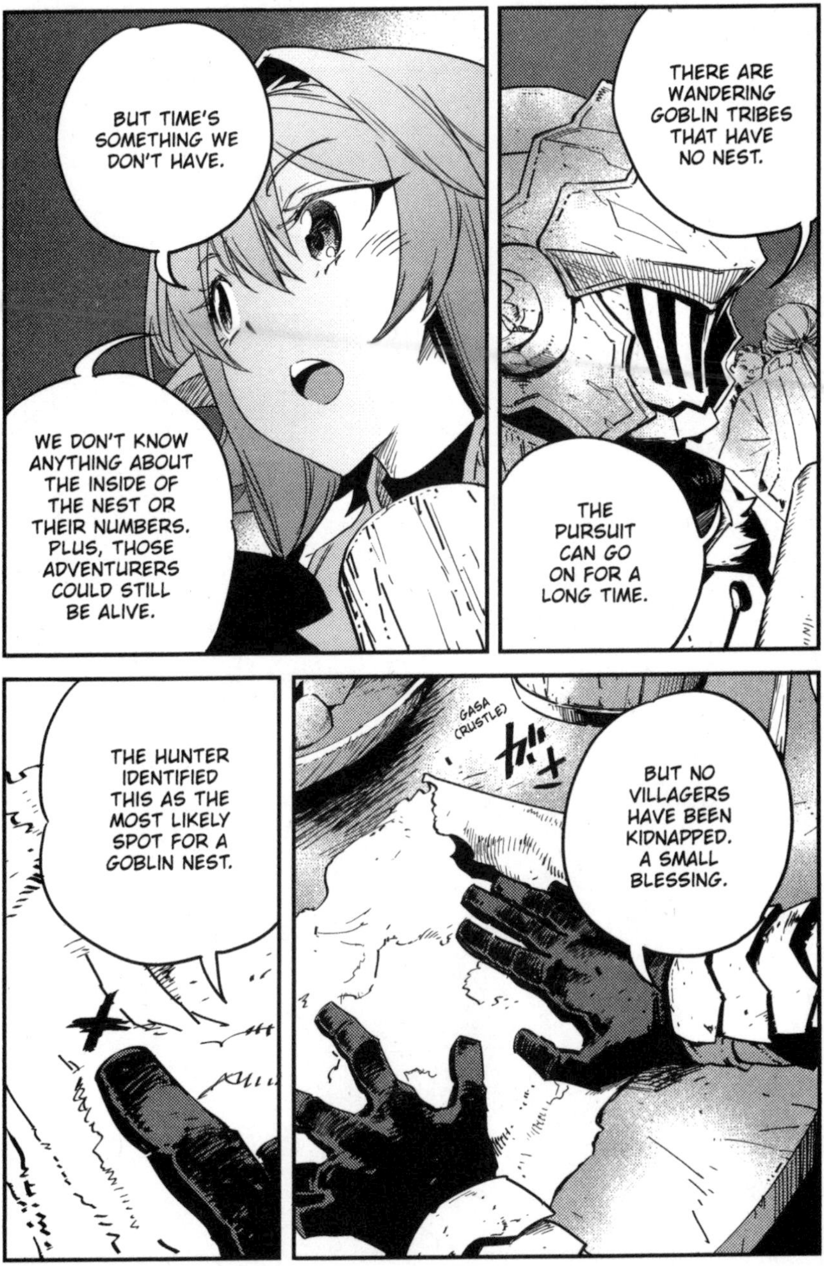
THERE ARE WANDERING GOBLIN TRIBES THAT HAVE NO NEST.
THE PURSUIT CAN GO ON FOR A LONG TIME.
BUT TIME'S SOMETHING WE DON'T HAVE.
WE DON'T KNOW ANYTHING ABOUT THE INSIDE OF THE NEST OR THEIR NUMBERS. PLUS, THOSE ADVENTURERS COULD STILL BE ALIVE.
GASA (RUSTLE)
BUT NO VILLAGERS HAVE BEEN KIDNAPPED. A SMALL BLESSING.
THE HUNTER IDENTIFIED THIS AS THE MOST LIKELY SPOT FOR A GOBLIN NEST.

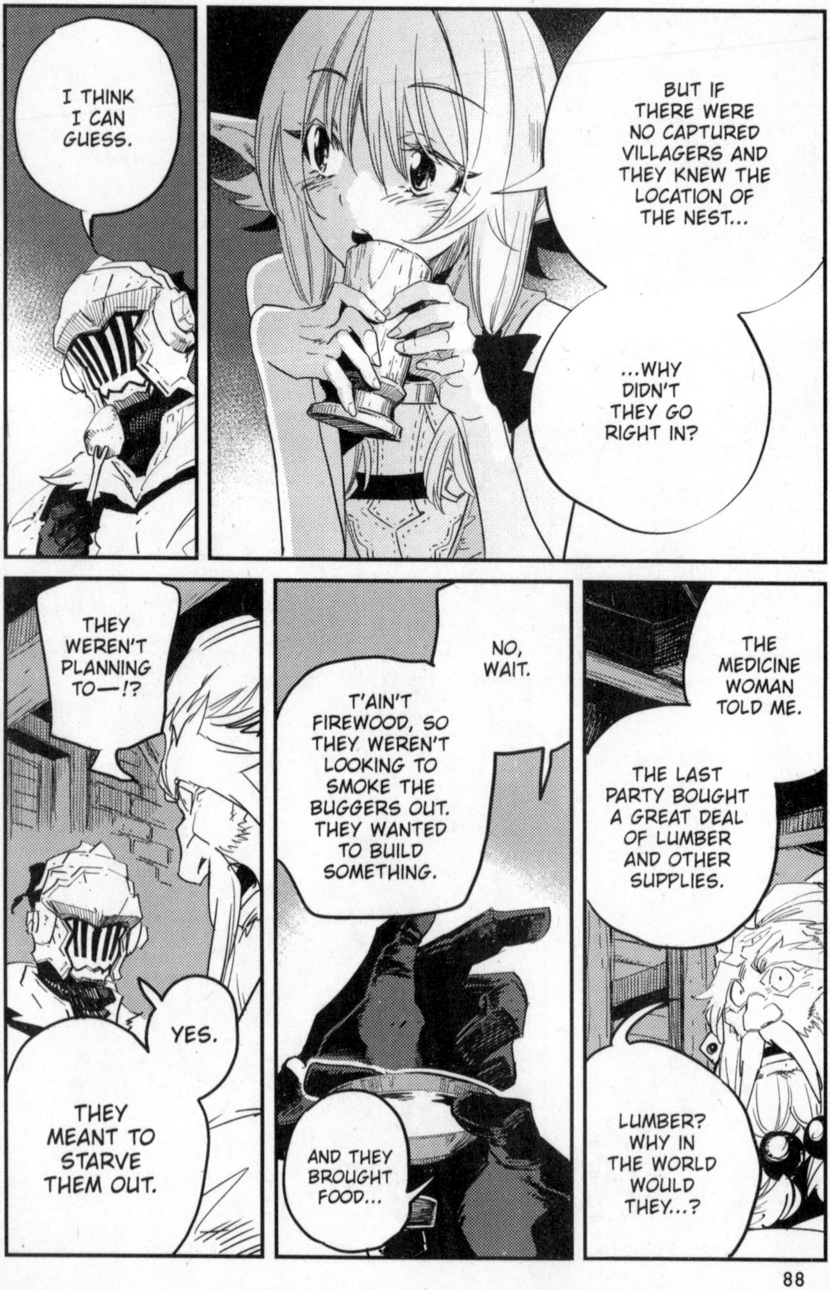
BUT IF THERE WERE NO CAPTURED VILLAGERS AND THEY KNEW THE LOCATION OF THE NEST...
...WHY DIDN'T THEY GO RIGHT IN?
I THINK I CAN GUESS.
THE MEDICINE WOMAN TOLD ME.
THE LAST PARTY BOUGHT A GREAT DEAL OF LUMBER AND OTHER SUPPLIES.
LUMBER? WHY IN THE WORLD WOULD THEY...?
NO, WAIT.
T'AIN'T FIREWOOD, SO THEY WEREN'T LOOKING TO SMOKE THE BUGGERS OUT. THEY WANTED TO BUILD SOMETHING.
AND THEY BROUGHT FOOD...
THEY WEREN'T PLANNING TO—!?
YES.
THEY MEANT TO STARVE THEM OUT.

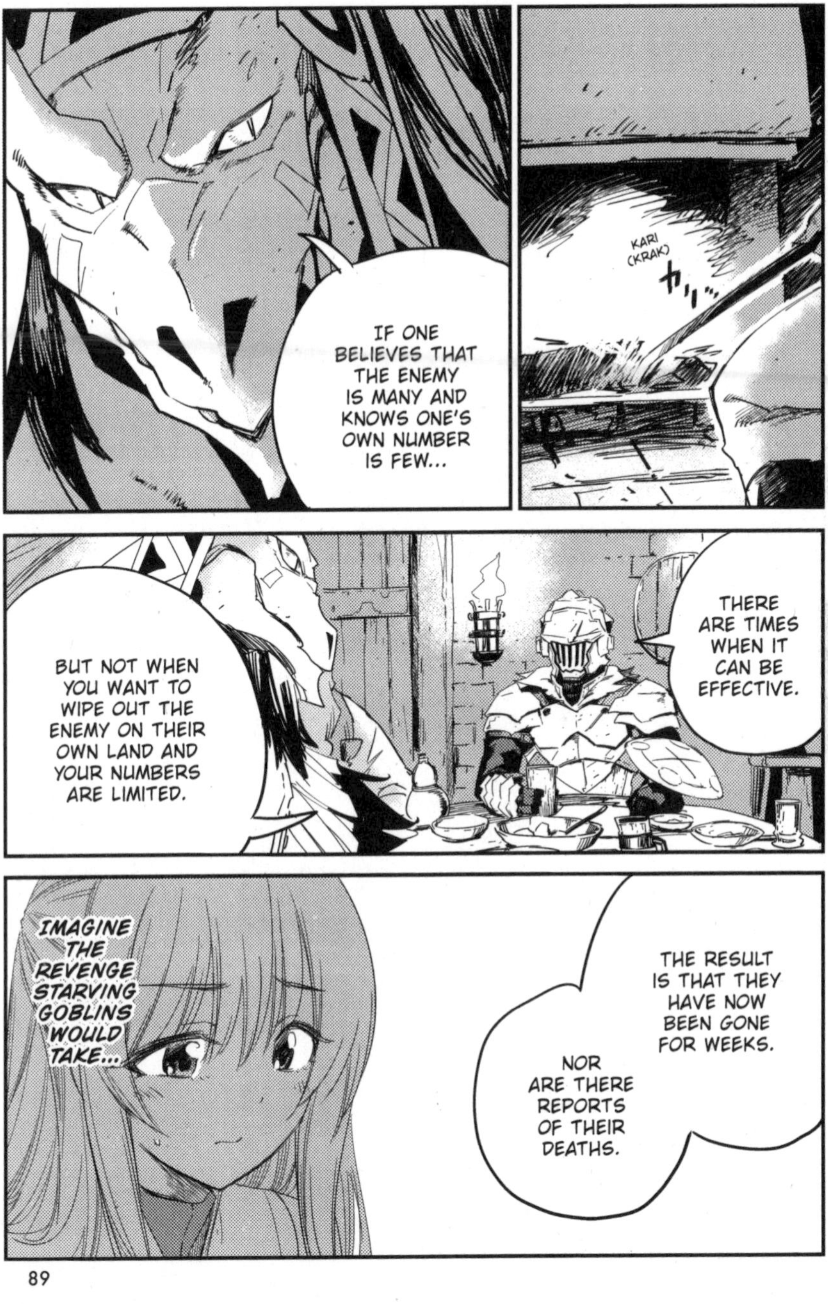
KARI (KRAK)
IF ONE BELIEVES THAT THE ENEMY IS MANY AND KNOWS ONE'S OWN NUMBER IS FEW...
THERE ARE TIMES WHEN IT CAN BE EFFECTIVE.
BUT NOT WHEN YOU WANT TO WIPE OUT THE ENEMY ON THEIR OWN LAND AND YOUR NUMBERS ARE LIMITED.
THE RESULT IS THAT THEY HAVE NOW BEEN GONE FOR WEEKS.
NOR ARE THERE REPORTS OF THEIR DEATHS.
IMAGINE THE REVENGE STARVING GOBLINS WOULD TAKE...

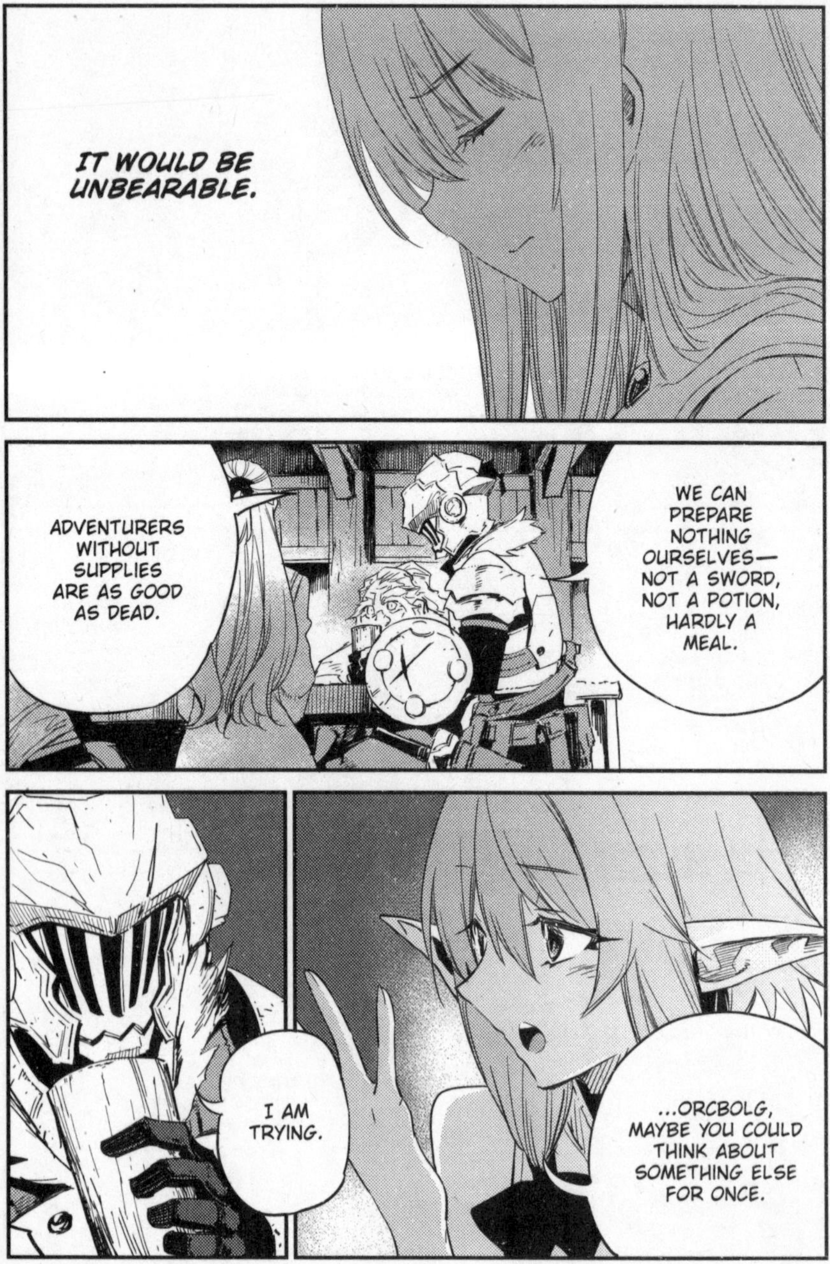
IT WOULD BE UNBEARABLE.
WE CAN PREPARE NOTHING OURSELVES—NOT A SWORD, NOT A POTION, HARDLY A MEAL.
ADVENTURERS WITHOUT SUPPLIES ARE AS GOOD AS DEAD.
...ORCBOLG, MAYBE YOU COULD THINK ABOUT SOMETHING ELSE FOR ONCE.
I AM TRYING.

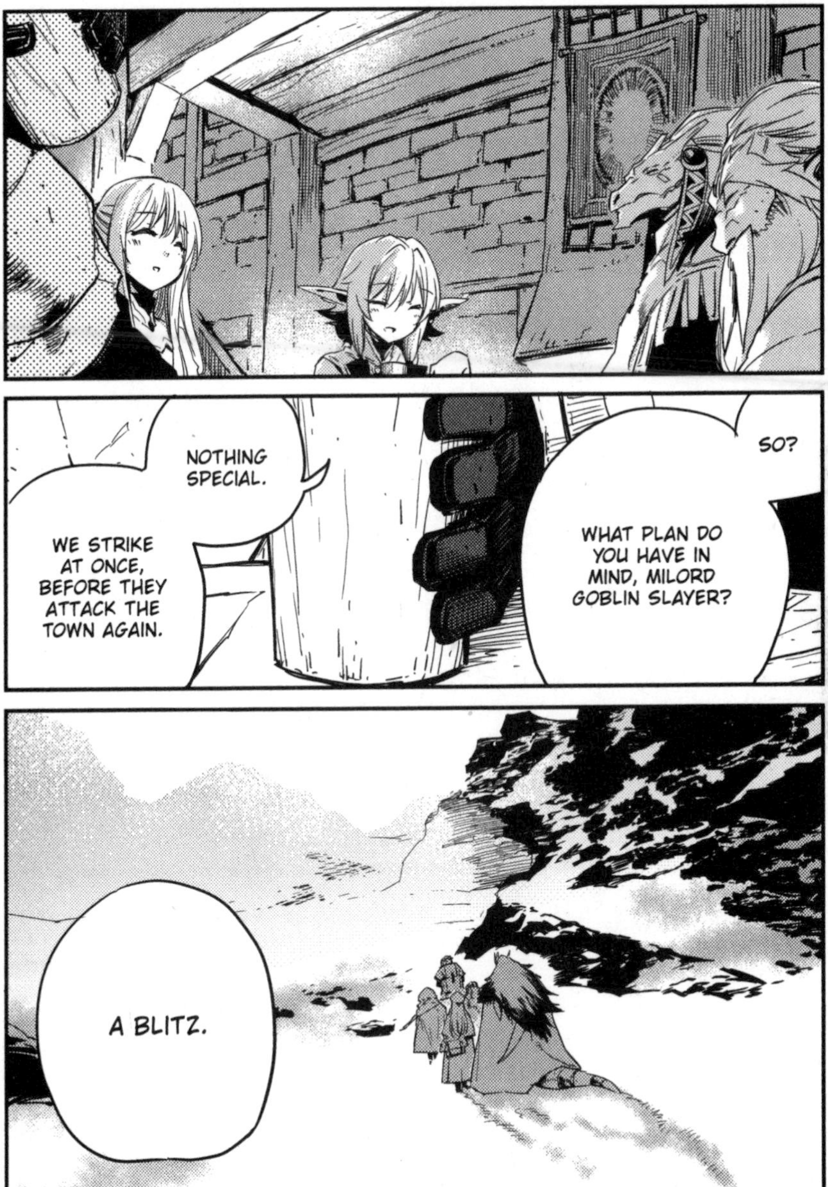
SO?
WHAT PLAN DO YOU HAVE IN MIND, MILORD GOBLIN SLAYER?
NOTHING SPECIAL.
WE STRIKE AT ONCE, BEFORE THEY ATTACK THE TOWN AGAIN.
A BLITZ.

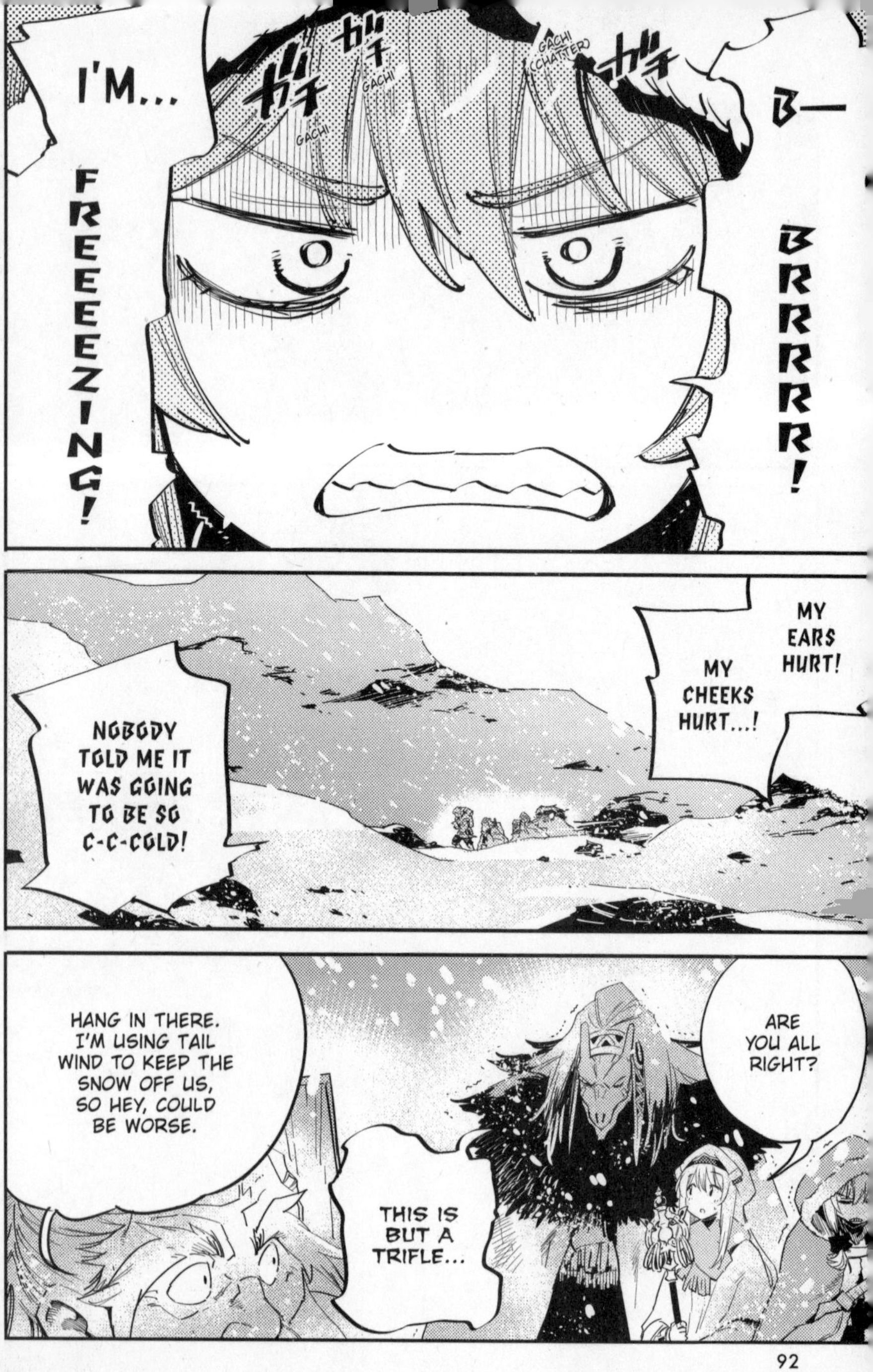
B—
BRRRRRR!
GACHI (CHATTER)
GACHI
GACHI
I'M...
FREEEEZING!
MY EARS HURT!
MY CHEEKS HURT...!
NOBODY TOLD ME IT WAS GOING TO BE SO C-C-COLD!
ARE YOU ALL RIGHT?
HANG IN THERE. I'M USING TAIL WIND TO KEEP THE SNOW OFF US, SO HEY, COULD BE WORSE.
THIS IS BUT A TRIFLE...

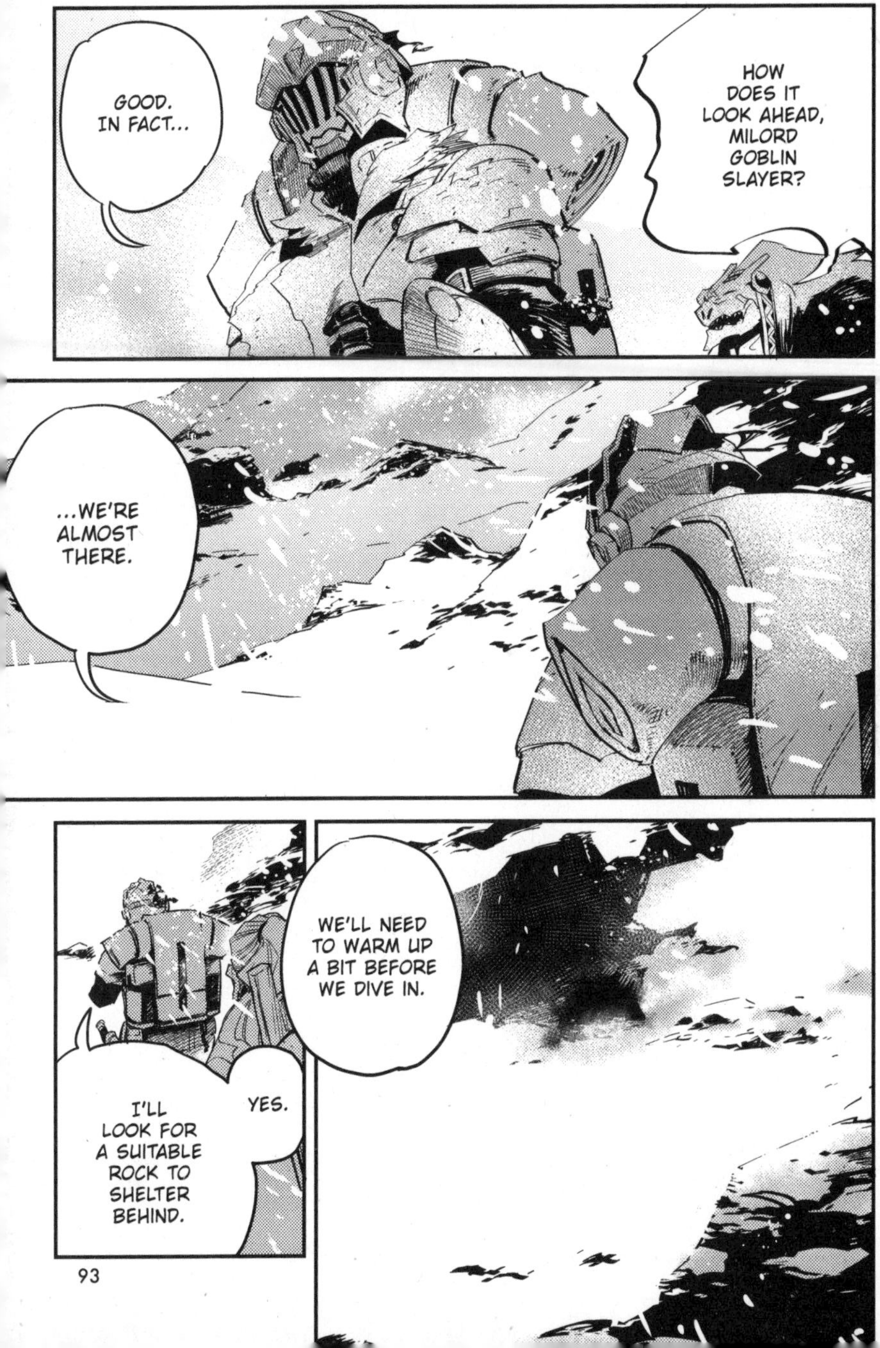
HOW DOES IT LOOK AHEAD, MILORD GOBLIN SLAYER?
GOOD. IN FACT...
...WE'RE ALMOST THERE.
WE'LL NEED TO WARM UP A BIT BEFORE WE DIVE IN.
YES.
I'LL LOOK FOR A SUITABLE ROCK TO SHELTER BEHIND.

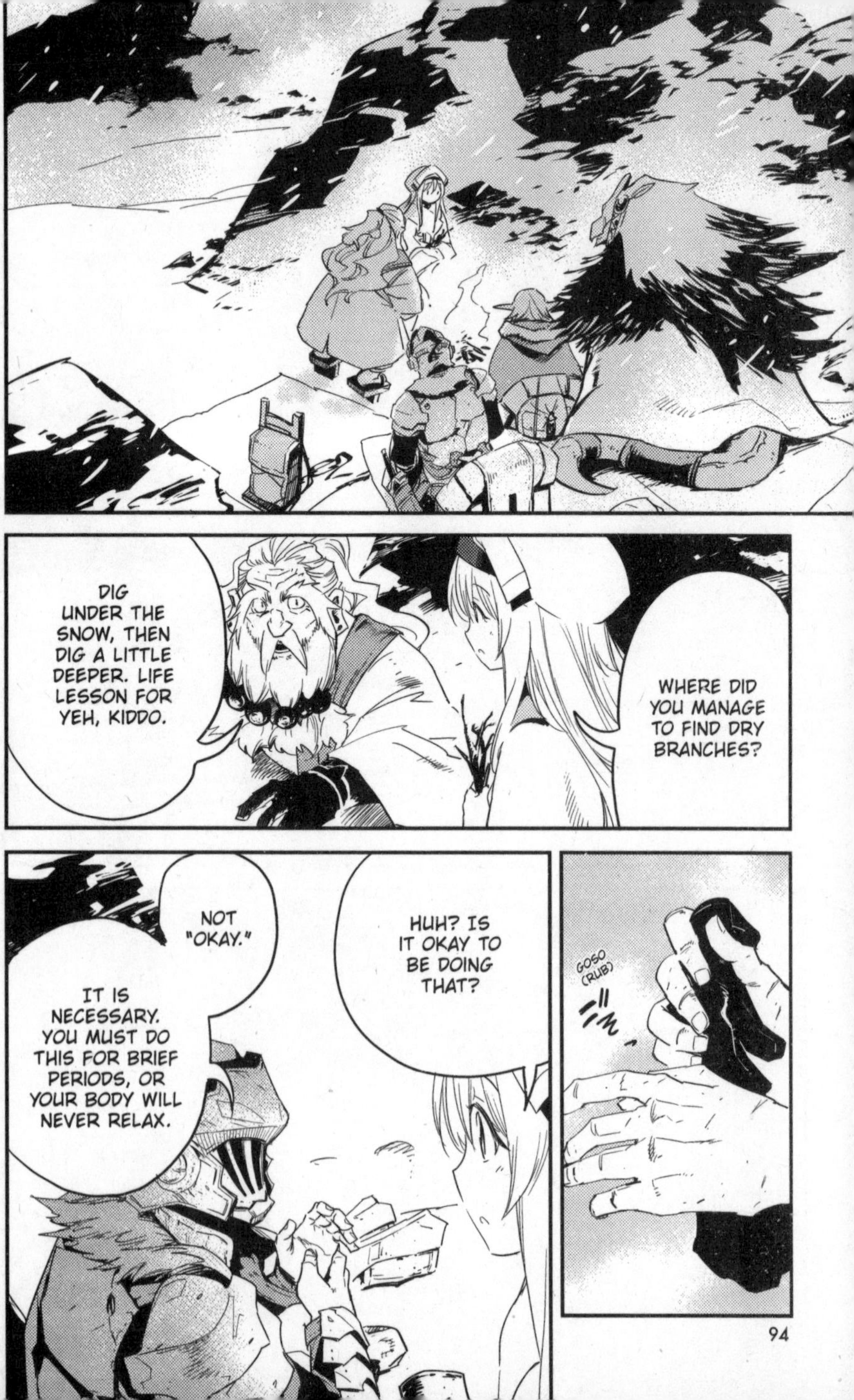
WHERE DID YOU MANAGE TO FIND DRY BRANCHES?
DIG UNDER THE SNOW, THEN DIG A LITTLE DEEPER. LIFE LESSON FOR YEH, KIDDO.
GOSO (RUB)
HUH? IS IT OKAY TO BE DOING THAT?
NOT "OKAY."
IT IS NECESSARY. YOU MUST DO THIS FOR BRIEF PERIODS, OR YOUR BODY WILL NEVER RELAX.

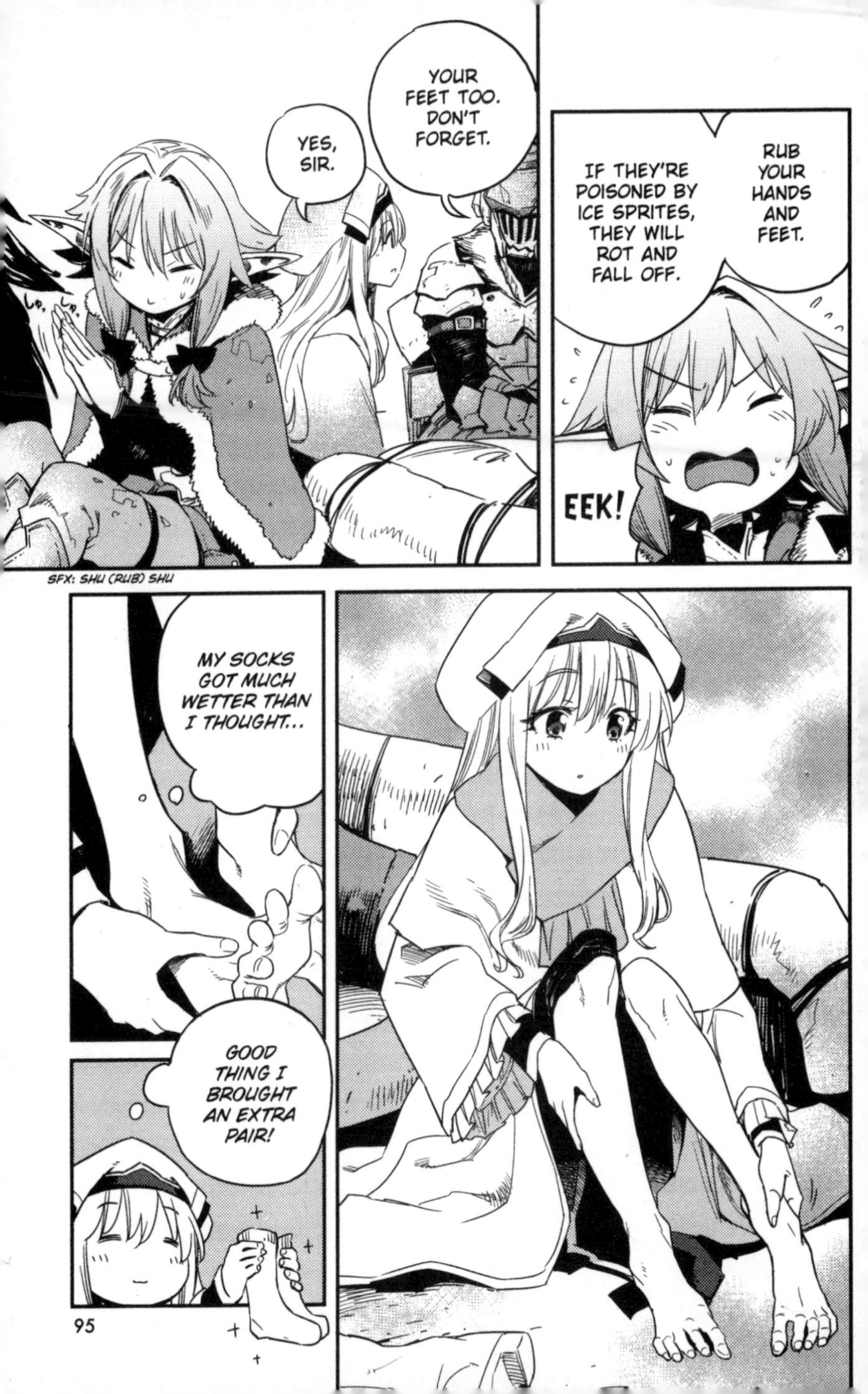
RUB YOUR HANDS AND FEET.
IF THEY'RE POISONED BY ICE SPRITES, THEY WILL ROT AND FALL OFF.
EEK!
YOUR FEET TOO. DON'T FORGET.
YES, SIR.
SFX: SHU (RUB) SHU
MY SOCKS GOT MUCH WETTER THAN I THOUGHT...
GOOD THING I BROUGHT AN EXTRA PAIR!

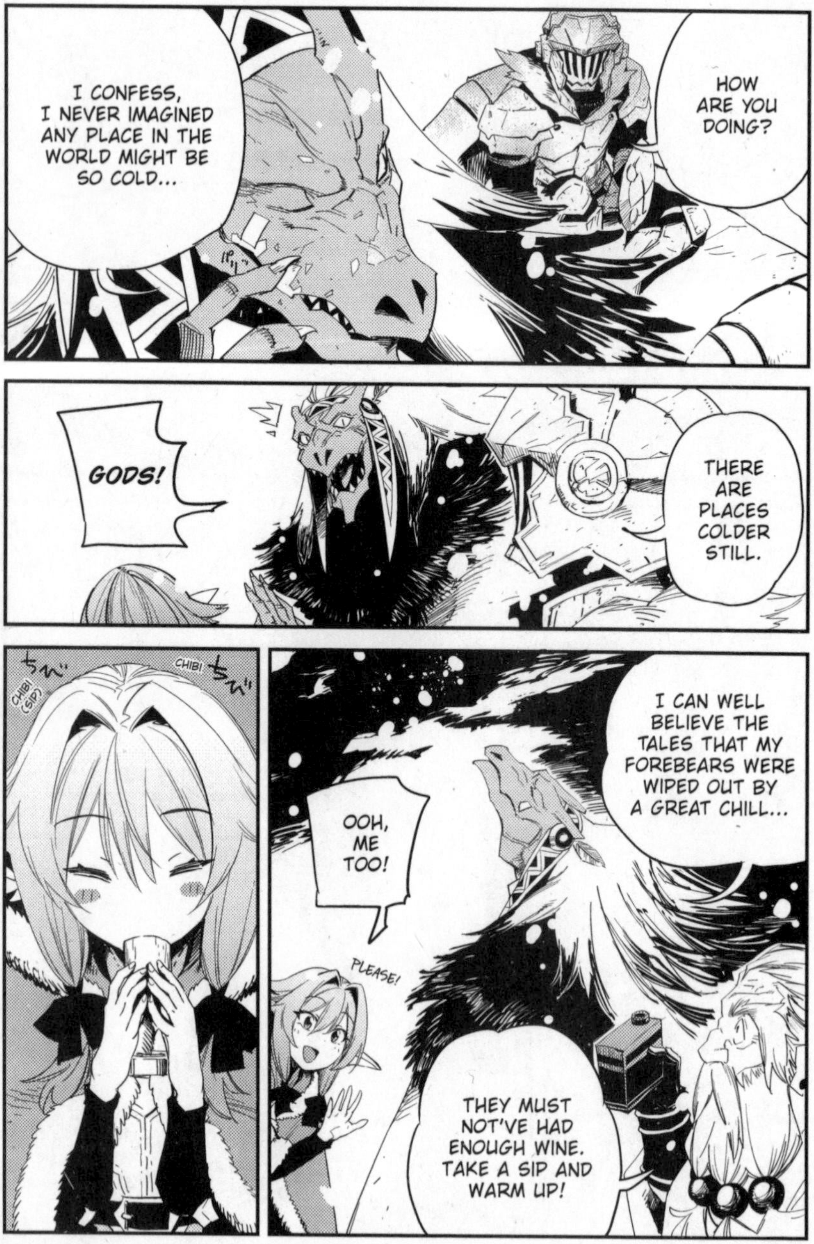
HOW ARE YOU DOING?
I CONFESS, I NEVER IMAGINED ANY PLACE IN THE WORLD MIGHT BE SO COLD...
THERE ARE PLACES COLDER STILL.
GODS!
I CAN WELL BELIEVE THE TALES THAT MY FOREBEARS WERE WIPED OUT BY A GREAT CHILL...
OOH, ME TOO!
PLEASE!
THEY MUST NOT'VE HAD ENOUGH WINE. TAKE A SIP AND WARM UP!
CHIBI
CHIBI (SIP)

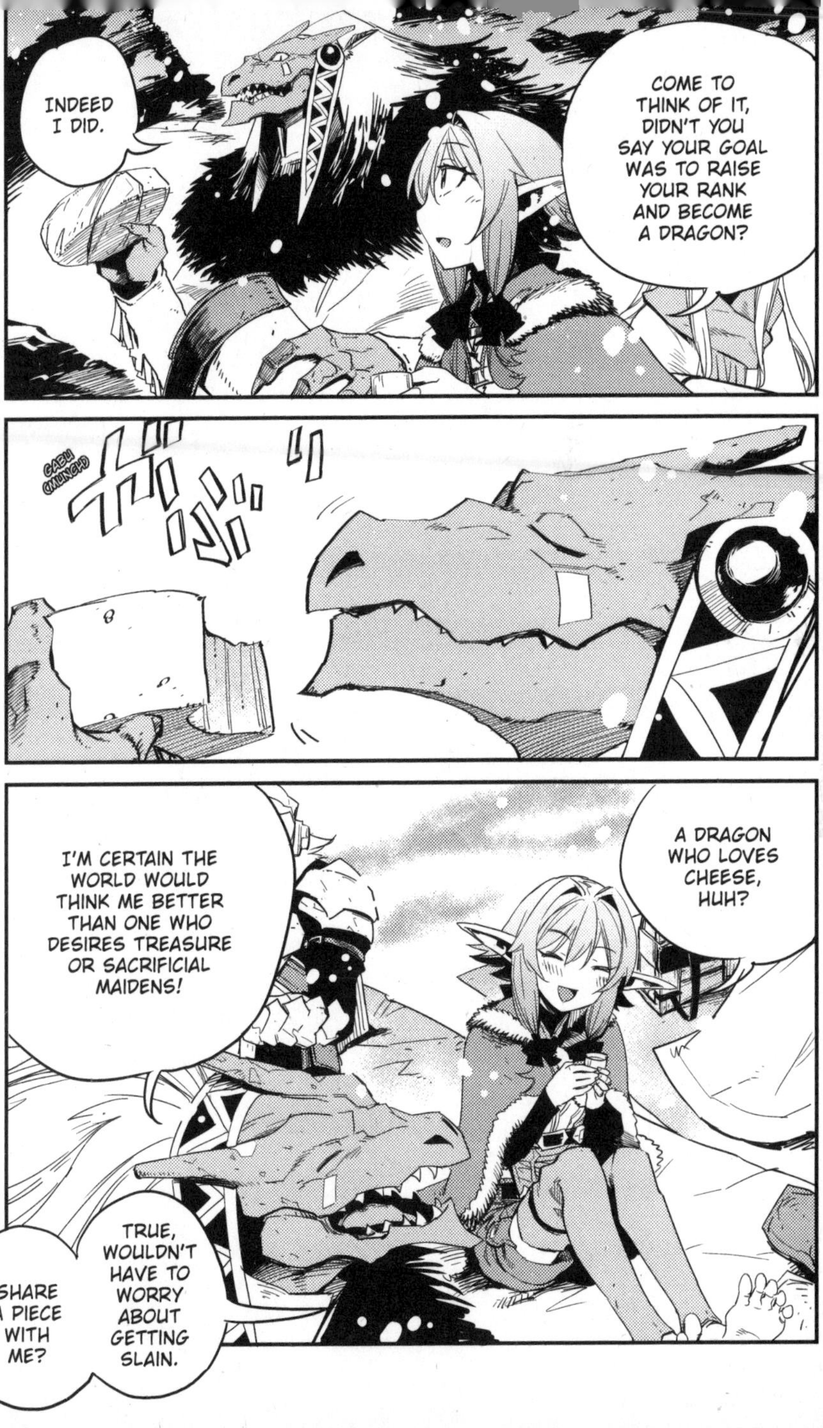
COME TO THINK OF IT, DIDN'T YOU SAY YOUR GOAL WAS TO RAISE YOUR RANK AND BECOME A DRAGON?
INDEED I DID.
GABU (MUNCH)
A DRAGON WHO LOVES CHEESE, HUH?
I'M CERTAIN THE WORLD WOULD THINK ME BETTER THAN ONE WHO DESIRES TREASURE OR SACRIFICIAL MAIDENS!
TRUE, WOULDN'T HAVE TO WORRY ABOUT GETTING SLAIN.
SHARE A PIECE WITH ME?

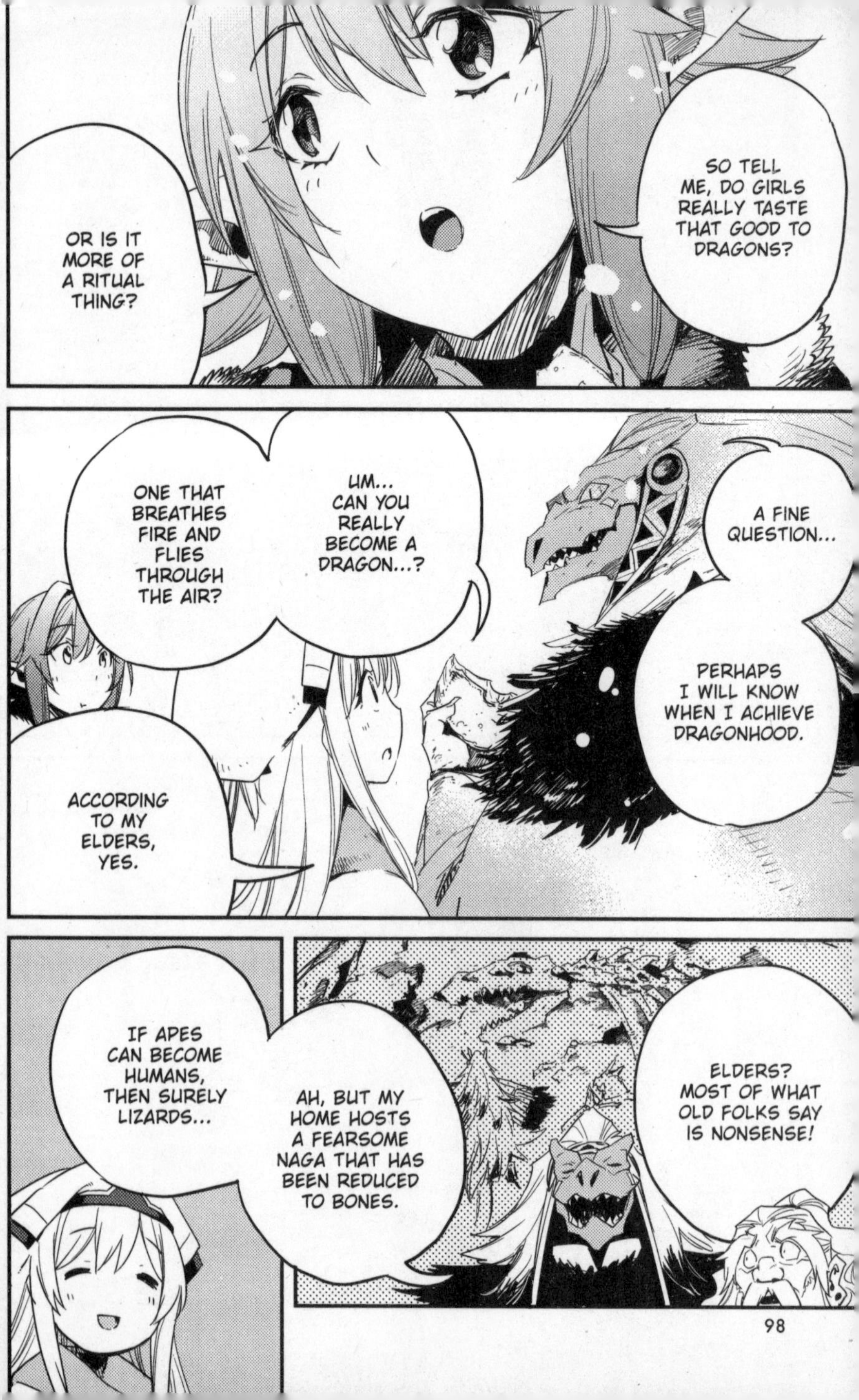
SO TELL ME, DO GIRLS REALLY TASTE THAT GOOD TO DRAGONS?
OR IS IT MORE OF A RITUAL THING?
A FINE QUESTION...
PERHAPS I WILL KNOW WHEN I ACHIEVE DRAGONHOOD.
UM... CAN YOU REALLY BECOME A DRAGON...?
ONE THAT BREATHES FIRE AND FLIES THROUGH THE AIR?
ACCORDING TO MY ELDERS, YES.
ELDERS? MOST OF WHAT OLD FOLKS SAY IS NONSENSE!
AH, BUT MY HOME HOSTS A FEARSOME NAGA THAT HAS BEEN REDUCED TO BONES.
IF APES CAN BECOME HUMANS, THEN SURELY LIZARDS...

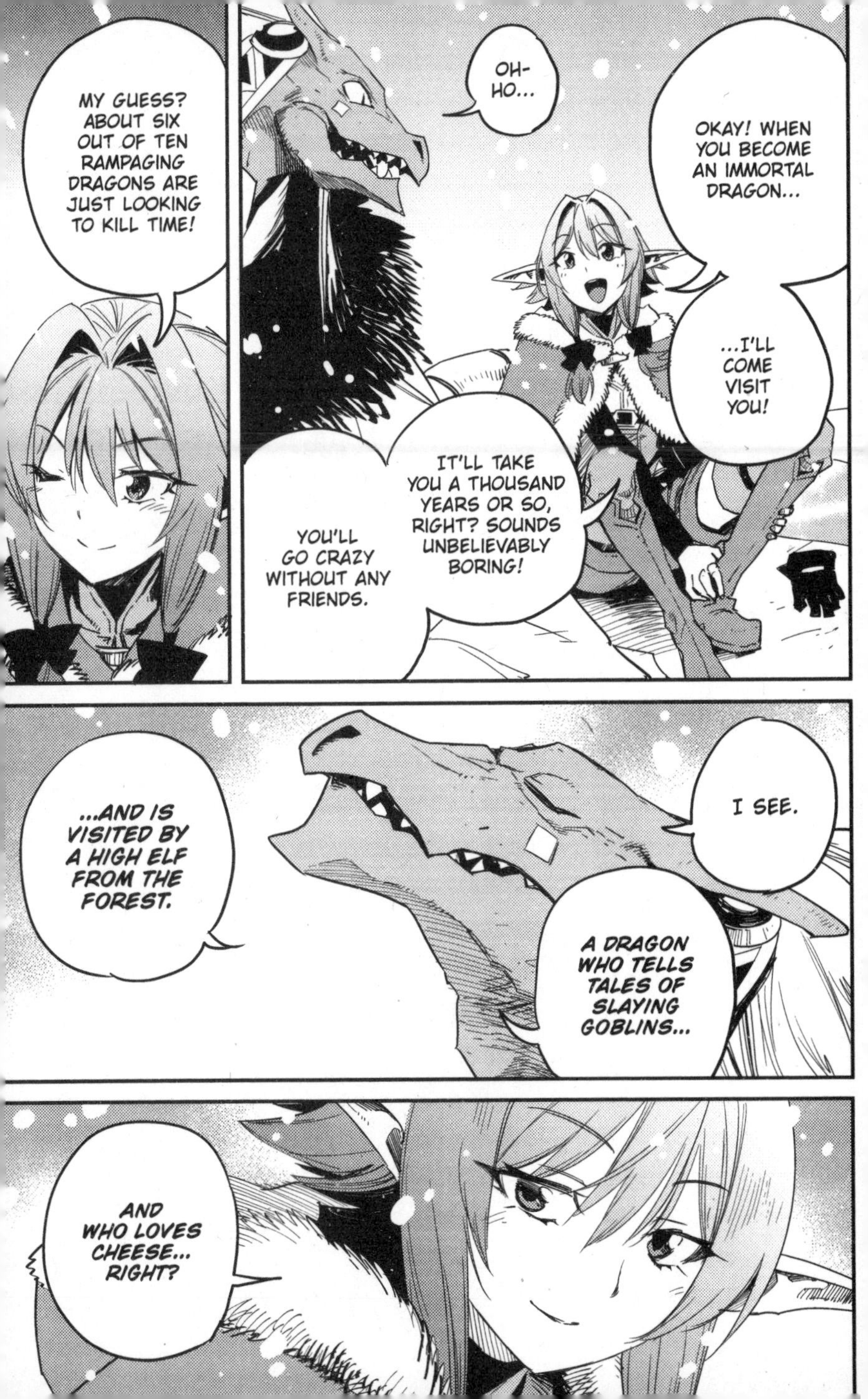
OKAY! WHEN YOU BECOME AN IMMORTAL DRAGON...
...I'LL COME VISIT YOU!
IT'LL TAKE YOU A THOUSAND YEARS OR SO, RIGHT? SOUNDS UNBELIEVABLY BORING!
YOU'LL GO CRAZY WITHOUT ANY FRIENDS.
OH-HO...
MY GUESS? ABOUT SIX OUT OF TEN RAMPAGING DRAGONS ARE JUST LOOKING TO KILL TIME!
I SEE.
A DRAGON WHO TELLS TALES OF SLAYING GOBLINS...
...AND IS VISITED BY A HIGH ELF FROM THE FOREST.
AND WHO LOVES CHEESE... RIGHT?

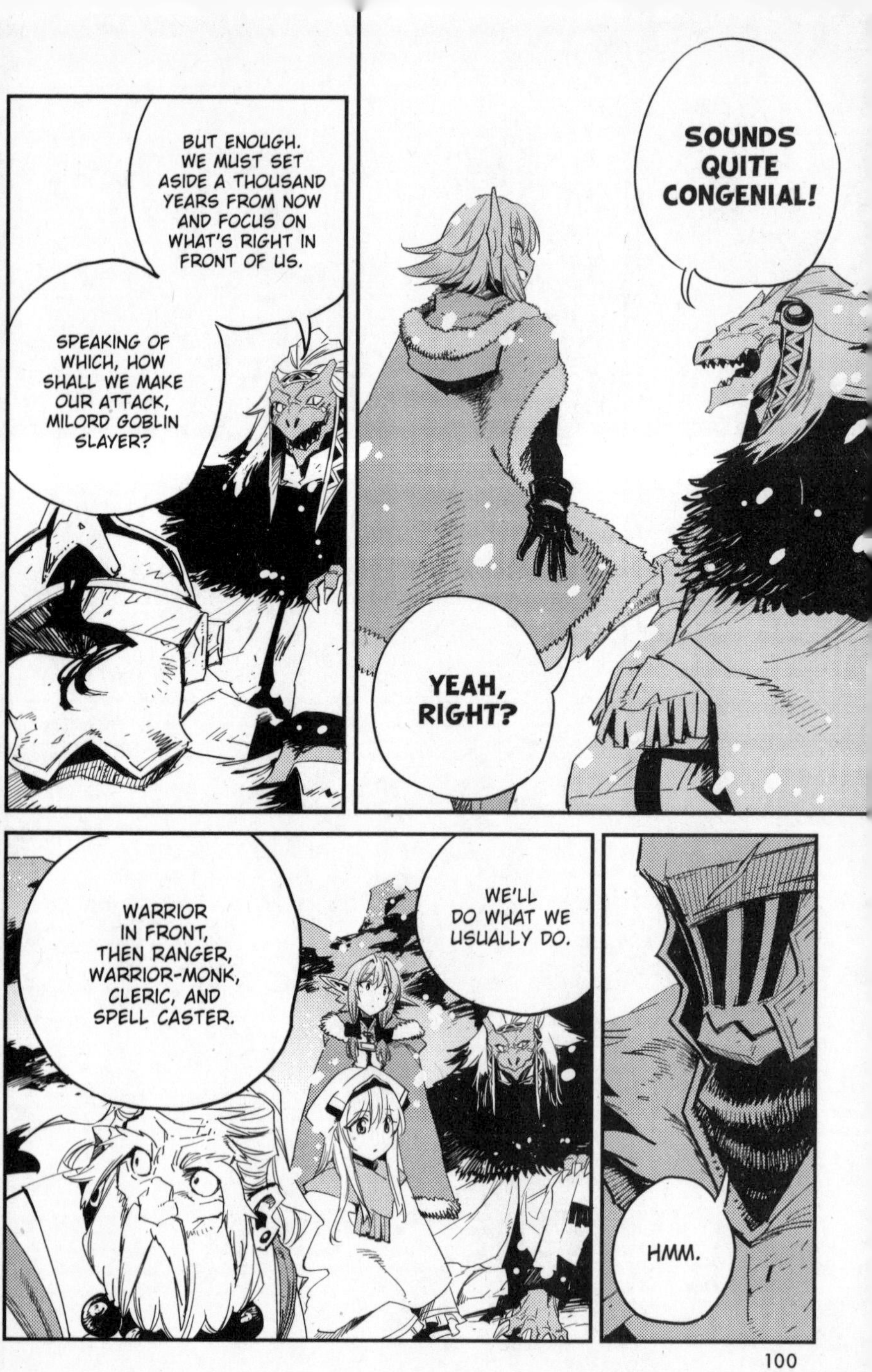
SOUNDS QUITE CONGENIAL!
YEAH, RIGHT?
BUT ENOUGH. WE MUST SET ASIDE A THOUSAND YEARS FROM NOW AND FOCUS ON WHAT'S RIGHT IN FRONT OF US.
SPEAKING OF WHICH, HOW SHALL WE MAKE OUR ATTACK, MILORD GOBLIN SLAYER?
HMM.
WE'LL DO WHAT WE USUALLY DO.
WARRIOR IN FRONT, THEN RANGER, WARRIOR-MONK, CLERIC, AND SPELL CASTER.

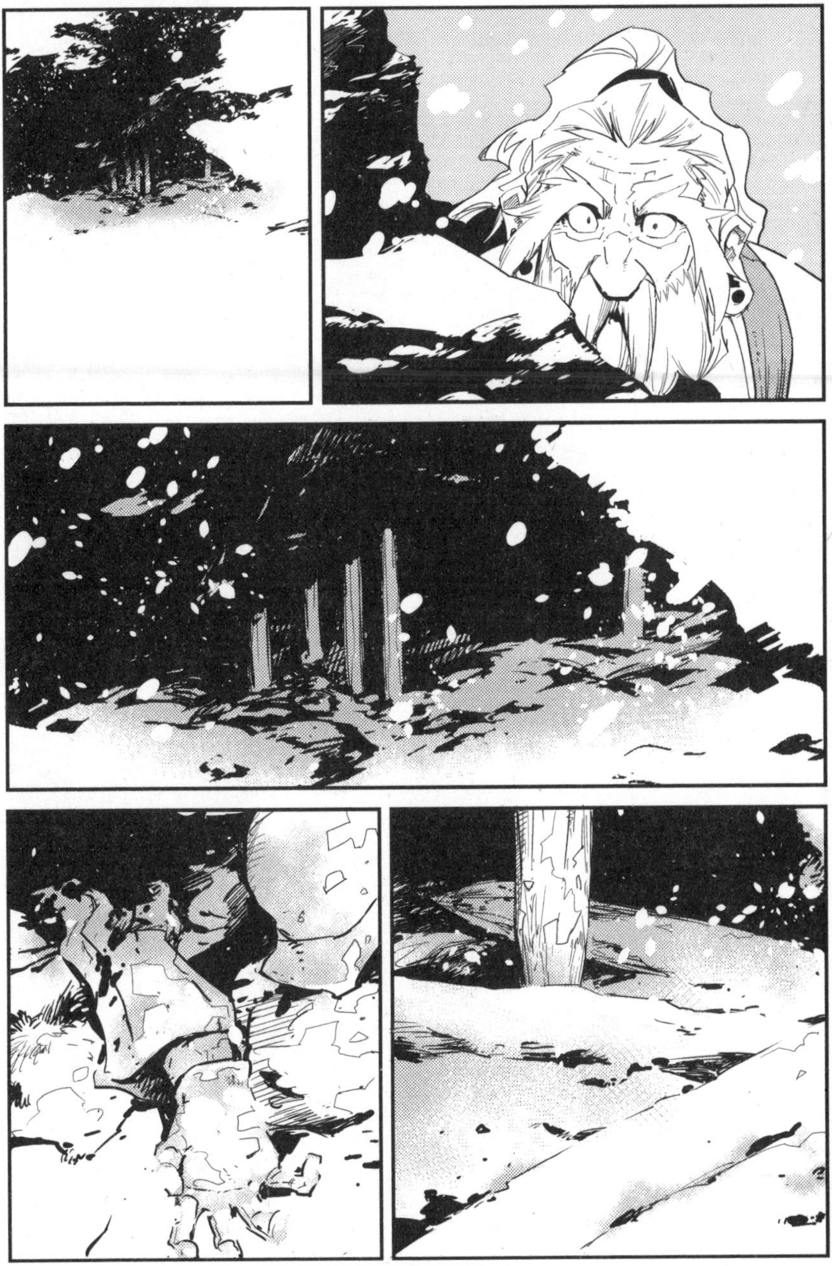

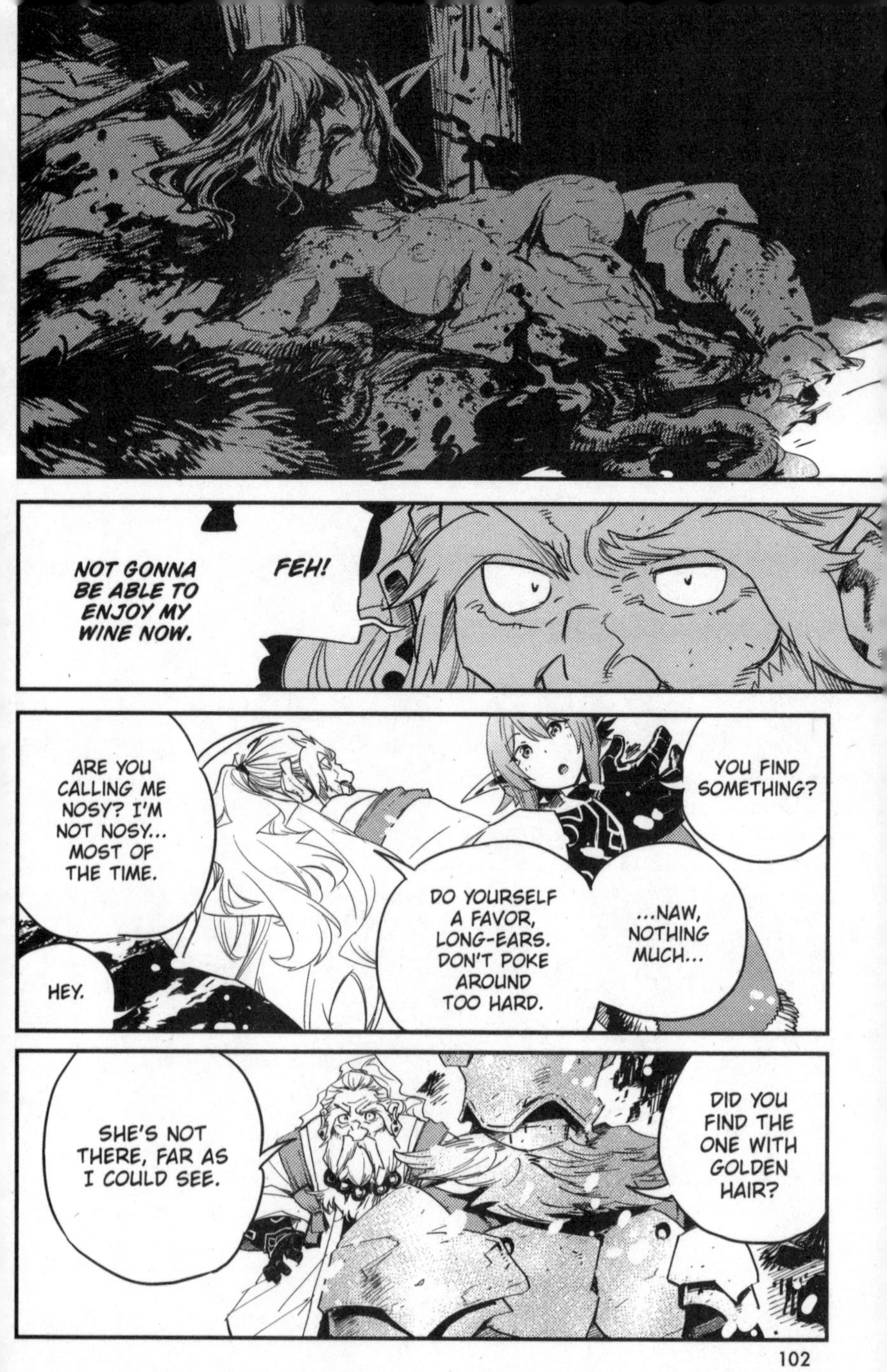
FEH!
NOT GONNA BE ABLE TO ENJOY MY WINE NOW.
YOU FIND SOMETHING?
...NAW, NOTHING MUCH...
DO YOURSELF A FAVOR, LONG-EARS. DON'T POKE AROUND TOO HARD.
ARE YOU CALLING ME NOSY? I'M NOT NOSY... MOST OF THE TIME.
HEY.
DID YOU FIND THE ONE WITH GOLDEN HAIR?
SHE'S NOT THERE, FAR AS I COULD SEE.

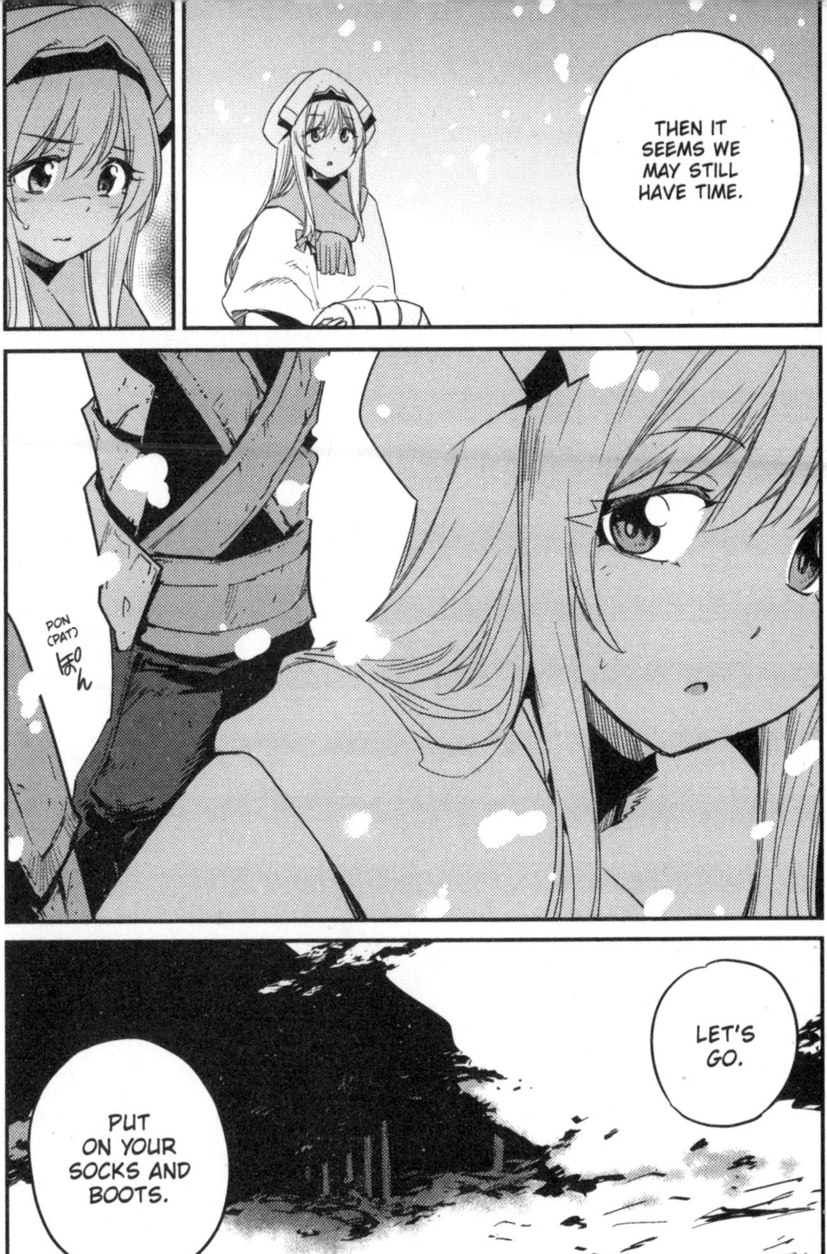
THEN IT SEEMS WE MAY STILL HAVE TIME.
PON (PAT)
ぽん
LET'S GO.
PUT ON YOUR SOCKS AND BOOTS.

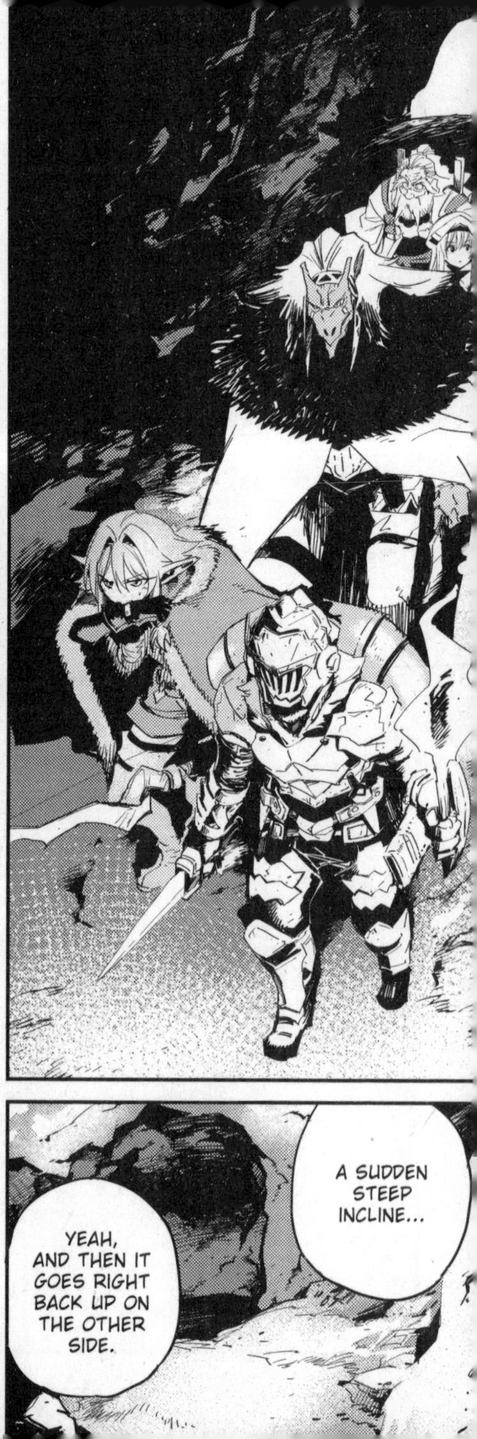
A SUDDEN STEEP INCLINE...
YEAH, AND THEN IT GOES RIGHT BACK UP ON THE OTHER SIDE.

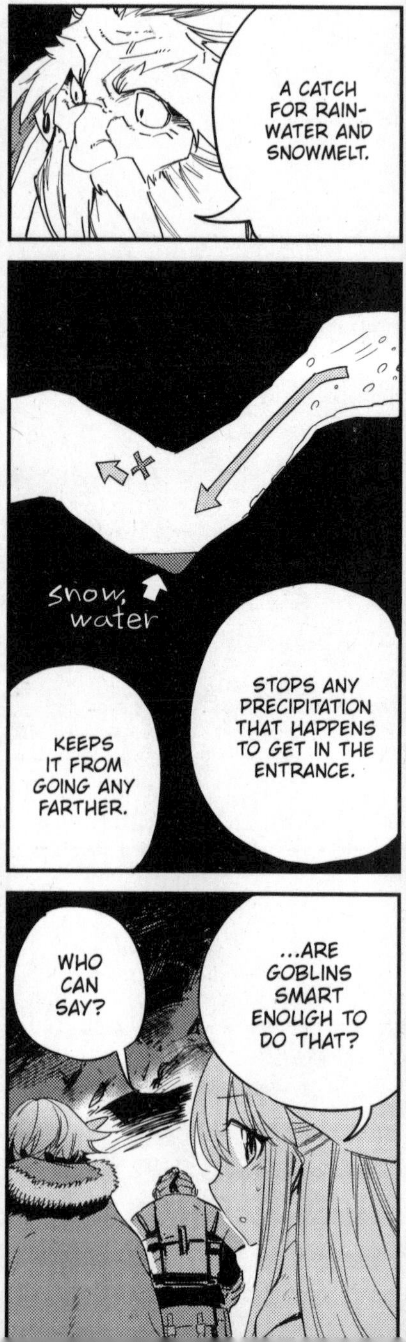
A CATCH FOR RAIN-WATER AND SNOWMELT.
snow, water
STOPS ANY PRECIPITATION THAT HAPPENS TO GET IN THE ENTRANCE.
KEEPS IT FROM GOING ANY FARTHER.
...ARE GOBLINS SMART ENOUGH TO DO THAT?
WHO CAN SAY?

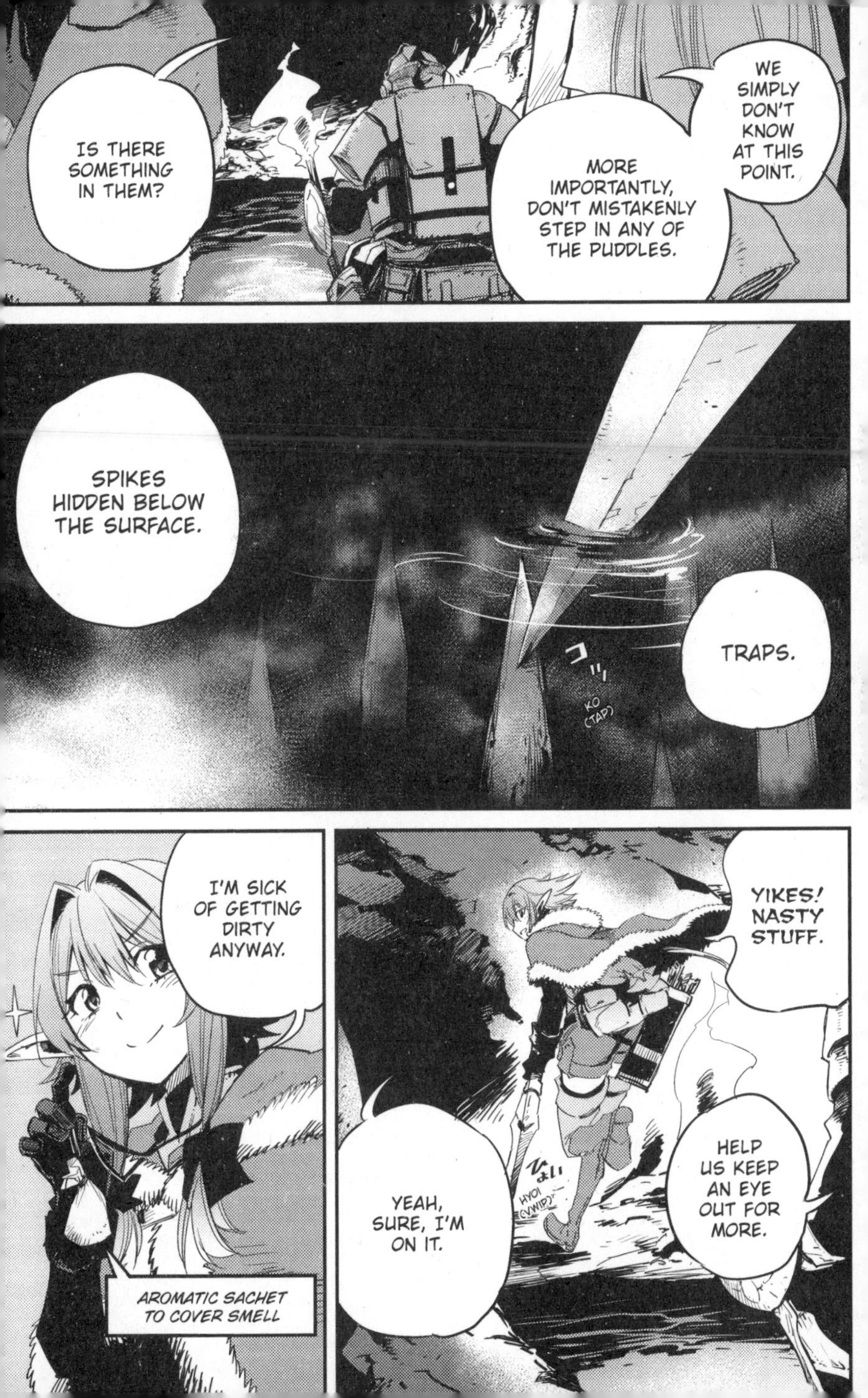
WE SIMPLY DON'T KNOW AT THIS POINT.
MORE IMPORTANTLY, DON'T MISTAKENLY STEP IN ANY OF THE PUDDLES.
IS THERE SOMETHING IN THEM?
TRAPS.
KO (TAP)
SPIKES HIDDEN BELOW THE SURFACE.
YIKES! NASTY STUFF.
HELP US KEEP AN EYE OUT FOR MORE.
HYOI (VWIP)
YEAH, SURE, I'M ON IT.
I'M SICK OF GETTING DIRTY ANYWAY.
AROMATIC SACHET TO COVER SMELL

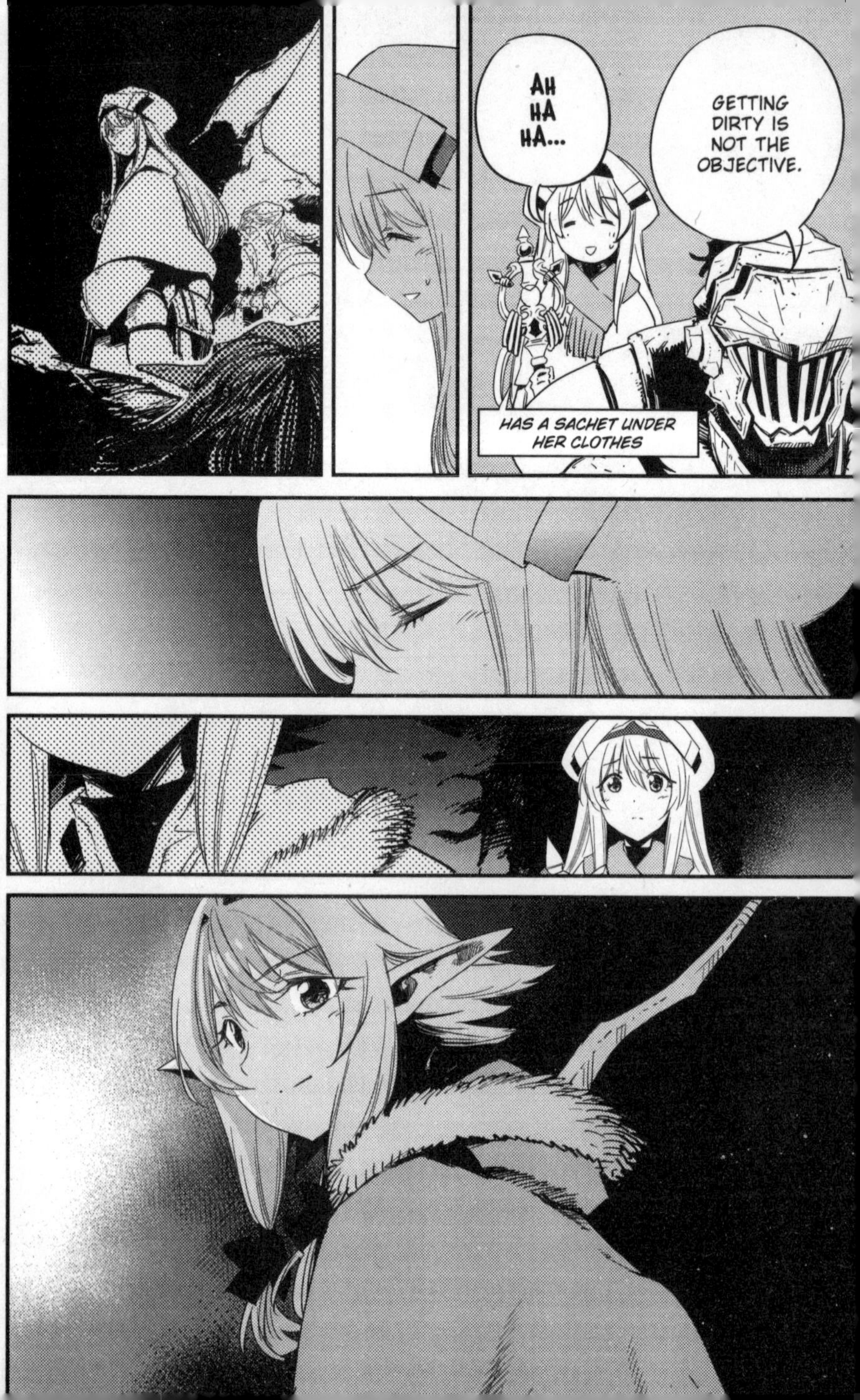
GETTING DIRTY IS NOT THE OBJECTIVE.
AH HA HA...
HAS A SACHET UNDER HER CLOTHES

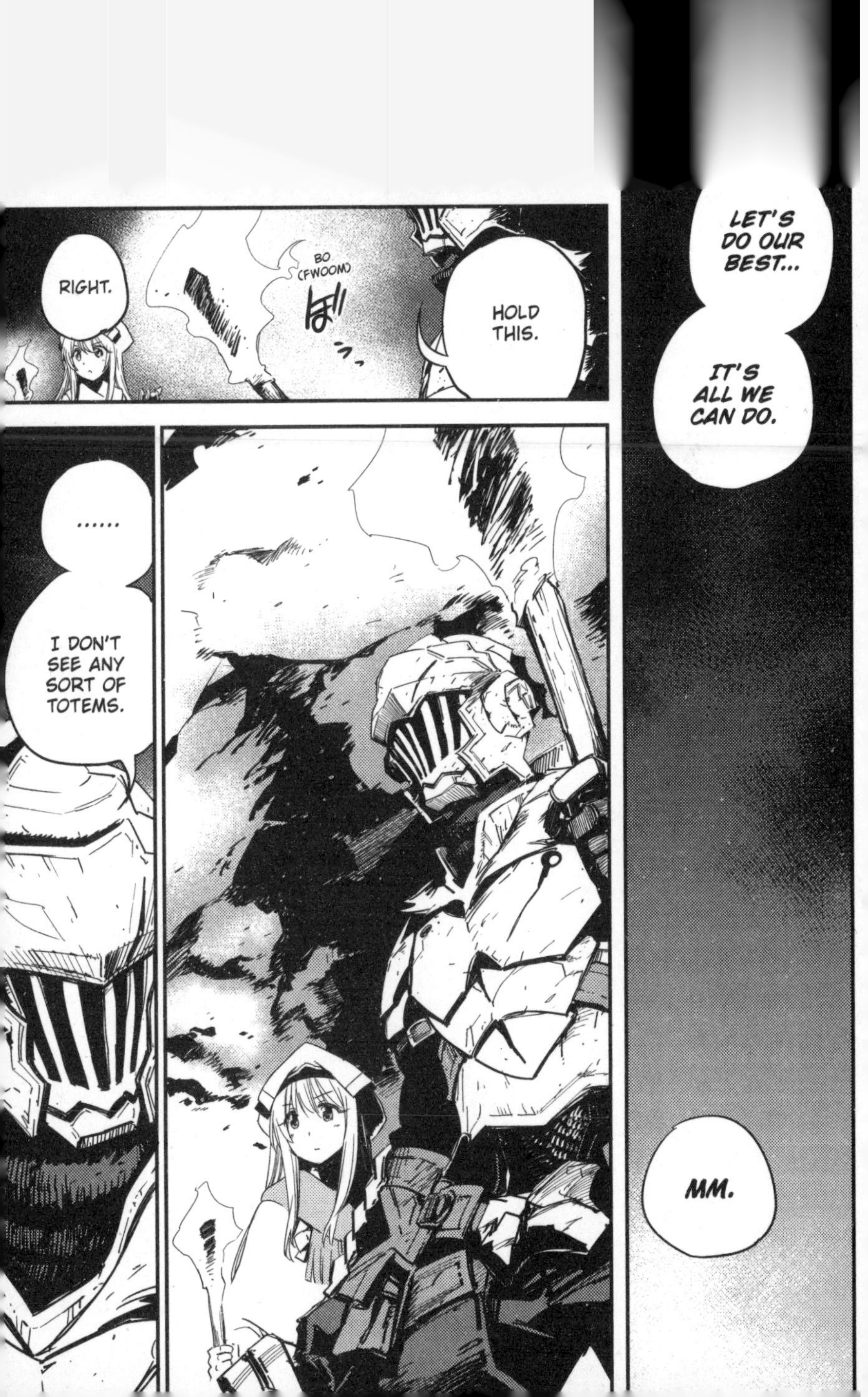
LET'S DO OUR BEST...
IT'S ALL WE CAN DO.
MM.
HOLD THIS.
BO (FWOOM)
RIGHT.
......
I DON'T SEE ANY SORT OF TOTEMS.

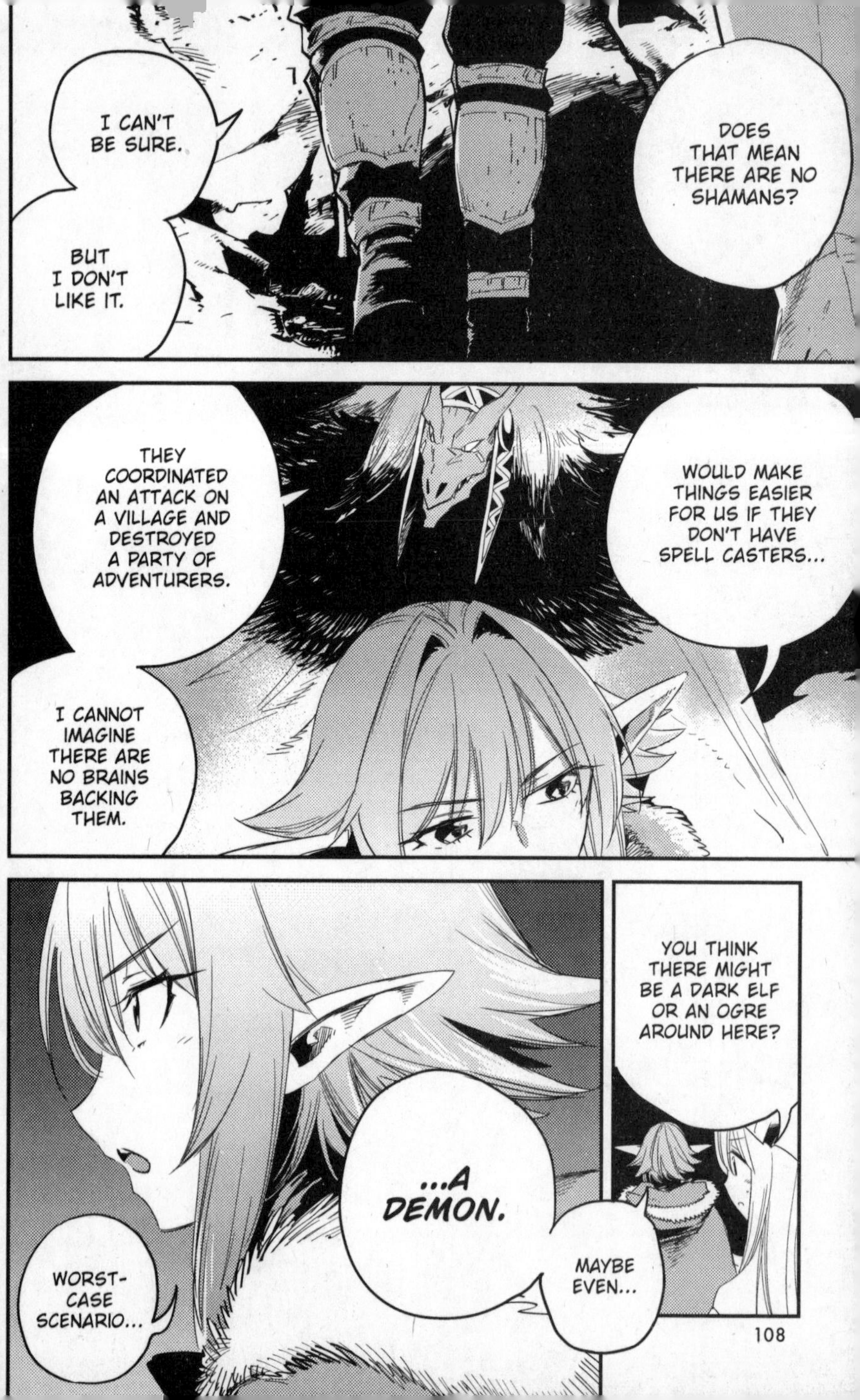
DOES THAT MEAN THERE ARE NO SHAMANS?
I CAN'T BE SURE.
BUT I DON'T LIKE IT.
WOULD MAKE THINGS EASIER FOR US IF THEY DON'T HAVE SPELL CASTERS...
THEY COORDINATED AN ATTACK ON A VILLAGE AND DESTROYED A PARTY OF ADVENTURERS.
I CANNOT IMAGINE THERE ARE NO BRAINS BACKING THEM.
YOU THINK THERE MIGHT BE A DARK ELF OR AN OGRE AROUND HERE?
MAYBE EVEN...
...A DEMON.
WORST-CASE SCENARIO...

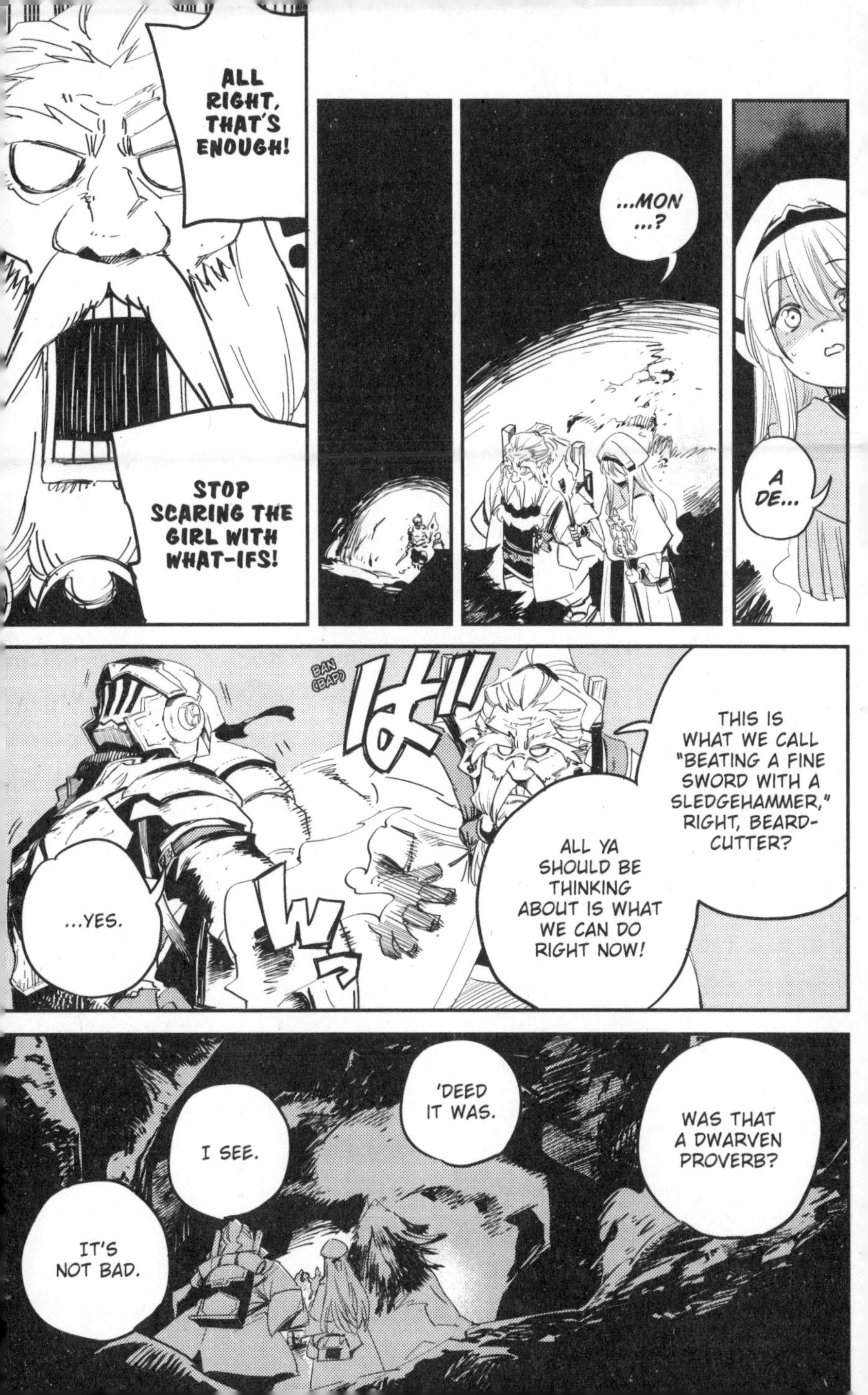
A DE...
...MON ...?
ALL RIGHT, THAT'S ENOUGH!
STOP SCARING THE GIRL WITH WHAT-IFS!
THIS IS WHAT WE CALL "BEATING A FINE SWORD WITH A SLEDGEHAMMER," RIGHT, BEARD-CUTTER?
ALL YA SHOULD BE THINKING ABOUT IS WHAT WE CAN DO RIGHT NOW!
BAN (BAP)
...YES.
WAS THAT A DWARVEN PROVERB?
'DEED IT WAS.
I SEE.
IT'S NOT BAD.

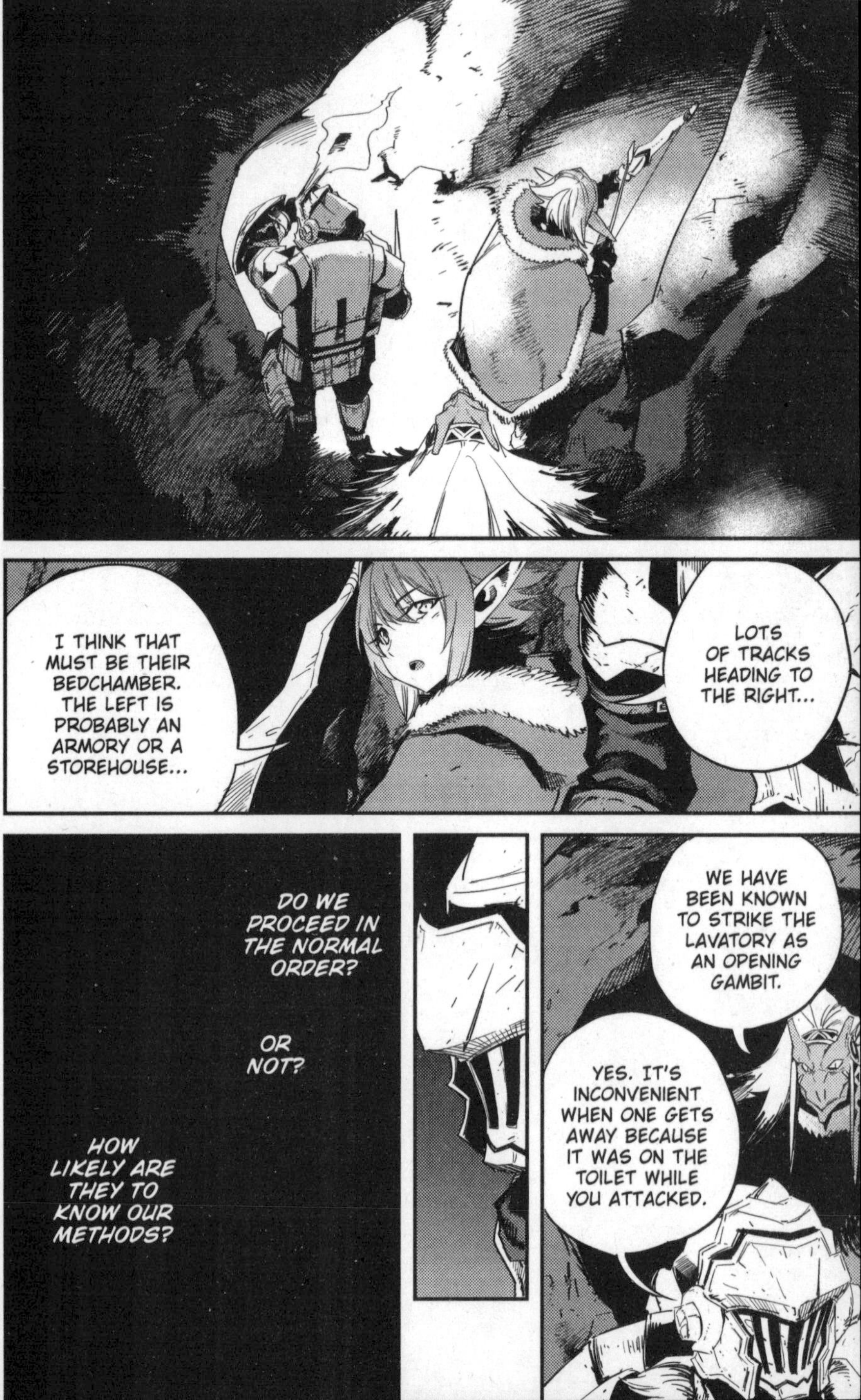
LOTS OF TRACKS HEADING TO THE RIGHT...
I THINK THAT MUST BE THEIR BEDCHAMBER. THE LEFT IS PROBABLY AN ARMORY OR A STOREHOUSE...
WE HAVE BEEN KNOWN TO STRIKE THE LAVATORY AS AN OPENING GAMBIT.
YES. IT'S INCONVENIENT WHEN ONE GETS AWAY BECAUSE IT WAS ON THE TOILET WHILE YOU ATTACKED.
DO WE PROCEED IN THE NORMAL ORDER?
OR NOT?
HOW LIKELY ARE THEY TO KNOW OUR METHODS?

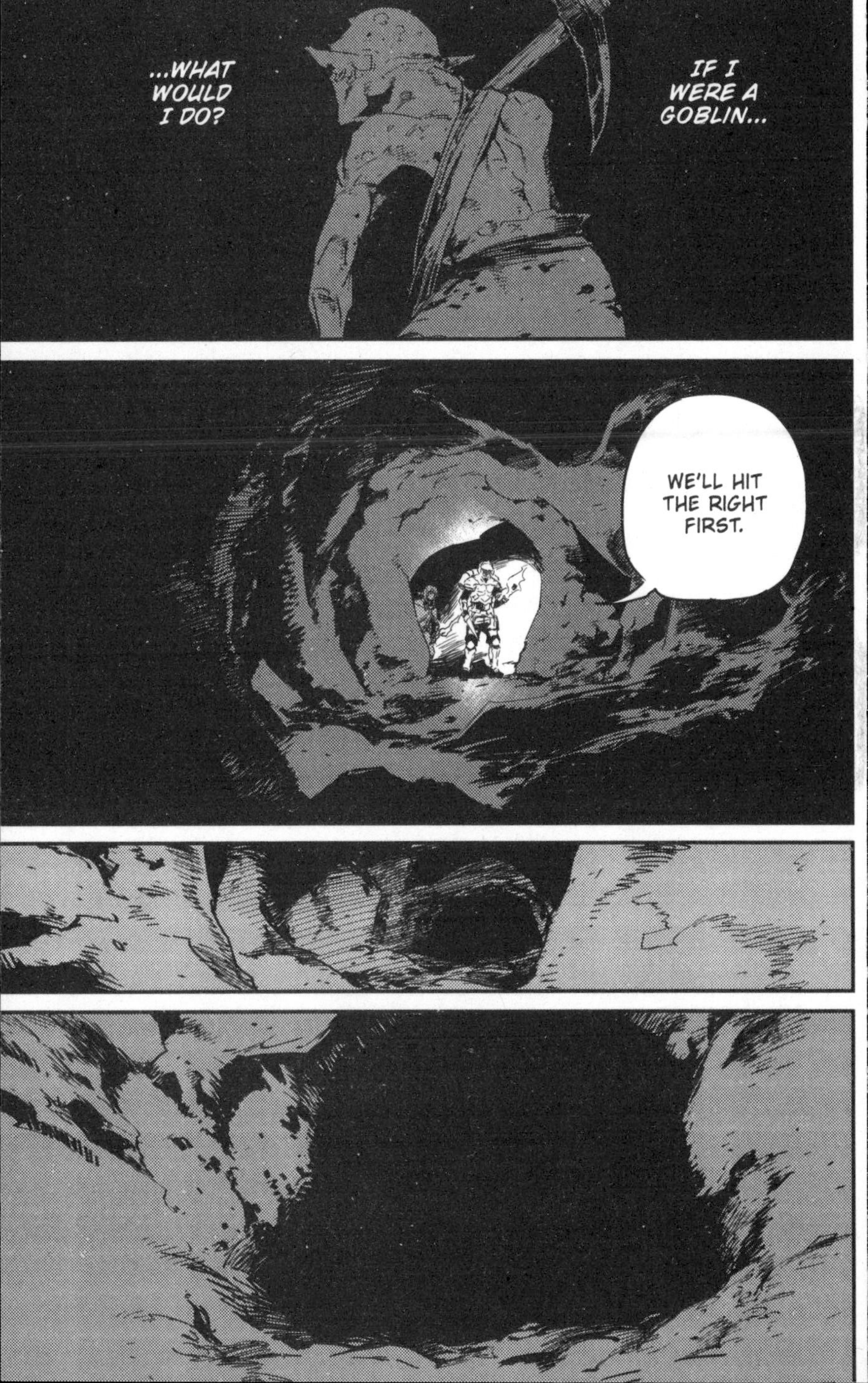
IF I WERE A GOBLIN...
...WHAT WOULD I DO?
WE'LL HIT THE RIGHT FIRST.

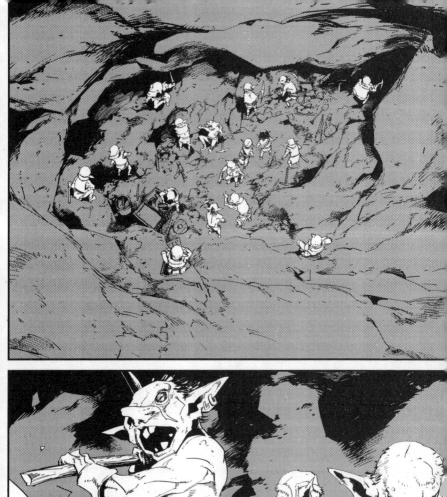

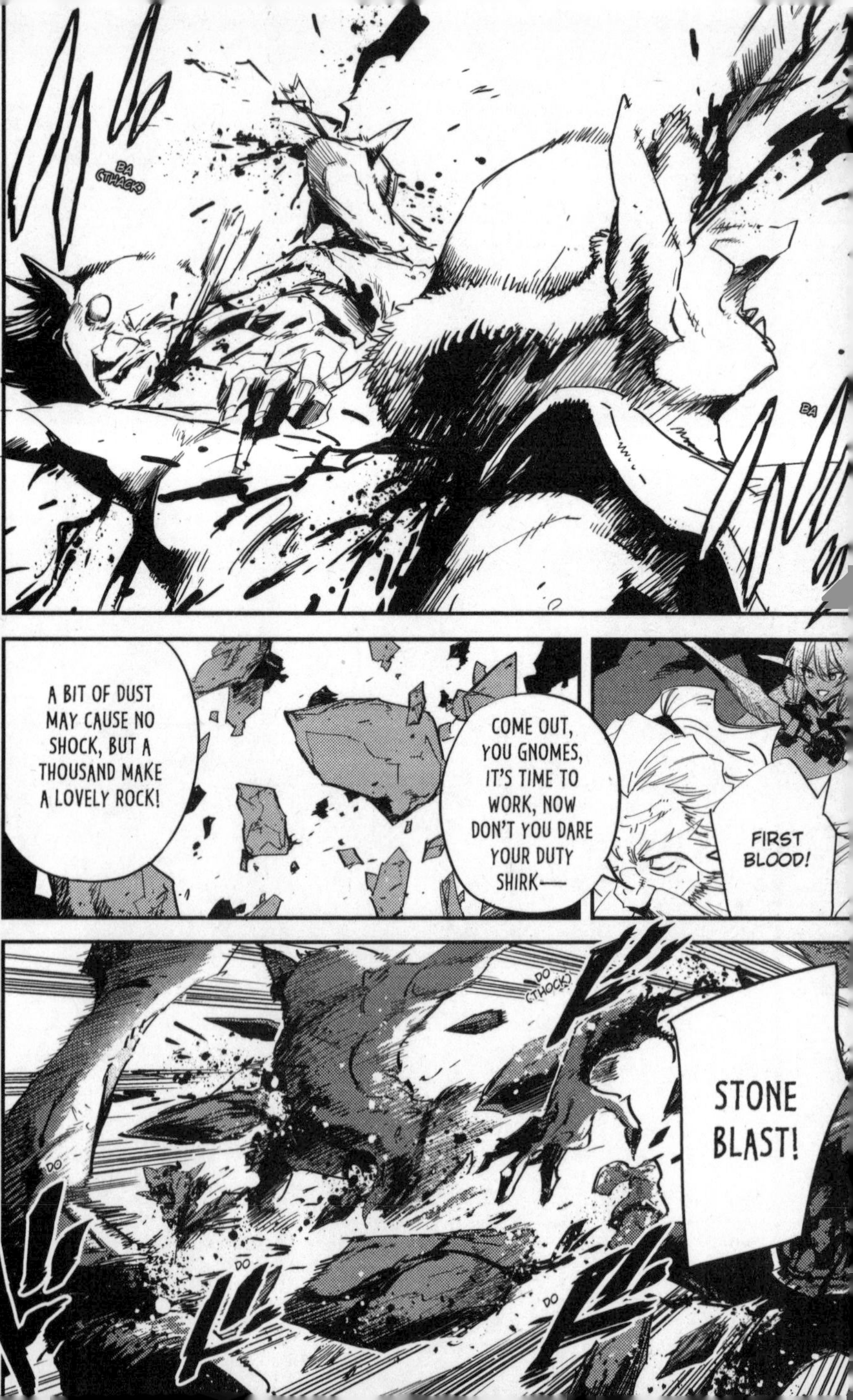
BA
BA (THACK)
FIRST BLOOD!
COME OUT, YOU GNOMES, IT'S TIME TO WORK, NOW DON'T YOU DARE YOUR DUTY SHIRK—
A BIT OF DUST MAY CAUSE NO SHOCK, BUT A THOUSAND MAKE A LOVELY ROCK!
STONE BLAST!
DO (THOCK)
DO
DO
DO

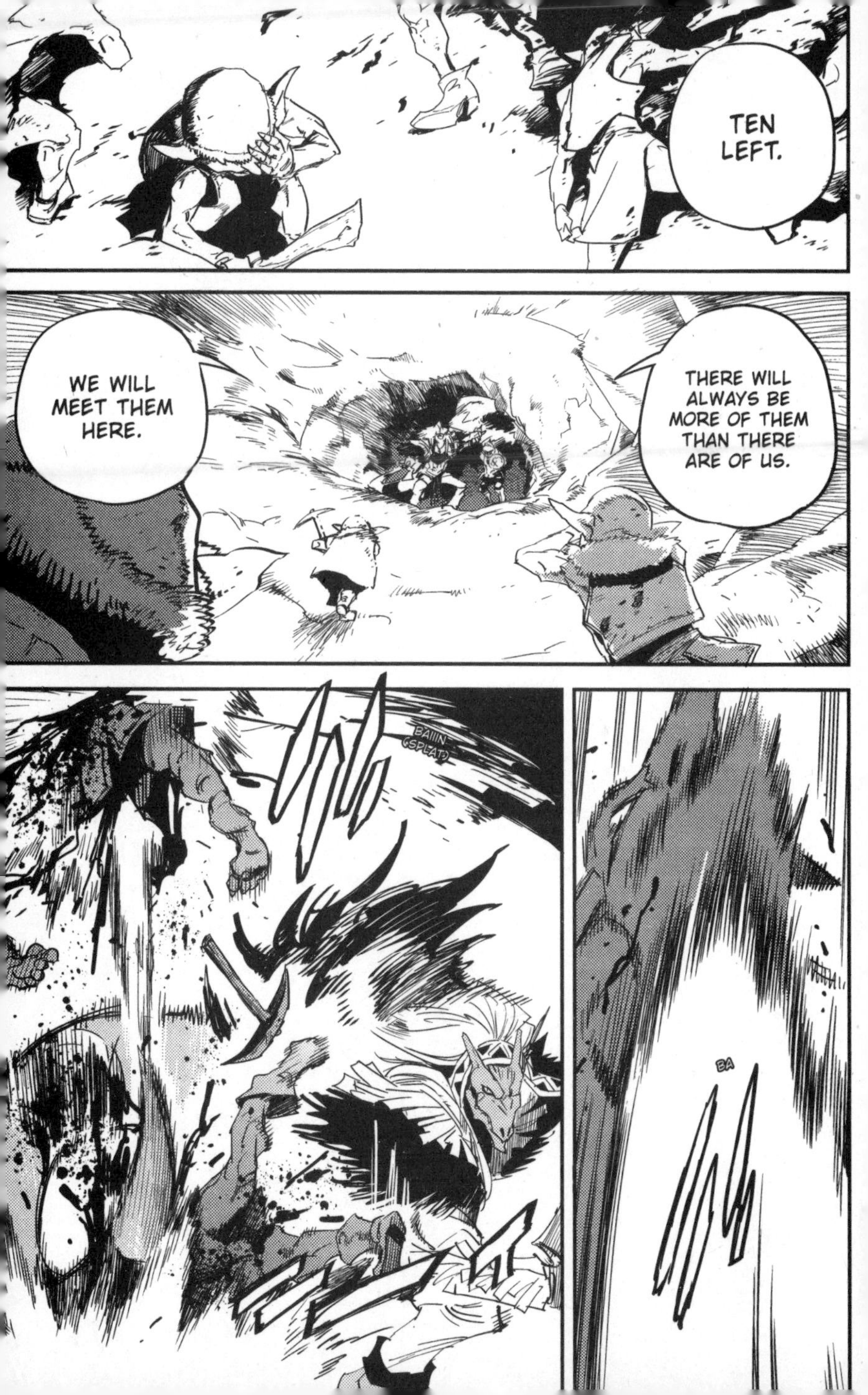
TEN LEFT.
THERE WILL ALWAYS BE MORE OF THEM THAN THERE ARE OF US.
WE WILL MEET THEM HERE.
BA
BAIIN (SPLAT)

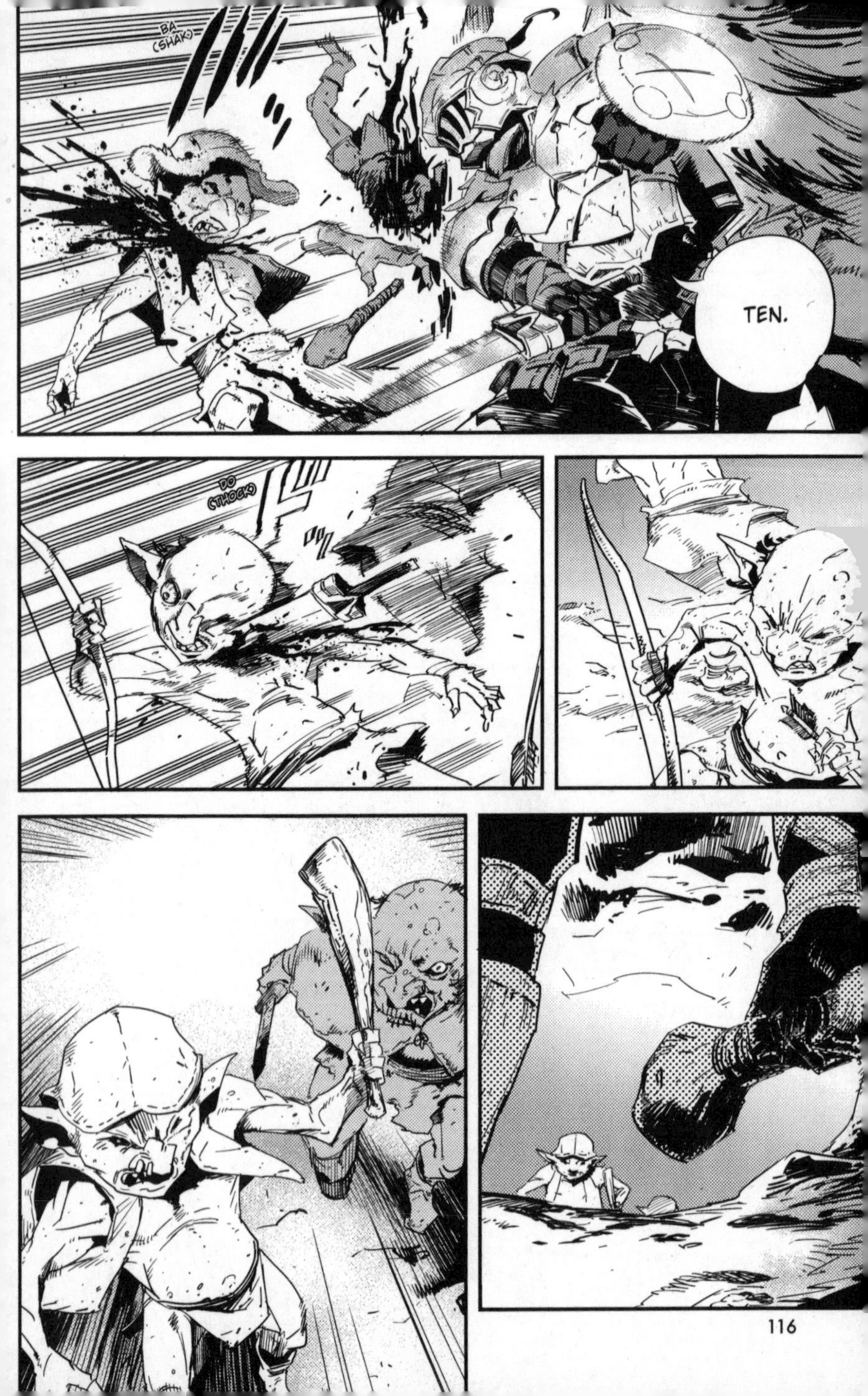
BA (SHAK)
TEN.
DO (THOCK)

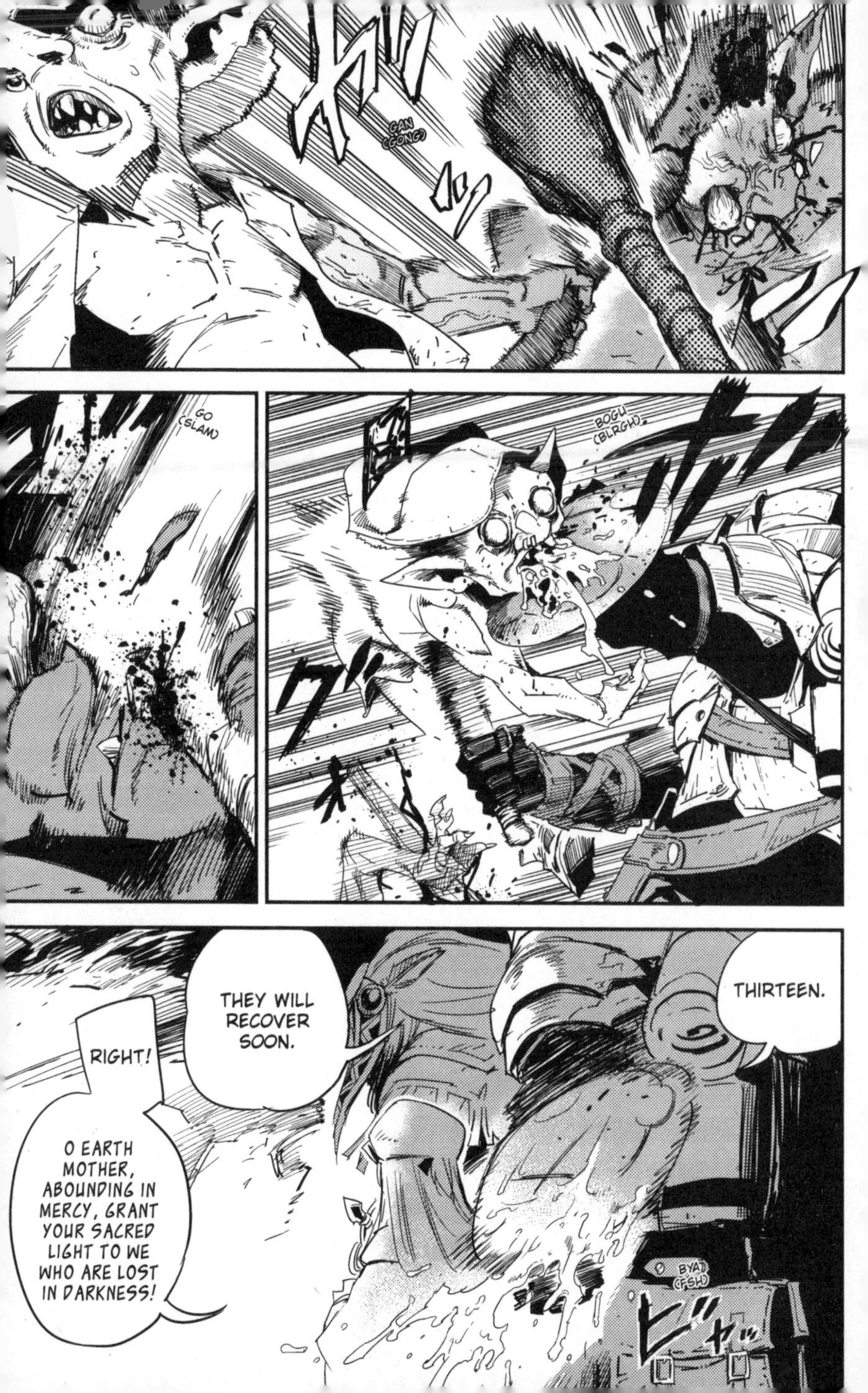
GAN (CONG)
BOGU (BLRGH)
GO (SLAM)
THIRTEEN.
BYA (FSH)
THEY WILL RECOVER SOON.
RIGHT!
O EARTH MOTHER, ABOUNDING IN MERCY, GRANT YOUR SACRED LIGHT TO WE WHO ARE LOST IN DARKNESS!

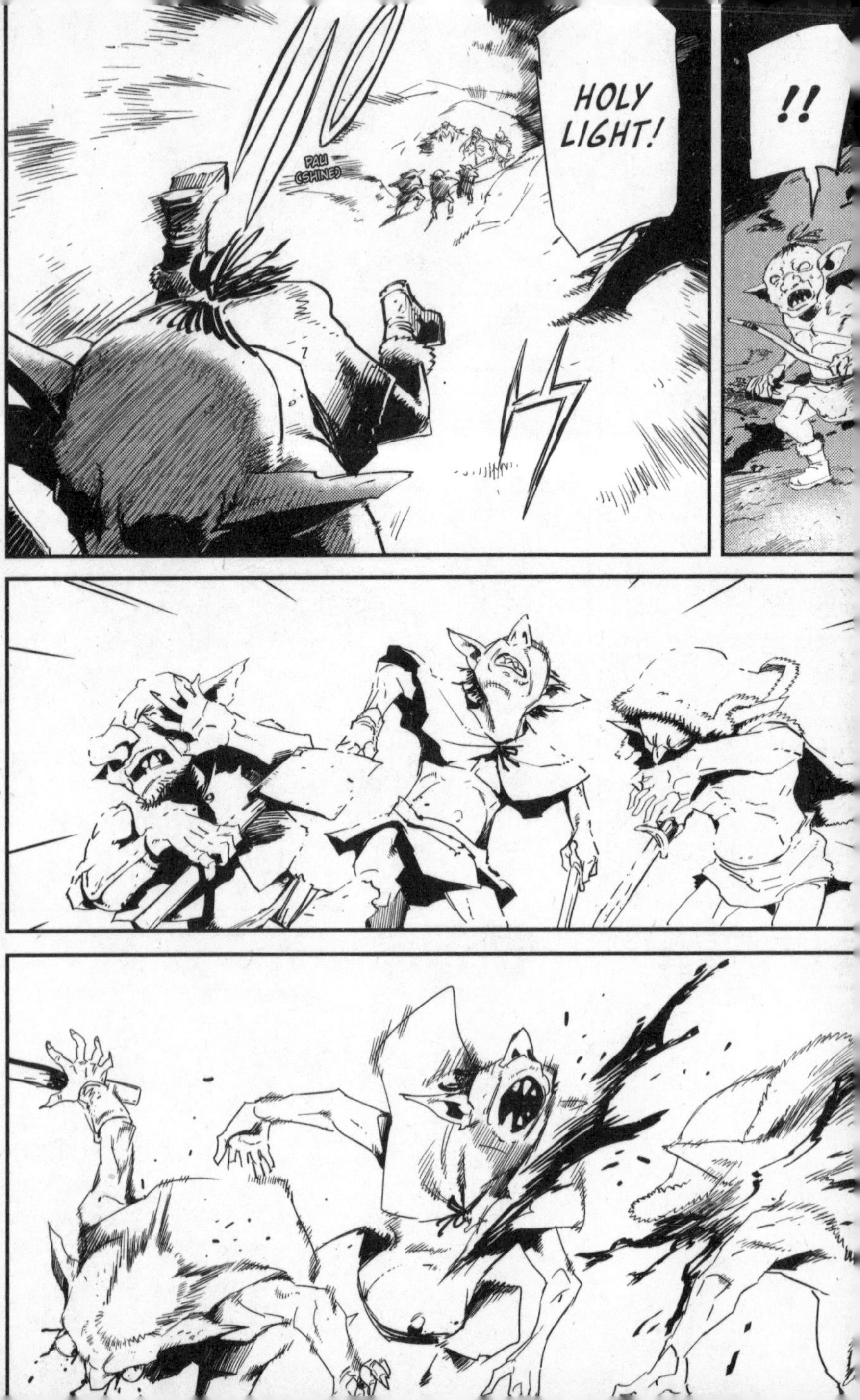
!!
HOLY LIGHT!
PAU
(SHINE)

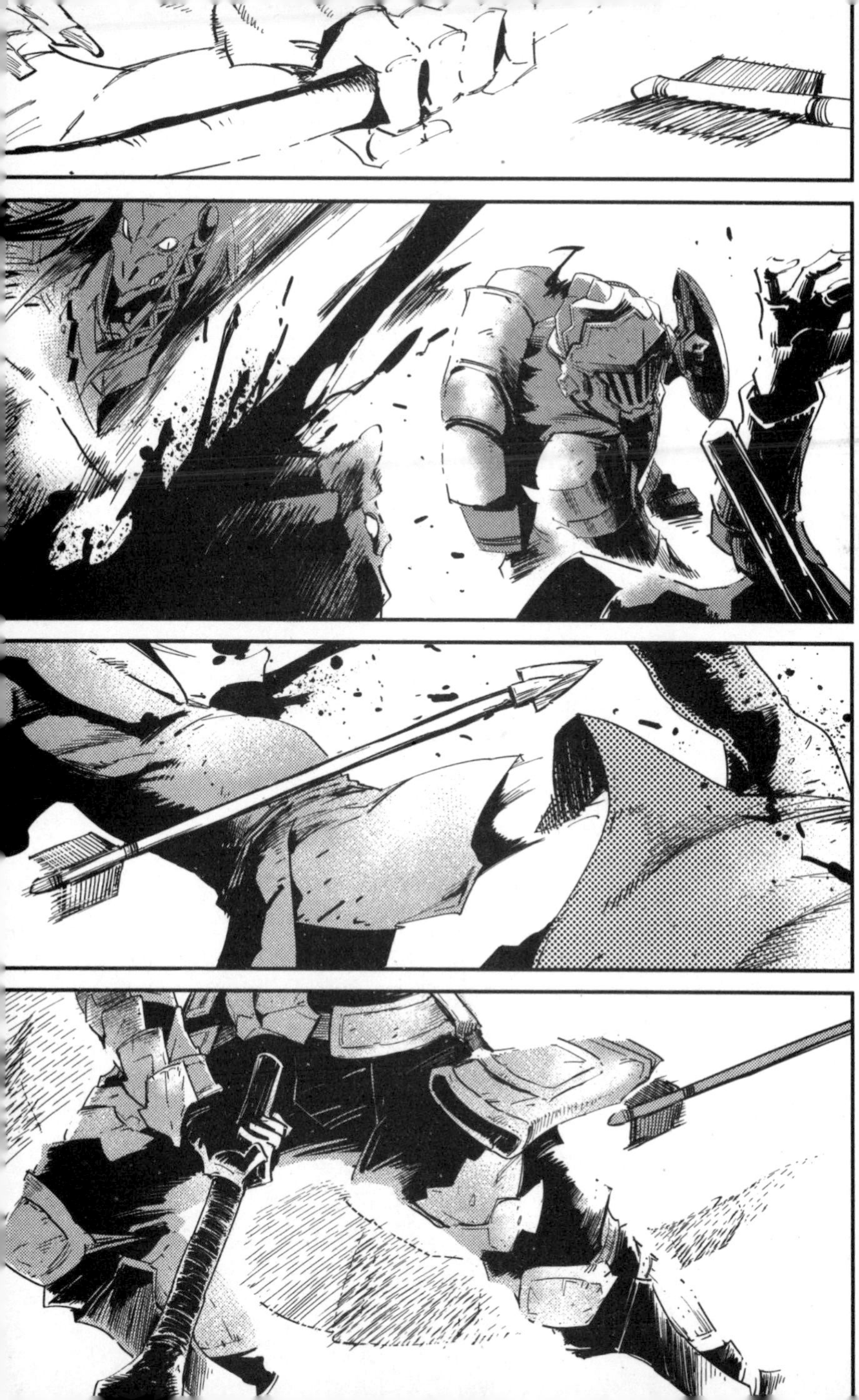

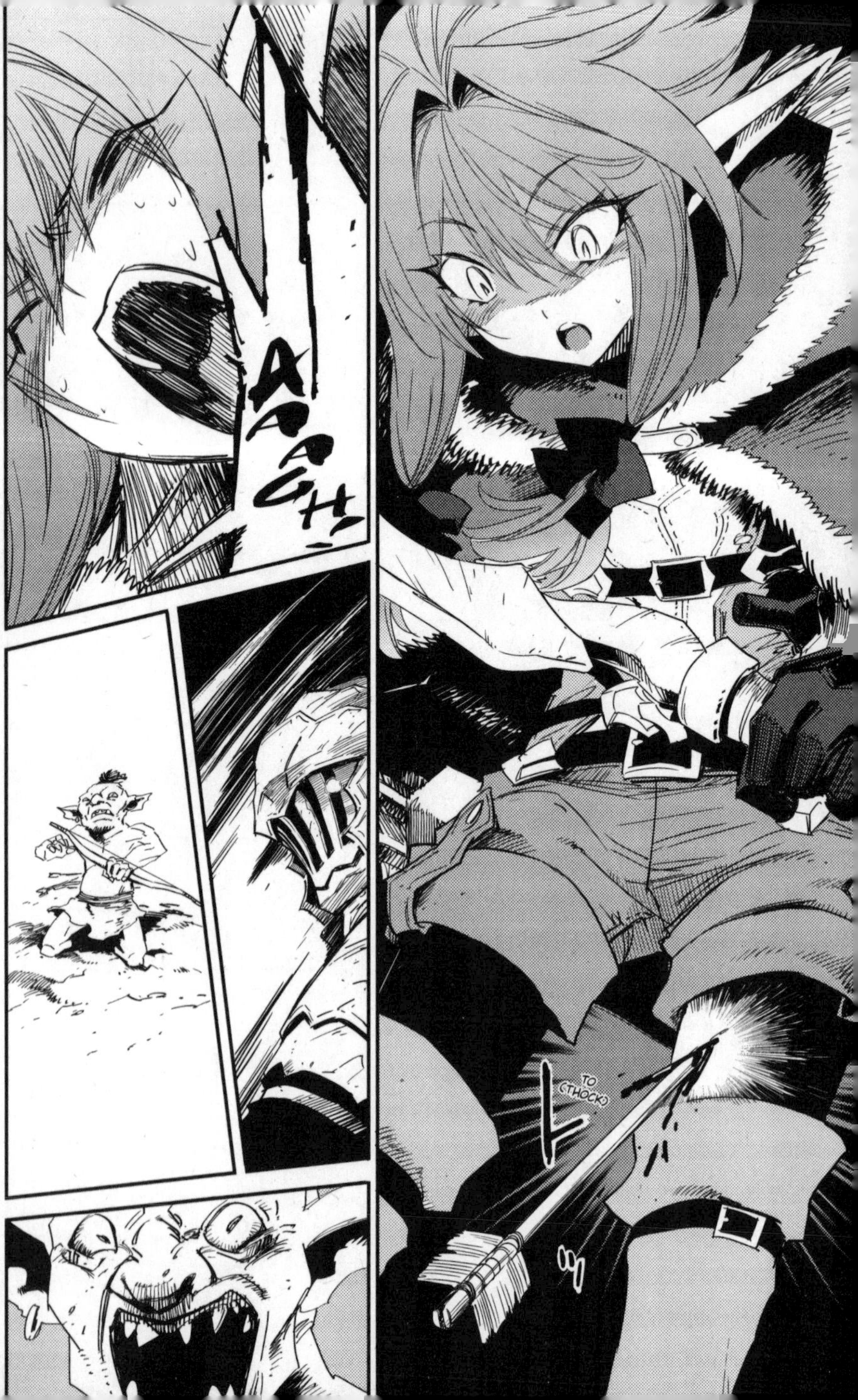
TO (THOCK)
AAAGH!

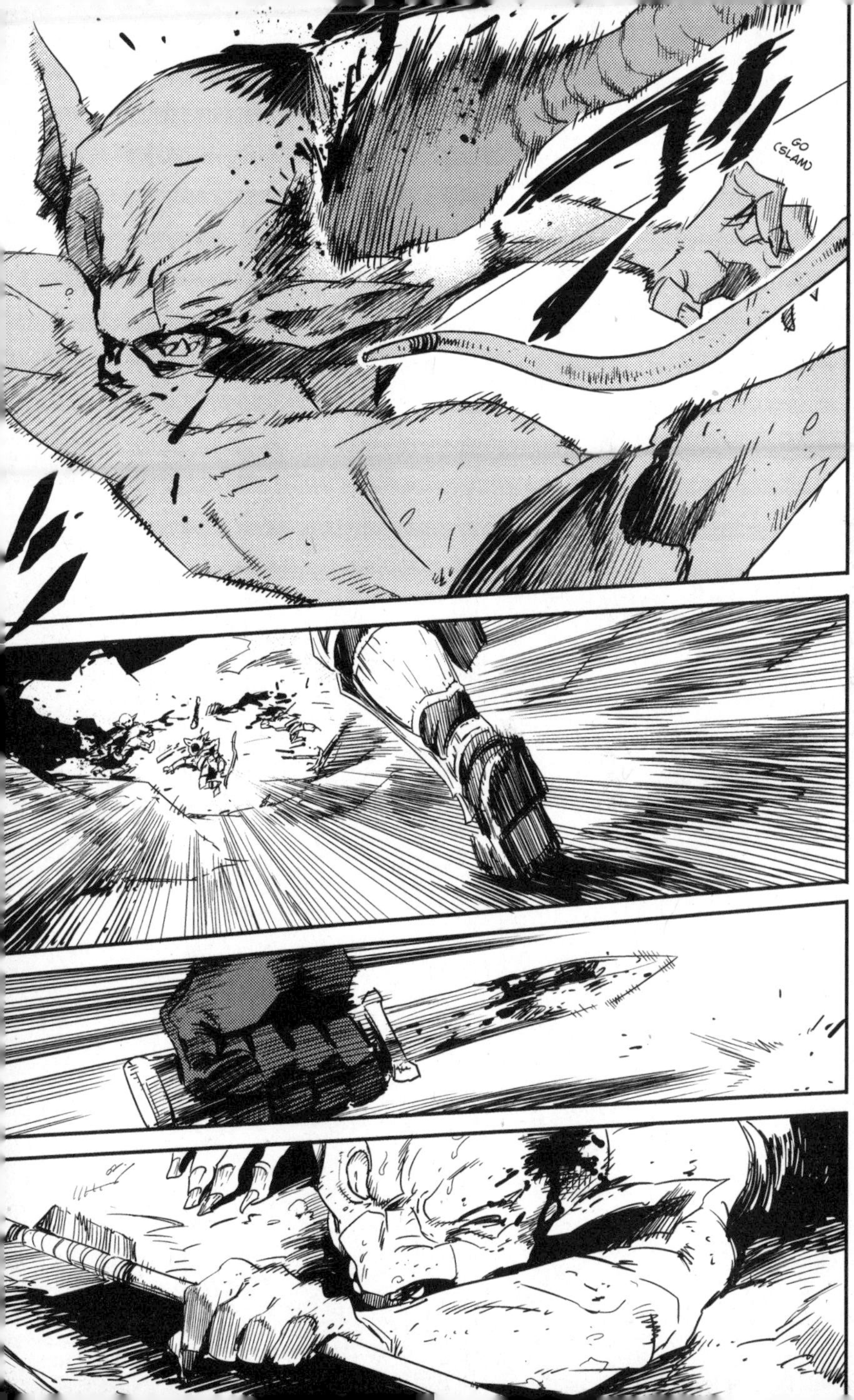
GO
(SLAM)

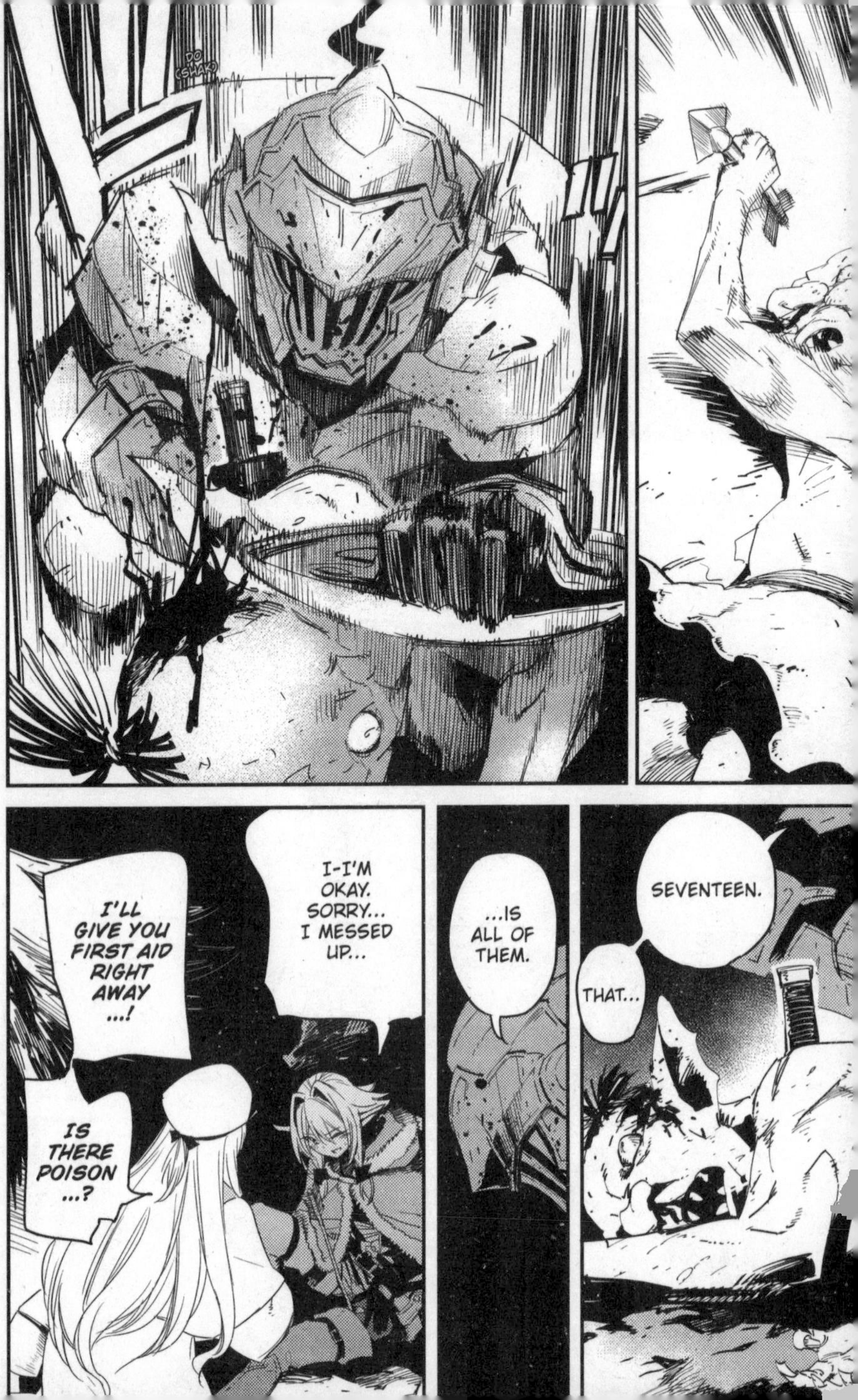
DO
(SHAK)
SEVENTEEN.
THAT...
...IS ALL OF THEM.
I-I'M OKAY. SORRY... I MESSED UP...
I'LL GIVE YOU FIRST AID RIGHT AWAY ...!
IS THERE POISON ...?

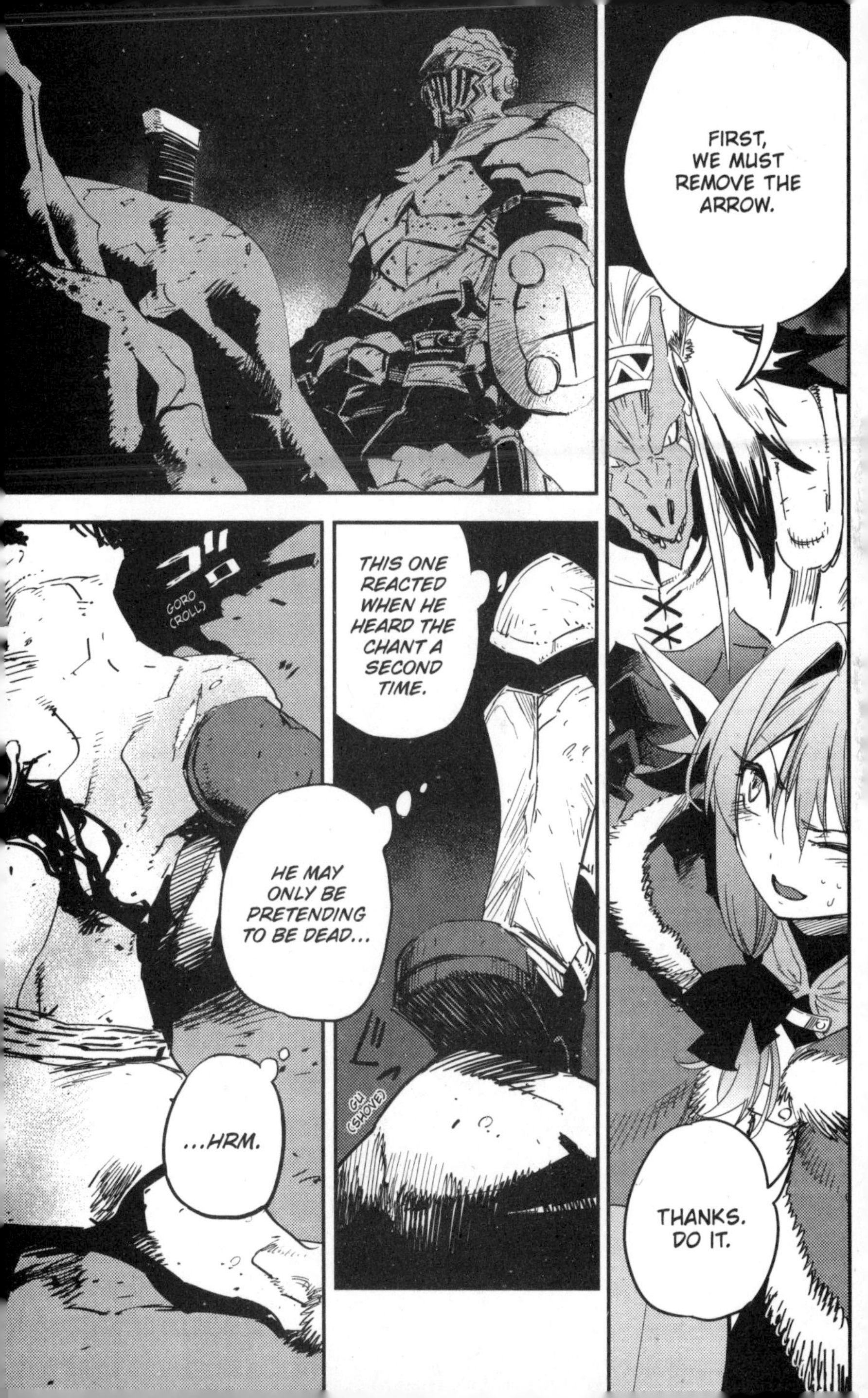

FIRST, WE MUST REMOVE THE ARROW.
THANKS. DO IT.
THIS ONE REACTED WHEN HE HEARD THE CHANT A SECOND TIME.
HE MAY ONLY BE PRETENDING TO BE DEAD...
GU (SHOVE)
GORO (ROLL)
...HRM.

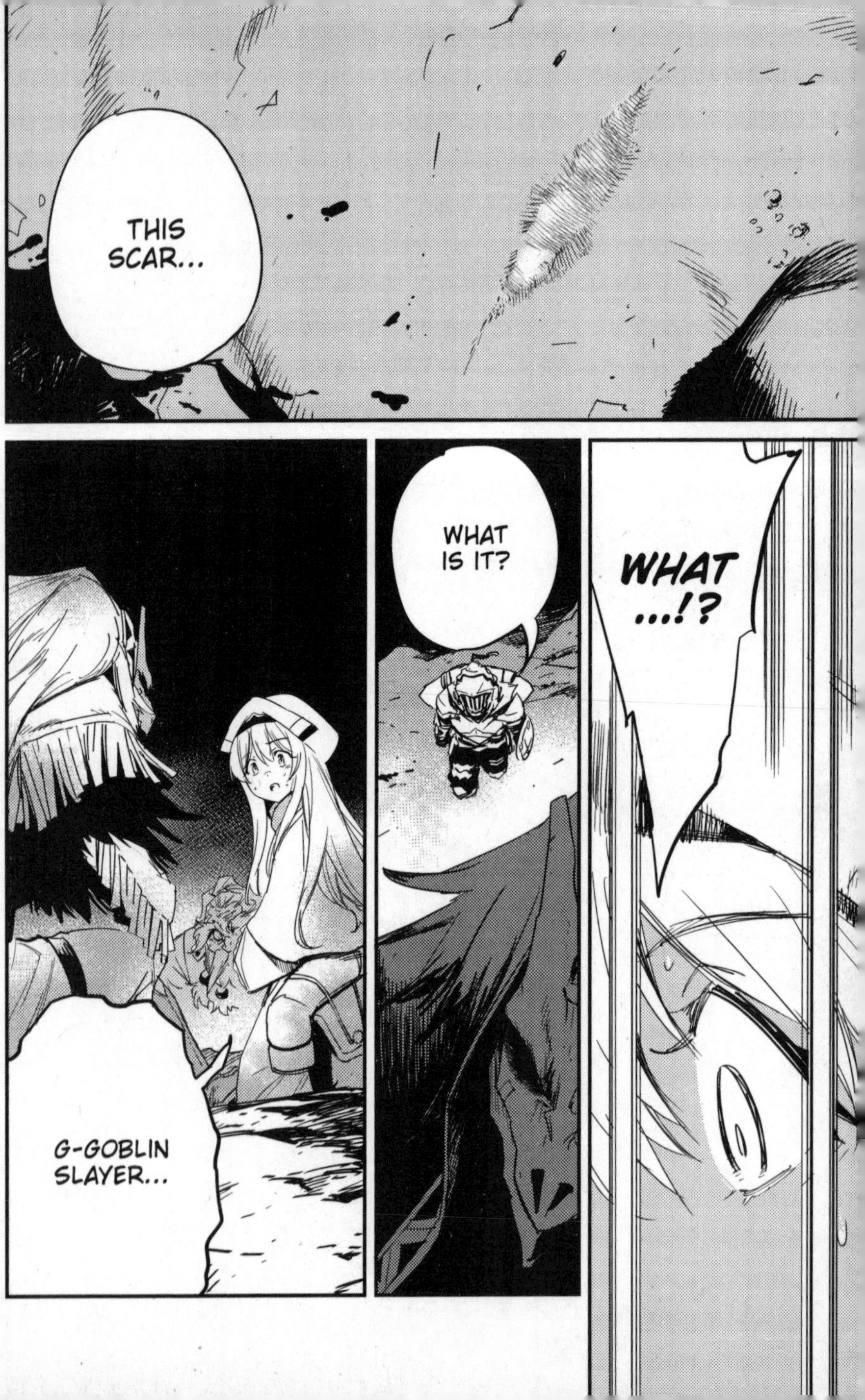
THIS SCAR...
WHAT ...!?
WHAT IS IT?
G-GOBLIN SLAYER...

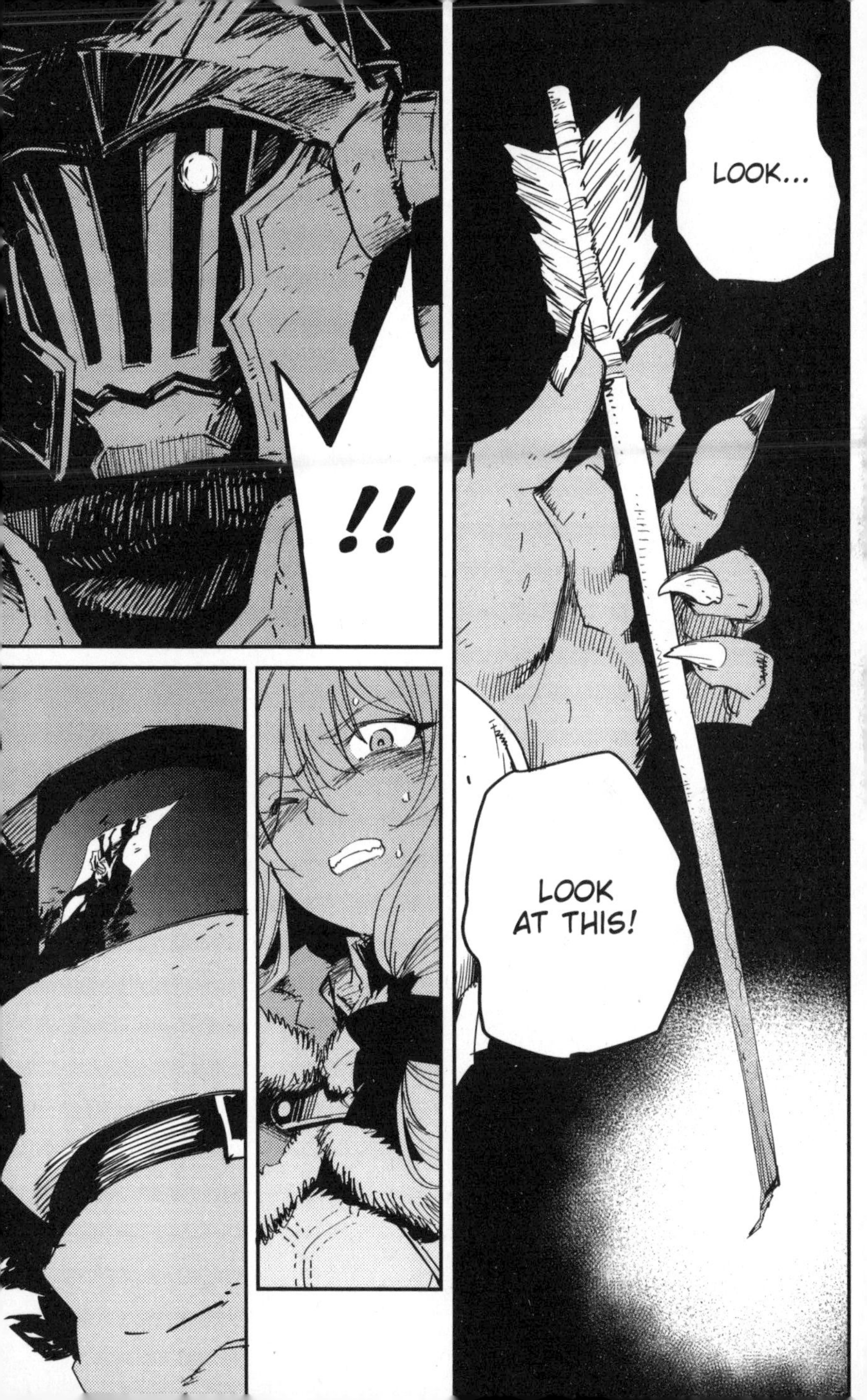
LOOK...
LOOK AT THIS!
!!

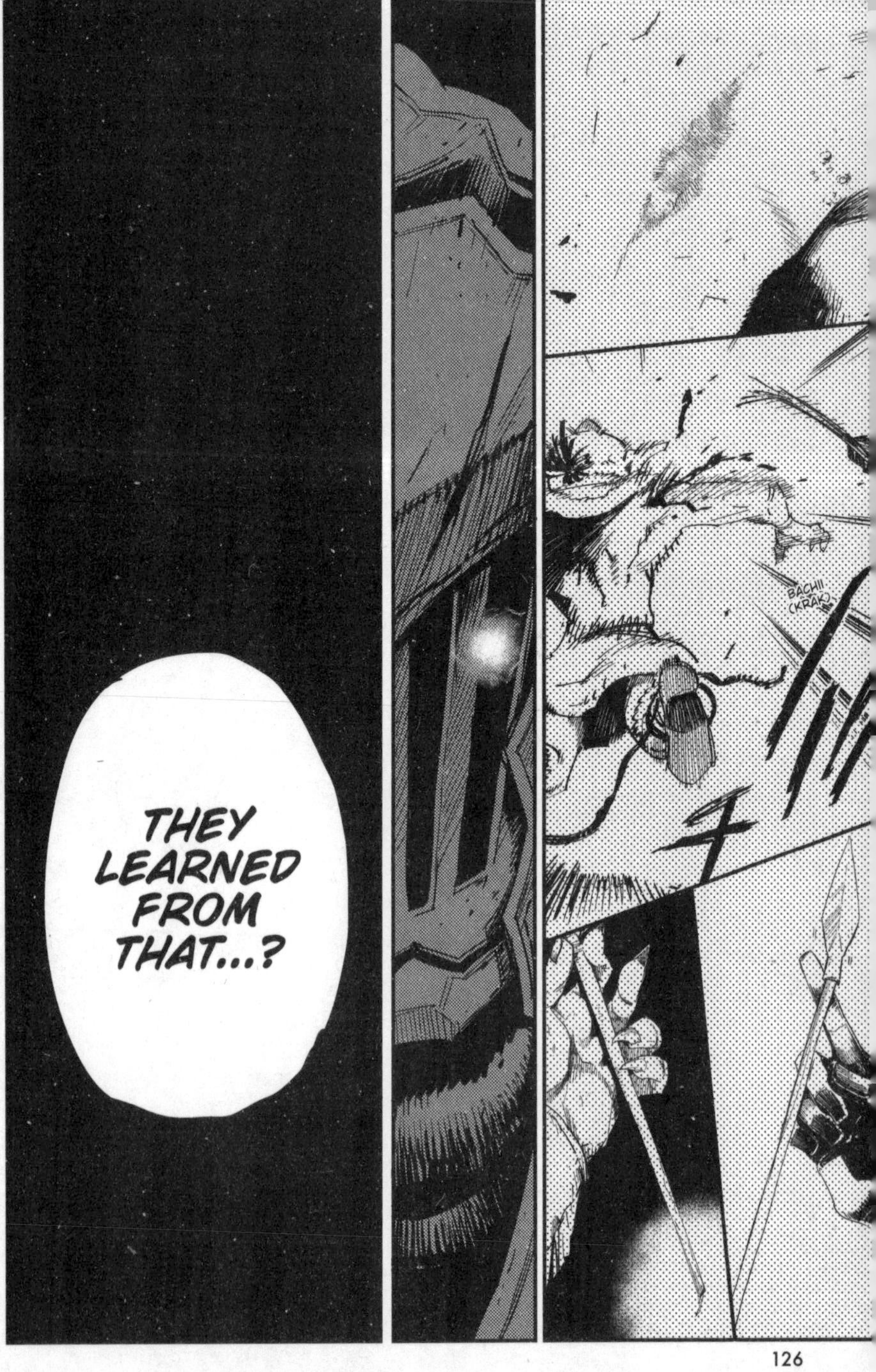
BACHII
(KRAK)
THEY LEARNED FROM THAT...?

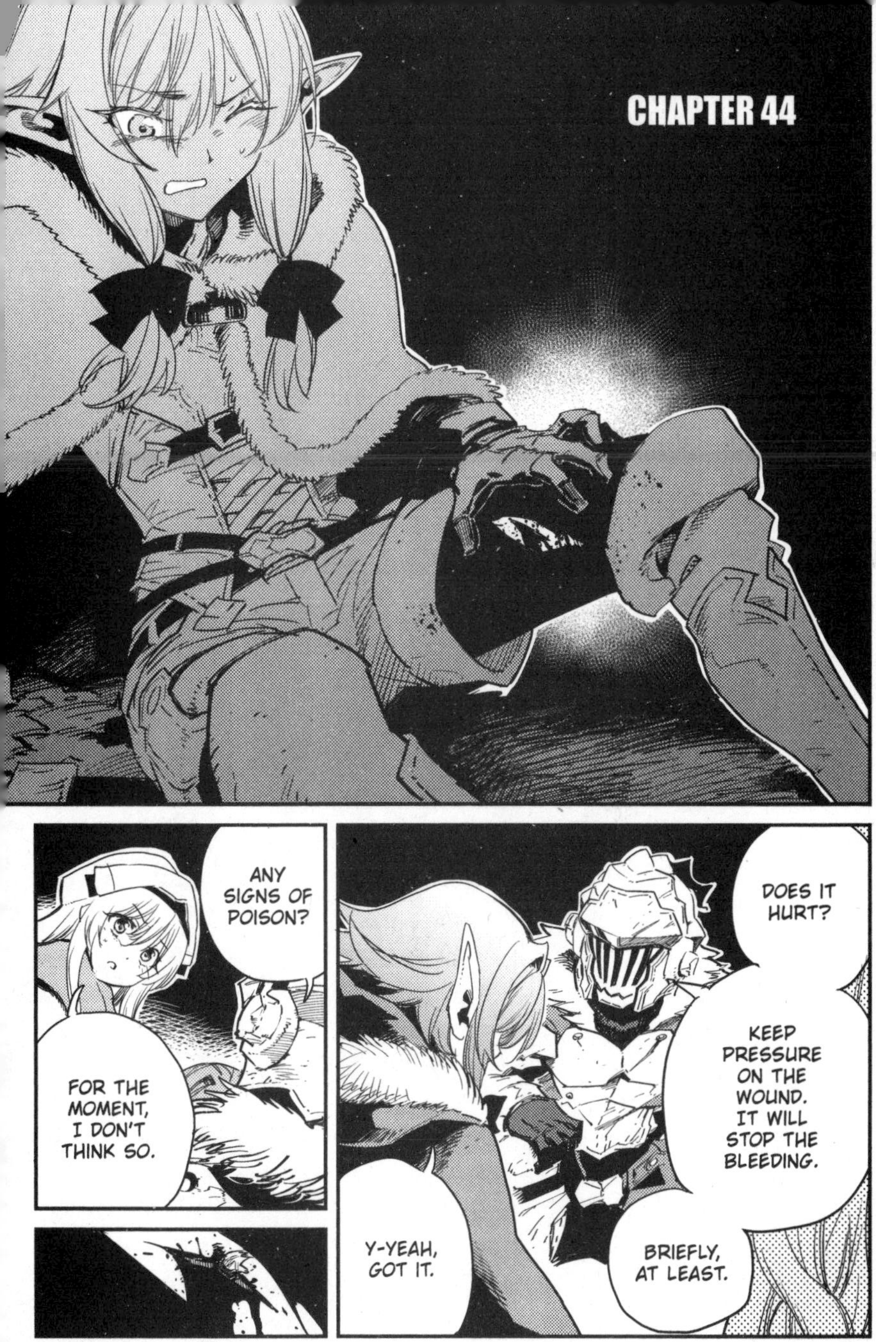
CHAPTER 44
DOES IT HURT?
KEEP PRESSURE ON THE WOUND. IT WILL STOP THE BLEEDING.
BRIEFLY, AT LEAST.
Y-YEAH, GOT IT.
ANY SIGNS OF POISON?
FOR THE MOMENT, I DON'T THINK SO.

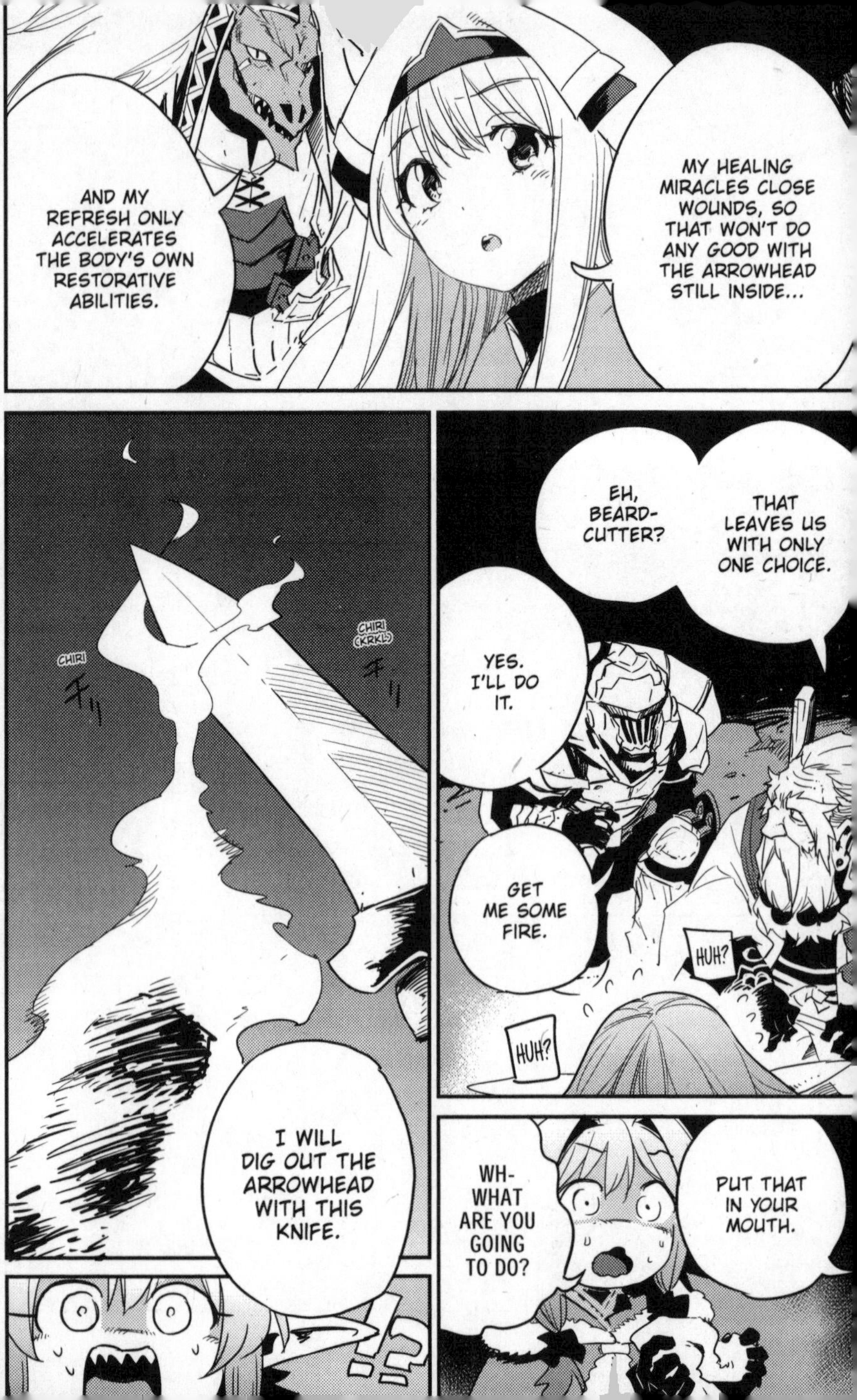
MY HEALING MIRACLES CLOSE WOUNDS, SO THAT WON'T DO ANY GOOD WITH THE ARROWHEAD STILL INSIDE...
AND MY REFRESH ONLY ACCELERATES THE BODY'S OWN RESTORATIVE ABILITIES.
THAT LEAVES US WITH ONLY ONE CHOICE.
EH, BEARD-CUTTER?
YES. I'LL DO IT.
GET ME SOME FIRE.
HUH?
HUH?
CHIRI (KRKL)
CHIRI
I WILL DIG OUT THE ARROWHEAD WITH THIS KNIFE.
PUT THAT IN YOUR MOUTH.
WH-WHAT ARE YOU GOING TO DO?

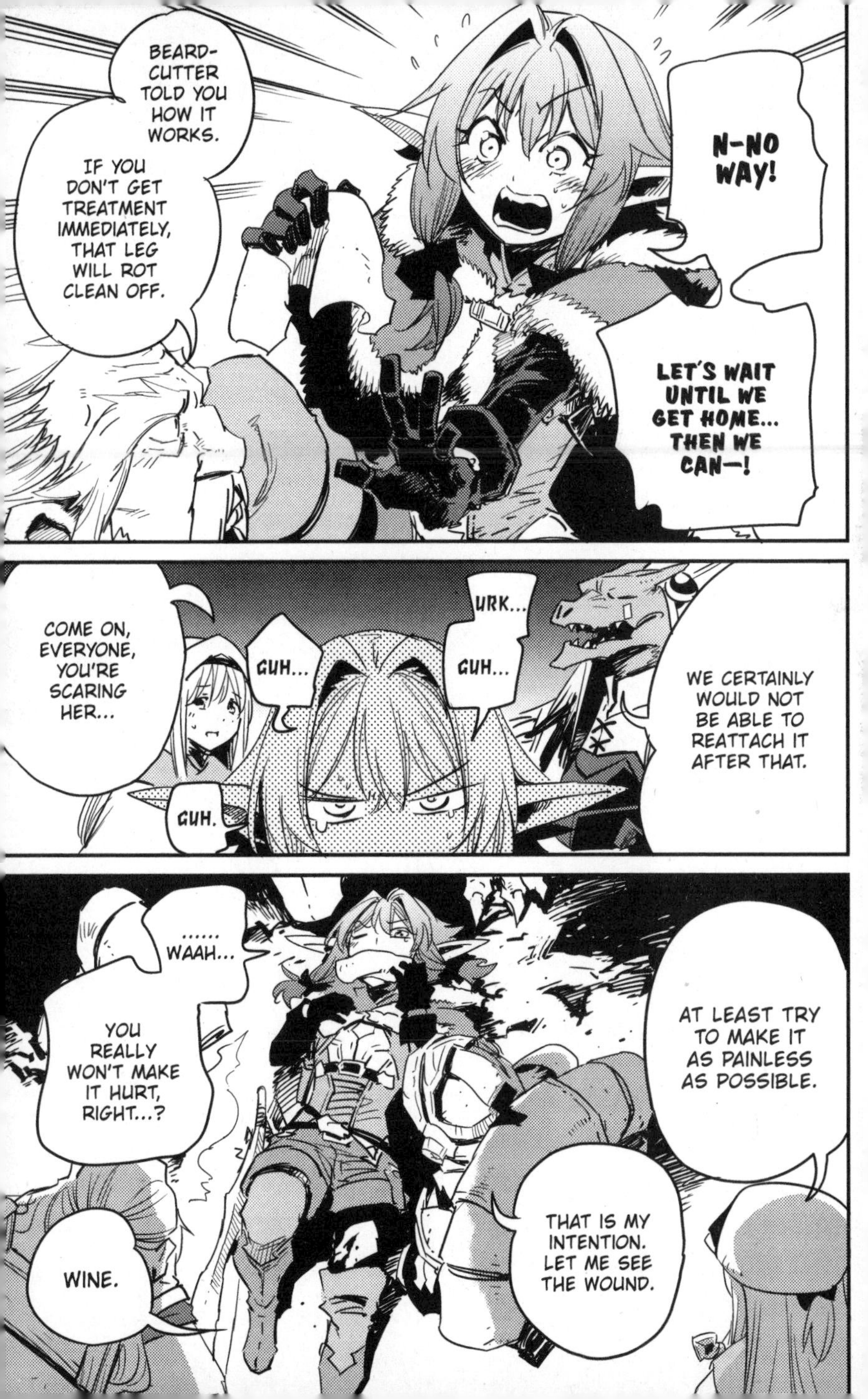
N-NO WAY!
LET'S WAIT UNTIL WE GET HOME... THEN WE CAN—!
BEARD-CUTTER TOLD YOU HOW IT WORKS.
IF YOU DON'T GET TREATMENT IMMEDIATELY, THAT LEG WILL ROT CLEAN OFF.
WE CERTAINLY WOULD NOT BE ABLE TO REATTACH IT AFTER THAT.
URK...
GUH...
GUH...
COME ON, EVERYONE, YOU'RE SCARING HER...
GUH.
AT LEAST TRY TO MAKE IT AS PAINLESS AS POSSIBLE.
...... WAAH...
YOU REALLY WON'T MAKE IT HURT, RIGHT...?
THAT IS MY INTENTION. LET ME SEE THE WOUND.
WINE.

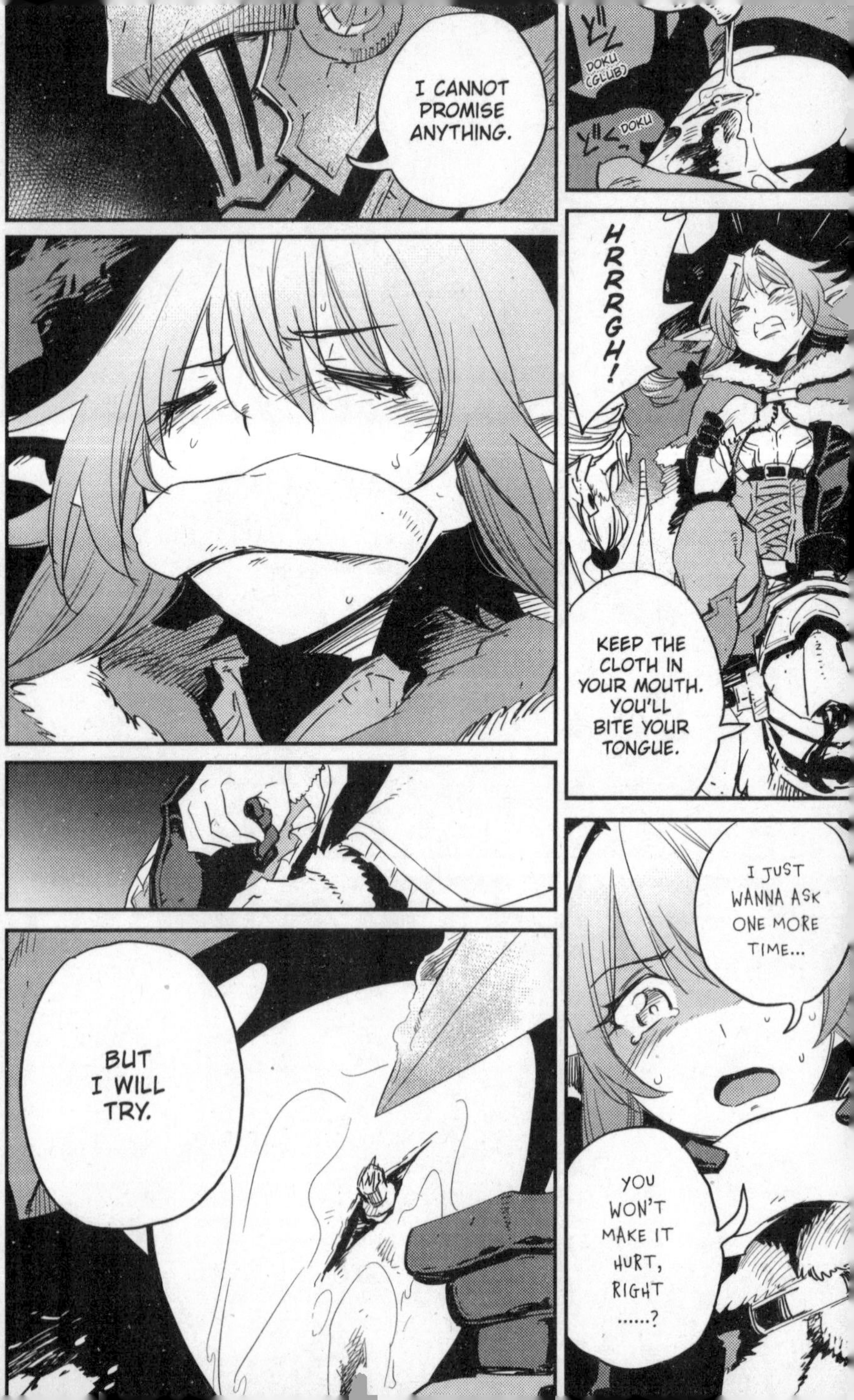
DOKU (GLUB)
DOKU
I CANNOT PROMISE ANYTHING.
HRRRGH!
KEEP THE CLOTH IN YOUR MOUTH. YOU'LL BITE YOUR TONGUE.
I JUST WANNA ASK ONE MORE TIME...
YOU WON'T MAKE IT HURT, RIGHT ......?
BUT I WILL TRY.

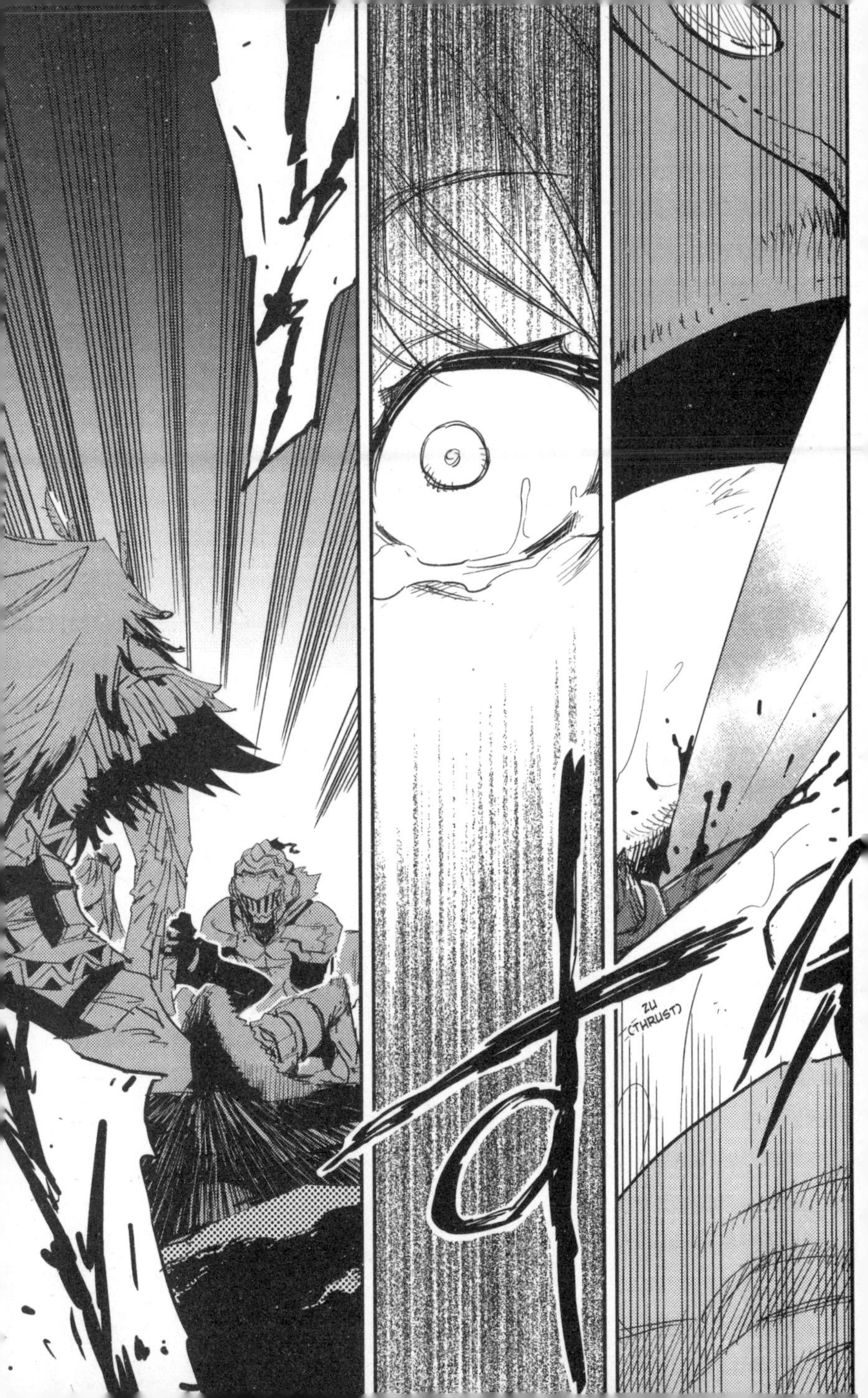
ZU
(THRUST)

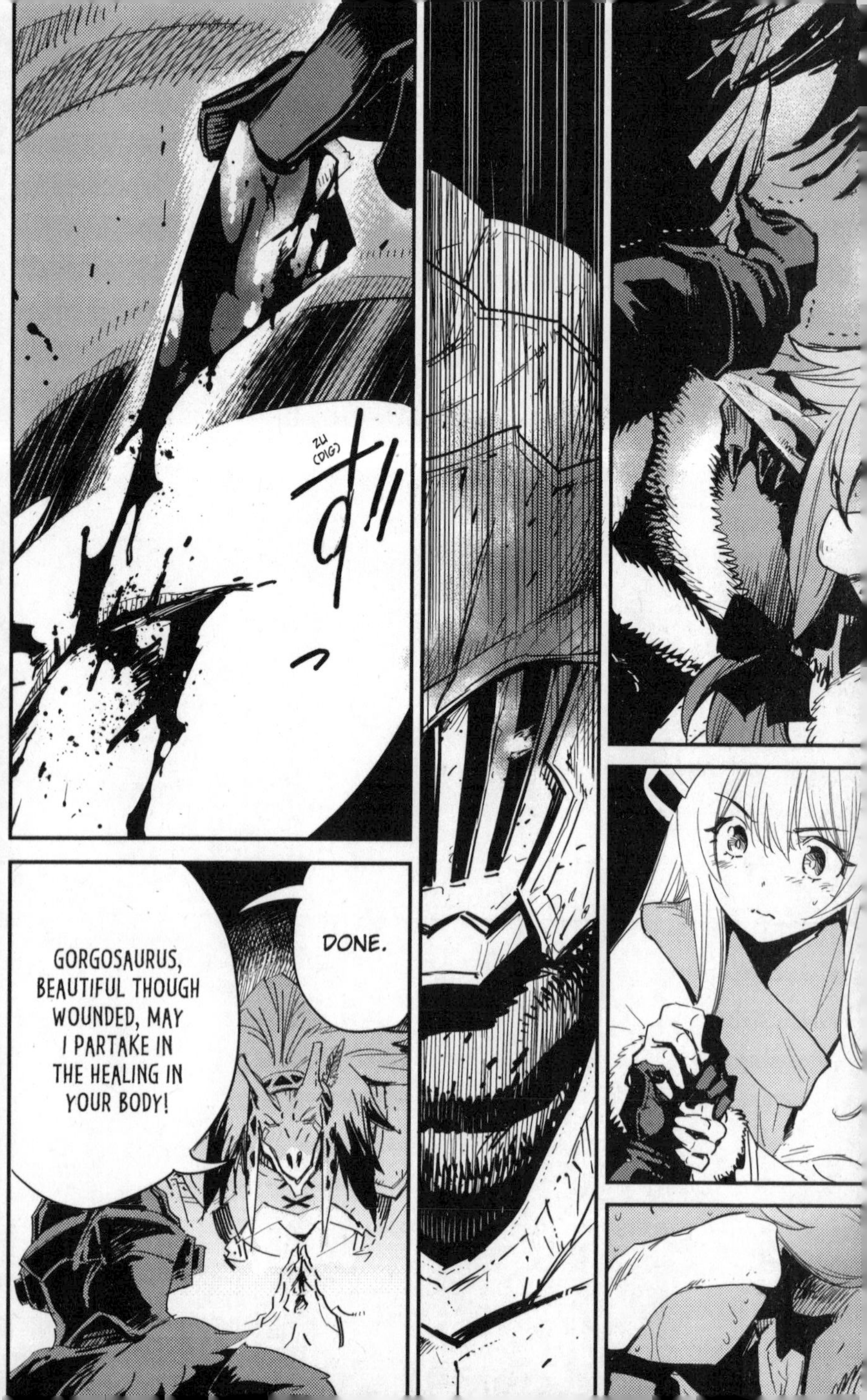
ZU (DIG)
DONE.
GORGOSAURUS, BEAUTIFUL THOUGH WOUNDED, MAY I PARTAKE IN THE HEALING IN YOUR BODY!

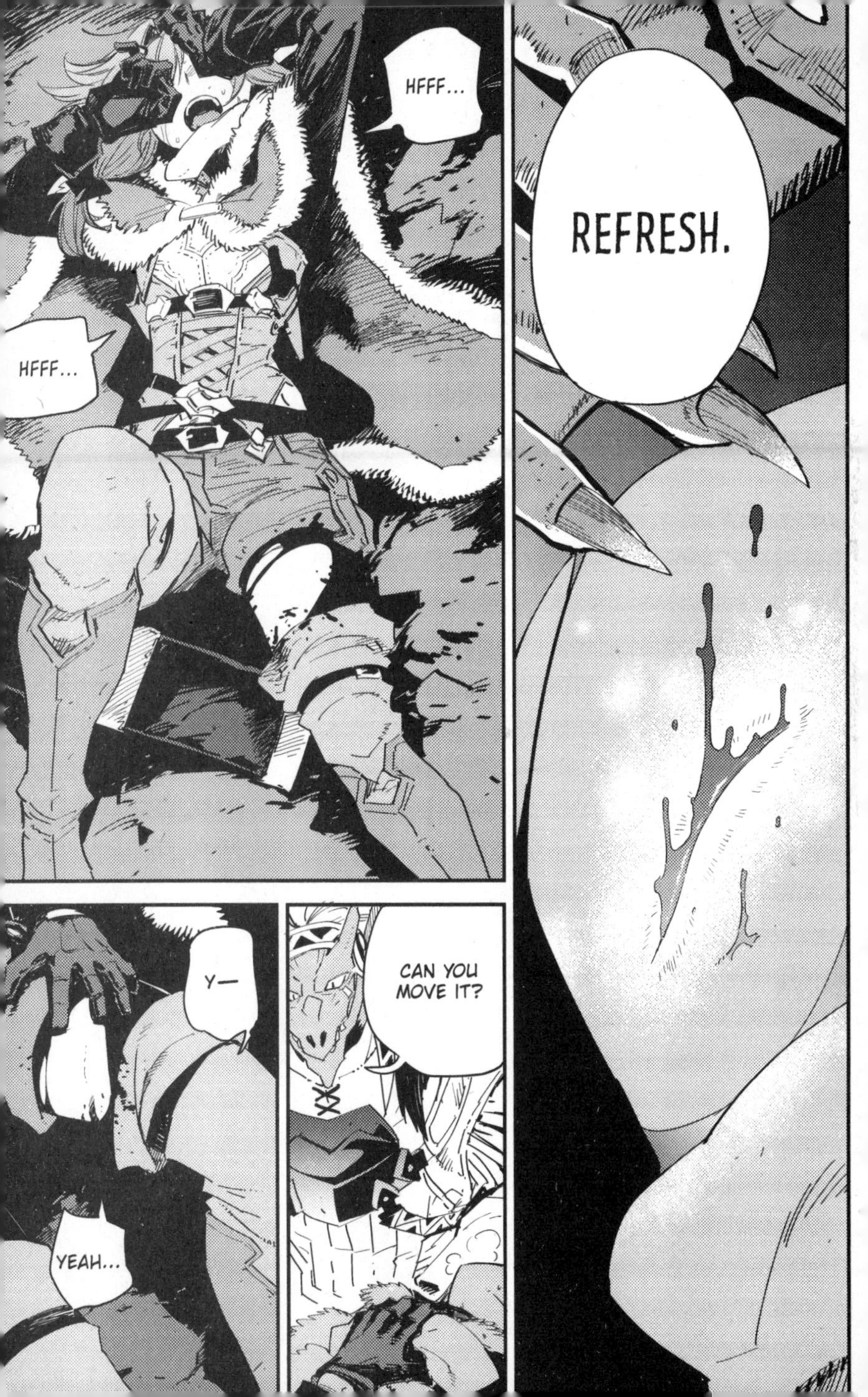
REFRESH.
HFFF...
HFFF...
CAN YOU MOVE IT?
Y—
YEAH...

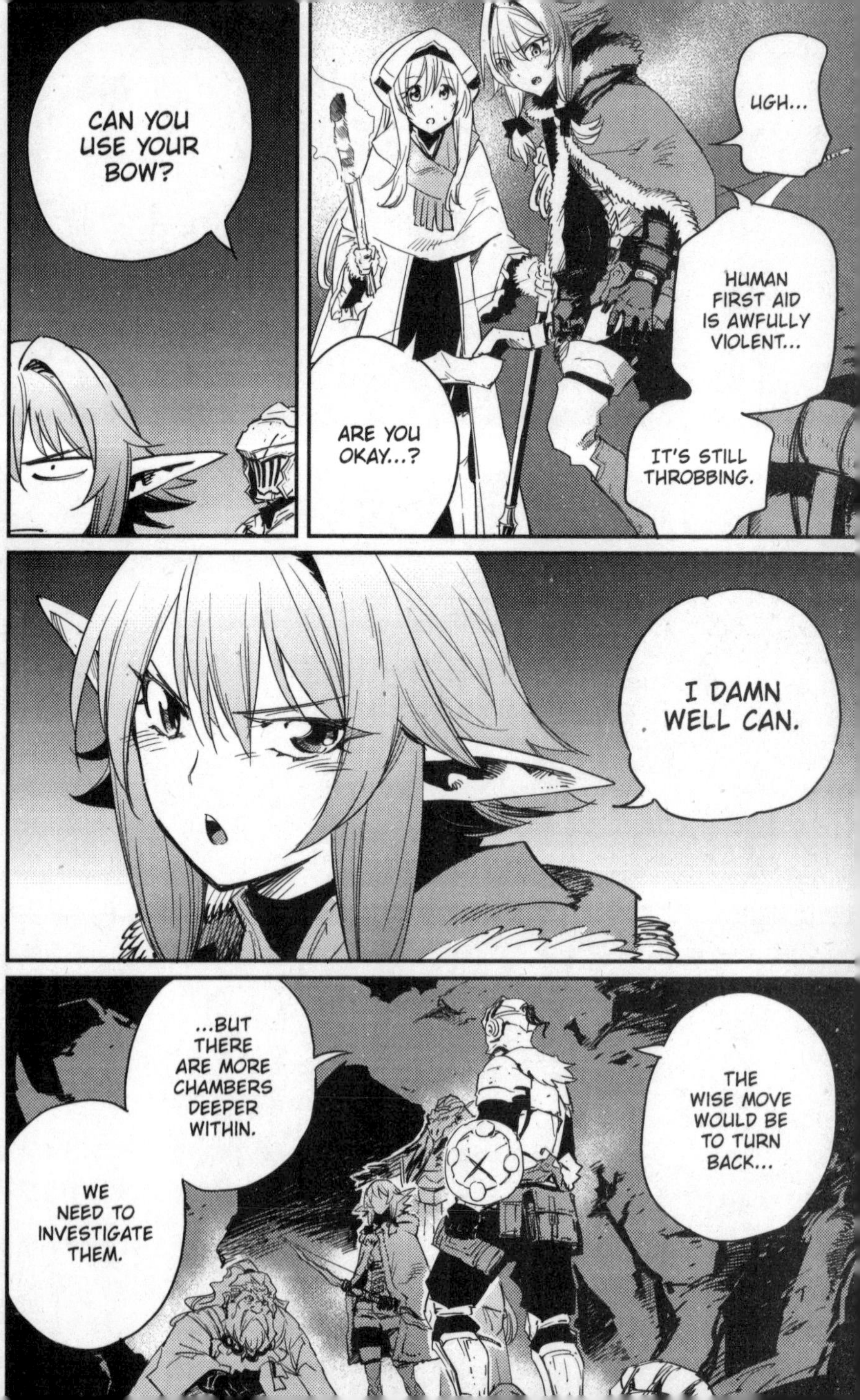
UGH...
HUMAN FIRST AID IS AWFULLY VIOLENT...
IT'S STILL THROBBING.
ARE YOU OKAY...?
CAN YOU USE YOUR BOW?
I DAMN WELL CAN.
THE WISE MOVE WOULD BE TO TURN BACK...
...BUT THERE ARE MORE CHAMBERS DEEPER WITHIN.
WE NEED TO INVESTIGATE THEM.

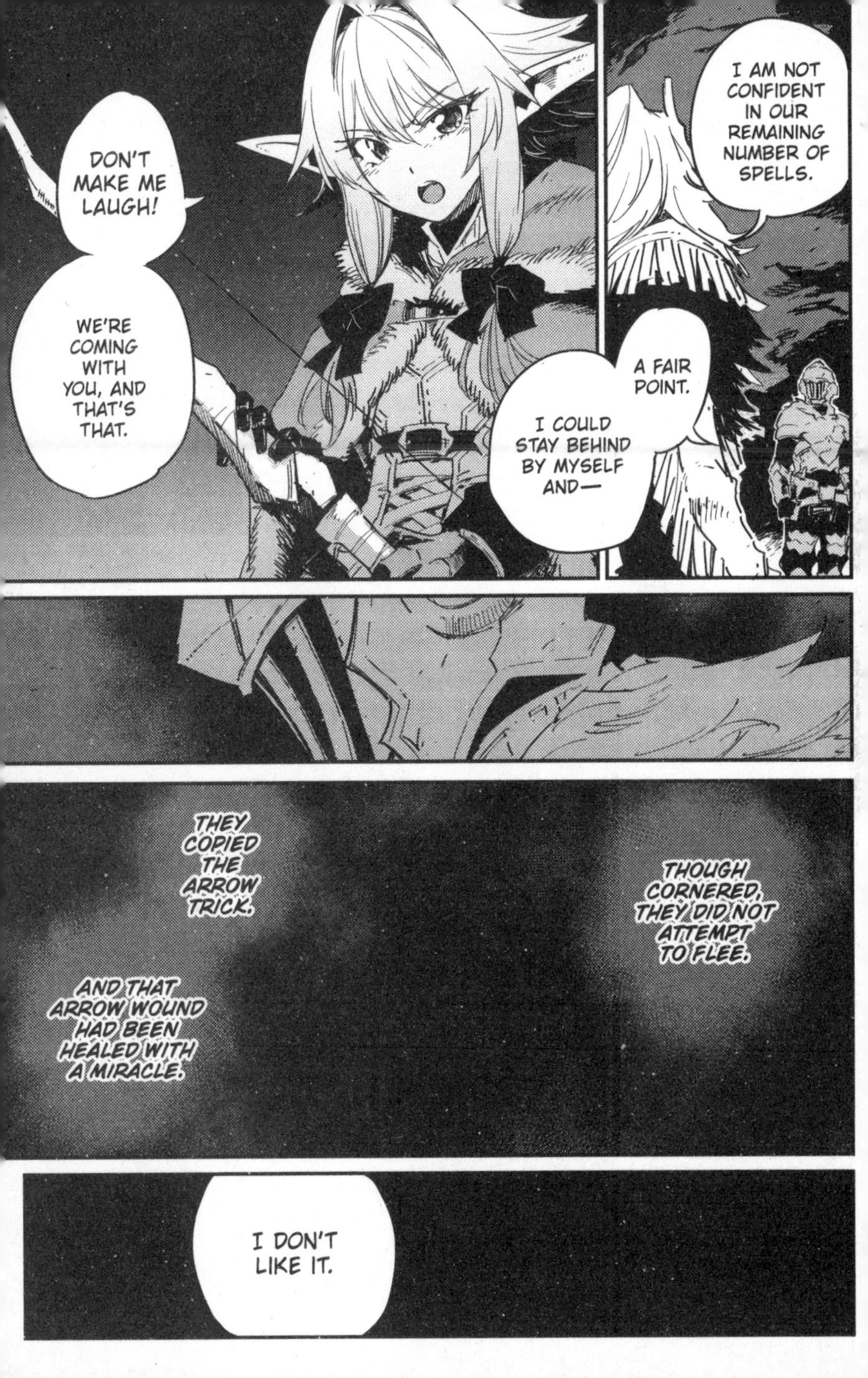
I AM NOT CONFIDENT IN OUR REMAINING NUMBER OF SPELLS.
A FAIR POINT.
I COULD STAY BEHIND BY MYSELF AND—
DON'T MAKE ME LAUGH!
WE'RE COMING WITH YOU, AND THAT'S THAT.
THOUGH CORNERED, THEY DID NOT ATTEMPT TO FLEE.
THEY COPIED THE ARROW TRICK.
AND THAT ARROW WOUND HAD BEEN HEALED WITH A MIRACLE.
I DON'T LIKE IT.

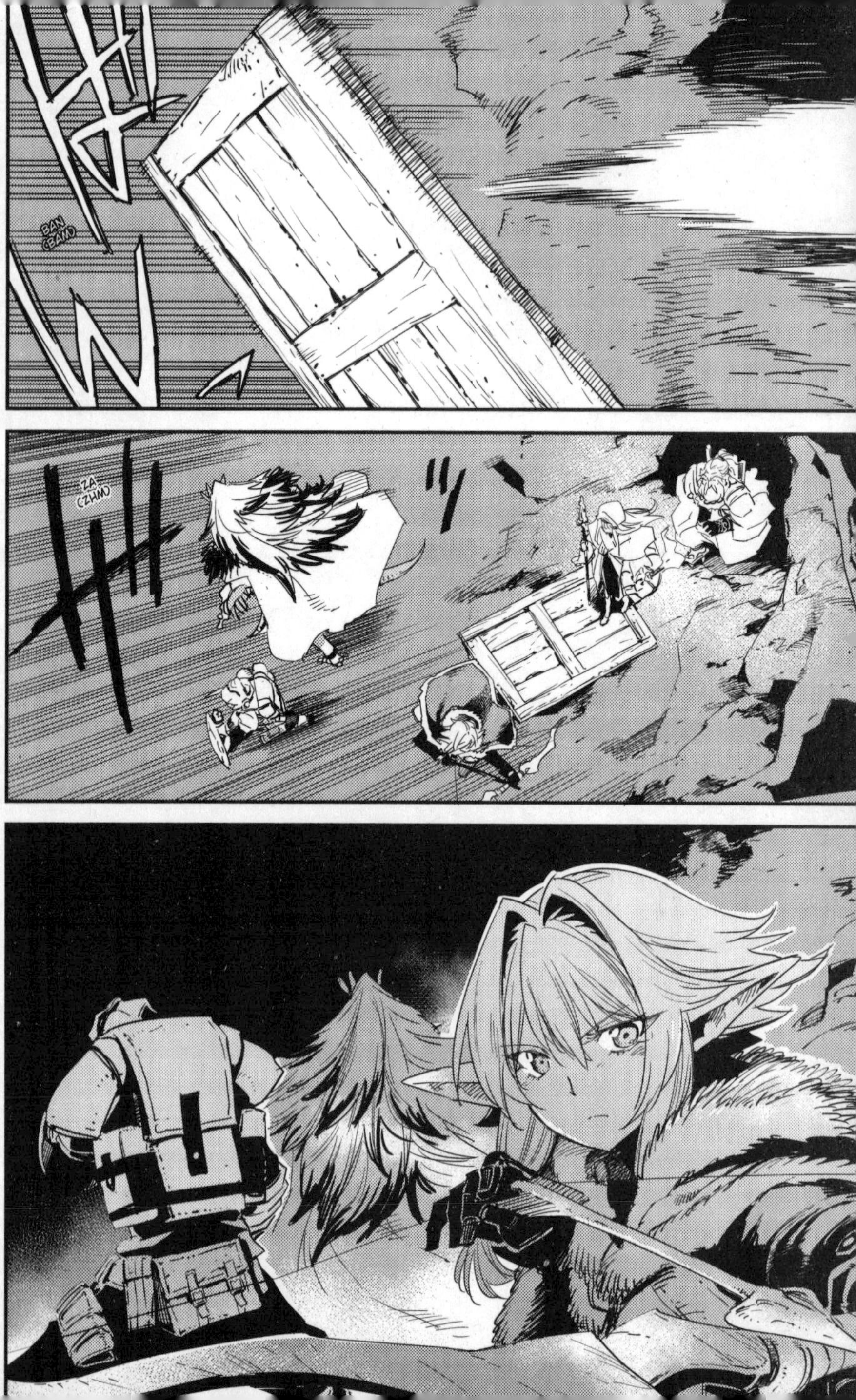
BAN (BAM)
ZA (ZHM)

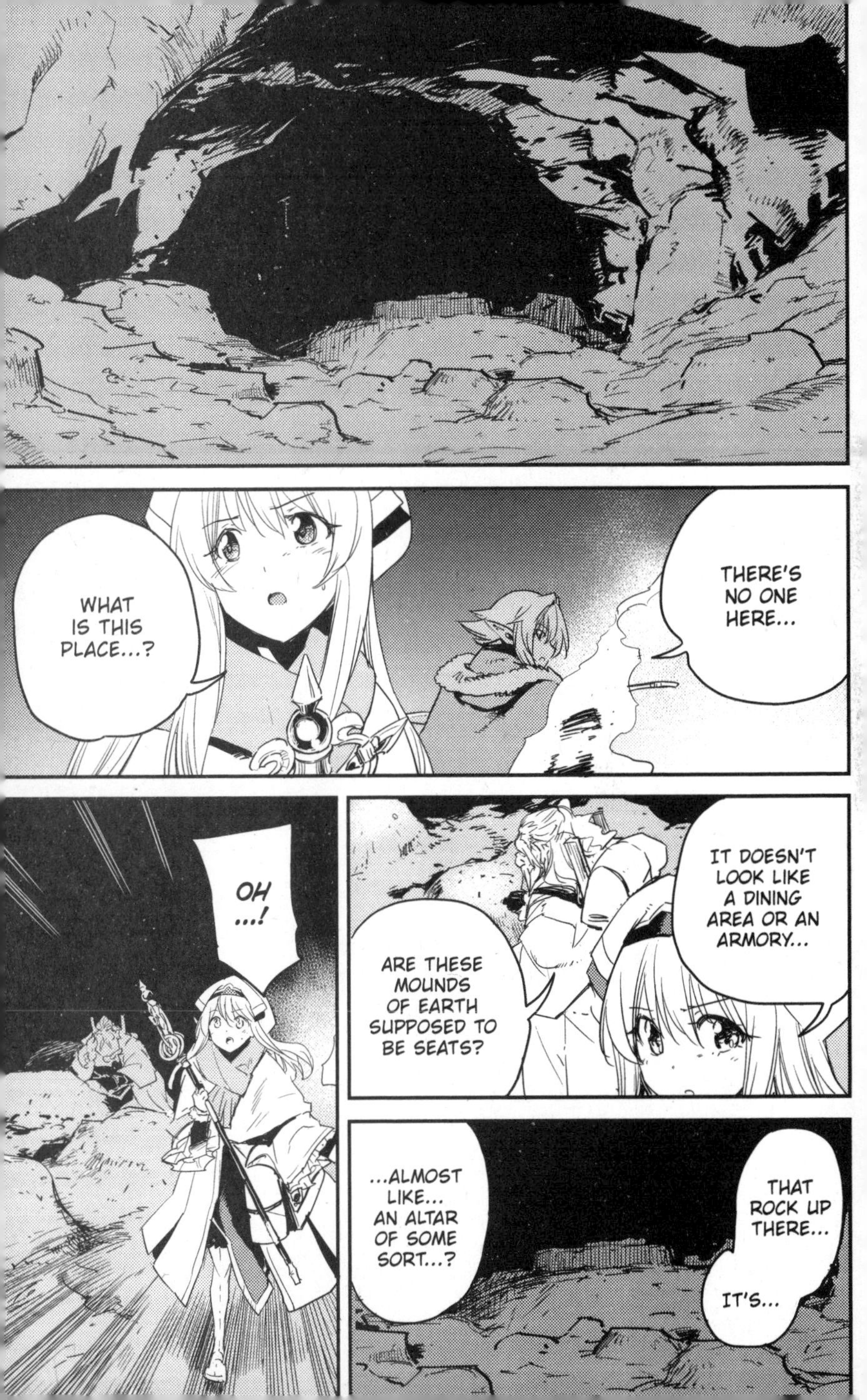
THERE'S NO ONE HERE...
WHAT IS THIS PLACE...?
IT DOESN'T LOOK LIKE A DINING AREA OR AN ARMORY...
ARE THESE MOUNDS OF EARTH SUPPOSED TO BE SEATS?
THAT ROCK UP THERE...
IT'S...
...ALMOST LIKE... AN ALTAR OF SOME SORT...?
OH ...!

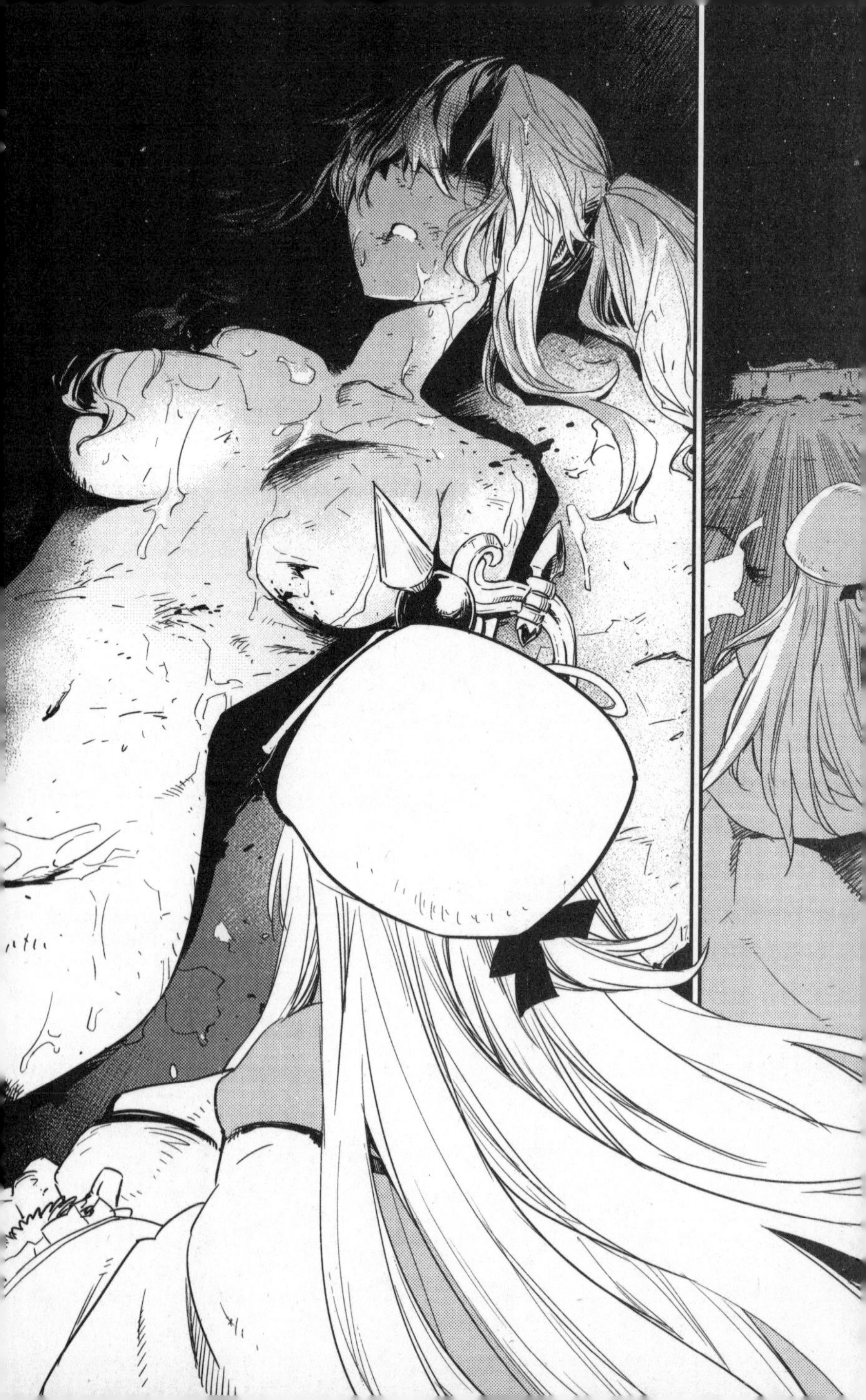

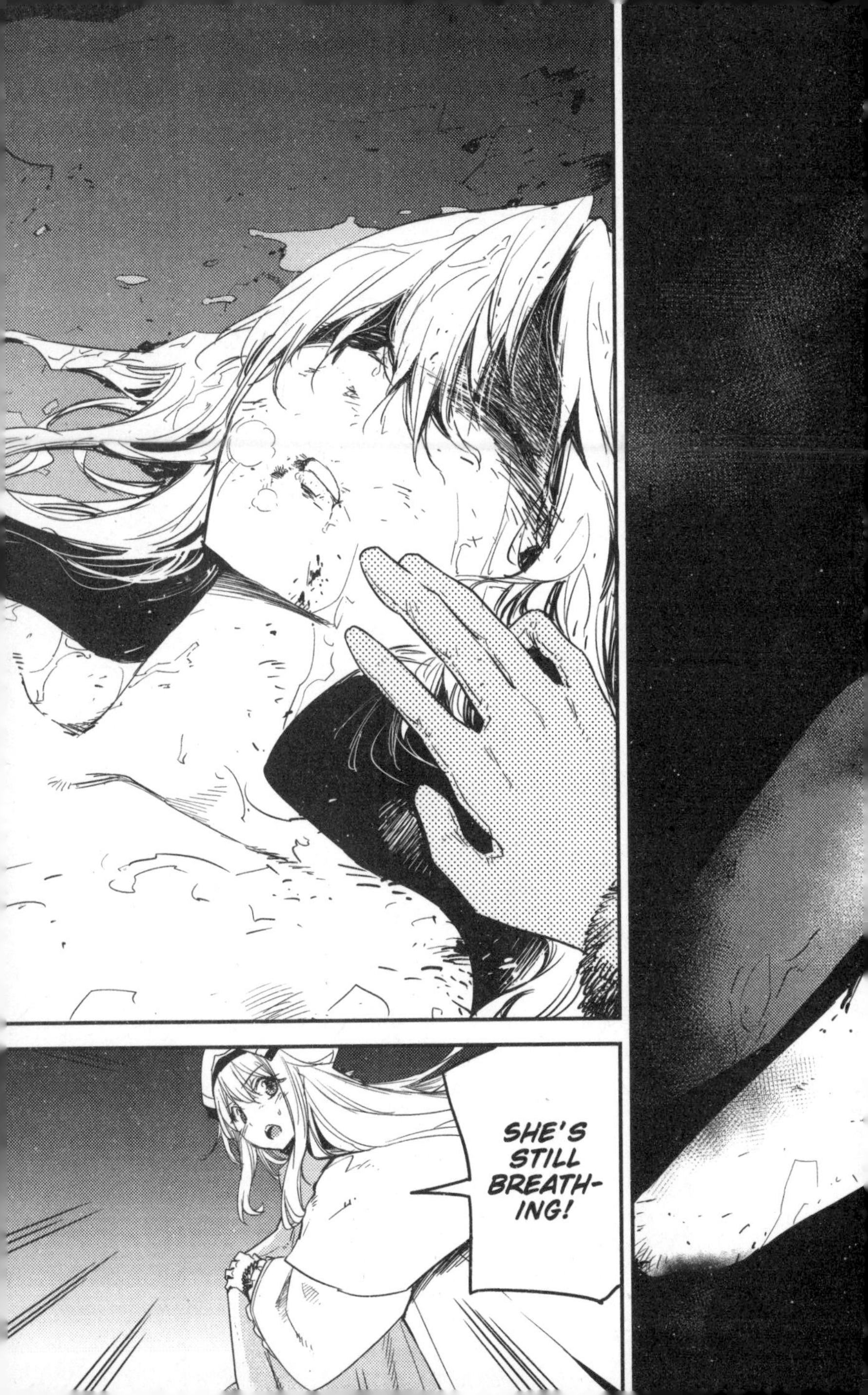
SHE'S STILL BREATH-ING!

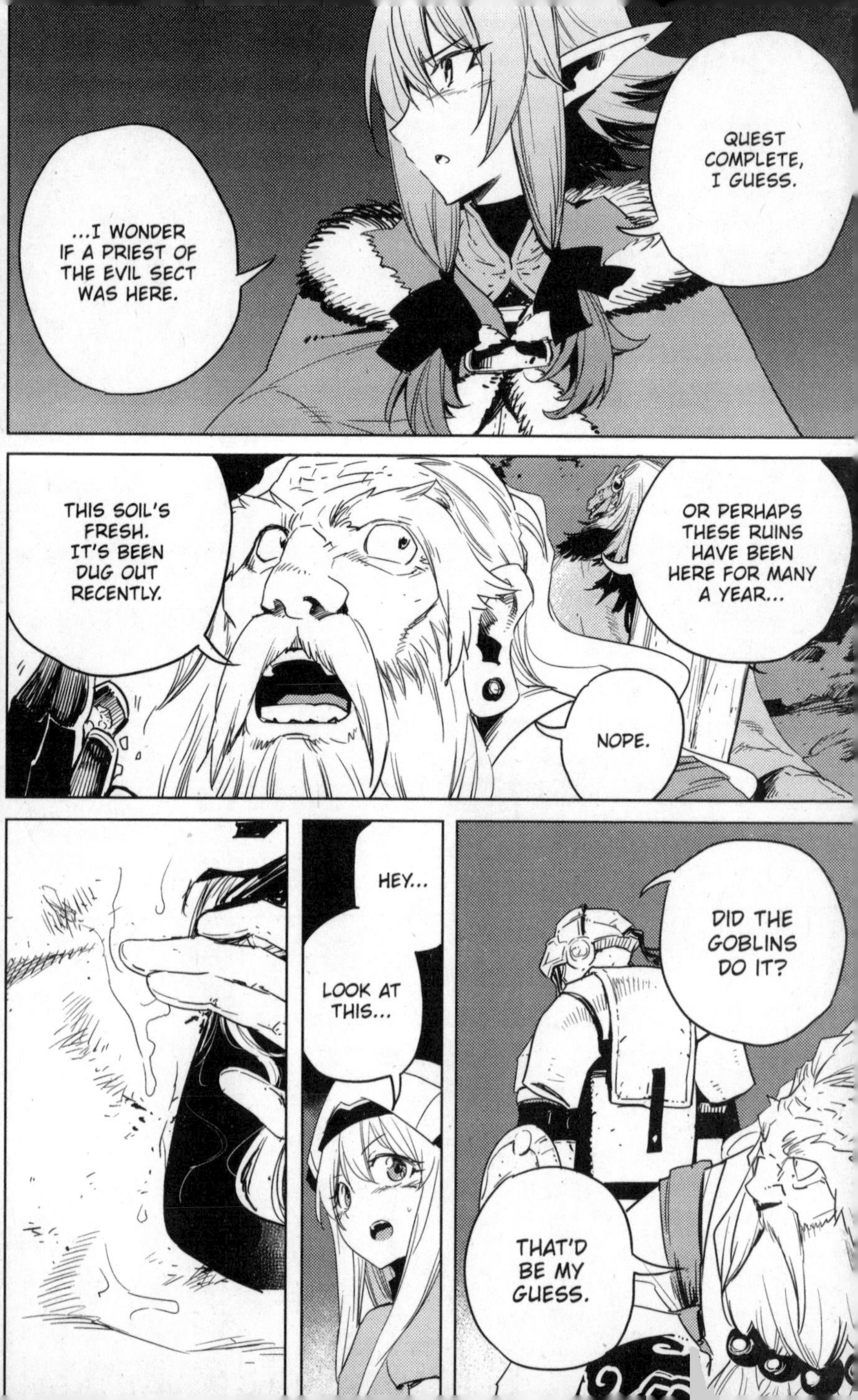
QUEST COMPLETE, I GUESS.
...I WONDER IF A PRIEST OF THE EVIL SECT WAS HERE.
OR PERHAPS THESE RUINS HAVE BEEN HERE FOR MANY A YEAR...
NOPE.
THIS SOIL'S FRESH. IT'S BEEN DUG OUT RECENTLY.
DID THE GOBLINS DO IT?
THAT'D BE MY GUESS.
HEY...
LOOK AT THIS...

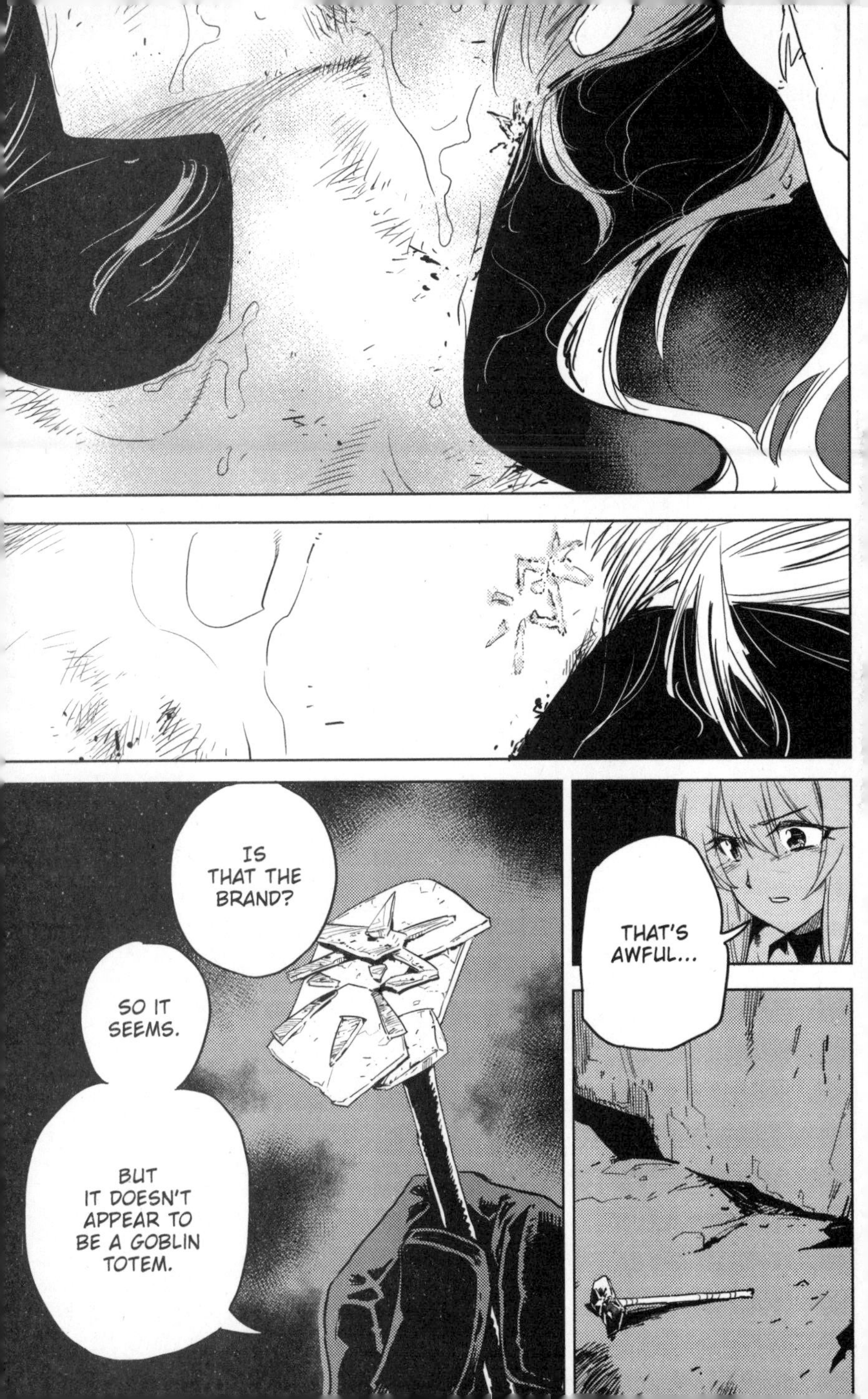
THAT'S AWFUL...
IS THAT THE BRAND?
SO IT SEEMS.
BUT IT DOESN'T APPEAR TO BE A GOBLIN TOTEM.

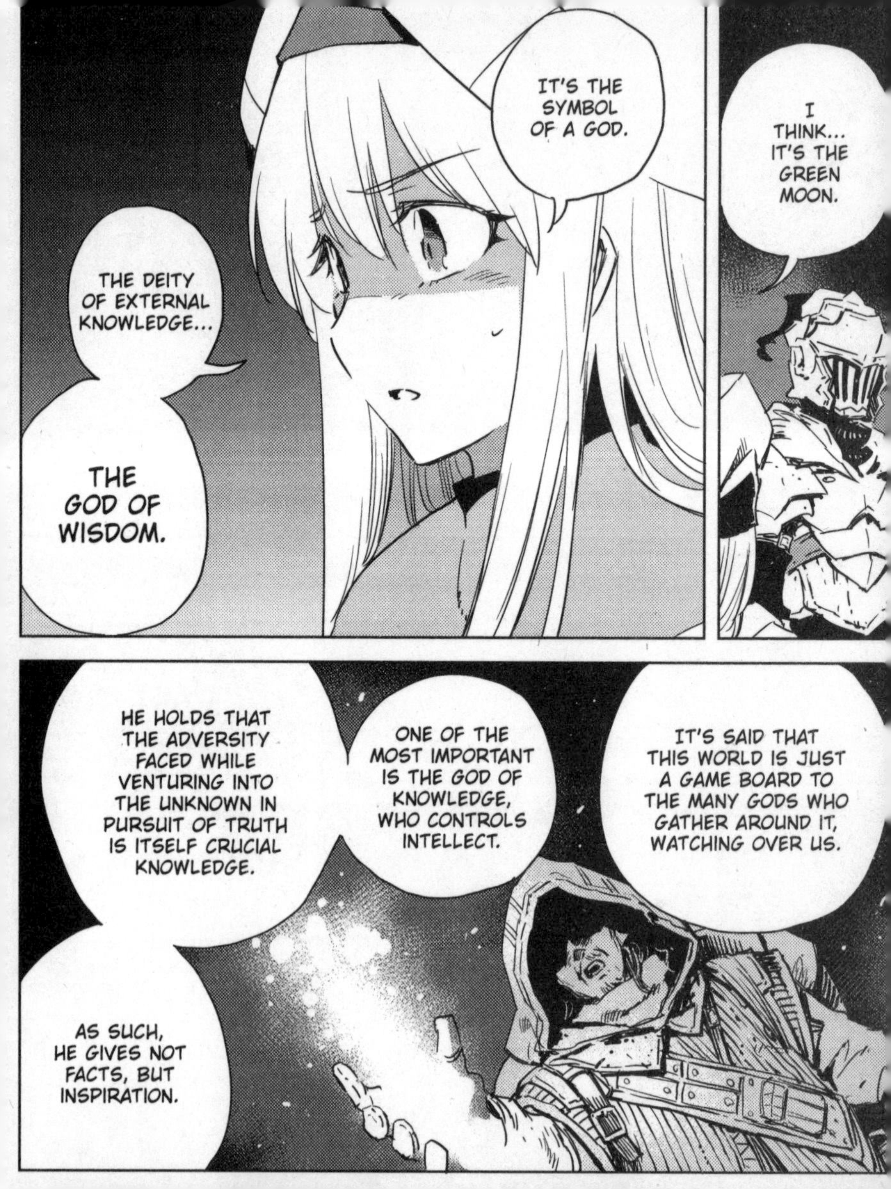
I THINK... IT'S THE GREEN MOON.
IT'S THE SYMBOL OF A GOD.
THE DEITY OF EXTERNAL KNOWLEDGE...
THE GOD OF WISDOM.
IT'S SAID THAT THIS WORLD IS JUST A GAME BOARD TO THE MANY GODS WHO GATHER AROUND IT, WATCHING OVER US.
ONE OF THE MOST IMPORTANT IS THE GOD OF KNOWLEDGE, WHO CONTROLS INTELLECT.
HE HOLDS THAT THE ADVERSITY FACED WHILE VENTURING INTO THE UNKNOWN IN PURSUIT OF TRUTH IS ITSELF CRUCIAL KNOWLEDGE.
AS SUCH, HE GIVES NOT FACTS, BUT INSPIRATION.

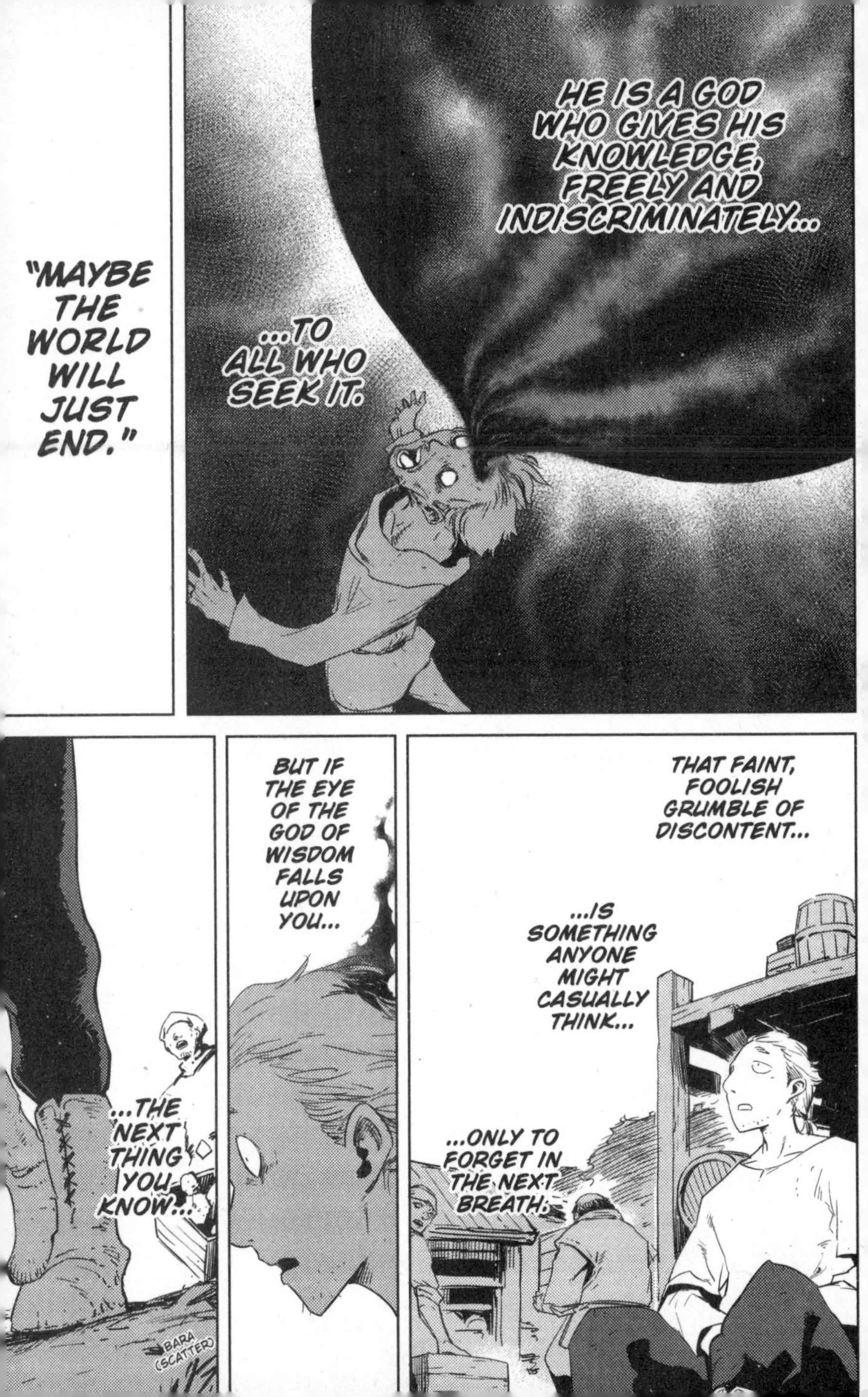
HE IS A GOD WHO GIVES HIS KNOWLEDGE, FREELY AND INDISCRIMINATELY...
...TO ALL WHO SEEK IT.
"MAYBE THE WORLD WILL JUST END."
THAT FAINT, FOOLISH GRUMBLE OF DISCONTENT...
...IS SOMETHING ANYONE MIGHT CASUALLY THINK...
...ONLY TO FORGET IN THE NEXT BREATH.
BUT IF THE EYE OF THE GOD OF WISDOM FALLS UPON YOU...
...THE NEXT THING YOU KNOW...
BARA (SCATTER)

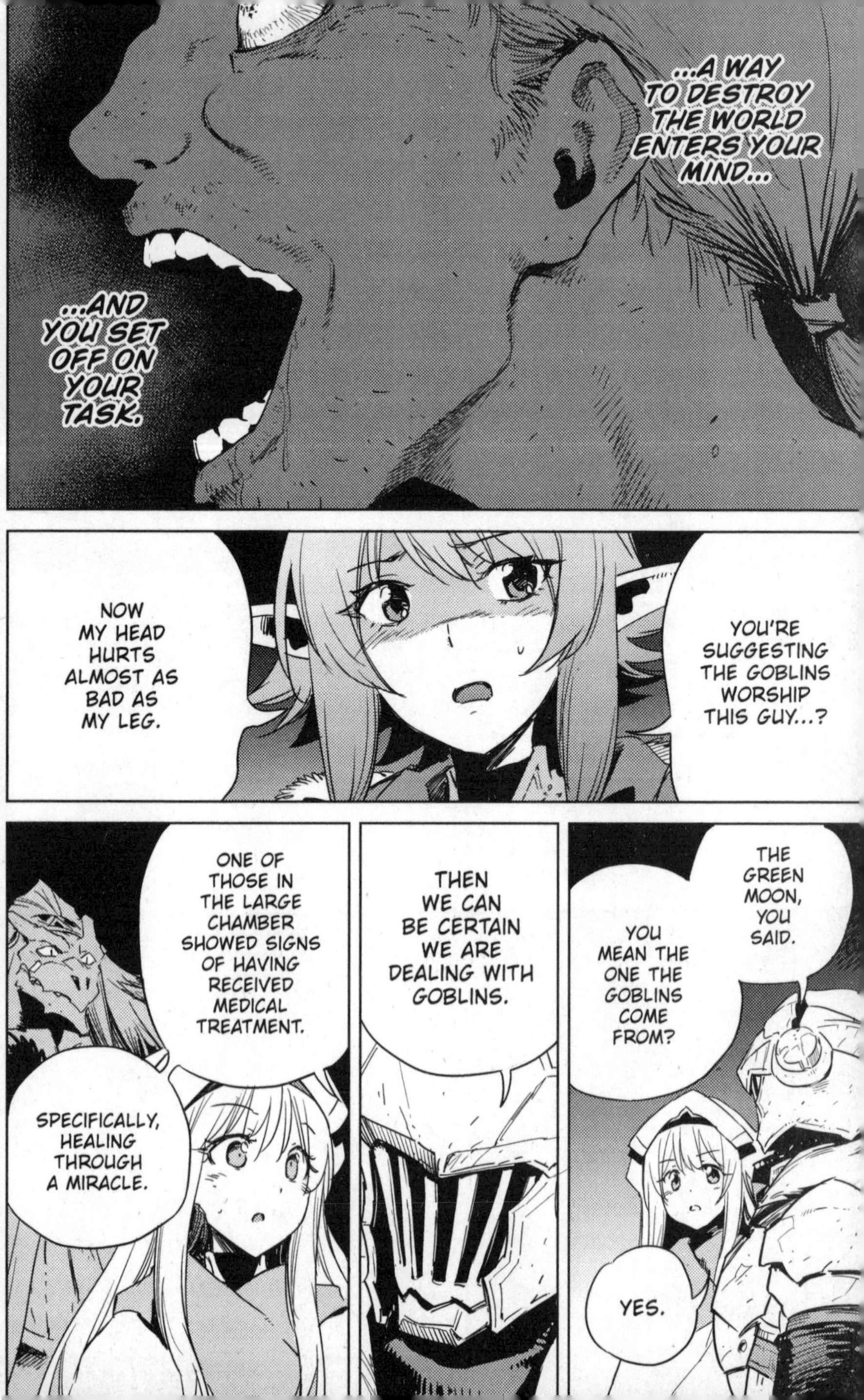
...A WAY TO DESTROY THE WORLD ENTERS YOUR MIND...
...AND YOU SET OFF ON YOUR TASK.
YOU'RE SUGGESTING THE GOBLINS WORSHIP THIS GUY...?
NOW MY HEAD HURTS ALMOST AS BAD AS MY LEG.
THE GREEN MOON, YOU SAID.
YOU MEAN THE ONE THE GOBLINS COME FROM?
YES.
THEN WE CAN BE CERTAIN WE ARE DEALING WITH GOBLINS.
ONE OF THOSE IN THE LARGE CHAMBER SHOWED SIGNS OF HAVING RECEIVED MEDICAL TREATMENT.
SPECIFICALLY, HEALING THROUGH A MIRACLE.

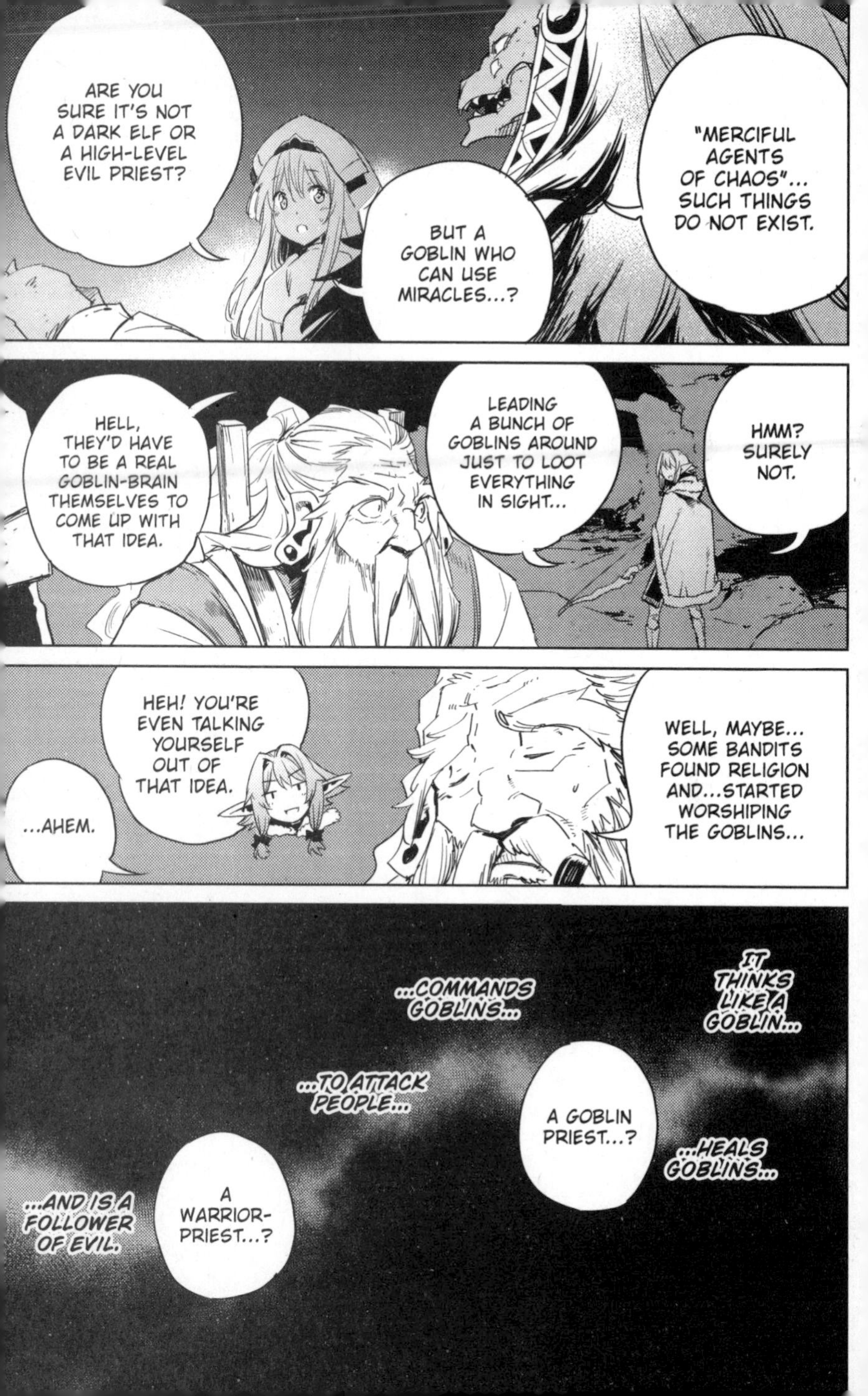
"MERCIFUL AGENTS OF CHAOS"... SUCH THINGS DO NOT EXIST.
BUT A GOBLIN WHO CAN USE MIRACLES...?
ARE YOU SURE IT'S NOT A DARK ELF OR A HIGH-LEVEL EVIL PRIEST?
HMM? SURELY NOT.
LEADING A BUNCH OF GOBLINS AROUND JUST TO LOOT EVERYTHING IN SIGHT...
HELL, THEY'D HAVE TO BE A REAL GOBLIN-BRAIN THEMSELVES TO COME UP WITH THAT IDEA.
WELL, MAYBE... SOME BANDITS FOUND RELIGION AND...STARTED WORSHIPING THE GOBLINS...
HEH! YOU'RE EVEN TALKING YOURSELF OUT OF THAT IDEA.
...AHEM.
IT THINKS LIKE A GOBLIN...
...COMMANDS GOBLINS...
...TO ATTACK PEOPLE...
A GOBLIN PRIEST...?
...HEALS GOBLINS...
A WARRIOR-PRIEST...?
...AND IS A FOLLOWER OF EVIL.

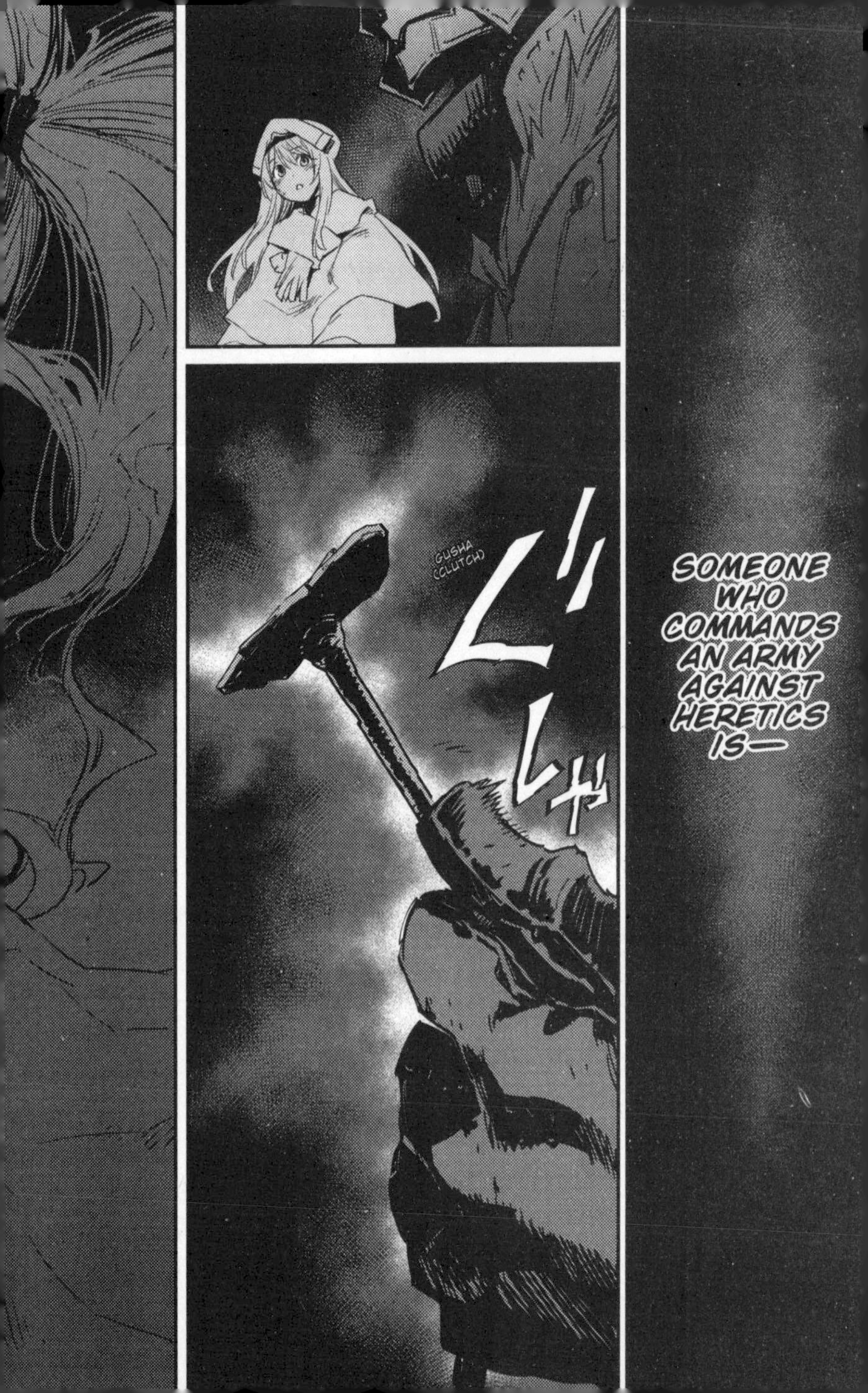
SOMEONE WHO COMMANDS AN ARMY AGAINST HERETICS IS—
GUSHA (CLUTCH)

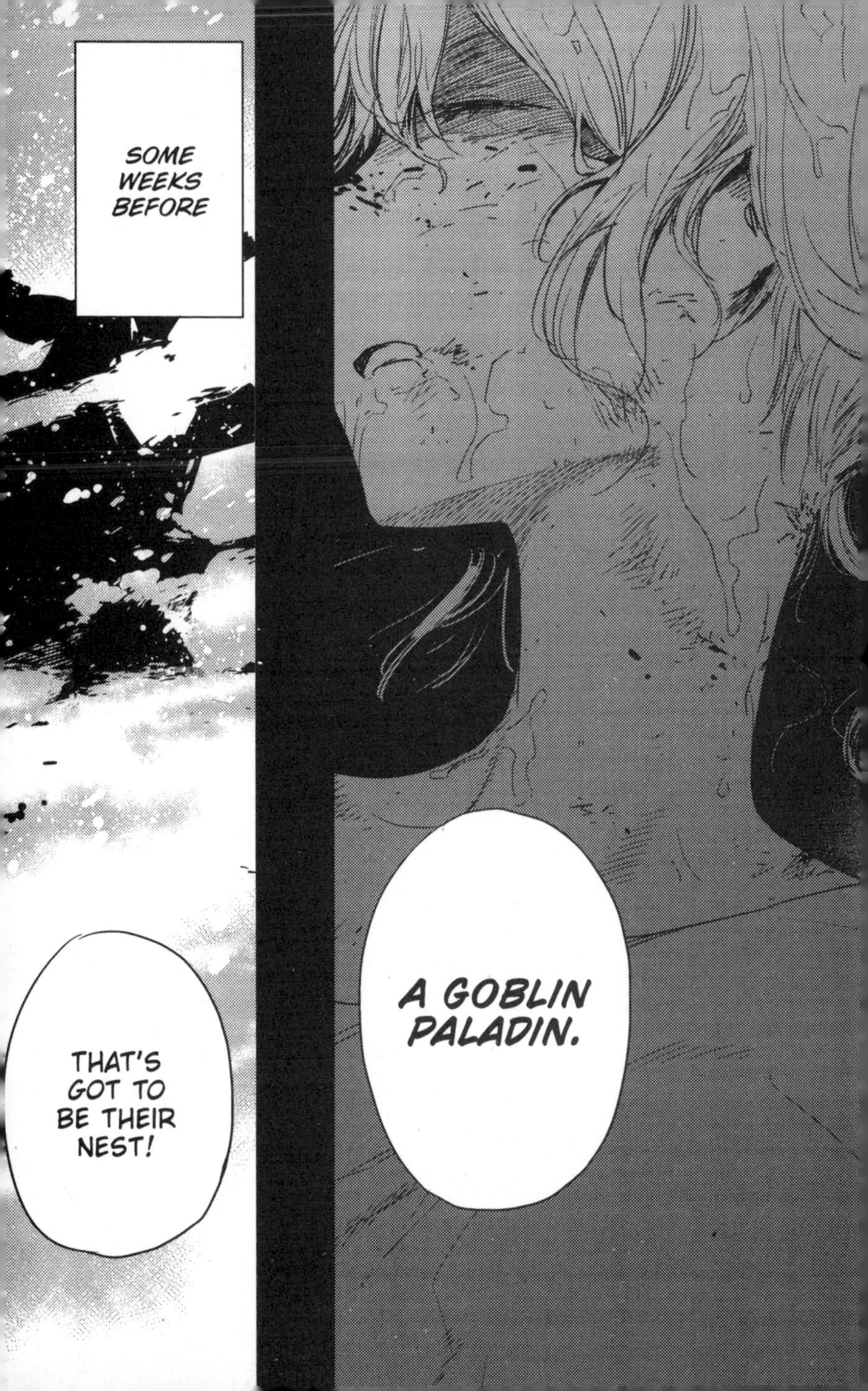
A GOBLIN PALADIN.
SOME WEEKS BEFORE
THAT'S GOT TO BE THEIR NEST!

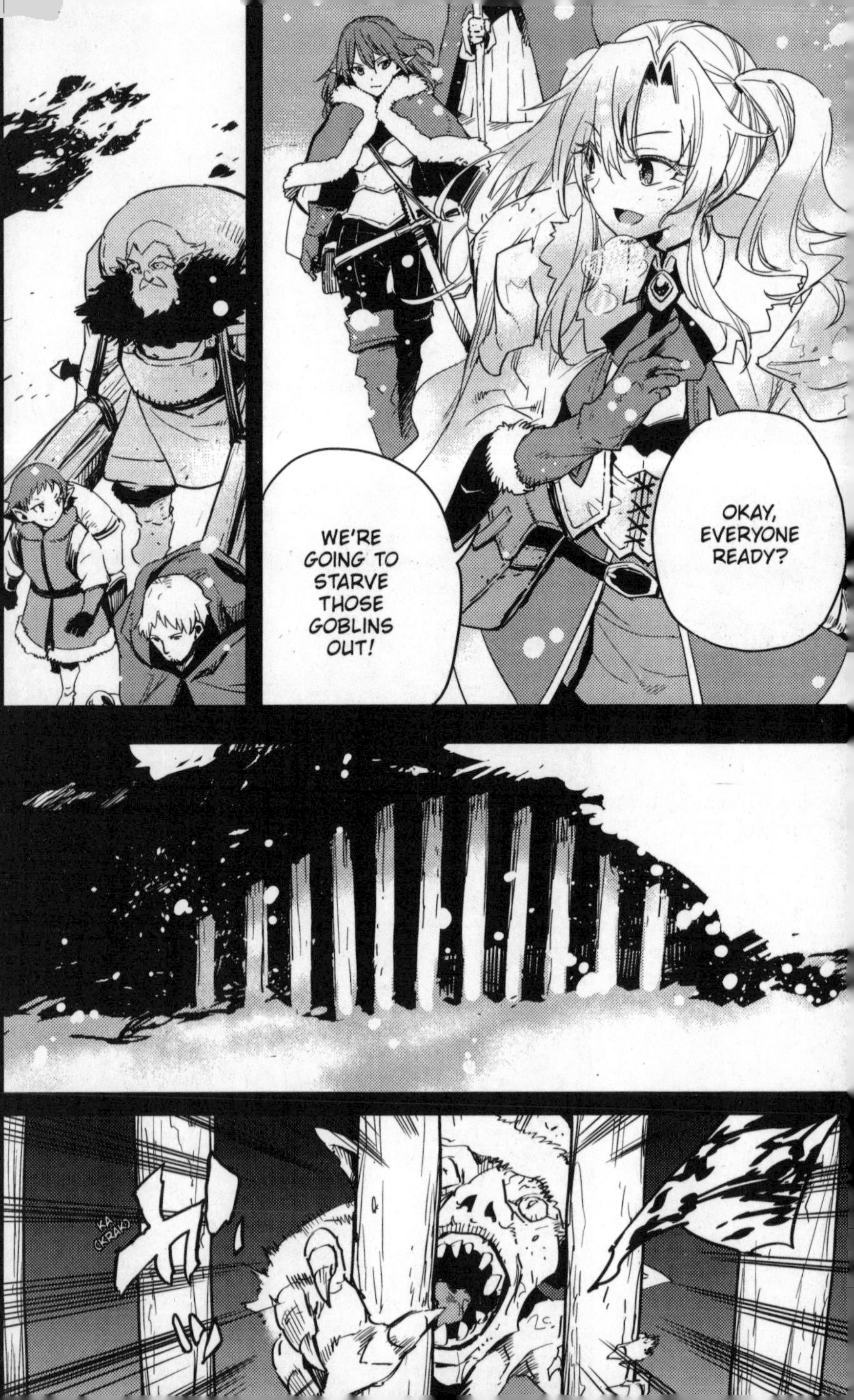
OKAY, EVERYONE READY?
WE'RE GOING TO STARVE THOSE GOBLINS OUT!
KA (KRAK)

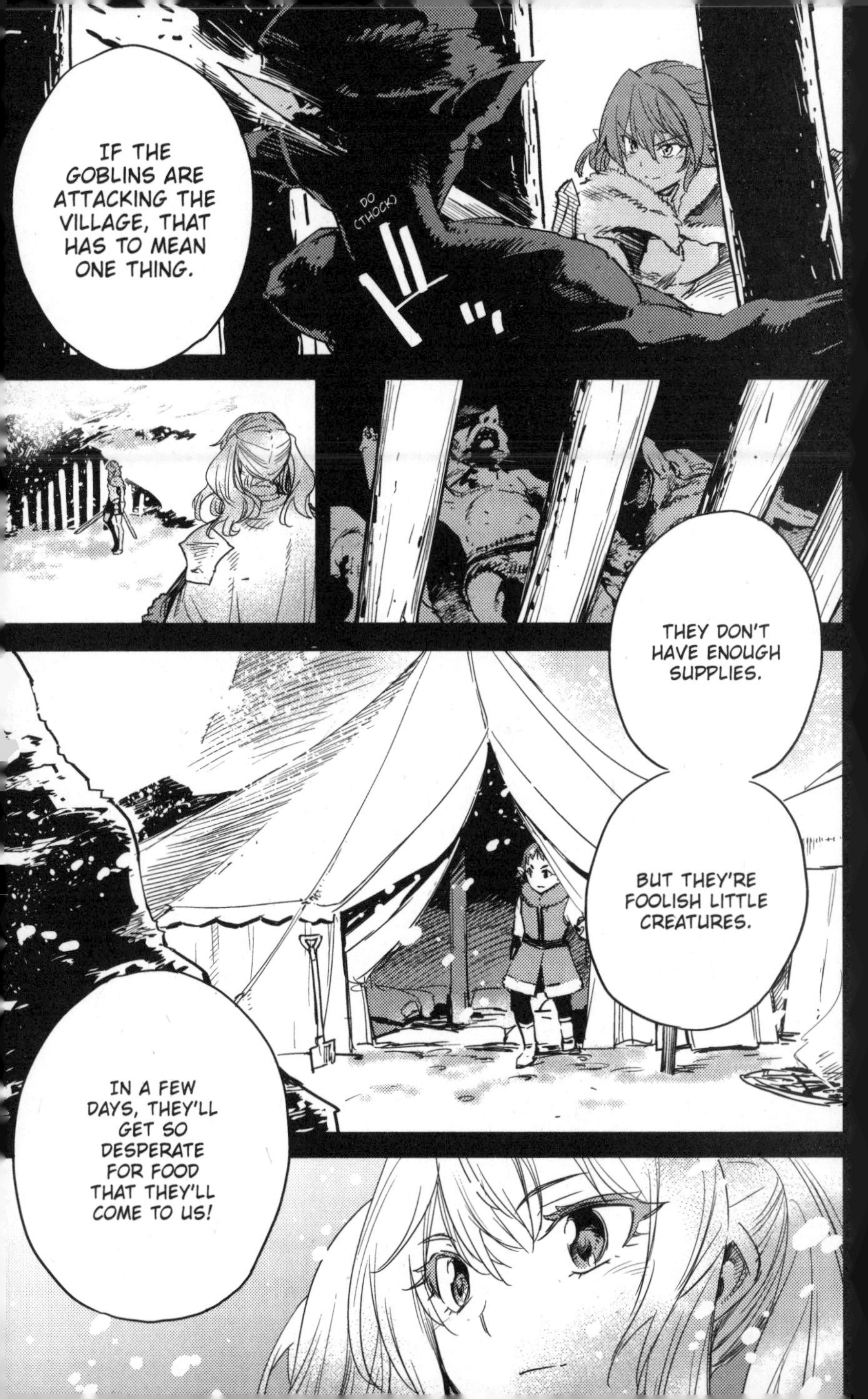
IF THE GOBLINS ARE ATTACKING THE VILLAGE, THAT HAS TO MEAN ONE THING.
DO (THOCK)
THEY DON'T HAVE ENOUGH SUPPLIES.
BUT THEY'RE FOOLISH LITTLE CREATURES.
IN A FEW DAYS, THEY'LL GET SO DESPERATE FOR FOOD THAT THEY'LL COME TO US!

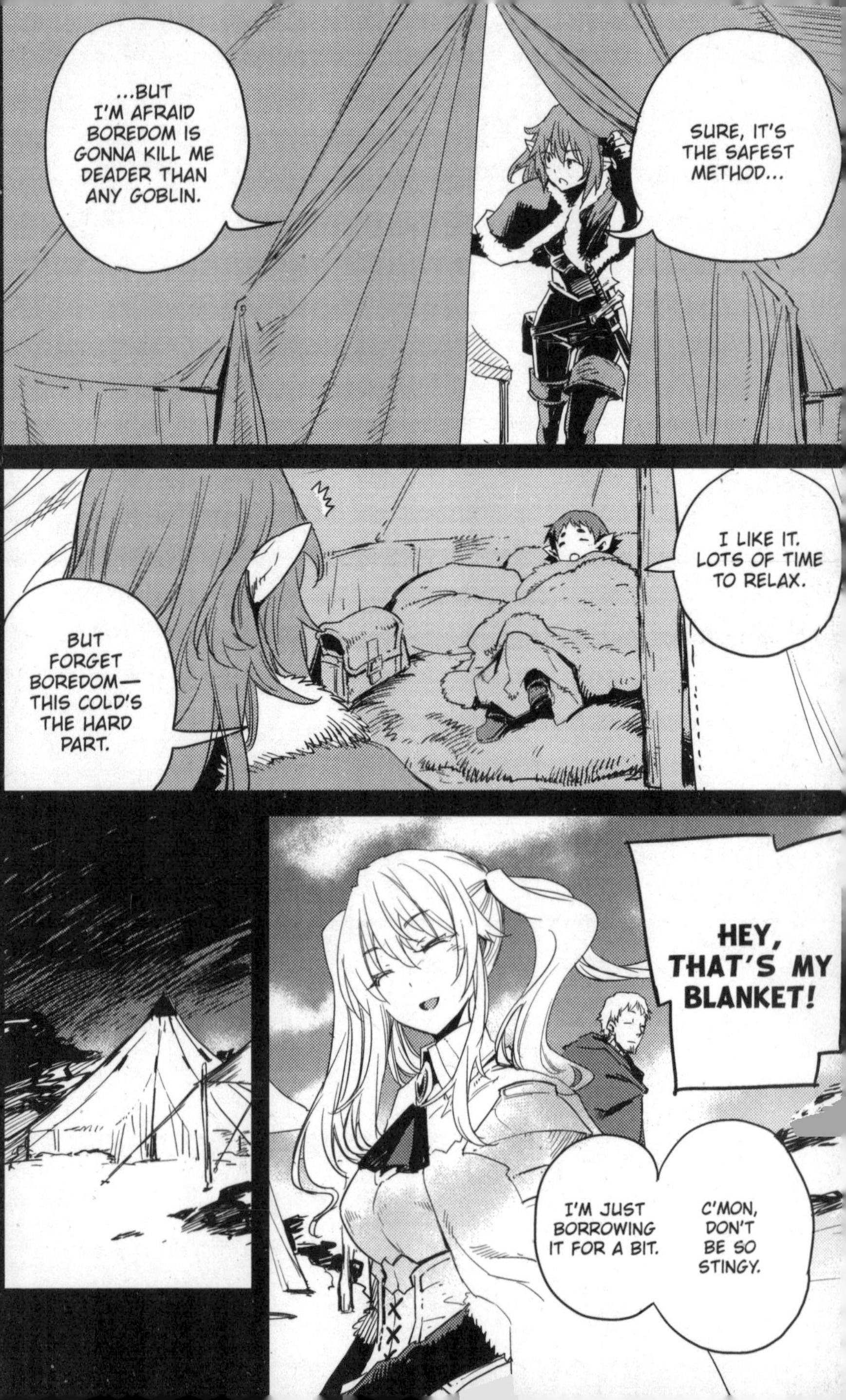
SURE, IT'S THE SAFEST METHOD...
...BUT I'M AFRAID BOREDOM IS GONNA KILL ME DEADER THAN ANY GOBLIN.
I LIKE IT. LOTS OF TIME TO RELAX.
BUT FORGET BOREDOM— THIS COLD'S THE HARD PART.
HEY, THAT'S MY BLANKET!
C'MON, DON'T BE SO STINGY.
I'M JUST BORROWING IT FOR A BIT.

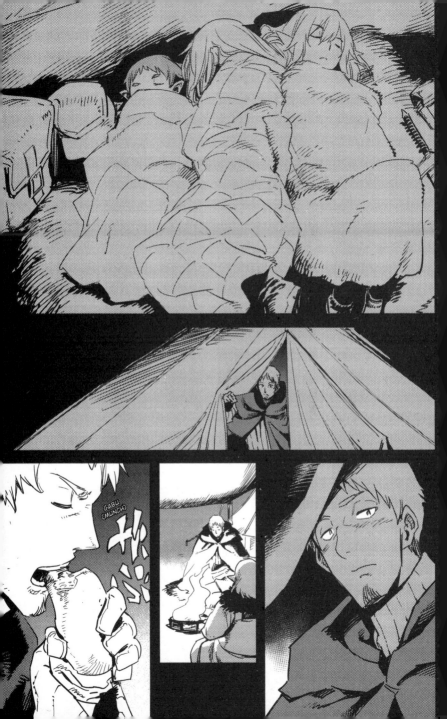

GABU
(MUNCH)

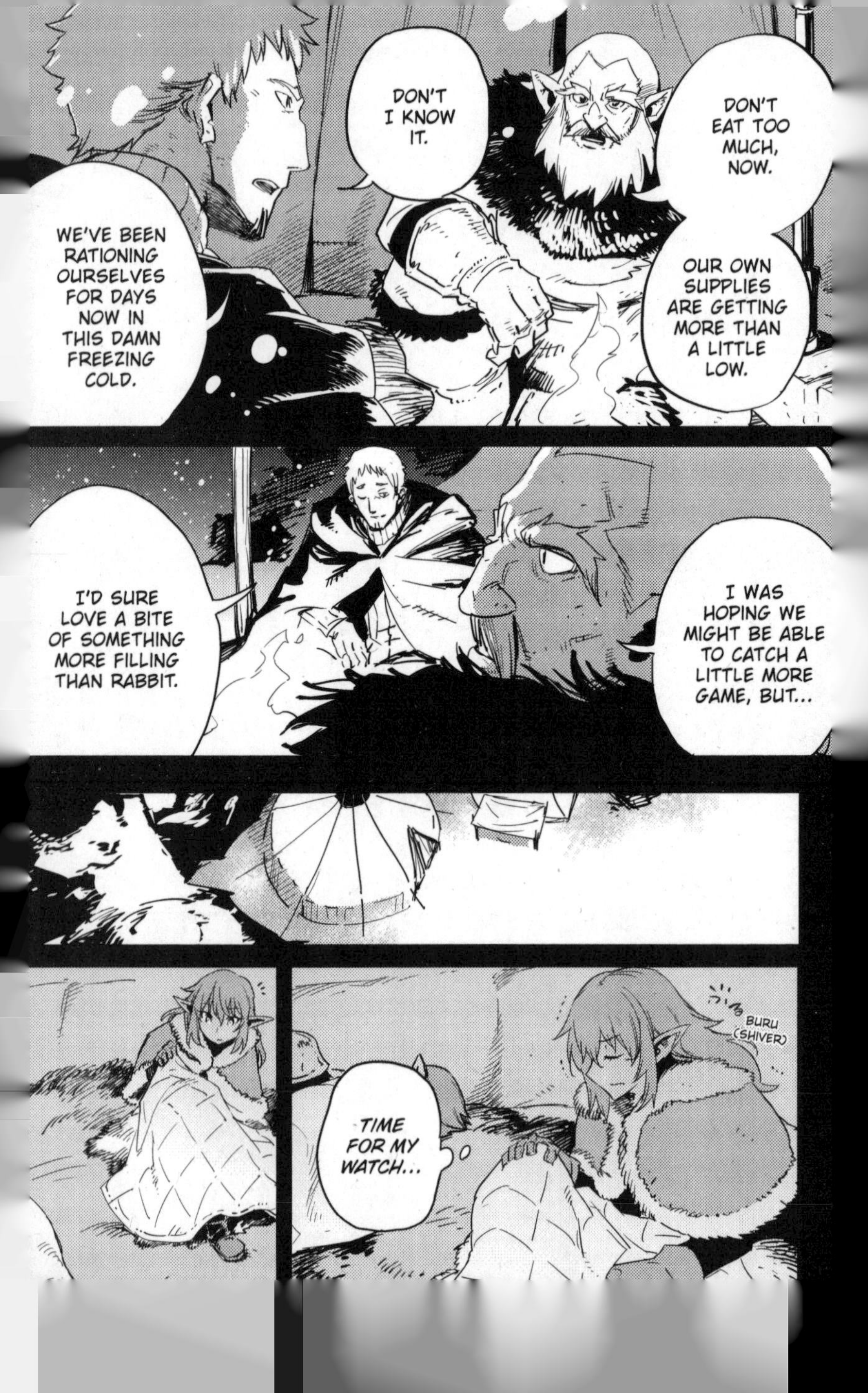
DON'T EAT TOO MUCH, NOW.
DON'T I KNOW IT.
WE'VE BEEN RATIONING OURSELVES FOR DAYS NOW IN THIS DAMN FREEZING COLD.
OUR OWN SUPPLIES ARE GETTING MORE THAN A LITTLE LOW.
I WAS HOPING WE MIGHT BE ABLE TO CATCH A LITTLE MORE GAME, BUT...
I'D SURE LOVE A BITE OF SOMETHING MORE FILLING THAN RABBIT.
BURU (SHIVER)
TIME FOR MY WATCH...

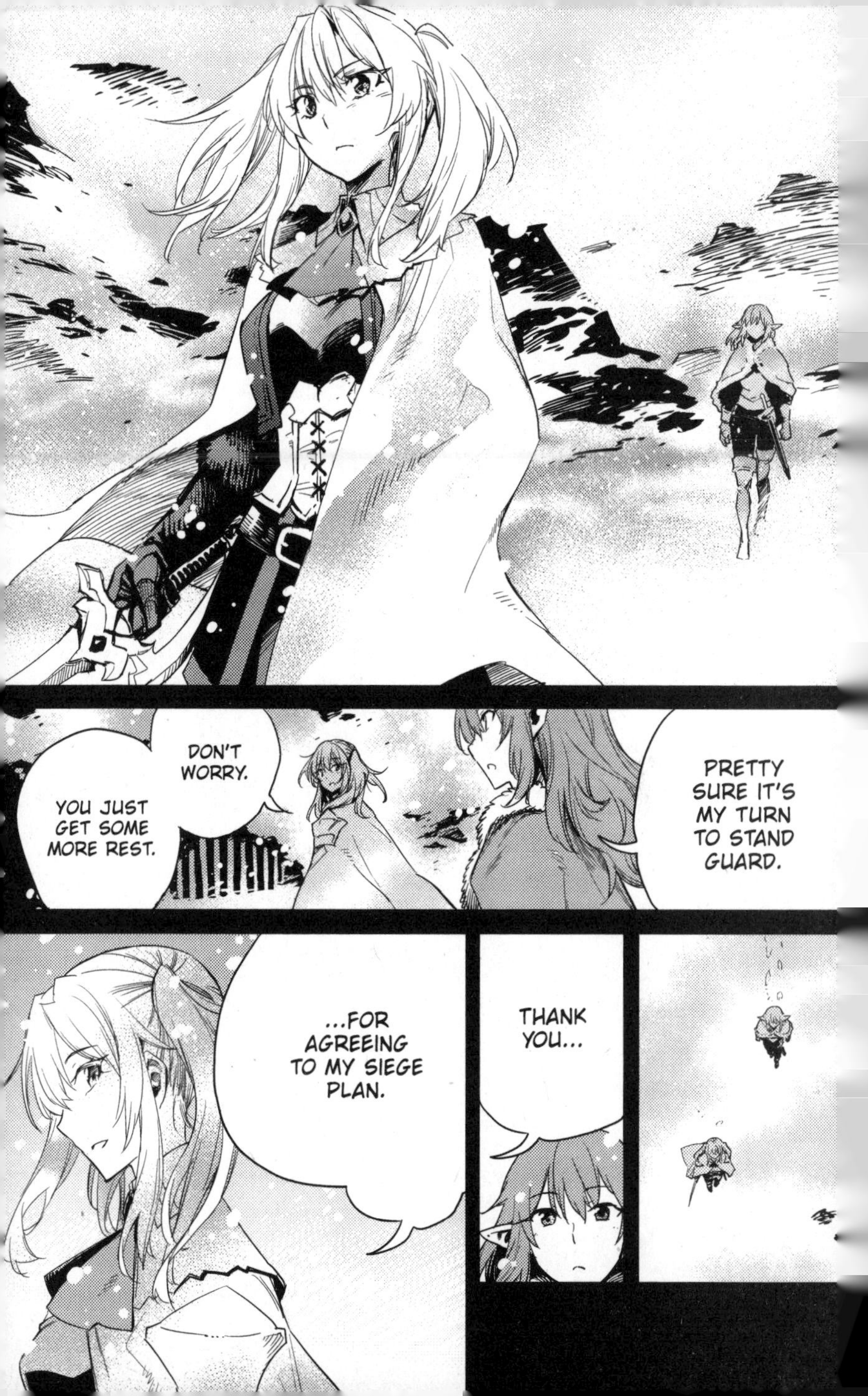
PRETTY SURE IT'S MY TURN TO STAND GUARD.
DON'T WORRY.
YOU JUST GET SOME MORE REST.
THANK YOU...
...FOR AGREEING TO MY SIEGE PLAN.

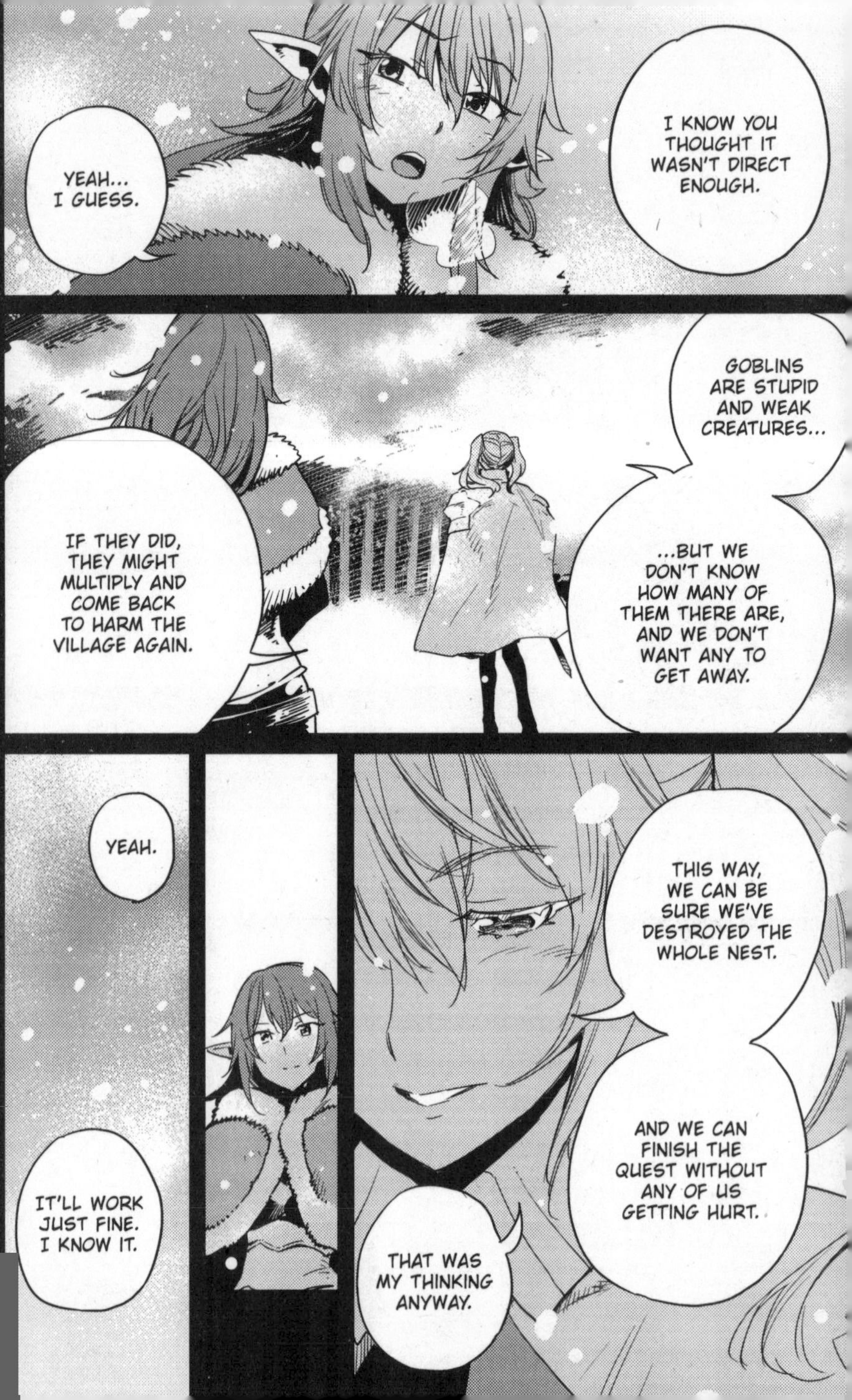
I KNOW YOU THOUGHT IT WASN'T DIRECT ENOUGH.
YEAH... I GUESS.
GOBLINS ARE STUPID AND WEAK CREATURES...
...BUT WE DON'T KNOW HOW MANY OF THEM THERE ARE, AND WE DON'T WANT ANY TO GET AWAY.
IF THEY DID, THEY MIGHT MULTIPLY AND COME BACK TO HARM THE VILLAGE AGAIN.
THIS WAY, WE CAN BE SURE WE'VE DESTROYED THE WHOLE NEST.
AND WE CAN FINISH THE QUEST WITHOUT ANY OF US GETTING HURT.
THAT WAS MY THINKING ANYWAY.
YEAH.
IT'LL WORK JUST FINE. I KNOW IT.

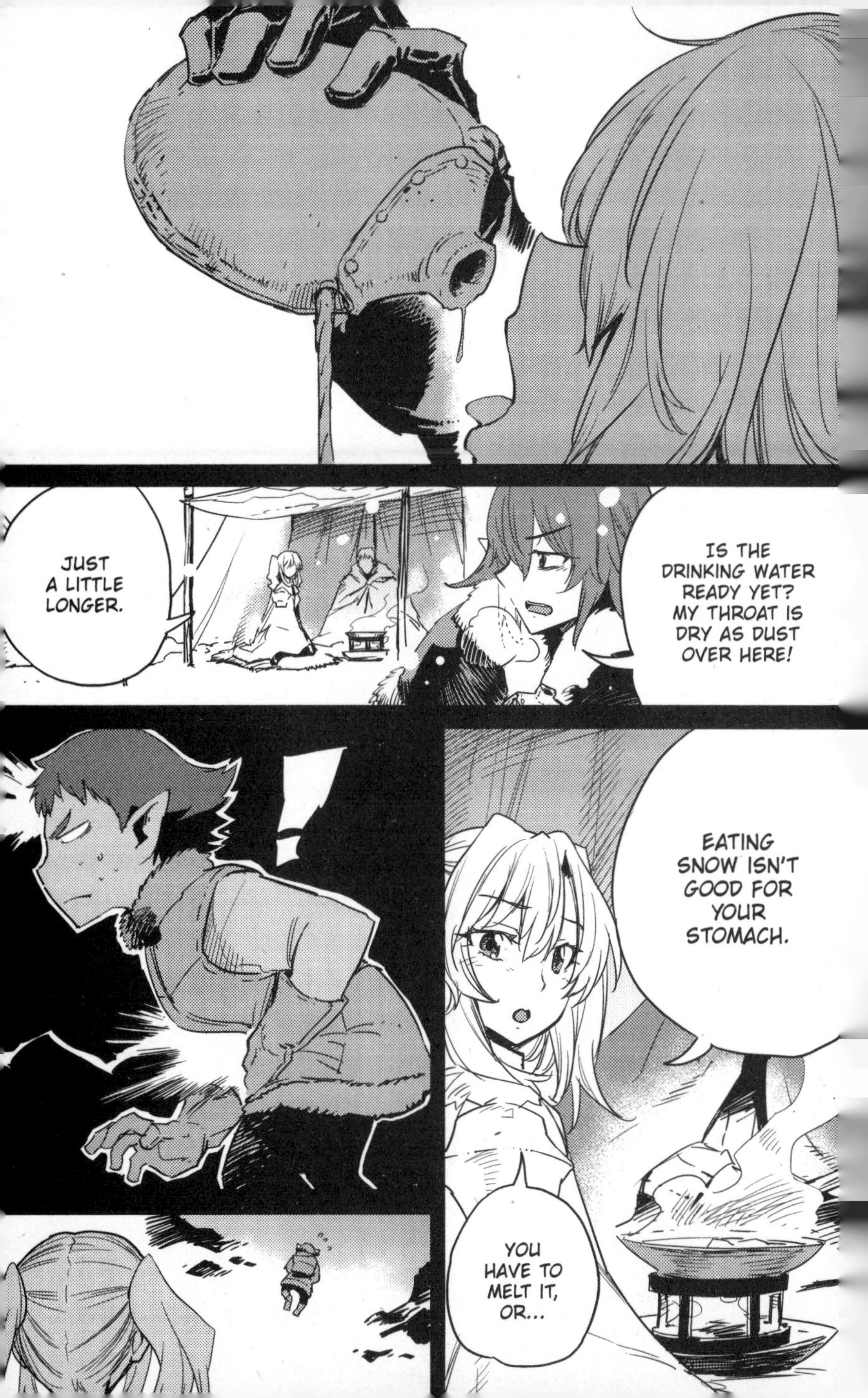
IS THE DRINKING WATER READY YET? MY THROAT IS DRY AS DUST OVER HERE!
JUST A LITTLE LONGER.
EATING SNOW ISN'T GOOD FOR YOUR STOMACH.
YOU HAVE TO MELT IT, OR...
!

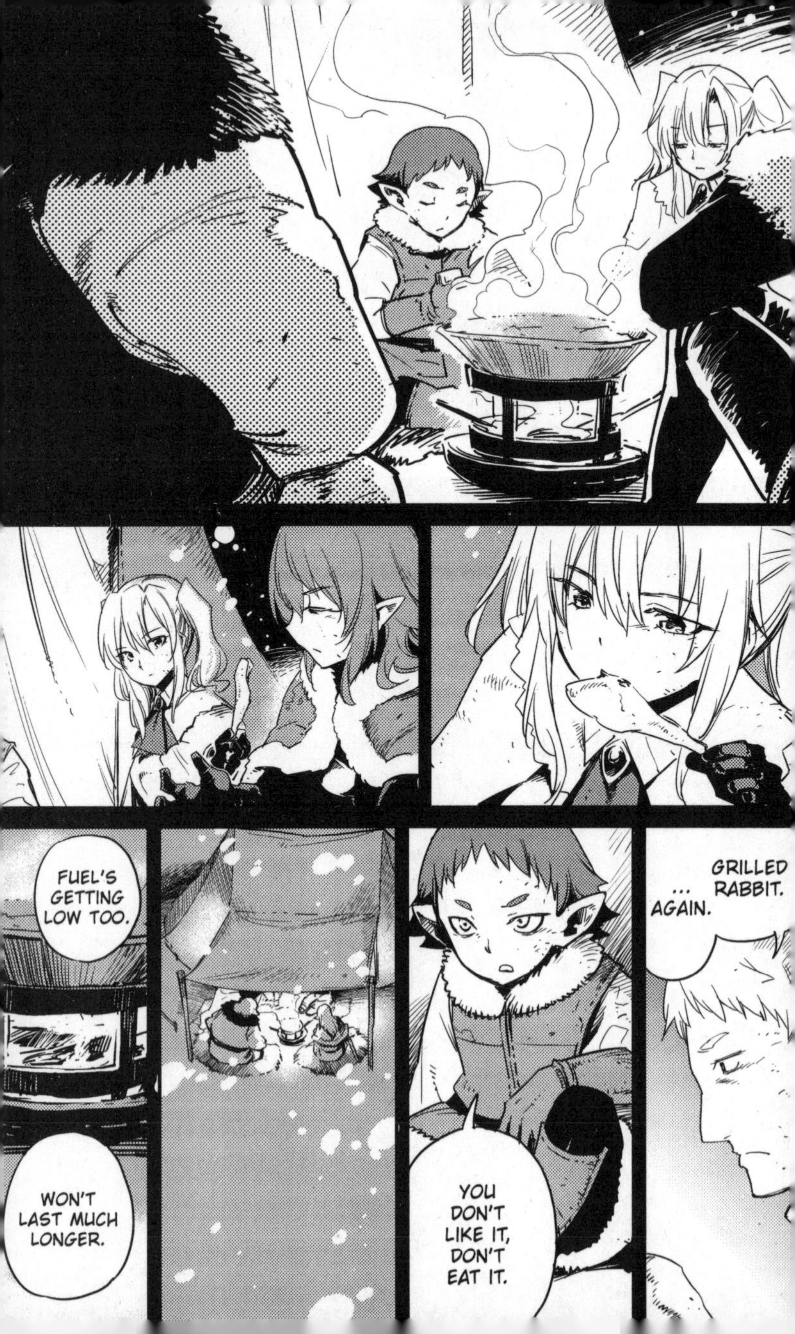
GRILLED RABBIT.
... AGAIN.
YOU DON'T LIKE IT, DON'T EAT IT.
FUEL'S GETTING LOW TOO.
WON'T LAST MUCH LONGER.

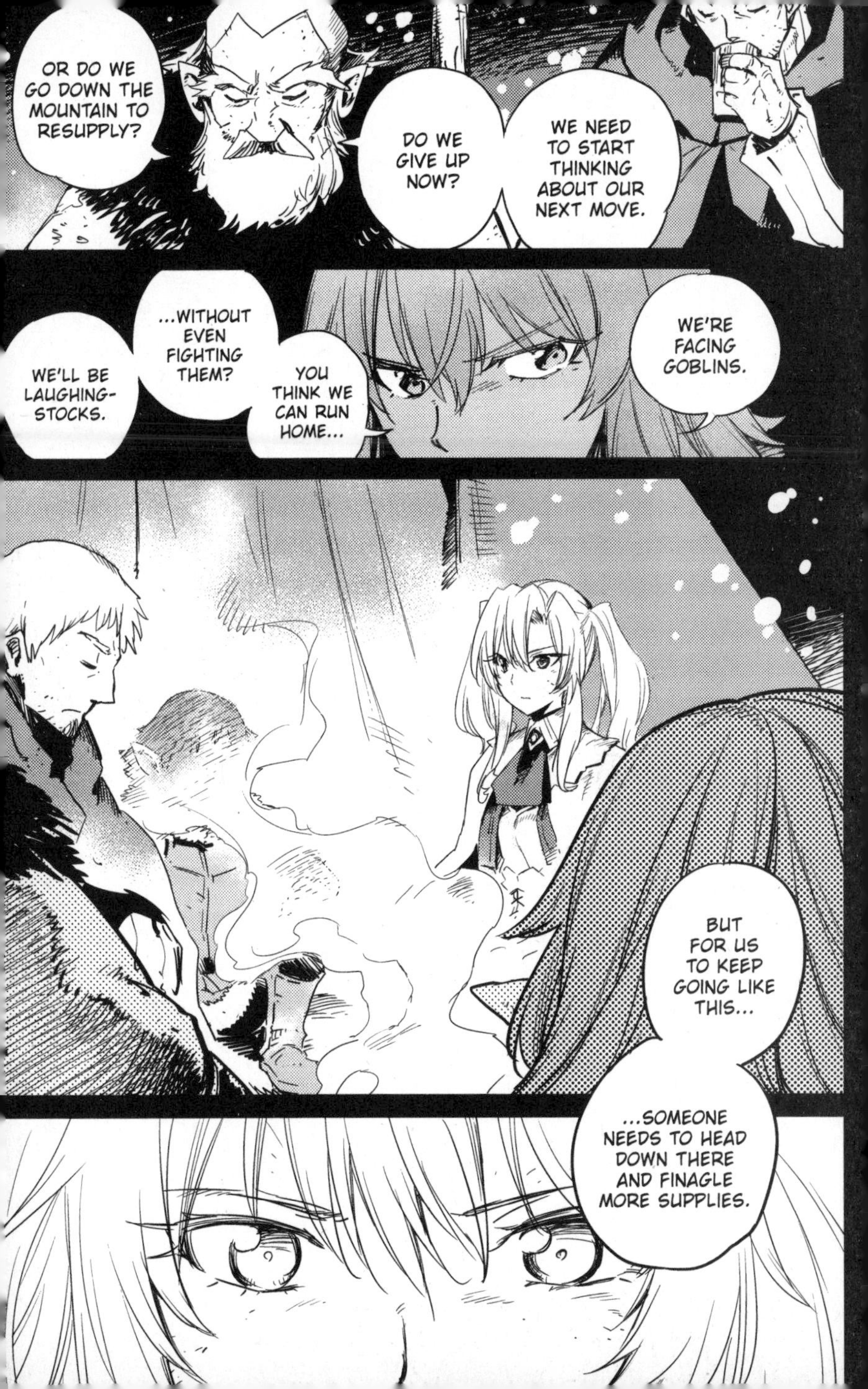
WE NEED TO START THINKING ABOUT OUR NEXT MOVE.
DO WE GIVE UP NOW?
OR DO WE GO DOWN THE MOUNTAIN TO RESUPPLY?
WE'RE FACING GOBLINS.
YOU THINK WE CAN RUN HOME...
...WITHOUT EVEN FIGHTING THEM?
WE'LL BE LAUGHING-STOCKS.
BUT FOR US TO KEEP GOING LIKE THIS...
...SOMEONE NEEDS TO HEAD DOWN THERE AND FINAGLE MORE SUPPLIES.

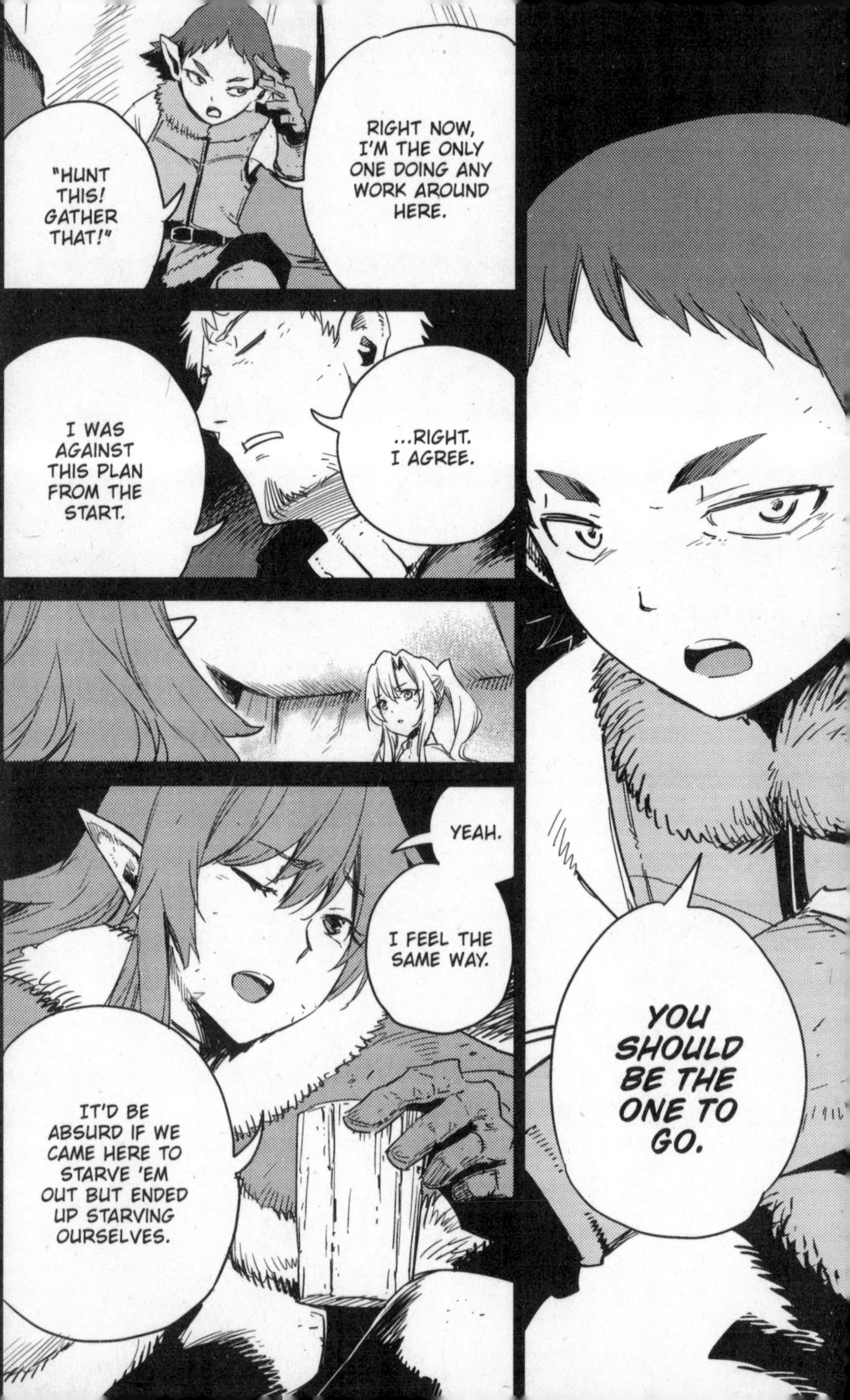
YOU SHOULD BE THE ONE TO GO.
RIGHT NOW, I'M THE ONLY ONE DOING ANY WORK AROUND HERE.
"HUNT THIS! GATHER THAT!"
...RIGHT. I AGREE.
I WAS AGAINST THIS PLAN FROM THE START.
YEAH.
I FEEL THE SAME WAY.
IT'D BE ABSURD IF WE CAME HERE TO STARVE 'EM OUT BUT ENDED UP STARVING OURSELVES.

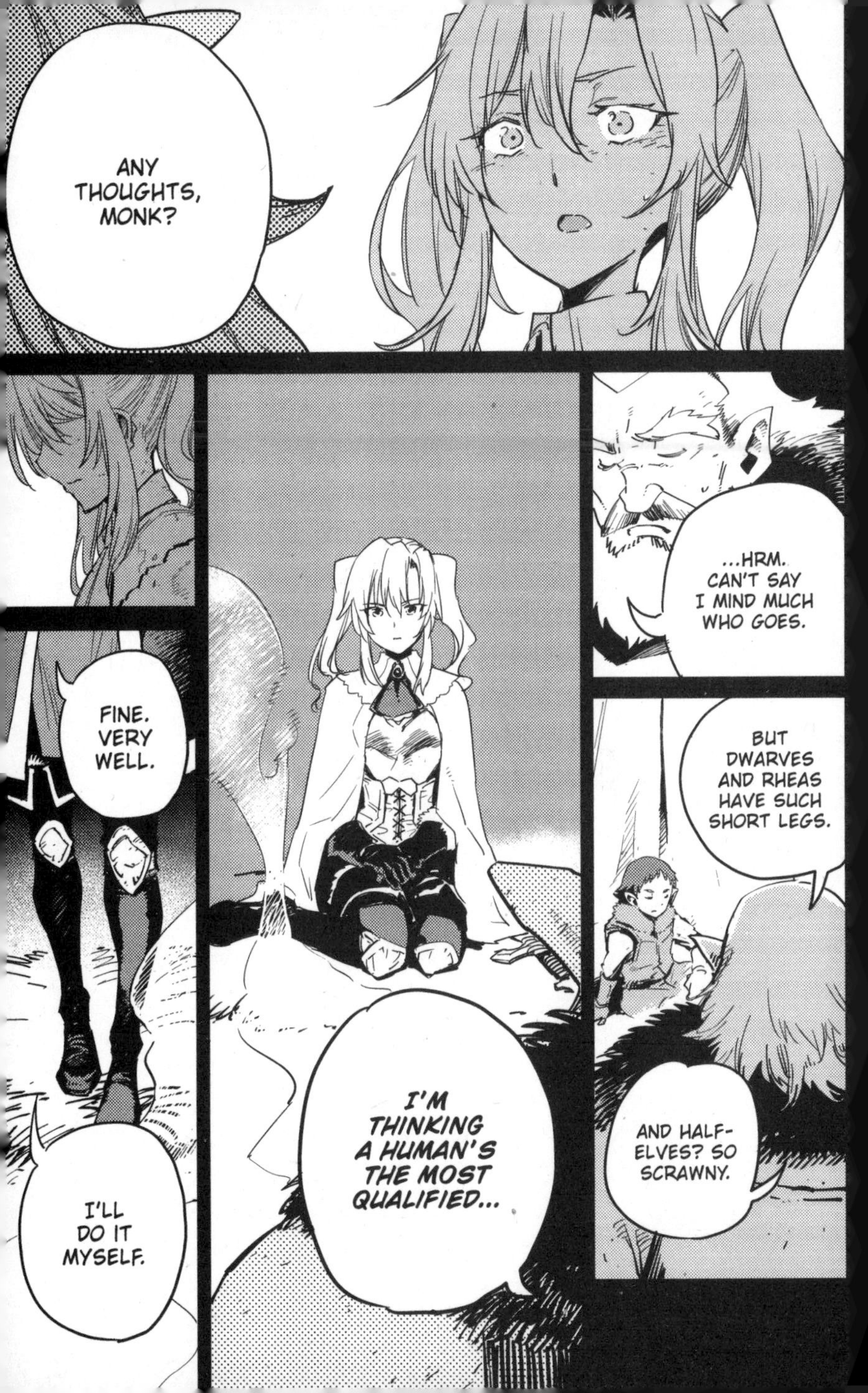
ANY THOUGHTS, MONK?
...HRM. CAN'T SAY I MIND MUCH WHO GOES.
BUT DWARVES AND RHEAS HAVE SUCH SHORT LEGS.
AND HALF-ELVES? SO SCRAWNY.
I'M THINKING A HUMAN'S THE MOST QUALIFIED...
FINE. VERY WELL.
I'LL DO IT MYSELF.

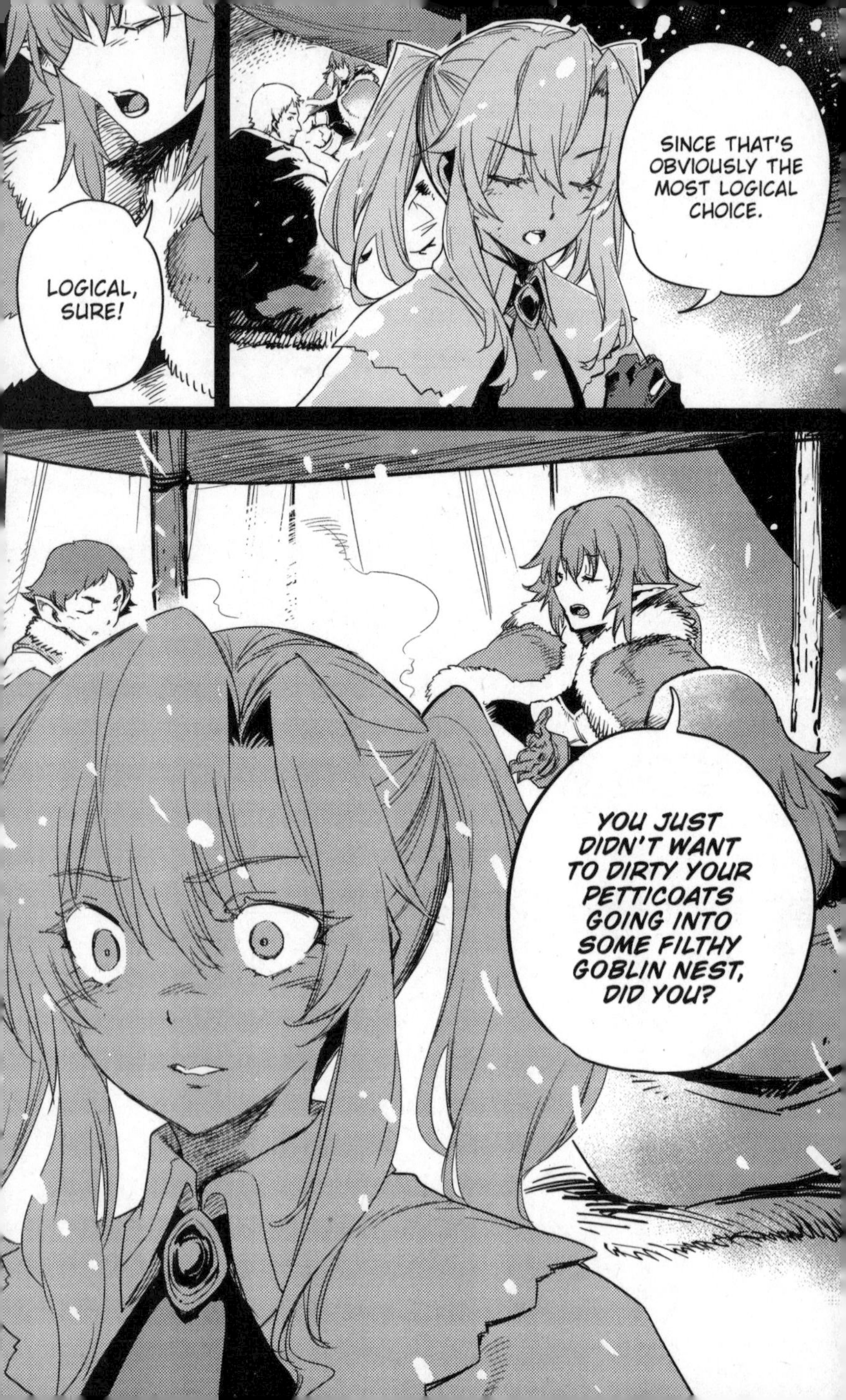
SINCE THAT'S OBVIOUSLY THE MOST LOGICAL CHOICE.
LOGICAL, SURE!
YOU JUST DIDN'T WANT TO DIRTY YOUR PETTICOATS GOING INTO SOME FILTHY GOBLIN NEST, DID YOU?

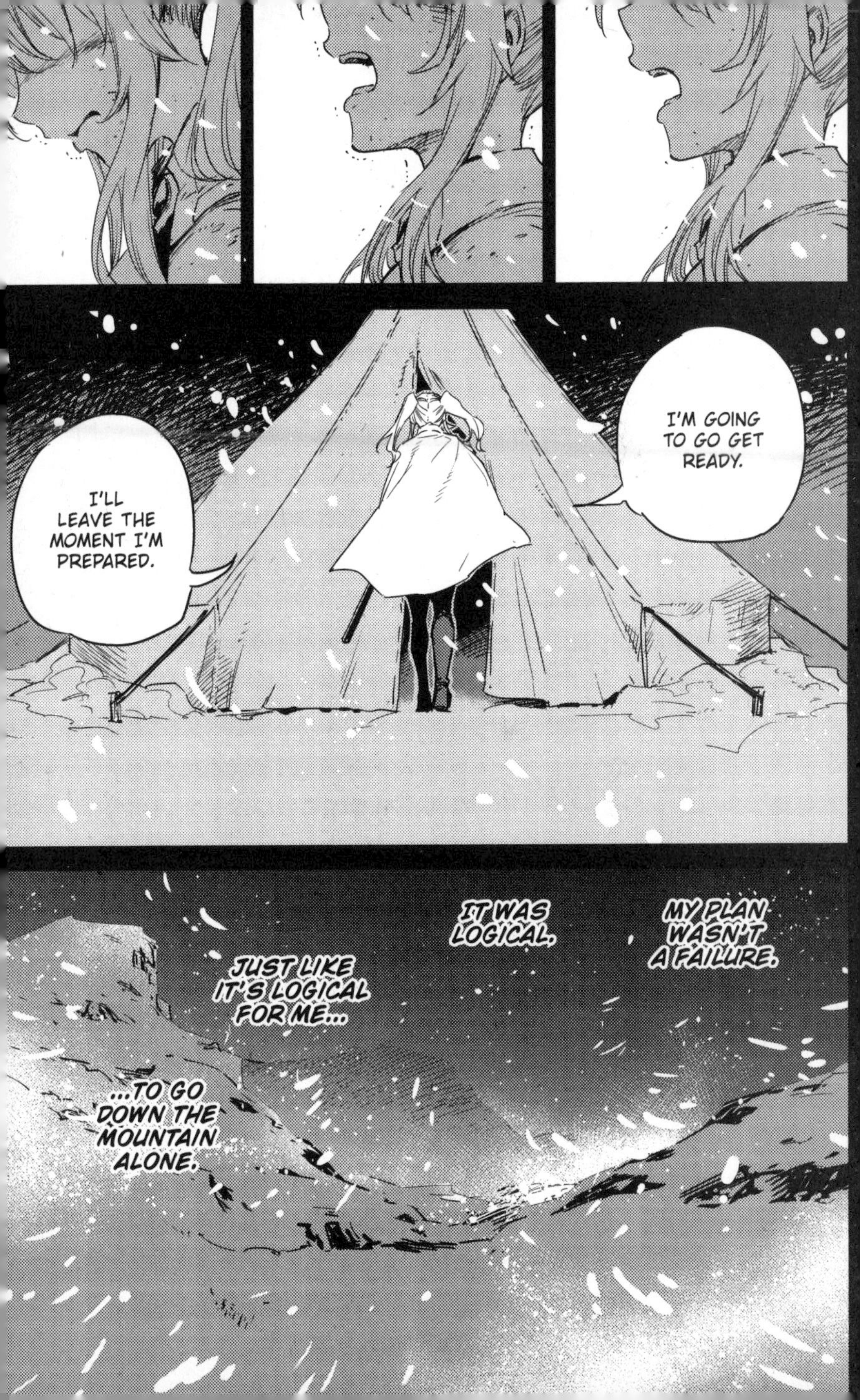
I'M GOING TO GO GET READY.
I'LL LEAVE THE MOMENT I'M PREPARED.
MY PLAN WASN'T A FAILURE.
IT WAS LOGICAL.
JUST LIKE IT'S LOGICAL FOR ME...
...TO GO DOWN THE MOUNTAIN ALONE.

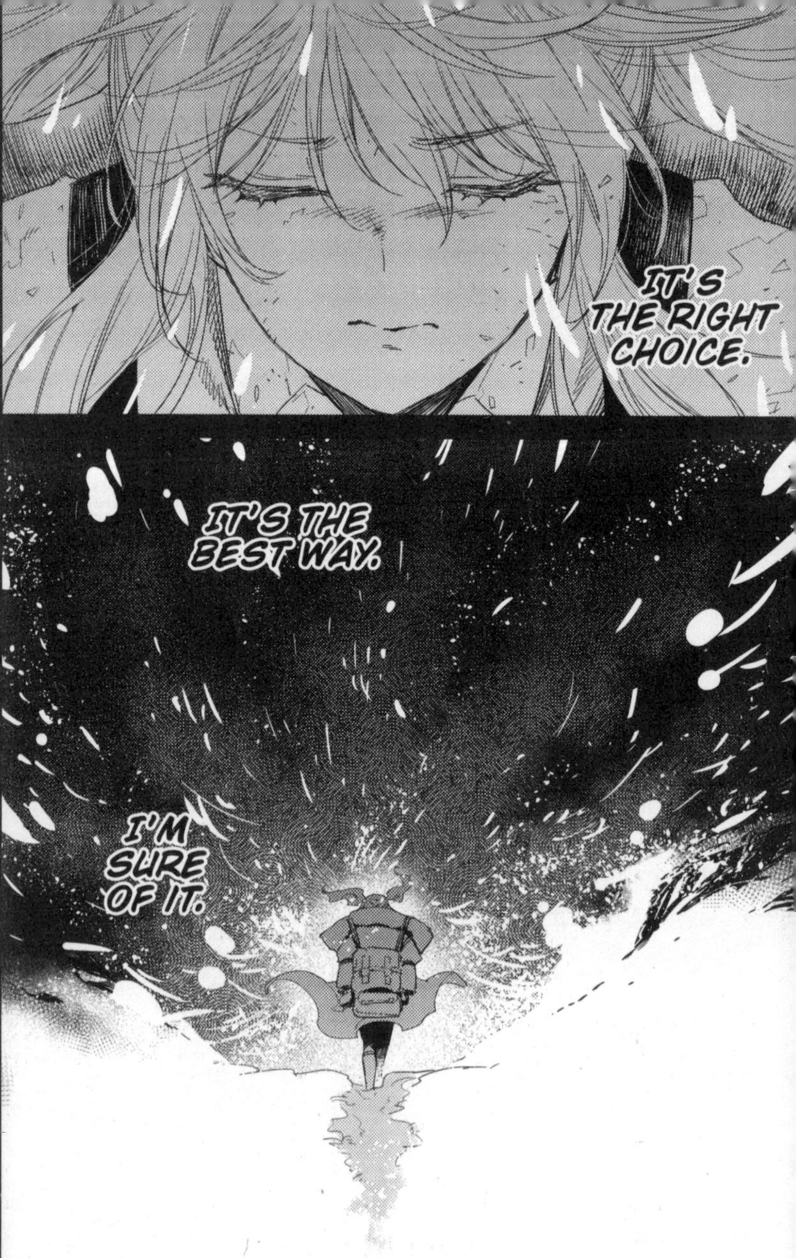
IT'S THE RIGHT CHOICE.
IT'S THE BEST WAY.
I'M SURE OF IT.

GOBLIN SLAYER 9 THE END

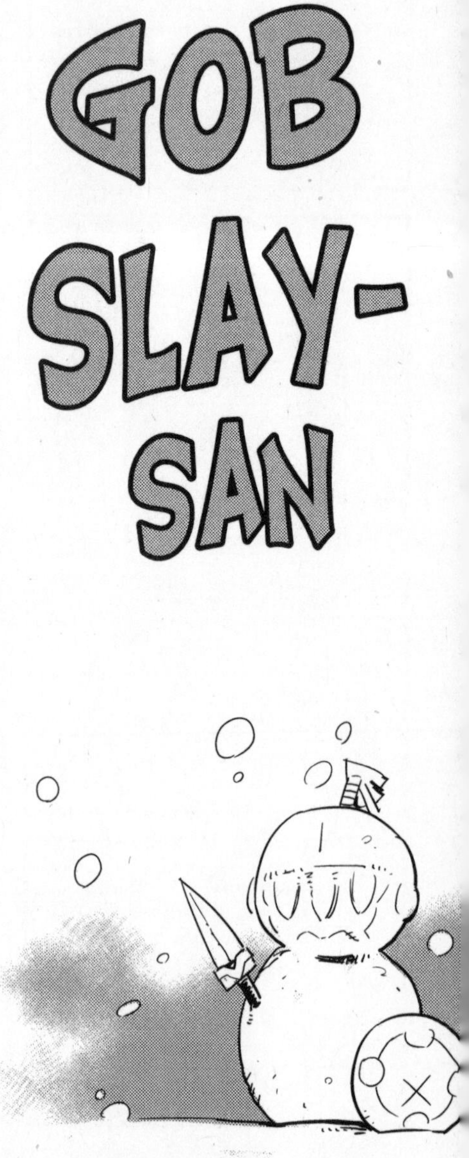
GOB SLAY-SAN

HUNTING

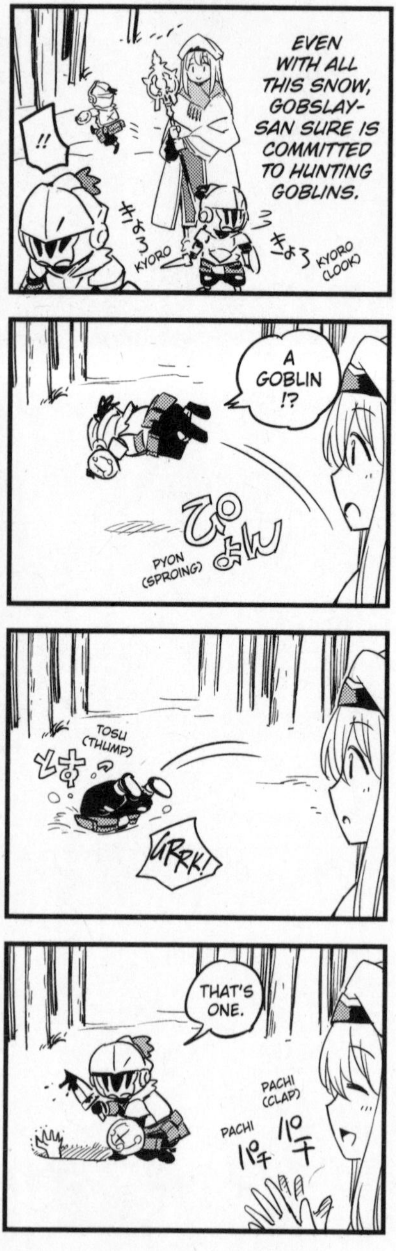
EVEN WITH ALL THIS SNOW, GOBSLAY-SAN SURE IS COMMITTED TO HUNTING GOBLINS.
!!
きょろ
KYORO (LOOK)
きょろ
KYORO
A GOBLIN !?
ぴょん
PYON (SPROING)
TOSU (THUMP)
とすっ
URRK!
THAT'S ONE.
パチ
PACHI (CLAP)
パチ
PACHI

IT'S A STRETCH

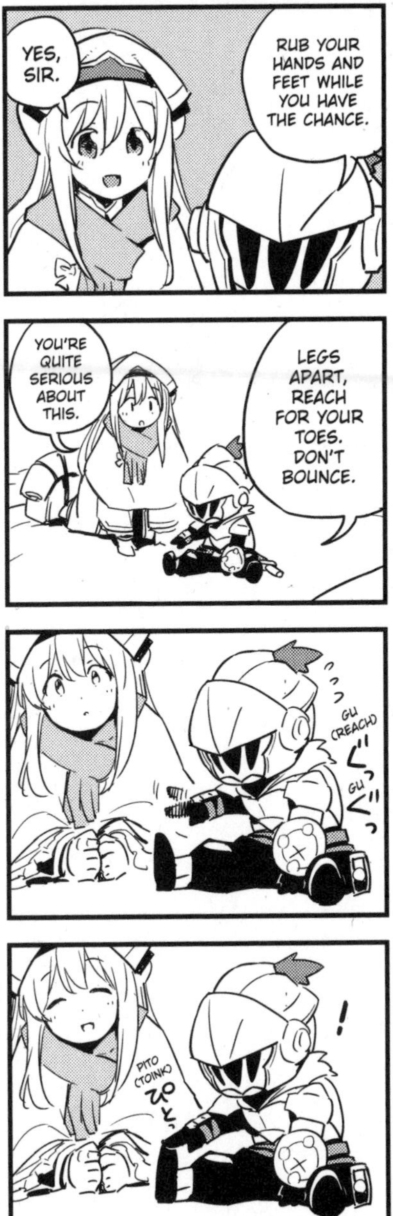
RUB YOUR HANDS AND FEET WHILE YOU HAVE THE CHANCE.
YES, SIR.
LEGS APART, REACH FOR YOUR TOES. DON'T BOUNCE.
YOU'RE QUITE SERIOUS ABOUT THIS.
GU (REACH)
GU
!
PITO (TOINK)

VERY ATHLETIC

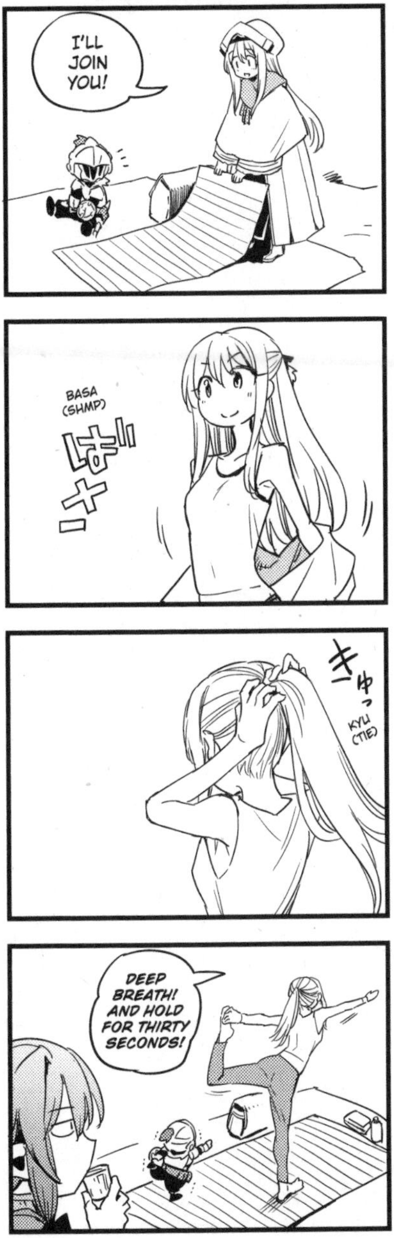
I'LL JOIN YOU!
BASA (SHMP)
KYU (TIE)
DEEP BREATH! AND HOLD FOR THIRTY SECONDS!

Turn to the back of the
book for a short story by
Kumo Kagyu!

GOBLIN SLAYER

HE DOES NOT LET ANYONE ROLL THE DICE.

A young Priestess joins her first adventuring party, but blind to the dangers, they almost immediately find themselves in trouble. It's Goblin Slayer who comes to their rescue—a man who has dedicated his life to the extermination of all goblins by any means necessary. A dangerous, dirty, and thankless job, but he does it better than anyone. And when rumors of his feats begin to circulate, there's no telling who might be coming calling next...

Light Novel
V.1-10
Available
Now!

Check out the simul-pub manga chapters every month!

Yen Press   YEN ON
www.yenpress.com

GOBLIN
SLAYER

a snowy mountain. She had no idea what might await her there, what might happen...

"Hee-hee...!"

As there was nobody around from whom she might need to hide it, Priestess let out a little chuckle at how fun that sounded.

hands, ears, and tail made her a little jealous. They were so cute, too. The Commandments strictly forbade high fashion or luxurious indulgence, but just a small something...

Surely, even the honored Earth Mother would be kind enough to look the other way...!

The thought gave her a smidgen of courage to indulge. That covered cold-weather gear and food. A map and other minor necessities could be acquired on-site, so that left only...

"Oh!"

"Hmm?" Padfoot Waitress perked up her ears quizzically, and Priestess quickly waved a hand to signal there was nothing wrong.

Oh, for—! Gosh. Silly me, forgetting the most important thing.

"The Adventurer's Toolkit..."

Never leave home without it!

She clenched her fist and thanked the Earth Mother profusely for reminding her. "Okay, thank you again!"

"Sure thing! Be careful out there!" Padfoot Waitress nodded politely, and Priestess energetically pattered out of the tavern. She was soon back in her room, confirming the full contents of her Adventurer's Toolkit were present and otherwise preparing her cargo.

She always had her hands full with all the things that had to be done before an adventure. They were heading out to help people in trouble, and it behooved them to take it seriously. After all, this would be her first trip to

"Cold makes a body hungry. Or...uh, does that not happen to humans?"

"I guess I don't know? But we do get hungry one way or another." Priestess responded to the question with an ambiguous tilt of her head. She wasn't exactly sure how much sharper padfoot senses were than humans'.

But, well...

As long as they didn't load you down completely, provisions could only help. You might be able to conserve by hunting game while on the road, but where food was concerned, it was better safe than sorry.

"Something we can even eat frozen... There probably isn't anything like that, is there?"

"If there is, I don't know about it!" Padfoot Waitress chortled. "Couldja just store some food in your clothes to keep it warm?"

"That's true." Priestess nodded, then pulled some coins out of her purse one at a time, placing them on the round table.

"Pleasure doing business!" Priestess returned the friendly smile Padfoot Waitress gave her, then collected the provisions and nodded in satisfaction.

I should probably go buy a cape or something as well.

Putting on too many layers would make it hard to move, but she could at least do with some simple outerwear. Another glance in her purse confirmed she had a few coins to spare...

Above all, the thought of Padfoot Waitress's fuzzy

"Oh, well," Priestess said, blinking. "Ummm..."

"Hmm?"

Priestess found herself a bit overwhelmed by Padfoot Waitress, who was leaning toward her, as she groped for the words to explain.

Isn't this exactly the "asking around" you said you weren't going to do?

This flicker of doubt briefly assailed Priestess, but she pushed it away and said, in a single breath, "I'm going to the snowy mountain in winter so I was wondering if you could get some provisions ready for me, just whatever you think would be best!"

"Sure thing!" Padfoot Waitress didn't appear fazed at all as she turned around and jogged over to a shelf. She reached out with the padded, furry hand that was her race's namesake. "You'll be needing something that stays edible even if it freezes, then!"

"Yes, thank you." Yes, that was it. Surely. That had to be right. Priestess nodded to herself. "If you have some things like that..."

"Then let me give you a few of my choice vittles!" Padfoot Waitress grabbed one preserved food after another, piling them up on an empty table. Dried fruits and berries, hard-cooked bread. Priestess realized none of it seemed that different from what she would take on any adventure. If anything...

"Walnuts... Dried meat... I feel like I see a lot of oily things..."

"Ummm... Well, for starters..."

Cold-weather gear would be...quick enough to secure—or so she thought.

"If I can't find any, I might really regret it once I'm there."

Though she had no idea how accurate her assumptions were, it would probably be best to immediately begin assembling what she needed. And once she started thinking that way, she realized the same might be true for provisions and the like...

With these thoughts running through her head, Priestess briskly walked into the tavern adjoining the Guild. Perhaps because she had been constantly going off on adventures, she wasn't used to the place yet and still hadn't caught the rhythm of when the tavern would be full of other adventurers and when it was more likely to be empty. When she poked her head inside, the place seemed fairly quiet, with only a few seats taken by customers.

"Um, excuse me..."

"Be right with you!" came the effusive answer from Padfoot Waitress, who suddenly popped into view. Her curvy body was barely contained by her waitress's uniform, and her tail wagged from under a short skirt as she jogged over.

I've heard lots of restaurants are staffed by padfoots...

It made a certain kind of sense, Priestess thought. They were sweet-looking and put customers at ease.

"Whatcha want?"

harvest festival, but after that had come...a goblin hunt.

"...Hrm."

She couldn't help but feel this was a little...*unbalanced*.

Though she had also been on the occasional adventure with High Elf Archer and the others...

It hasn't all been goblin hunting, has it...?

No. Surely not. Surely.

Priestess took a moment to nod to herself, then pointedly redirected her thoughts once she had a firmer grip on her emotions.

Yes, the real issue at hand was this snowy mountain. She'd be marching through snow. So what would she need?

"Hmm..."

Maybe she should just start asking people for their opinions... No, that didn't seem quite right.

True, you had to ask people for advice sometimes. Nobody started with the knowledge or experience they needed, and it was hard to put it into practice even once you had it. You could get all your calculations right, and your timing, and everything about the situation, and still run into trouble. Priestess had learned that much during her short time adventuring.

So maybe I could do just a little by myself.

She could try to apply what she had learned. Priestess clenched her fists, determined to show she had grown.

§

Interlude:

Of Her First Departure — by Kumo Kagyu

"Hmm... What should I do...?"

These were the first words out of Priestess's mouth when she received her new quest.

She had found herself a little space in the corner of the Adventurers Guild away from the reception desk, where none of her companions or other adventurers were around to disturb her. It was, in fact, the perfect place to quietly, almost inadvertently mutter to herself. Words inexorably tumbled from her lips, though she knew she could find the will to clam up if Goblin Slayer happened to be nearby.

"A snowy mountain? What do I need for that...?"

She had no idea. That was the problem.

It had been about a year since she became an adventurer. She tried to think of all the places she had been and the things she had done in that time, counting them off on her fingers as she went.

In spring, a goblin hunt. Then a goblin hunt. A goblin hunt in some old ruins, then another goblin hunt.

In summer, a goblin hunt. Then a goblin hunt in the water town. Then the battle with the Giant Eyeball, followed by a goblin hunt.

In fall, she had been busy with preparations for the

GOBLIN SLAYER  9

Original Story: Kumo Kagyu

Art: Kousuke Kurose

Character Design: Noboru Kannatuki

Translation: Kevin Steinbach ✛ Lettering: Bianca Pistillo

This book is a work of fiction. Names, characters, places, and incidents are
the product of the author's imagination or are used fictitiously. Any resemblance
to actual events, locales, or persons, living or dead, is coincidental.

GOBLIN SLAYER Volume 9
©Kumo Kagyu / SB Creative Corp.
Original Character Designs: ©Noboru Kannatuki / SB Creative Corp.
©2020 Kousuke Kurose / SQUARE ENIX CO., LTD. First published in Japan in 2020 by
SQUARE ENIX CO., LTD. English translation rights arranged with SQUARE ENIX CO.,
LTD. and YEN PRESS, LLC through Tuttle-Mori Agency, Inc., Tokyo.

English translation ©2020 by SQUARE ENIX CO., LTD.

Yen Press
150 West 30th Street, 19th Floor
New York, NY 10001

Visit us at yenpress.com
facebook.com/yenpress
twitter.com/yenpress
yenpress.tumblr.com
instagram.com/yenpress

First Yen Press Edition: December 2020
The chapters in this volume were originally published as ebooks by Yen Press.

Yen Press is an imprint of Yen Press, LLC.
The Yen Press name and logo are trademarks of Yen Press, LLC.

The publisher is not responsible for websites (or their content) that are
not owned by the publisher.

Library of Congress Control Number: 2017954163

ISBNs: 978-1-9753-1791-1 (paperback)
        978-1-9753-1792-8 (ebook)

10 9 8 7 6 5 4 3 2 1

WOR

Printed in the United States of America